Y0-BRR-803

WITHDRAWN

Library
College of St. Scholastica
Duluth, Minn.

Theory and Method in the
Social Sciences

Theory and Method in the

SOCIAL SCIENCES

by ARNOLD M. ROSE

The University of Minnesota Press, Minneapolis

Copyright 1954 by the

UNIVERSITY OF MINNESOTA

All rights reserved. No part of this book
may be reproduced in any form without the
written permission of the publisher. Permission is hereby granted to reviewers to quote
brief passages in a review to be printed in
a magazine or newspaper.

PRINTED AT THE LUND PRESS, INC., MINNEAPOLIS

Library of Congress Catalog Card Number: 54–6369

The following chapters, first published elsewhere, are reprinted here, in revised form,
by permission of the editors of the publications: Chapter 11, "Public Opinion Research
Techniques Suggested by Sociological Theory," copyright Summer 1950 by *Public
Opinion Quarterly*; Chapter 16, "Conditions of the Social Science Experiment," copyright October 1948 by *American Sociological Review*; Chapter 17, "A Weakness of
Partial Correlation in Sociological Studies," copyright August 1949 by *American Sociological Review*; Chapter 18, "Attitude Measurement and the Questionnaire Survey,"
copyright February 1949 by *Scientific Monthly*; Chapter 21, "Popular Logic: A
Methodological Suggestion," copyright October 1946 by *American Sociological Review*.

H
61
.R66

PUBLISHED IN GREAT BRITAIN, INDIA, AND PAKISTAN BY
GEOFFREY CUMBERLEGE: OXFORD UNIVERSITY PRESS, LONDON, BOMBAY, AND KARACHI

Preface

THE series of essays which comprise this book should have for their title, in place of the title which convention has dictated, "Some Aspects of Theory and Research in Social Science with Particular Attention to Sociology and Social Psychology." This is to say that the book is not intended to be a comprehensive, much less an exhaustive, work. The major reason for its publication is that it may encourage research in sociology along certain neglected channels and with certain relatively neglected research tools. There are other reasons for its publication: (1) Many of the essays have not been published before and hence have not been available. Most important among these essays is the one entitled "A Theory of Social Organization and Disorganization," which won the 1952 prize given by the American Association for the Advancement of Science for essays in social theory. (2) Several of the previously published articles are out of print, and the author is no longer able to satisfy requests for reprints. Some of the articles were first published in fairly inaccessible journals. (3) A number of the essays were written several years ago and needed considerable revision in the light of recent developments in theory and research. All but one of the hitherto published essays have been revised for publication in this book, and some have been so changed that their resemblance to their originals can be seen only in their titles and subject matters. I certainly do not believe that any of the present chapters are definitive statements; I hope that I may make further drastic revisions during the coming years.

The book is intended primarily for two audiences: (1) mature social scientists, who may find the discussion useful even when they are not in agreement with the author; and (2) students in advanced courses and seminars in social theory, methods of social research, social psychology, social organization, and the philosophy of the social sciences. While the book is addressed primarily to sociologists and social psychologists, it has relevance for other social scientists. Stu-

32805

v

Library
College of St. Scholastica
Duluth, Minn.

dents of the law are directed especially to chapters 4, 6, and 13; economists to chapters 10 and 22; psychologists to chapters 7, 8, 11, and 12, and sections IV and V generally; political scientists to chapters 2, 4, and 6; historians to chapters 2, 3, 4, and 14; anthropologists to 4, 14, 19, and 21; and students of the logic of the social sciences to the whole volume. Practitioners of public opinion polling may find use for Chapter 11 and Section V. Intergroup relations specialists may have a special interest in chapters 5, 6, and 8.

The major limitations of the book will be obvious from an examination of the Table of Contents. No effort is made to acquaint the reader systematically with all of the issues and problems in theory and method in the social sciences. The selection made represents the particular interest, and the particular bias, of the author. While the book is not systematically integrated, the considerable extent to which there is mutual dependence of the chapters is suggested by the frequent cross references. Some of the matters discussed in the book are controversial, and there is no body of research experience to give adequate support to the positions taken. Since the chapters were written at different times, with slightly different terminologies, there may appear to be inconsistencies among them, but a close reading would reveal that the inconsistencies are in terminology rather than in logic. There is, however, a certain amount of repetition and overlap as the same point is taken up in different contexts. Specific research contributions have deliberately not been included except for the paper on "Voluntary Associations in France," in which data and theory are so intimately interwoven that to present the theory without the data would be to render it virtually meaningless. The other essays, even though they contain no research themselves, make frequent reference to published studies in sociology and allied fields.

The concept of "theory" is defined at the beginning of the first essay; for this Preface it is sufficient to point out that I mean by it a framework of definitions, assumptions, and hypotheses (tested and untested) that is developed in intimate contact with research and that can be used to guide research. This definition is somewhat at variance with the dominant usage of the term "theory" among sociologists, whose courses in "Social Theory" usually consist of a history of thought regarding the nature of society or a presentation of one or more "systems" that attempt to explain all of human behavior. The narrower definition used here follows that of an increasing number of research sociologists. I also do not equate theory with untested hypothesis, which—when verified—is considered to pass from the realm of "theory" to that of "fact."

The term "method" is here used to mean a consideration of the ways in which knowledge is acquired. The concern with method thus ranges from a consideration of assumptions underlying research to a presentation of specific research tools that may or must be used to acquire knowledge of various kinds. Both theory and method are essential in science, which may be broadly defined as a body of knowledge which permits us to make predictions that prove to be more accurate than chance or everyday experience alone would allow us to make. By "predictions" is meant informed expectations, not only for future events, but also for past events (in order not to exclude certain kinds of historical research) and for events occurring under very unrealistic, controlled conditions.

I deplore the tendency to consider science solely as the product of a single experimental method—which has proved useful in physics but which has been found insufficient in much of the research in astronomy, biology, economics, history, and sociology—or of statistical method, which has contributed so much to social science knowledge but which is inadequate to answer certain research questions. The major purpose of most of the chapters dealing with research techniques is to indicate how such techniques have to be adapted to the kinds of research problems found in sociology. Thus this book provides no systematic exposition of research techniques—a task well performed by such authors or editors as Chapin; Goode and Hatt; Jahoda, Deutsch, and Cook; Festinger and Katz; Lundberg; Parten; and P. V. Young—but considers the adaptation of research techniques to the various kinds of researches found in sociology.

In a work of this sort the author's intellectual obligations must necessarily be many and deep. In a very real sense all of my teachers and colleagues, past and present, have contributed to this book. Special acknowledgment must be made of the debt to Herbert Blumer, Ernest Burgess, Gunnar Myrdal, and Samuel Stouffer and to the late Henry C. Simons and Louis Wirth. Through their writings, Charles H. Cooley, Emile Durkheim, and George H. Mead have had a profound influence on me. I have had the benefit of criticisms on several of the chapters from May Brodbeck, Caroline B. Rose, and Hans L. Zetterberg. Individual chapters have benefited from critical reading by persons acknowledged in footnotes to the titles of those chapters. For clerical aid I am indebted to David Shaw and Maryann Cadwell, whose services were provided by means of a grant from the Rockefeller Foundation. I am also very grateful to the University of Minnesota for making available the free time and facilities necessary for scholarly writing and research.

ARNOLD M. ROSE

University of Minnesota
January 1954

Acknowledgments of Previous Publications

SOME of the chapters of this book are reworked versions of previously published articles. Editors or publishers of the journals in which these pieces originally appeared have kindly given their permission to republish, and in most cases have turned over the copyright to the University of Minnesota Press. Appreciation is expressed to these editors and publishers. The chapters based on previously published articles are listed below, with their original source.

Chapter 2. "The Problem of a Mass Society," *Antioch Review*, 10 (September 1950), 378–394.

Chapter 7. "The Selection of Problems for Research," *American Journal of Sociology*, 54 (November 1948), 219–227.

Chapter 8. "Where Social Action and Social Research Meet," *Sociology and Social Research*, 36 (May–June 1952), 283–290.

Chapter 10. "The Potential Contribution of Sociological Theory and Research to Economics," *American Journal of Economics and Sociology*, 12 (October 1952), 23–33.

Chapter 11. "Public Opinion Research Techniques Suggested by Sociological Theory," *Public Opinion Quarterly*, 14 (Summer 1950), 205–214.

Chapter 13. "Problems in the Sociology of Law and Law Enforcement," *Journal of Legal Education*, vol. 6, no. 2 (1953), pp. 191–202.

Chapter 15. "Generalizations in the Social Sciences," *American Journal of Sociology*, 59 (July 1953), 49–58.

Chapter 16. "Conditions of the Social Science Experiment," *American Sociological Review*, 13 (October 1948), 616–619.

Chapter 17. "A Weakness of Partial Correlation in Sociological Studies," *American Sociological Review*, 14 (August 1949), 536–539.

Chapter 18. "Attitude Measurement and the Questionnaire Survey," *Scientific Monthly*, 68 (February 1949), 97–101. The present chapter also includes "Interviewing to Test for Validity and Reliability,"

International Journal of Opinion and Attitude Research, 1 (January 1947), 100–101.

Chapter 19. "A Research Note on Experimentation in Interviewing," *American Journal of Sociology,* 51 (September 1945), 143–144.

Chapter 21. "Popular Logic: A Methodological Suggestion," *American Sociological Review,* 11 (October 1946), 590–592.

Chapter 22. "A Deductive Ideal-Type Method," *American Journal of Sociology,* 56 (July 1950), 35–42.

Contents

SECTION IV. METHODOLOGICAL ISSUES IN SOCIOLOGY

SECTION V. SOME SPECIFIC TECHNIQUES OF SOCIOLOGICAL RESEARCH

SECTION I

Social Theory

1

A Theory of Social Organization and Disorganization

THE *introductory chapter defines the nature of theory, describes its strength and weaknesses, and provides an example of theory from subject matter at the core of sociology. The purpose of the chapter is to integrate the largely uncoordinated traditions of sociological thinking and research of certain French, German, and American writers with regard to the hitherto discrete sets of concepts and researches on "social structure" and "social problems." The tradition of Durkheim and Thomas is followed in that research in the one area is suggested as having value for research in the other area. There are many inadequacies in the following formulation, but it is hoped that it provides a step toward suitable sociological theory.*

THE NATURE AND SHORTCOMINGS OF THEORY

A *THEORY* may be defined as an integrated body of definitions, assumptions, and general propositions covering a given subject matter from which a comprehensive and consistent set of specific and testable hypotheses can be deduced logically. The hypotheses must take the form "If *a,* then *b,* holding constant *c, d, e* . . . ." or some equivalent of this form, and thus permit of causal explanation and prediction.

A *good* theory is one which (1) has its definitions, assumptions, and general propositions consistent, insofar as possible, with previous research findings and with careful, although perhaps not systematic, observations; (2) has a minimum number of definitions, assumptions, and general propositions; (3) has its deduced hypotheses in readily testable form; and, crucially, (4) gets its deduced hypotheses verified by proper scientific methods.

It is quite possible to be scientific without using theory. If we include in the realm of science anything which permits accurate prediction, some of the most scientific work in the social sciences has been

3

in the nature of actuarial research, which involves no theory whatsoever. The formation of scales by compiling items that elicit significant differences in response from two groups that are known to be respectively high and low on the variable to be predicted also permits accurate prediction and is therefore scientific even though the scales are not based on theory. Simple hypotheses, which spring from casual observation, can be tested scientifically and, if proven accurate, will lead to valuable insights and predictions. These, too, are not based on theory.

There are certain values to theory, however, which have led many investigators in the older disciplines to make extensive use of it. (1) It is a guide to the formation of hypotheses and trains investigators to look for facts which may ordinarily not be readily apparent. (2) It permits research to be cumulative; that is, it allows the conclusions of older studies to gain support from new research and allows older studies to provide some of the data for new research. (3) It indicates what studies are crucial; that is, it provides one guide for the selection of research problems from among the infinitely large number of possible hypotheses. (4) It permits research to proceed systematically and allows conclusions to take a shorthand form so that they are readily communicable.

There are also certain dangers to the use of theory in science. It may be argued that these dangers are not inherent in the utilization of theory but result, rather, from the misuse of theory. As logically accurate as that may be, it is nevertheless apparent that the use of theory as a guide to research seems always to bring in its train some undesirable consequences:

1. Theory channelizes research along certain lines; it does not encourage equally all lines of investigation. If the theory ultimately proves to be wrong, many years of work are wasted and new ideas have not had a fair chance for expression.

2. Theory tends to bias observation; there are certain assumptions and definitions inevitable in theory, and these limit observation sometimes more than is desirable in a young science. Without a theory we might tend to have alternative definitions and assumptions in a given piece of work. Theory usually limits us to one consistent set of definitions and assumptions.

3. The concepts that are necessary in theory tend to get reified. The

tendency to reify concepts may be a general characteristic of human behavior, but the use of theoretical definitions seems to stimulate this human weakness.

4. We are faced with the fact in social science, seldom mentioned but readily verifiable, that replications of a study seldom reach an identical conclusion.[1] This may be the result of poor measuring devices, or it may be due to the fact that we have as yet failed to come to grips with the great diversity and complexity of our subject matter. Until we resolve these difficulties and secure consistent replications for simple hypotheses, are we justified in formulating elaborate theories which assume consistency in findings?

5. Until a theory can be completely verified, which is practically never, it tends to lead to overgeneralization of its specific conclusions to areas of behavior outside their scope. In social science we have been faced with the phenomenon that studies of the maze learning of rats have been used to guide the development of children and that conclusions arising from the investigation of neurotic behavior among adults have been suggested as a chief guide for the understanding of politics. The history of social science shows enough natural tendency to overgeneralize without having the stimulation of theory to encourage this unscientific procedure.

6. If there are rival theories of human behavior, and there will inevitably tend to be in a democratic and pluralistic society, the rivalry seems to encourage distortion of simple facts. Quite frequently scientists can agree on statements of fact but have very serious disagreements concerning the significance or explanation of these facts on a theoretical level. Sometimes even the immediate causes of the facts are subject to agreement but the more basic ones suggested by theory are not. I wish to emphasize these shortcomings of theory, because they apply in one degree or another to the theory which will be advanced on the following pages.

DEFINITIONS, ASSUMPTIONS, AND GENERAL PROPOSITIONS
IN THE THEORY

The theory of social organization and disorganization to be presented has its roots in three independent, and hitherto largely unco-

---

[1] For evidence, see Chapter 15.

ordinated,[2] traditions of sociological thinking and research: (1) the
French tradition of Emile Durkheim and his students, especially
valuable for its concepts of collective representations, anomie, and solidarity, and for its studies of suicide, religion, social solidarity, and child
development; (2) the German tradition of Georg Simmel and Max
Weber and those they directly influenced, especially valuable for
its concepts of action, meaning, and understanding, and for its studies
of urbanization, money, and the relation of ideology to social structure; (3) the American tradition of C. H. Cooley, John Dewey, W. G.
Sumner, G. H. Mead, W. I. Thomas, R. E. Park, and their students, especially valuable for its concepts of self, person, role, conduct, primary group, folkway, the act, generalized other, social disorganization, definition of the situation, and secondary group, and for
its researches on child development, acculturation, urbanism, and
disorganization. A major purpose of this chapter is to integrate these
and other concepts into a systematic theory and to derive from the
theory testable hypotheses for research, within the limits of the previously stated drawbacks and dangers of theory. Preceding the statement
of the theory itself there will be a specification of its assumptions and
definitions.

Assumption 1. Human behavior is in part characterized by a social
factor. The *social factor* in human behavior can quite simply be defined as behavior in which one individual takes into account the perceived expectations of other individuals and which in itself implies
expectations for certain kinds of behavior on the part of others.[3] The
expectations may be unconscious as well as conscious, despite the
connotation of consciousness usually connected with the term. The
social factor might, in the future history of science, be reducible to
a statement of physiological relations, just as all physiological rela-

---

[2] Talcott Parsons, in his *The Structure of Social Action* (New York: McGraw-Hill,
1937), has taken a major step toward the coordination of two of the three traditions—
namely those associated with the names of Weber and Durkheim. His aim, however,
was limited to demonstrating that both men were working toward a theory of social
action, rather than showing how their specific concepts and research findings were
similar or complementary. Parsons limited himself further by trying to find out something that was common, not only to Weber and Durkheim, but also to Pareto and
Marshall. In the development of the specific theory presented here, it has not been
found useful to borrow any of the concepts or research findings of Pareto or Marshall.

[3] Weber and his followers used the term "action" to refer to behavior determined by
the social factor defined in this way. Dewey and Park used the term "conduct" in an
equivalent way. Mead used the term "the act" to refer to the same type of behavior
in units rather than collectively.

tions might someday be reducible to a statement of chemical or physical relations. But at the present stage of our knowledge we have practically no basis for making this reduction; and we can make much more reliable and accurate predictions about many types of human behavior with research that seeks manifestations of the social factor as herein defined than we can with reductionistic statements in physiological or chemicophysical terms. It is not necessary to take sides in the controversy over reductionism if we can agree that, even if possible, reduction will not be feasible or useful for hundreds of years of future research.

This assumption is not in opposition to the neobehaviorist theory of learning associated with the name of Clark Hull,[4] if the concept of cue, or stimulus, in this theory is considered as broad enough to include significant symbols and the imagined responses of others.[5] The neobehaviorists, as distinct from the older behaviorists, apparently do have this broad definition of stimulus; and they also recognize the role of motivation ("drive") from within the individual as a prerequisite to learning. Their major interest in learning, through reinforcement or tension reduction, is of course tangential to our interest in the adjustive responding to social cues.

Assumption 2. The *social group* exists, not as a physical entity, a "group mind," nor as a mere collection of individuals, but as a number of persons who have a set of perceived (not necessarily "conscious") expectations in relation to one another.[6] The expectations are either that others will behave in a certain way under certain conditions or that others expect one to act in a certain way under certain conditions. Each set of consistent and communicable expectations held by a biological *individual* may be called a *person* or *self* or *role*,[7] so that—as William James said—an individual may have as many selves as there are discrete groups to which he belongs, and—as Cooley said—the person and the group are two aspects of the same set of expectations,

---

[4] Clark Hull, *Principles of Behavior* (New York: Appleton-Century-Crofts, 1943).

[5] These are specifically included in the statement of neobehaviorist learning theory by John Dollard and Neal Miller, *Personality and Psychotherapy* (New York: McGraw-Hill, 1950), pp. 37–39.

[6] Mead used the term "generalized other" to refer to the social group defined in this way. In this book, as in most other social science writings, the term "society" will be used to refer to a group or groups that occupy all of a given geographical territory and that have something of a common culture.

[7] What Park called the *person,* James and Cooley called the *self,* and Mead called the *role,* but they are essentially synonymous terms.

depending on whether the individual or collective aspect of the behavior is under consideration.

Assumption 3. The expectations of a number of individuals in interaction specify or refer to a number of (1) *meanings* and (2) *folkways*
or *values,* which together make up the *culture* or subculture of the
group.[8] A meaning is simply a definition of an object, whether the
object is material or nonmaterial, "real" or "imagined." The meaning
usually indicates how an individual *may* act toward the object; that
is, it usually indicates the "purpose" of the object and how it will
respond to action toward it. For example, the meaning of "pillow"
is a soft, flattened object for resting the head and raising it slightly
when the person is in a prone position. This meaning tells how a person may use a pillow, but it does not coerce him into using it in the
way indicated. The meaning seldom indicates how an individual
should or *must* act toward an object; such a specification is made by
a folkway or value. As Sumner indicated, folkways may be subdivided
into *usages* (which indicate how individuals should act toward an
object, according to customary belief) and *mores* (which indicate how
individuals must act to avoid endangering the society, according to
customary belief).[9]

We may more properly consider the elements of a culture as being
distributed along a continuum, according to the degree of coercion
which the group imposes on the individual, with meanings designating
the cultural elements toward one pole, the mores and pseudomores
designating usually only a small portion of the cultural elements at
the other pole, and the usages designating the elements between.

---

[8] Durkheim did not differentiate between meanings and folkways but considered
them together under the rubric "collective representations." As a result, he gave the
impression that the group was much more coercive of the individual than either he
or his critics believed. The distinction between meanings and folkways is arbitrary—
that is, there is a continuum of degree of coercion—but it may be advisable to use
type terminology to avoid giving the impression that Durkheim did.

[9] It might be suggested that a section of the continuum be distinguished between
the mores and usages and be called the *pseudomores.* The pseudomores are values
which were formerly in the mores but at the present are considered as mores by only
a minority of the group. The prohibition of public discussion carries over, however,
so that people generally believe that almost everyone but themselves regards these
values as mores. Some individuals, of course, actually do regard these values as
mores, and they are usually the ones who punish violation or who most vociferously
demand punishment. Since most people regard these values merely as usages, they
will occasionally discuss the values with their close friends, and some even deviate
from them in their behavior if they believe they will not be observed. I would guess
that most of what appear to be mores in American culture actually are pseudomores.

Derivations to be presented more fully later will hypothesize that this continuum of coercion is also a continuum of uniformity-variation and of social structure to implement conformity. These derivations are mentioned here simply to indicate that the theory by no means requires uniformity in behavior among the members of a social group, nor does it require—as Durkheim's functionalism required—that formal steps always be taken by a group to restore itself (that is, to restore the expectations) when an individual member does not conform. Probably a larger portion of cultural elements consists simply of meanings than of values, although this ratio varies for different cultures, and the meanings are only slightly coercive.

General Proposition 1 (derived, but too broad to be verified directly). A person is able to predict the behavior of other persons most of the time, and thereby adjust his behavior to theirs (both in cooperation and in conflict), because he has internalized approximately the same meanings and values as the others have. This process of *internalization,* or *socialization* as it is more frequently called, is a learning process, and therefore one which the psychologist is best able to study. This accurate prediction can extend a long way into the future, and adjustment of a certain type can be planned on a long-time basis, because meanings and values are integrated into complex wholes wherein behavior, in conformity with some of the meanings and values, leads after a time to an expectation that there will be behavior in conformity with other meanings and values. These integrated complexes of meanings and values are *social structures* (which can be classified as institutions, class and caste systems, "ways of life," etc.). The social structures, plus miscellaneous meanings and values that are *ad hoc* for specific situations and are not integrated into complexes, collectively make up the *culture* or subculture of a group.

General Proposition 2. There are circumstances under which a number of biological individuals may be in physical contact with one another (that is, some sense organ of each one is directly stimulated by the others) over a period of time and yet do not form a group, because they can make no accurate predictions with respect to one another's behavior (that is, they have no expectations that receive reinforcement because of behavior in conformity with expectations). This situation arises when the individuals do not have a sufficient number of common meanings and values (either through a failure in the learning process or through a loss of meanings and values once learned). This situation has been defined as one of *social disorganization* by Thomas and Znaniecki.[10]

We may consider two logical types of social disorganization. The first type is one in which a number of individuals in physical contact with one another form discrete subgroups, each of which has a large proportion of meanings and values common to its members, but between which there are relatively few meanings and values in common. Depending on the character of the specific meanings and values of each of the subgroups, and the distribution of power (which is a function of numbers and access to implements of power) among them, this situation can be described either as one of *symbiosis* or one of *conflict*.

I do not mean to suggest the basic *cause* of conflict here, but merely to indicate that subgroup formation and isolation necessarily *result* in either group conflict or symbiosis. The underlying causes may be a difference of interest or mere accidental separation or something else which separates groups. I do imply that groups which are in physical contact but which have few important meanings and values in common are likely to get into conflict, even if that conflict is not violent. This should not be taken to mean that cultural pluralism leads to conflict, since groups in a pluralist society may understand one another perfectly well, and have correct expectations for one another's behavior, even if they behave differently. There may, of course, be other paths to conflict—this is frequently true in the case of industrial and marital conflict—but with these I am not concerned here.

Conflict can be subdivided (again depending on the specific meanings and values and on the distribution of power in relation to the other subgroups) into war, civil war or revolution, minority-group conflict, and most types of deliberate crime.

The second type of social disorganization is one in which a number of individuals in physical contact with one another do not share a large number of meanings and values; that is, it is like the first type except that there are no subgroups, or each individual can be considered as his own subgroup. This is a situation which Durkheim defined as *anomie* (literally, "without values"—that is, without meanings and values in common). Anomie, of course, is a matter of degree

[10] W. I. Thomas and Florian Znaniecki, *The Polish Peasant in Europe and America* (Boston: Badger Press, 1918), Vol. IV, Introduction.

for different individuals and for different human situations, but the most common manifestation seems to be one in which a majority of individuals have a sufficient number of meanings and values in common to keep the group going, and the minority of individuals have different degrees of isolation. Such a situation of anomie is productive of certain nonorganic types of mental disorder, suicide, alcoholism, and other individualistic forms of social disorganization.

Further Definitions. Various sociologists have had occasion to use other terms which readily fit into this theory. Park, for example, used the terms "accommodation" and "assimilation" to refer to situations in which subgroups formerly in conflict had acquired a larger proportion of meanings and values in common. Park and Stonequist have defined the "marginal man" as "one whom fate has condemned to live in two societies and in two, not merely different but antagonistic, cultures." [11] Park and Stonequist, sometimes explicitly and sometimes implicitly, often indicate that the marginal man is disorganized. However, Simmel defines the "stranger" in substantially the same way, and for him the stranger is not disorganized.[12]

The apparent opposition might be resolved if the different situations the authors had in mind were analyzed and more precisely specified: Simmel had primarily in mind the middle-class Jewish tradesman in a gentile community of central Europe who "does not belong in it from the first, [who] . . . brings qualities into it that are not, and cannot be, native to it." [13] Park and Stonequist, on the other hand, had primarily in mind the lower-class immigrant from rural Europe to the cities of the United States (by some peculiar misinterpretation of an essay of DuBois,[14] they also had in mind the mulatto in the United States).

The Durkheim school, seeking terms to describe a situation opposed to anomie, described it with the concepts of *social solidarity* and *morale*; [15] such a situation would be one in which all the individuals

[11] Robert E. Park, Introduction to Everett V. Stonequist's *The Marginal Man: A Study in Personality and Culture Conflict* (New York: Scribner, 1937), p. xv.

[12] Georg Simmel, *Soziologie* (Leipzig: Duncker und Humblot, 1908), pp. 685-691.

[13] From a translation of Simmel by Robert E. Park and Ernest W. Burgess, *Introduction to the Science of Sociology* (Chicago: University of Chicago Press, 1924), p. 322.

[14] W. E. B. DuBois, *The Souls of Black Folk* (Chicago: McClurg, 1903), p. 3.

[15] Recent students of minority groups, such as Lewin and Rose, have used the terms "group identification" and "group belongingness" in a sense equivalent to that of the French sociologists' use of the terms "solidarity" and "morale." See Kurt Lewin,

have a large proportion of meanings and values in common. Durkheim distinguished between mechanical and organic solidarity as follows: In the former, the expectations in accord with common meanings and values were that all individuals (at least all those in the same sex-age category) would act in the same way; in the latter, the expectations were that the individuals would act in different but complementary ways ("division of social labor"). The French sociologists used the term "sacred society" to refer to an organization of all members of the group which produced a mechanical solidarity, and "secular society" to refer to an organization of all members of the group which produced an organic solidarity. Ferdinand Toennies used the terms "Gemeinschaft" and "Gesellschaft" in substantially the same way, and other sociologists have presented a lengthy series of dichotomous terms coordinate to this pair.

There is not much point in continuing to list and define terms that are not central to the theory. Suffice it to say that a significant number of concepts used by sociologists since 1890 can be integrated into the theory and that some of them will be specified and defined where concrete hypotheses derived from the theory suggest their use. For some of the specific hypotheses derived below, additional special assumptions not common to all the hypotheses will have to be made; these will be indicated in their proper context.

Summary Statement of the Theory. The theory of social organization and social disorganization may now be stated in summary form: People are able to act together in an organized manner over an indefinitely long period of time because they have internalized a large number of meanings and values, commonly understood and adhered to, which permit them to make fairly accurate predictions about one another's behavior. Social disorganization—in the form of one or more of the familiar social problems—occurs when a significant proportion of meanings and values are no longer sufficiently internalized to guide the behavior of a significant proportion of the individuals still in physical contact with one another.

Before turning to specific derivations from this theory, it might be

Resolving Social Conflicts (New York: Harper, 1948); Arnold M. Rose, *The Negro's Morale* (Minneapolis: University of Minnesota Press, 1949). S. Frank Miyamoto has used the original term "solidarity" in a comparable way in describing a minority group in *Social Solidarity among the Japanese in Seattle* (Seattle: University of Washington, 1939).

well to make explicit one aspect of it which has been overlooked by sociologists in the three traditions that have contributed to the theory. A culture includes meanings and values of which the persons participating in it are not "conscious" as well as those of which they are "conscious." People show by their behavior that they have expectations for the behavior of others which are in accord with these *covert* meanings and values, and they themselves conform to them in their responses to others, even though no one in the group seems to be aware of the covert meanings and values.

The covert culture elements of the group are very similar to the unconscious attitudes and impulses that the psychoanalysts have noted in individuals. By definition, the covert culture elements differ only in that they are common to most members of the group and in that they play a role in mutual expectations which allows persons to adjust to one another. They are expressed in camouflaged ways; they are apparently opposed to certain overt meanings and values; and when verbally presented, they cause much more emotional reaction (as in "resistance") than is called for. These characteristics suggest that covert culture elements are "repressed" somewhat as the psychoanalysts believe certain individual motivations and memories are repressed. To provide tentative examples, merely by way of illustration, it might be that a favorable attitude toward war and a mild support for certain "white-collar crimes" are covert culture elements for significant segments of the American people. The anthropologist generally has a difficult time in discerning covert culture elements in societies he studies, because they seem to be camouflaged and seldom discussed, but it is even more difficult to discern them in one's own culture because of the observer's resistances.[16] It is not known what proportion of culture elements are covert, but that there are some and that they make a culture appear inconsistent should not be overlooked. It is possible also that there are cultural elements which people are not aware of, but which they are not repressing and which do not cause apparent inconsistencies.

DERIVATIONS FROM THE THEORY

Some derivations from the theory may now be stated as hypotheses for research. For some of these hypotheses, earlier research has already

[16] Some techniques for eliciting the covert culture are suggested in Chapter 21.

provided some evidence, and this will be summarized insofar as it is known to me.

1. If communication is for some reason blocked between an individual and others in his society, or between subgroups in the society, or between a group and the rest of the society, the behavior of one will manifest an increasing divergence from that of the other. This proposition makes the special assumption that societies and subgroups within societies are constantly changing their meanings and values. Thus, a more complete statement of the hypothesis is the following equation: The amount of divergence of behavior between two (or more) subgroups in a society (where one individual can be considered as a subgroup) that develops within any given time period is a direct function of the amounts of change occurring within each of them and an inverse function of the amount of communication (direct, or indirect through other subgroups) between them. In symbolic form, the equation may be expressed in the following way, if we assume measurable (or at least orderable) entities:

$$d_{ij} = F_1(h_i, h_j, c)$$

where d is divergence between any groups i and j, h_i and h_j are amounts of change in the two groups respectively, c is the amount of communication, and F_1 is an increasing function of h_i and h_j and a decreasing function of c.

History demonstrates the increasing divergence in culture between persons or groups who were once part of a common culture but whom circumstances have isolated. Numerous case studies of individuals who have moved from one society to another suggest that those individuals either slough off the meanings and values of their former society and adopt those of the new society or else form subgroups with their fellow migrants which try to maintain the old meanings and values after the old society itself has changed. However, these studies need to be made more systematically and with proper controls. The most important type of study along this line has scarcely been attempted: What happens to a person completely cut off from his fellows? It might be thought that he retains the culture of his former group, as Robinson Crusoe is alleged to have done, whereas the theory considered here would lead to the hypothesis that isolation results in increasingly "goalless" and "non-value-oriented" behavior. Incidental case reports of voluntary and involuntary hermits, of feral men, and of persons who live in the social isolation of rooming houses suggest that this hypothesis is the correct one, but more systematic research is called for.

2. Collectively expressed hostility to deviations from a cultural element varies directly with the amount of conformity demanded and inversely with the amount of deviation from the cultural element usually found (that is, the heterogeneity within the culture):

$$m = F_2(n, d_{10})$$

where m is collectively expressed hostility when there is deviation from a cultural element, n is the amount of conformity demanded to the cultural element, d_{10} is the divergence of the deviating group from the society's cultural element (a specific case of d_{ij}), and F_2 is an increasing function of n and a decreasing function of d_{10}. That is, considering the continuum from meanings through usages to mores, the degree of collectively expressed hostility forms a similar continuum. A research supporting this proposition is that by Myrdal, Sterner, and Rose, which shows that the "no social equality" taboo between Negroes and whites becomes stronger as the behavior approaches the sexual—both in the verbal statements of the whites and in the behavior of the Negroes—and that Negro violations of the taboo are collectively punished by whites also to the extent that they approach the sexual.[17] Data provided by the Kinsey report could also be used to support the hypothesis, although the authors do not themselves draw the relevant conclusion.[18] Further tests of the hypothesis could be made with available statistics on crime and a content analysis of the law of punishment; with a content analysis of canon law and a study of its application (in real life or in fiction[19]); with available ethnological reports on crime, punishment, and immorality; and with any other data on "unmoral" behavior.

Several subhypotheses can also be derived: (a) Deviations from the mores will be perceived as much more dangerous to social welfare and

[17] Gunnar Myrdal, with the assistance of Richard Sterner and Arnold Rose, *An American Dilemma* (New York: Harper, 1944), Chaps. 3, 29, 30.

[18] Alfred C. Kinsey, W. B. Pomeroy, and C. E. Martin, *Sexual Behavior in the Human Male* (Philadelphia: Saunders, 1948).

[19] It is to be noted that Dante conceived the deeper circles of Hell to be smaller and less densely populated than the upper circles.

will provoke more collective hostility than behavior not in accord with the usages and meanings. (b) There is less discussion about the merits and demerits of behavior in accord with the mores than there is of behavior in accord with the usages and meanings. (c) There are fewer jokes about deviations from the mores than about deviations from the usages and meanings. (Note here the few jokes about incest compared to other forms of sex deviation, and the fewer jokes among white southerners about Negro male–white female relations than about white male–Negro female relations.) (d) The social situations which the group creates for its members will seldom be such as to encourage or tempt violations of the mores. If nature or chance circumstance creates such situations, they will also acquire an element of taboo.

3. It is to be noted that "deviation in behavior" referred to in the first hypothesis is the same phenomenon as that referred to in the second, although in the first it is dealt with as an "effect" and in the second as a "cause." Hence it is possible to bring the two hypotheses together to derive a third: Collectively expressed hostility to deviations from a cultural element varies directly with the amount of communication among members of the society (as well as with the amount of conformity demanded to the cultural element, as noted in hypothesis 2) and inversely with the amount of change generally taking place within the society and the amount of change of the deviators:

$$m = F_2(n, F_1'(h_1, h_0, c))$$
$$= F_3(n, h_1, h_0, c)$$

where F_3 is an increasing function of n and c, and a decreasing function of h_1 and h_0.

Anthropologists have often pointed out that the highly integrated societies—those having few barriers to internal communication so that there is general understanding of the meanings and values and a high accuracy to predictions that behavior will conform to them—are the ones most capable of expressing collective hostility to deviations from cultural demands. Within our own society it can be observed that lynchings (or other collective violence against deviants) are much more likely to take place in small communities where there is more intercommunication than in large cities. Further, as our society has increased its rate of change, there are fewer and fewer expressions of collective hostility toward individual deviants. No evidence comes to mind concerning the inverse relation, predicted in the equation, between collective hostility toward a deviant and the rate of change characteristic of that deviant, but this is a hypothesis that can be tested both in the laboratory and in the field.

4. If group expectations are incompatible with the organic needs of the biological individual, the increasing pressure of those needs will tend to "disorganize" the individual (that is, to restrict his ability to understand and respond to the expectations of others). This hypothesis makes the special assumption that there is a physiological limit to the capacities of the individual and that organic needs must be satisfied within limits or the individual will perish. In support of this hypothesis, observations have been made that physical deprivation and torture cause socially disorganized behavior.

5. The fifth hypothesis makes the special assumption that each individual who belongs to many groups hierarchizes or assigns a relative value to these groups and the roles he takes in each of them.[20] In cases where two or more of these groups are in opposition or conflict, the individual is faced with a dilemma concerning the direction of his personal behavior. If the value to him of one group is low and the other high, his behavior will tend to conform to the expectations demanded by the latter group. If both groups are fairly low in his hierarchy, his behavior will take the form of escape from the demands of both of them and will conform to the demands of some other, higher group. If both groups are high in his hierarchy, his behavior will either be inconsistent because it is in conformity to both sets of social expectations or disorganized because it is in conformity to none. This hypothesis brings in other assumptions which can best be tested with a technique such as that developed by Stouffer.[21]

6. An adult individual who has not internalized the meanings and values of the group or groups in which he lives, or one who cannot internalize them because of mental deficiency or disease, will be forcibly isolated from the group, since his behavior constantly deviates from the expectations of others in serious ways (i.e., in ways that violate the folkways) and since his behavior cannot express communi-

[20] This is the assumption of reference groups first stated by Herbert Hyman (*The Psychology of Status*, Archives of Psychology No. 269, 1942).

[21] Samuel A. Stouffer, "An Analysis of Conflicting Social Norms," *American Sociological Review*, 14 (December 1949), 707–717.

cable expectations to others (i.e., he cannot "adjust" to the group). Some societies might kill all such individuals or otherwise incarcerate or exile them as criminals; whereas other societies, which understand the distinction between following antisocial values and the inability to internalize any set of values, would treat the persons guilty of the former behavior as criminals but place the persons characterized by the latter disability in special institutions for the feeble-minded or mentally disordered.

Verification of this hypothesis would involve observing the way different societies treat nonconformists to group expectations and determining whether the feeble-minded and psychotics understand the meanings and values common in our society. It is to be noted that children can be defined socially as feeble-minded individuals who are recognized to be unable to act socially because of biological imma- turity and who are likely to overcome this biological immaturity in time and to be able to act socially if they are taught the meanings and values of the society. Thus children are not forcibly isolated, but their deviations are tolerated and they are treated in such ways as are believed to be best for the acquisition of the meanings and values.

Variant theories have been advanced, of course, to explain feeble- mindedness and psychosis and to indicate how one or both might be cured. From the theory advanced here a hypothesis may be deduced which would predict one essential element in any cure: If the mentally deranged individual has been isolated from the larger society for any length of time, he will have to be taught the meanings and values of the society which he "forgot," or which he never learned because of his isolation, before he can act socially. If he does not know many of the meanings and values, the society will not accept him; and even if he has only a relatively few to learn, such rapid learning without guidance puts a special strain on the individual—comparable to adjustment to a new society.

7. To the extent that an individual has not adequately internalized the meanings and values of his group, he tends to ascribe power over the group to certain mysterious and sinister, though perhaps earthly, powers. This is derived from the theory in the following manner: If the individual does not perceive the basis of mutual expectations and mutual adjustment in common meanings and values, he will seek the explanation in terms of other forces which actually have

nothing to do with the group. This does not refer, of course, to a situation in which the culture itself includes a myth (which may be either a meaning or a value) that a certain supernatural force is the source of power over the group, but about a situation where a minority of the members believe this or its equivalent.

Support for this theory comes from studies showing that the type of anti-Semitism in which mysterious and evil powers are attributed to Jews is most likely to occur among disorganized and disturbed people.[22]

8. Insofar as new meanings and values arise in a social group through one-way communication from the mass media rather than through continued multilateral communication among all or most members of the group, the individual members get a feeling that they are being manipulated and that the powers manipulating them have no "right" to manipulate them (as would be true in a monarchy or dictatorship). When problems arise for the group, blame can readily be attached to these dimly comprehended powers and, by false identification of the powers, the phenomenon of scapegoating occurs. Thus, the more a society is manipulated through the mass media, or through other means by unperceived forces, the more it will tend to engage in scapegoating when mass frustration occurs. This hypothesis does not contradict the frustration-aggression hypothesis[23] but adds an amendment to it.

9. Social disorganization affecting individuals rather than sub-groups is most frequent in times when the values of the society seem most uncertain and impermanent and among those who have least communication with organized groups or communities. This hypothesis requires a study of the incidence of onset of psychosis, neurosis, and panic behavior, and the incidence of suicide, in relation to political-economic events and to certain social characteristics of the individuals affected.

To indicate how this hypothesis can be distinguished from the frustration-aggression theory, we may note a few types of incidents which would be frustrating but would not involve a decreased

[22] Nathan W. Ackerman and Marie Jahoda, *Anti-Semitism and Emotional Disorder* (New York: Harper, 1950). Also see T. W. Adorno *et al.*, *The Authoritarian Personality* (New York: Harper, 1950).

[23] John Dollard *et al.*, *Frustration and Aggression* (New Haven, Conn.: Yale University Press, 1939). Also see Department of Psychology, Harvard University, *ABC's of Scapegoating* (Chicago: Central Y.M.C.A. College, n.d.).

influence of values, and vice versa. For example, this hypothesis would predict a decrease of personal disorganization at the outbreak of a crisis about which no one could do anything, since the crisis would bring people into increased intercommunication, whereas the frustration-aggression theory would seem to call for an increase of personal disorganization at such a time, since there would be frustration without the possibility of direct, aggressive response to its source. This theory would predict an increase of personal disorganization during a time when major governmental policy was being debated (e.g., the "great debate" in the American Congress over "troops to Europe" and war with China in 1950–1951), whereas the frustration-aggression theory would predict a decrease of personal disorganization at that time, since the debate opened avenues for verbal aggression and created the possibility that frustrations caused by war and heavy military expenditures would be reduced. Systematic studies of situations of this type need to be made to test this hypothesis. Studies of family disorganization during the depression—by Angell, Cavan and Ranck, and Koos [24]—found that the depression was disorganizing only to those families that had little integration before it began, and thus tend to support the hypothesis. Hill and Boulding's study of the effect of wartime dislocation on families found similar results.[25] Studies of the incidence of functional mental disorder show that it occurs most frequently among those who are isolated from any kind of social group.[26]

10. When the whole group or society experiences a weakening of values, its members have a lower sense of social security,[27] which can result either in personal disorganization, as mentioned in hypothesis 9 above, or in successful efforts to re-create meanings and values. One constructive response of society to a weakening of values is

---

[24] Robert C. Angell, *The Family Encounters the Depression* (New York: Scribner, 1936); Ruth S. Cavan and K. Ranck, *The Family and the Depression* (Chicago: University of Chicago Press, 1938); Earl L. Koos, *Families in Trouble* (New York: King's Crown Press, 1946).

[25] Reuben Hill and Elise Boulding, *Families under Stress* (New York: Harper, 1949).

[26] Robert E. L. Faris and H. Warren Dunham, *Mental Disorders in Urban Areas* (Chicago: University of Chicago Press, 1939).

[27] It is to be recalled that the "social factor" has been herein defined as a conscious or unconscious taking into account the expectations and expected reactions of other persons. "Social security" thus refers to confidence that one knows the expectations and expected reactions of others. The popular use of the term "social security" refers, of course, to the *economic* security of the individual.

a great deal of public discussion, which may lead to the formation of interest groups—that is, more permanent structures for the achievement or maintenance of certain values. To test this point, it would be necessary to determine the social circumstances and historical times under which there is much organization of pressure groups, unions, businessmen's organizations, reform movements, etc. The hypothesis is that these would be times shortly following a period of rapid social change.

Another reaction to a large-scale loss of values is to form small groups that oppose the larger society, rather than work within it to reform it. These groups substitute their own formulation of standards for those that might be worked out for the society as a whole. Such groups exist in several forms, depending on their specific standards and activities: escapist literary societies, utopian community groups, criminal gangs, revolutionary movements, etc. Such groups, of course, do not re-establish the social security and values of individuals who are not among their members.

In still another type of reaction, the person may restore values and social security based on them by personal isolation and communication within himself. He can thus become a hermit, or engage in fantasy communication with fictitious persons who can be "controlled" mentally, or he can isolate himself for a good portion of the waking day with fictional persons who can be "controlled" by selection (e.g., of books, movies, radio programs).

These three modes of behavior are regarded as alternative means of re-establishing values and hence social security. Studies need to be made, not only to verify this hypothesis regarding their function, but also to determine the various circumstances and personality types that favor one mode of reaction rather than the other. Since the three modes are regarded as social-psychological equivalents, it can be hypothesized that those who are following one mode can less readily be induced to follow another mode than can a person whose original values have just been weakened and whose social security is consequently low. Insofar as an individual may be induced to follow one mode, it can be hypothesized that he will reduce his activities in other modes. These hypotheses can be tested by field experiments which induce persons in criminal gangs or persons given to excessive and indiscriminate movie-going or novel-reading to participate in reform or interest groups; such persons should be more resistant to such induction than those not so engaged, but when induced should reduce their "criminal" or "escapist" activities. This, of course, is the hypothesis underlying the "area project" experiment in Chicago, directed by Clifford Shaw.

11. The various forms of social disorganization tend to be concentrated among the same elements of the population. This follows from the theory since those with low internalization of the meanings and values of the society are the ones most likely to manifest social disorganization. Numerous researches by urban ecologists show the high concentration of functional psychosis, crime, suicide, prostitution, alcoholism, and so on, among those who live in the slum sections of the city and indicate that this cannot be due to hereditary factors, since the offspring of these people—practically all of whom move to other sections of the city as immigrants move in—do not have high rates of such social problems.[28] A subhypothesis is that those who have the first type of social disorganization (crime, prostitution, etc.) are not the same individuals as those who have the second type of social disorganization (psychosis, suicide, etc.). This hypothesis has been confirmed in Dunham's study of Chicago.[29]

12. Even when their native intelligence is high, criminals who are members of criminal groups have a low understanding and awareness, not to speak of acceptance, of the values of the larger society. That their meanings and values are at odds with the values of the larger society has been demonstrated by the Chicago group of criminologists,[30] but the above hypothesis has not yet been directly tested. Minority and majority ethnic groups also have been shown to have a low degree of understanding and awareness of one another's meanings and values.[31]

13. If a society undergoes a progressive trend toward weakening

[28] These researches are summarized in recent texts on human ecology and urban sociology such as James A. Quinn, *Human Ecology* (New York: Prentice-Hall, 1950); Amos H. Hawley, *Human Ecology* (New York: Ronald Press, 1950); Noel P. Gist and L. A. Halbert, *Urban Society* (3rd ed.; New York: Crowell, 1948); Stuart A. Queen and David Carpenter, *The American City* (New York: McGraw-Hill, 1952).

[29] H. Warren Dunham, "The Interrelationship of Criminal Behavior and Schizophrenic Psychosis," unpublished Ph.D. thesis, University of Chicago, 1941.

[30] Clifford Shaw and Henry D. McKay, *Juvenile Delinquency and Urban Areas* (Chicago: University of Chicago Press, 1942).

[31] Francis J. Brown and Joseph S. Roucek, *One America* (New York: Prentice-Hall, 1945); Arnold and Caroline Rose, *America Divided* (New York: Knopf, 1948).

and loss of common meanings and values, an increase of crime and civil disorder will be an earlier manifestation of the resultant social disorganization than will suicide and mental disorder. At a later stage in this development, criminals and revolutionists will be found to have a stronger internalization of the remaining social values than will people who have unsuccessfully attempted suicide or who are showing signs of mental disorder. A study by Porterfield[32] supports this hypothesis by showing that among those segments of our society that approach the secular-ideal type there is more suicide than among other segments, while among those segments of our society that approach the folk-ideal type there is more crime.

14. When a person moves out of a given social role into another, and the society fails to provide as full and clear-cut a set of meanings and values for the guidance of behavior in the second role as in the first, the person will experience a relative loss of contact with meanings and values (which Durkheim called anomie, and which is experienced subjectively as a sense of "meaninglessness of life"). This situation occurs in American society (1) for a man when he retires from his life occupation; (2) for a married woman when the last of her children leaves home or is about to leave home; (3) for an unmarried woman when she passes from the age of "young woman" to "old maid." This experience is temporary if the individual succeeds in carving out a new role for himself which has as complete a specification of meanings and values as his earlier role. But if he fails to take this active step, the permament anomie would soon assume some psychopathic form. To verify this hypothesis, it is necessary to examine the age, sex, and marital status incidence of functional psychoses (especially melancholia), suicide, and first visits to the psychiatrist. Tentative support for the hypothesis is offered by the fact that diagnoses of involutional melancholia are most frequent for women between the ages of 40 and 60, and for men between the ages of 60 and 70. Studies of the incidence of suicide since Durkheim first proposed, and tested, a similar hypothesis also support this hypothesis.[33]

15. The adequacy of the advance expectations for future social

[32] Austin L. Porterfield, "Suicide and Crime in Folk and in Secular Society," *American Journal of Sociology*, 57 (January 1952), 331–338.
[33] Emile Durkheim, *Suicide: A Study in Sociology* (1st ed.; Paris: Felix Alcan, 1897; American ed., Glencoe, Ill.: Free Press, 1951).

roles is a function of the definiteness and specificity of the meanings and values included in the future roles themselves. An operational definition of adequate expectations is that they are consistent, specific (rather than vague), and realistic (in the sense of being closely related to probable events in the future). In the one completed study known to have tested this hypothesis, it was shown that the roles of middle-class women are less definite and specific than those of middle-class men. The hypothesis was then given support by demonstrating that among middle-class college students the girls had less adequate expectations for adult social roles than did the boys.[34]

16. A person who communicates in a "responsible" and "facilitating" way in a group is better able than a person who communicates only his own attitudes and information to empathize with other members of the group. By responsible communication is meant such behaviors as encouraging the expression of all present points of view, relating facts and points of view expressed, pointing up differences or similarities in attitudes, clarifying or repeating important points, and helping the group to arrive at some consensus. By empathy is meant the ability to select, from among the vast number of cues emitted in group discussion, those which are significant for ascertaining the attitudes, interests, motivations, intentions, and so on, of other persons in the group and the ability to give a correct interpretation of these cues. Social psychologists in the Cooley-Mead tradition have assumed this hypothesis about the "social factor" (see assumption 1) to be true but have never submitted it to rigorous testing, so far as I know.

This list of hypotheses and subhypotheses derived from the basic theory of social organization and disorganization could be greatly extended. A more systematic specification of all tangential and implicit assumptions would be desirable, as would also a symbolic formulation of the hypotheses in the manner indicated for the first three hypotheses.

[34] See Arnold M. Rose, "The Adequacy of Women's Expectations for Adult Roles," *Social Forces*, 30 (October 1951), 69–77. Leonard S. Cottrell, Jr., has independently suggested a similar hypothesis in his challenging paper, "Some Neglected Problems in Social Psychology," *American Sociological Review*, 15 (December 1950), 709–711.

2

The Problem of a Mass Society

THE *preceding chapter was abstract and systematic; the next one, which is broadly descriptive and concrete, proposes to analyze the problems that arise from the relative lack of communication among people and their consequent difficulty in integrating themselves into modern society. The decline of the older society, based on organized group behavior, and the rise of the mass society are briefly traced, and a discussion of the widespread occurrence of the unstable "audience" and the importance of the "public"—the only kind of stable society possible in modern Western civilization—is presented.*

THE CHARACTERISTICS OF A MASS SOCIETY

MANY of those who probe into current social problems discover at the core a condition in which individuals find themselves without genuine contacts with one another. The individual finds it difficult or impossible to communicate satisfactorily with his fellows and consequently cannot orient his own values or put himself into harmony with society. As early as 1897 the great French sociologist Durkheim investigated suicide and found its chief modern cause in what he called *anomie*.[1] This was a sense of isolation, of estrangement from the fellowship and values of the social group, of anonymity. Later Faris and Dunham provided evidence that schizophrenia, the most common type of mental disease, was much more likely to occur in those whose life circumstances prevented them from developing close personal ties to their fellows.[2] Angell demonstrated that a major decline of income resulted in family disorganization only when there were few ties of intimacy and understanding among family members to begin with.[3] This list of scientific studies could

[1] Emile Durkheim, *Suicide* (American ed.; Glencoe, Ill.: Free Press, 1951).
[2] Robert E. L. Faris and H. Warren Dunham, *Mental Disorders in Urban Areas* (Chicago: University of Chicago Press, 1939).
[3] Robert C. Angell, *The Family Encounters the Depression* (New York: Scribner, 1936).

be greatly extended, but enough examples have been given to indicate a major conclusion of social science research into certain contemporary social problems. These problems in large measure result from the atomization of social groups into mentally isolated individuals.

It is highly illuminating to view these and other social problems in conjunction with the forms of human association typical of our time. This chapter proposes to analyze the problems rising from people's relative lack of communication and integration into a society in terms of three sociological constructs: "the organized group," "the audience," and "the public."

We can conceptualize the organized group as an association with multilateral communication and with common expectations for individual behavior formulated in terms of traditional meanings and values and known to all members. Thus the members of the organized group tend to behave in traditionally expected ways, and their behavior is only slowly modified over time as gradual extensions of the traditional meanings and values occur.[4]

The audience, on the other hand, may be defined as a form of association whose members act in similar ways because of a common source of stimulation but do not have much contact with one another.[5] Etymologically the term means "hearers" or "listeners" but it is used here to refer to recipients of communications through all sense organs, not only the ear. An almost ideal illustration of the sociological audience is the audience at a motion picture theater. People enter the darkened theater at different times and have practically no interaction with one another. They concentrate their attention on the screen, the common source of stimulation, and any influence on their behavior that arises out of their experience, either at the moment or after they leave, comes from the screen rather than from one another. The stimulation is one-way: Members of the audience usually do not respond to the screen with significant symbols, and

[4] The expectations are different for different age categories, so that the behavior of any one individual is modified drastically as he goes through his life cycle even though the society's meanings and values do not change.

[5] Floyd Allport has used the term "coacting group" to refer to what is here called the audience, but his term has unfortunately not been widely adopted. Several sociologists, including myself, have used the term "mass" to refer to what is here called the audience, but that term has been used in so many different ways that it has been a source of confusion. The term "audience" is not adequate for general use either, since it popularly connotes a purely receptive, passive group, whereas it will be shown here that important behavior results from participation in an audience.

even when occasionally they do respond they have no effect on the source of stimulation. The only influence members of the audience have on one another is through the vague feeling that there are other people who are also attentive to the screen; this keeps them from deviating significantly from culturally expected patterns of behavior as they might if they were completely alone. Communication in the audience, therefore, tends to be one-way rather than mutual. Members of the audience may act in *similar* ways because of their common stimulation but they do not act together *cooperatively* because there are no bonds among the members.

The members of the audience do not have to be in physical contact with one another. A radio audience, for example, is scattered widely, perhaps over an entire nation, and yet it fits perfectly the definition of audience. People who congregate in the street through the course of several hours or a day to watch an accident or a steam shovel in operation form an audience. One of the most important kinds of audience in contemporary American society is that which sees the billboards, car cards, and other forms of advertising. As already indicated, those who receive the communications of all mass media—radio programs, movies, newspapers, magazines, etc.—are audiences.

We may speak of the source of communication in the audience as a "propagandist," because the communication is one-way, without implying any derogatory connotation to that term. Since the sociologist is interested in the behavior of people, he is interested in the source of communication merely as a stimulus to a common behavior. Thus the sociologist is primarily concerned with the propagandist for his effects on the members of the audience. The propagandist may have the intention of influencing the audience or he may have no such intention. Regardless of the intent, the stimulus provided by the propagandist is an experience to the members of the audience and, especially if it is prolonged or frequently repeated, tends to have an influence on most of the members.

It would be incorrect to think of propaganda as generally bad or the intentions of the propagandist as always evil or selfish. Propagandists include those who try to get people to behave in a more rational fashion or in ways that are more beneficial or wholesome for themselves. Consequently, doing just the opposite of what the propagandist desires may be the most stupid and irrational kind of behavior. Similarly, ignoring all known forms of propaganda simply because they are propaganda would tend to make one immune to change and to improvement of any sort. It would include resistance to any form of education. Being a member of an audience, therefore, is not in itself a bad thing. The mass media are important and valuable sources of common action in a worth-while direction in our society. They are dangerous to the individual only when he is subject *solely* to their influence. If he has no specific information, general knowledge, or critical ability to resist them under any circumstances, then he is simply responding as an automaton to their influence.

Thus far only the direct positive effect on the behavior of individuals of being a member of an audience has been considered. There is another, indirect influence which is important for us to note. Members of an audience are not interacting with one another. They are more or less passive recipients of communications, rather than active initiators of communications. There is no adequate taking of the "role of the other" among members of an audience, nor is there much opportunity for the interplay of human emotions. This is another influence which reduces the human character of the member of an audience and makes him more like an automaton. A certain amount of time spent as a member of an audience has no effects on a person's ability to act as a human being, but if he spends a very large portion of his time as a member of an audience, he loses something of his ability to experience human reactions or human emotions, just as when he is physically isolated from his fellows.[6]

For example, students of the movies have long noted that those who are very frequent attenders at movies have less opportunity to participate as members of a family or a social group. The family and other forms of intimate association are the developers of the human personality and human emotions. It has been observed that people who are excessive movie-goers tend to act as though they were living in a dream world.[7] This is not only because they are imagining themselves in the plot of the movie but also because in the course of time they have lost some of their contact with reality,

[6] Robert E. Park and Ernest W. Burgess, *Introduction to the Science of Sociology* (Chicago: University of Chicago Press, 1924), Chap. IV, "Isolation." Also see the literature on "feral men" and on children who have been raised in isolation.

[7] Herbert Blumer, *Movies and Conduct* (New York: Macmillan, 1933).

owing to lack of regular human association and human interaction. Some observers have said that the radio has counteracted the effects of the movies by bringing people together in small groups to listen to the radio and providing an occasion for people to comment on the radio programs, to observe one another's emotional responses, and to participate in a collective experience. This is true insofar as attention is not completely absorbed by the mass medium. The radio allows a good deal of independence for the individual, since only his ears are engaged by the mass stimulation, and even they may be disengaged for direct conversation. With the advent of television, however, the eyes as well as the ears are focused and it is likely that television has almost as much desocializing effect on people as do the movies.

Just as the prevalence of the audience restricts the time available for organized group activities and face-to-face conversation, so it restricts the time available for privacy.[8] To the extent that one-way communication absorbs the time of the member of the mass, it prevents him from communicating with himself. Privacy as well as social interaction has a certain function in the formation of the human personality and emotions. Extensive thinking and planning can go on only in privacy because the individual must rationally examine the possible consequences of any pattern of behavior and think through all the future contingencies of his own and others' behavior. Past experience is enriched if the individual has the time afterward to go over it in his mind and think through the implications and values of it for himself. Insofar as the individual spends his time as a member of an audience, he has less privacy and consequently less time to do any of the above-mentioned things. This again is a question of degree, and one can profitably spend only a certain amount of time in privacy, so that being a member of an audience becomes dangerous to the individual only when he is a member of it for a large part of his waking time.

THE DEVELOPMENT OF MODERN MASS SOCIETY

Students of society have been aware for some time that there has been a trend ever since the Middle Ages toward an increase in the frequency of occurrence of audiences and of behavior based

[8] The distinction between privacy and isolation is that of Park and Burgess, *op. cit.*

upon audience experience and away from the kind of behavior that
is based on the organized group. It is because of this that one frequently hears contemporary society characterized as a "mass society,"
since the term "mass" is a technical equivalent of "audience." [9]

With some exaggeration we can characterize the older society out
of which the mass society developed as one based upon organized
group behavior.[10] Communities had to be somewhat isolated from
one another, and their members were governed by strong traditions.
In their limited circle people were in adequate communication with
one another and they had a strong sense of belonging and of loyalty
to the community. Their values were clear to them and were believed
to be practical as well as "true." People believed they understood
the controlling forces of their society, even though modern scientists
know that these beliefs had little relationship to reality. Outside
influences may have existed in their experience but were regarded
simply as beyond their ken and had little challenge for them, little
meaning in their daily lives.

The trend toward increasing frequency of occurrence of the audience has been due to several causes. The most obvious one has been
the invention of a large number of mass media and of conditions
through which these mass media could have a wide audience. To
a considerable extent the mass media force the formation of audi-

[9] We use the term "mass society" in a way different from that of some other sociologists. Duncan and Artis and Hatt use it to refer to the general American society, as
distinguished from the local community. (O. D. Duncan and J. W. Artis, "Some Problems of Stratification Research," Rural Sociology, 16 [March 1951], 17–29; Paul K.
Hatt, "Stratification in the Mass Society," American Sociological Review, 15 [April
1950], 216–222). Bennett and Tumin use it to refer to a type of social organization
where large numbers of people use approximately the same cultural practices. (J. W.
Bennett and M. M. Tumin, Social Life [New York: Knopf, 1948].) Brown uses the
term "cultural mass" in about the same way—to refer to the common elements of
culture in a pluralistic society. (James C. Brown, "Cooperative Group Formation: A
Problem in Social Engineering," unpublished.) Ortega represents an old tradition among
political scientists and publicists in using the term "mass society" to refer to a political
situation in which power is held by the large bulk of the people as distinguished from
one in which power is held by an elite group. (José Ortega y Gasset, Revolt of the
Masses [London: Allen and Unwin, 1932].) Marx and his followers have referred to
the "masses" in this way as meaning the bulk of the population as distinguished from
a property-owning or intellectual elite. The term "mass society" is used in this book
to refer to a social situation characterized by numerous and frequent formations of
people into audiences—in which communication is one-way from a leader or propagandist, with very little interaction among the members.

[10] Redfield's term "folk society" has gained currency to refer to societies based on
organized group behavior. (Robert Redfield, Tepoztlán, a Mexican Village [Chicago:
University of Chicago Press, 1930].)

ences and before they existed there was less opportunity for audiences to form. A second influence in the augmentation of the audience has been the decline of the organized group. With the Commercial and Industrial revolutions came a good deal of geographical mobility, especially from rural to urban areas.[11] Economic influences broke up a large number of the old communities and placed people in cities, where it is more difficult to form the highly integrated forms of social existence that are possible in isolated rural areas and small villages.

Coincident with this trend was the breakup or decline of some of the institutions which formerly buttressed much of the value system of medieval European society. The extended family, which gave the whole community a family-like unity and intimacy, has all but disappeared in the United States and has declined considerably in most of the countries of Western Europe. The church, which taught, interpreted, and expressed the social values, has declined sharply in its influences since the Middle Ages, and here the decline has been more rapid in Western Europe than it has in the United States.

The Industrial Revolution also weakened the integrating effect of certain institutions by forcing people to segmentalize their lives to a certain extent. The conjugal family no longer provides economic occupations, the primary source of recreation, or education for the young. There are now specialized institutions where one works, plays, goes to school, and so on, and each of these is distinct from the family. This segmentalization, or division of labor in the broad sense of the term, has further broken up the organized community in which people once had a high degree of mutual interaction with one another. While these changes have released individuals from the tyranny of community pressure to a considerable extent, and have opened up the possibility of greater freedom of thought and action in an individualistic sense, they have also opened the way for the audience to substitute for the organized community.

Most historians have failed, somehow, to tell us what these drastic changes meant to the average citizen. By far the keenest analysis has come from the pen of an economist and editor, Karl Polanyi.[12]

[11] A most important historical description of the initial effects of the Commercial Revolution is Henri Pirenne's *Economic and Social History of Medieval Europe* (London: Kegan Paul, Trench, Trubner, 1936).

[12] Karl Polanyi, *The Great Transformation* (New York: Farrar and Rinehart, 1944).

He points out that these changes, especially the "almost miraculous" improvement in the tools of production, were accompanied by "a catastrophic dislocation of the lives of the common people." Before the Industrial Revolution, most of the ordinary people had a basic economic security. The feudal serf was treated almost as a slave and had a minimum of legal and political rights. But he "belonged" to a plot of land, and no one could force him off it even though he was not the titular owner. The medieval village also had "common land," out of which a bare living could be eked by sheep raising. The serf and peasant before the nineteenth century subsisted on an extremely low standard of living, but they felt that there were minimum economic resources on which they could always rely. Then the "enclosure movement" dispossessed most of them of their land and the Commercial and Industrial revolutions transformed a majority from farmers into workers.

At first the sudden uprooting from the basic security of the land was met in England by a sort of minimum wage law (the Speenhamland Act) whereby a worker who did not earn the minimum would have his wages supplemented up to the minimum by the government. This was a last gesture at maintaining the old security under the new system of industrial capitalism. It failed to work because employers found they could depress wages below the minimum without starving their workers and because workers found that they could loaf on the job without getting fired or lowering their total incomes below the minimum specified by law. After the law was repealed, in 1834, each worker found that his economic security was completely at the mercy of an employer, and each employer had to meet the competition of an impersonal market. Whenever confidence in the employer was shaken, either because of his personal arbitrariness or because he was not competing effectively, there was a drop in the worker's sense of security. Even though the average income per worker rose markedly under industrial capitalism, the *feeling of security* sagged. Each depression, with successively larger unemployment rates, provided a new blow to the worker's feeling that he was economically safe. This led to personal demoralization on the one hand and the demand for security on the other.

The demand for security took two forms: the organization of trade-unions and pressure for laws to provide minimum security. The growth of unions and farmers' organizations and the passage of social security laws, minimum wage laws, relief laws, and the like have compensated somewhat for the basic economic security previously provided by the land. But many workers are not members of effective unions, the unions do not have complete control over firing, the farmers' organizations do not have complete control over pricing, and many workers and most farmers are not covered by the security laws, so the economic problem of the mass society remains.

A comparable history could be traced for the businessman. During the Middle Ages, his production was protected by guilds, and his return by a conception of a "just price." These did not make for efficiency or initiative and so kept his financial return low, but they did give security. When the free enterprise system developed at the end of the eighteenth century, the businessman had more chances to grow very wealthy, but he also had a greater chance to fail. He was now subject to the vicissitudes of cutthroat competition, of depressions, of fashion in demand for his product, of inventions that would make his product quickly obsolete. So he gradually developed monopolistic combines, "fair trade" laws, techniques to suppress new inventions, and so on. But most businessmen have not completely solved their problems of insecurity, as is evident in their panicky behavior whenever a depression seems to threaten.

Another aspect of the transition from folk society to mass society has been investigated by Mayo and his followers.[13] While studying industrial fatigue and spontaneous featherbedding in industrial plants, Mayo found that such changes as rest periods and improvements in lighting helped to increase worker efficiency. The only difficulty with his early experiments was that *everything* helped; in fact production stayed high even when all the good things were removed. Interviewing the workers revealed that it had been the sympathetic attention given to the workers while the experiment was going on that had the effect, not the mechanical changes. Similar results have been demonstrated throughout industry by Golden and Ruttenberg.[14] They show that even pay raises, bonuses, and profit sharing have seldom, if ever, increased worker output. After extended investiga-

[13] Elton Mayo, *Human Problems of an Industrial Civilization* (New York: Macmillan, 1933).

[14] Clinton S. Golden and Harold J. Ruttenberg, *The Dynamics of Industrial Democracy* (New York: Harper, 1942).

tion, the Mayo group came to the following conclusion: When the worker felt he was treated as an impersonal cog in an industrial machine, he did not care much about doing a good job for the employer; but when personal interest was taken in the problems of the employee, when he was consulted on all matters concerning his job, and when rewards and punishments were given out with strict attention to all the factors in the worker's situation, his job morale and efficiency rose.

Viewed historically, the factory system under capitalism did transform most workers into impersonal cogs—labor was regarded as an ingredient in production, just as were materials and capital. The worker consequently felt a loss of individuality; he became one of the sheep portrayed so realistically by Charlie Chaplin in *Modern Times*. As a number rather than a man, he felt little incentive, even when a raise in pay might be held out as bait to him. A study by Professor W. Lloyd Warner and his associates of a strike in a New England city during the mid-1930s revealed that the strike had been building up in the workers' minds for eighty years.[15] The strike occurred in a shoe factory, where—eighty years previously—machine production had replaced skilled hand production. Workers no longer owned their tools; there was little opportunity to exercise skill; there was no way of knowing how the productive process might next be altered. Ownership changed hands, passing from the enterprising, responsible, paternalistic local leaders to an unknown corporation with headquarters in New York. The new bosses were simply well-paid agents for an impersonal power, and they seemed to care little about the workers or their town. There seemed to be little chance of getting ahead, and there could be little pride in work when the workers' jobs were so petty. The strike, out of which a union developed, was simply one manifestation of decades of frustration.

Drucker reports a telling story of what happened in an airplane factory toward the end of World War II.[16] The factory was playing a crucial role in war production, yet the turnover and absentee rates were very high and the production rate low. The workers were "fed up" with war shortages of consumers' goods, the difficulties of transportation to and from work, the inadequate housing, the confusion

---

[15] W. Lloyd Warner and J. O. Low, *The Social System of the Modern Factory. The Strike: A Social Analysis* (New Haven, Conn.: Yale University Press, 1947).

[16] Peter F. Drucker in a personal conversation.

of working in a rapidly expanded plant. Government officials and plant managers grew frantic as output continued to slip and no appeal seemed to work.

Then the Army put on exhibition a war-battered bomber plane that had been produced at that very factory several years earlier. With it came the crew that had flown the bomber on dozens of missions over Germany and that was now back in the States for a deserved rest. Members of the crew were "guides" to the plane; it was thought they would tell the workers about the bombing flights. It had not been expected that many workers would stay after hours to see the plane. But the workers came in droves and most of them asked questions. The questions were pretty much of the same pattern: "My job is to do thus-and-so. Would you please tell me where the part I handle is in the plane, and what it does?" The workers did not know what they were doing! Naturally they did not see their relation to the war effort. When the part at which each worked was pointed out, its function explained, and perhaps an anecdote passed along as to how that part had once been hit or how it protected a flier, the workers were delighted. It sounds incredible to those who have never felt as these workers apparently did, but production immediately jumped. As far as anyone could tell, the bomber exhibit— or, rather, the workers' discovery of the significance of their jobs in the total war effort—was the cause. The specialists had regained a conception of the whole, at least temporarily.

Economists and industrial relations experts like Polanyi, Mayo, Warner, and Drucker have done a good job of analyzing the shift from folk society to mass society insofar as it is manifested in the economic sphere of life. Sociologists, as we noted earlier, have paid a good deal of attention to the consequences of a mass society, but they have not analyzed the social consequences in historical terms. What happens to the individual, for example, when recreation shifts from the participant form to the passive, vicarious form? At present, we can only speculate, but certain hypotheses seem likely.

When individuals participate in games or other sociable recreation, they are obliged to communicate constantly with one another and to adjust their behavior and attitudes to those of the other participants. Social bonds grow out of such adjustments and readjustments. But when individuals take their recreation by observing other people play, they are not "interacting," they are not adjusting their behavior and attitudes to those of other people. Of course, there is a certain amount of interaction within the audience, especially when an individual comes to the sports event with other people. But, on the whole, the interpersonal relations consist largely of the members of the audience observing the players and the players communicating to one another and to the audience, with the audience having only a small reaction back on the players and not as individuals but as a mass. Modern man, of middle or lower income, has much more time for recreation than did his ancestors, but an increasing proportion of that recreational time is spent in a passive audience type of situation in which the individual is not communicating with, learning from, or adjusting to, his fellows.

Let us be more concrete in examining some of the trends through which the audience has become a more important factor in the life of the modern citizen. In 1790, only 5 per cent of the people of the United States lived in cities; in 1950, 63.7 per cent lived in cities, and the proportion has undoubtedly risen since then. A major adjustment is involved in moving from a rural area to a city, and not enough study has been devoted to the social consequences of this trend, which is still going on. Most urban neighborhoods, especially those in which people with middle and upper incomes live, are not highly integrated in the sense that all the people know one another and that a common set of stores and other facilities serve all of them. Whereas in rural areas or villages a resident will know all those who live within a radius of several miles, an urbanite may not know his next-door neighbor. There are special occasions in the village when most people will come out at one time and talk to one another— while attending a fair or an auction, or simply while watching the train come through. The absence of these things in the city creates for it a reputation of being cold and unfriendly.

Actually, of course, it is easy to make more friends in the city than in the country, because more people are available and there is a greater possibility of finding those who are temperamentally congenial. But one makes friends in a different way—by associating with fellow workers on the job; by joining a club, a church, or a union; or by going to a skating rink or bowling alley. One's friends may be scattered over many parts of a city rather than living close by. For the person who moves from the country to the city, it may be difficult to learn that physical closeness of residence is not a necessary basis of association. Consequently, he is lonely and isolated. This is especially significant in view of the fact that most immigrants to the city are unattached people rather than family groups, and so do not even have spouses, parents, or children to turn to for companionship. The isolated individual is a member of an audience, not of an organized society.

The city is heterogeneous, made up of groups of many divergent interests and backgrounds. This diversity, coupled with the large size of the urban population, which permits even a well-known individual to walk down most streets unnoticed, creates opportunities for freedom of personal behavior that is rare in villages and that scarcely existed before the rise of the large city in the nineteenth century.[17] Freedom and diversity have been two of the great attractions of city life, and they have been essential elements in the development of artistic and intellectual activities wherever they have appeared. But freedom imposes a responsibility on the individual to make up his own mind as to what kind of behavior he wishes to engage in. There are fewer standards to which the individual must conform, and the concepts of "right" and "good" are made more relative. To an individual without the training to make up his own mind on such ethical matters, or the strength of character to conform to standards which he thinks proper, freedom may be demoralizing. The demoralized individual is also a member of an audience, not of an organized society.

The city is also complex, or rather it reflects the complexity of modern life, which impinges on rural areas also. Complexity is confusing to the average individual. Just as industrial relations experts like Mayo[18] and Drucker[19] have shown that the complexity of machine production confuses the industrial worker and makes him unhappy, so could it be observed that the increasing complexity of other aspects of modern life creates new sources of confusion for most citizens.

[17] Louis Wirth, "Urbanism as a Way of Life," *American Journal of Sociology*, 44 (July 1938), 1–24.

[18] *Op. cit.*

[19] Peter F. Drucker, *The Future of Industrial Man: A Conservative Approach* (New York: Day, 1942).

Take politics, for example: The activities and structures of government are far more complex today than they were a hundred years ago. The government touches the lives of the average citizen at many more points. Despite the higher level of formal education, it is probable that the average citizen today understands the government less than ever at those points at which it impinges on him. This perhaps explains the widespread belief that corrupt and evil forces have control of the government (even when its head—Roosevelt, Truman, or Eisenhower, for example—may be widely trusted and respected, and even when there is a popular demand that the government engage in a greater number of activities to aid ordinary people). And a rumor that the Jews are widely infiltrated into the government will catch as a reasonable explanation of why the operations of government are so mysterious. In the organized-group society of premodern times clearly specified powers were known to have control of government, and the common people were not supposed to bother their heads with it. In today's democracy, the people are supposed to take responsibility for government, but it has become too complicated for them to understand. So they are confused and feel alienated from their "government" in some ways (not from their flesh and blood president, senator, representative, or Supreme Court justice, however). A confused people form an audience also, not an organized society.

There are other aspects of modern society which give the individual a sense of insecurity and alienation, and social forces are tending to increase these feelings. There is space only to list them here. First, the functions of women have decreased sharply since the day when a woman was a major helpmate to her husband in breadwinning and when she was the chief educator for a large brood of children. The mechanical revolution greatly reduced and simplified household tasks. Yet society imposes no demands that she seek substitute functions.[20] She can try her hand at a paid job or at social welfare activity, but usually no one says that she must. And so the modern wife, after her youngest child has started school, is partly functionless, which means that she is likely to raise questions to herself about her very reason for existence and to feel a vague but pervasive

[20] Arnold M. Rose, "The Adequacy of Women's Expectations for Adult Roles," *Social Forces*, 30 (October 1951), 69–77.

dissatisfaction. Since she has related herself to other people only at marginal points, and since she is uncertain as to her own role in society, she is a member of an audience, not of an organized society.

While the spread of formal education has increased modern man's sophistication, and in one sense has helped him to understand the forces which control him, it has concomitantly increased his skepticism regarding the sources of his information. This would tend to decrease false beliefs if the citizen knew how to secure alternative sources of facts and if he could weigh all the evidence and apply the scientific historian's rules of internal and external criticism. But the education of most people has not proceeded that far. They have learned only up to the point that propagandists are all about and that few sources of news are to be trusted. Consequently some people are generally in as bad a predicament as the several hundred women who, in early 1946, waited outside a hosiery store hoping to buy a pair of nylons. An hour earlier the proprietor had put up a sign saying "No More Nylons" and had locked his door as he could not transact other business with hundreds of women milling about in pursuit of nonexistent nylons. A policeman tried to persuade the women to move along: "Really, ladies, there ain't any more nylons today." Responded one of the hopefuls, "I never believe rumors." While this woman had not yet reached the state of bewilderment arrived at when people find out that sometimes it pays to believe signs and sometimes it doesn't, most Americans have arrived at that stage. When people do not know what to believe, and yet feel a need for information, they are members of an audience, not of an organized society.

While this analysis of contemporary society could be greatly extended, it should be quite clear that folk society has turned into mass society to a considerable extent. Consensus among people on values and ways of behaving hardly exists any longer because tradition and closely knit social structures have been weakened. People have increasingly become mentally isolated from one another, and they are confused by and suspicious of the forces that seem to control them.

REACTIONS TO THE MASS SOCIETY

Imaginative laymen and social scientists have been aware of this essential weakness caused by the excessive development of the audience in contemporary society, but the general public has reacted in a much more confused and emotional way. There has arisen, for example, a widespread hatred of city life and a sharp criticism of it in terms of its evils coupled with a desire to return to the "neighborliness" of the country. It may be hypothesized that the city represents, in the minds of these people, the audience structure of society which urbanization has historically fostered. This attitude has contributed also to the fascination for movements which seek to "incorporate" individuals completely and provide them with channels for communication from which there can be no deviation. Thus the popular reaction to the audience may have dangers for society even more extreme than those created by the audience itself.

For example, many of the current isms—not the least of which are fascism and anti-Semitism—appeal to the masses in terms of their promise to reintegrate the individual into the social order.[21] They hold out to the isolated, anonymous, modern man an offer to rejoin society, to regain his sense of social belonging, and to eliminate his conflict of values which arises from an unintegrated existence. This is no small offer to the mass man beset by extreme loneliness and mental conflict. The mass society we live in today is not and cannot be stable or progressive in an orderly way. It is likely to run to extreme panaceas—to orgiastic religious movements on the one hand, and to all-explaining, all-dominating dictatorships on the other hand. Neither of these will solve the problem, since they rely on false explanations and maintain the audience condition of society in order to perpetuate themselves.

There are those who would get rid of mass society by seeking to return to a folk society. Included among them are the agrarians who would abolish cities and return the populations to farms, the medievalists who would abolish diversity and set up one moral and intellectual authority, the primitivists who would re-establish ancient cultural forms and abolish modern ones. All these people, with their "quest for certainty," see the problems engendered by modern mass society but do not see the unplanned results of their solutions. The population is now too large and too specialized to return to the farm; the agrarian solution could be achieved only by killing off some

---

[21] Paul Massing, *Rehearsal for Destruction* (New York: Harper, 1950); Robert F. Byrnes, *Anti-Semitism in Modern France* (New Brunswick, N.J.: Rutgers University Press, 1950).

90 per cent of the people. The population is now too well educated and too heterogeneous to accept the medievalist solution of setting up one leader to answer all moral and intellectual questions. The population is too sophisticated and too adjusted to modern technology to accept the primitivist solution of abolishing modern culture forms. Short of a catastrophic destruction of most of the people and our culture, it would appear that the major sources of mass society are here to stay: the large cities, modern machine methods and other types of labor-saving technology, at least an elementary education for most children, people with diverse background and interests, and so on.

Most people seem to feel that these things are not bad in themselves, and the great majority seems anxious to take advantage of them. The question facing most people, then, seems not simply to be how to abolish the mass society but how to eliminate its unhappy consequences while retaining its beneficent causes. A great deal of thinking and research needs to be done to answer this question.

Philosophers and sociologists have given this problem their attention for over a generation. As early as 1909, Charles Horton Cooley deplored the trend toward mass society, toward a "dead level of culture" in which every individual was cut in the same mold as every other one and all were subjected to the same influences without the opportunity to discuss matters adequately.[22] Cooley observed that nationality groups were declining in the United States and would no longer provide the diversity of culture that would be essential for culture growth. He foresaw and advocated the growth of groups that would develop specific aspects of culture according to their own special interests, abilities, or backgrounds. Cooley was far more democratic than some of our later-day cultural pluralists who insist that nationality is the sole basis of cultural diversity and demand that individuals devote all aspects of their life to their nationality group; he would not only encourage cultural development in all kinds of groups, including the nationality groups, but would also allow individuals to join these groups on a voluntary basis instead of being involuntary members on the basis of birth alone.

Robert E. Park was an outstanding sociologist who was concerned about the trend toward a mass society.[23] In order to make it clear

---

[22] Charles H. Cooley, *Social Organization* (New York: Scribner, 1909).
[23] Park and Burgess, *op. cit.*, pp. 791–796.

that the mass is not the only form of a modern democratic society, Park and his follower Herbert Blumer[24] delineated the "public" in sharp distinction to it. Their ideas had roots in the writings of the publicist Walter Lippmann[25] and the university president A. Lawrence Lowell.[26] The public is a huge informal discussion group. When any problem arises or when anything happens that concerns them collectively, members of the public talk the matter over, argue it out in such a way that everyone's attitude is influenced by everyone else's. That does not mean that the resulting "public opinion" is completely unanimous; it simply means that every person understands the other's point of view and has somehow given it consideration. It also does not mean that everyone is considering the same subject or pursuing the same line of cultural development; there are many publics, each with a different interest, and one may join or leave them freely and voluntarily. While there is this element of volition in membership, the public—for any specific issue—is a definite enough group with adequate communication among its members. There is thus no social isolation, no sense of loneliness, no unsatisfied longing to belong to some group or movement.

While all the members of a public are subjected to the same influences, including propaganda, the influences are not taken at their face value and so are not directly determining. Members of a public do not respond directly to outside stimuli as members of a mass do; rather they evaluate every influence to see how it fits in with their knowledge, beliefs, and expectations. The public has a culture and a set of ideals with which to make these evaluations.

Leadership in the public tends to shift. Anyone who sets forth a distinctive and interesting point of view, or sometimes merely an important fact, draws the attention of other people, and for a while the discussion centers around what he has to say. When someone else has a more attractive point of view or bit of information to express, the leadership of the public shifts to him. Some persons are adept in forms of expression and hold leadership of the public for considerable lengths of time if they keep attuned to what is of public

[24] Herbert Blumer, "Collective Behavior," in Alfred M. Lee (ed.), *New Outline of the Principles of Sociology* (New York: Barnes and Noble, 1946), pp. 185–193.

[25] Walter Lippmann, *Public Opinion* (New York: Harcourt, Brace, 1922).

[26] A. Lawrence Lowell, *Public Opinion and Popular Government* (New York: Longmans, Green, 1913).

interest; they are not innovating leaders—as propagandists of the audience often are—but rather the well-known type of "leaders who follow."

Clearly the public is the only kind of stable society which is possible in modern Western civilization, since the isolation and unbroken tradition required by the folk society can no longer exist. The public can exist for a long time only in a democracy, since it requires freedom of expression and freedom of belief. Much of American, British, Scandinavian, and Dutch society has been that of the public type, and this helps to explain the long devotion to democracy which has characterized these nations. Some of the Central European nations—notably Germany, Austria, and Italy—have less of a tradition of free discussion and therefore urbanization and secularization in them have created the mass rather than the public. When modern democratic governments developed in these countries, they proved to be unstable. Some of the Eastern European nations have never ceased to be folk societies, at least in their rural areas, and an authoritarian type of government that does not too strongly violate local traditions is satisfactory to them.

The distinction between the audience and the public is a most important one for the analysis of contemporary society. In the first place, it should be noted that while both may exist in a democratic society, the audience, when it is the dominant form of group in a society, is such an unstable and unsatisfying condition that it is actually conducive to totalitarianism. But dictatorship provides only superficial satisfaction to the needs created by mass society. While the totalitarian state provides something for the people to belong to, it still keeps people apart and out of communication with one another. No dictatorship can survive if the common people form publics and freely discuss their situation, their culture, and their ideals. For if they do so, they threaten the dictatorship, or at least prevent it from doing what it wishes to do.

Fascism, therefore, sets up the strongest barriers to certain kinds of communication among citizens and yet tries to create the illusion that they are fully integrated members of an understanding and protective state. The dictator must subject his people to frequent propaganda and expect them to respond to it directly. Thus every totalitarian state in these days of high average education and easy

means of communication must be a mass society, even though it may
have a camouflage of stability. The mass society is no more stable
under dictatorship than it is under democracy. Fascism eventually
turns out to be a mirage. While it recruits members in its early stages
because it seems to be a way out of the mass society, it becomes an
extreme form of the mass society once it has achieved power and is
seeking to keep people in line.

The Soviet Communist dictatorship has been much cleverer than
the Fascist in avoiding some of the unpleasantness and ill effects of
the mass society.[27] The Communist leaders know that a sense of
participation in the processes of government and a *feeling* of being
free to discuss the matters relevant to political affairs are important
for the satisfaction and mental health of the ordinary citizen. They
therefore outline a set of discussion topics which are considered by
them to be of greatest significance and yet which can be discussed
without endangering the leadership in the exercise of power. To make
sure the discussion does not take a "dangerous" turn, they specify
in great detail what are the "right solutions" at which the discussion
should eventually arrive.

Every adult and adolescent in the Soviet state is urged and pressured into being a member and attending the meetings of a small
discussion group composed of people who work or live in the same
place. The discussion topics are handed over to a trusted group
leader who is a member of the Communist party, and with every
sort of moral pressure people are encouraged to discuss the topics
and to arrive at the predetermined solutions. In one sense the discussion is free, or at least gives the appearance of being free, since any
kind of argument can be raised if it is properly refuted when it does
not lead to the predetermined conclusion. There is considered to be
only one right answer and all deviations from it show incorrect thinking. In addition to engaging in the discussions, the average member
of the Soviet state is urged to participate in all sorts of activities for
the physical, mental, and moral improvement of the community and
the society at large, as specified by the Communist leaders. This high

---

[27] Some of the better sources on what is currently going on within the Soviet Union
are the publications of the Russian Research Center of Harvard University. See
especially Alex Inkeles, *Public Opinion in Soviet Russia* (Cambridge, Mass.: Harvard
University Press, 1952); Raymond A. Bauer, *The New Man in Soviet Psychology*
(Cambridge, Mass.: Harvard University Press, 1952).

degree of community participation and interpersonal communication removes much of the sense of isolation which is the basis of the problems created by the mass society. There is a great deal of friendly sociability in these activities and the individual citizen perhaps gets the feeling of participating in the important activities of his time. He is generally unhampered by the state unless he consistently refuses to be convinced of the right solution of all the social problems as specified by his leaders. He is aware that there is a threat of power in the background pushing him into conformity with the line specified by the Communist party, but his more immediate sensation is one of not being isolated and of belonging first to the small group and through it to the whole Communist state which considers itself not only national but international.

In the discussions the Soviet citizen is given full "explanations" of the forces controlling the social world. These explanations stem from basic Marxist theory, and while they seem utterly bizarre and unrealistic to the outsider whose mind is not completely adapted to the framework of Communist theory, the Soviet citizen learns through long practice to work his thinking through to an acceptance of these explanations. Through his extensive participation in community activities and through the "election" of lower party leaders, the Soviet citizen is given the impression that he is one of the controllers of the Soviet state. He, of course, is given only a choice of voting for the "right" candidate or not voting at all, and of participating in the "right" activities as determined by his leaders or not participating at all. A great deal of community and other pressure is used on him to participate and to vote and talk and think in the "right" way.

The Soviet state by these means avoids the *appearance* of being a mass society and tries to give its citizens the *feeling* that they are not simply an audience for the leaders. Actually, however, the Soviet state is still one large audience because there is no connection between the tremendous amount of communication and participation at the lower level and the ultimate control of important activities and even of social values by the top leaders. The important communications are still one way, from the top down, and the only thing that is characteristic of the audience and is avoided in the Soviet state is the block against the intercommunication of the members of the audience. The leaders pay attention to the discussion at the lower level only insofar as they are interested in measuring the current amount of deviation from the party line which they specify.

The fact that the state is one large audience, however, is apparent only to the more sophisticated people and to those who are themselves within the middle or upper levels of the party hierarchy. They are the ones who are aware of the huge, impersonal, audience-controlling mechanism that the Soviet state is, and they are the ones who not infrequently become prey to the diseases of the mass society. For the ordinary citizen who has never been aroused to what is going on around him or has never shown any willingness to deviate, the satisfactions of the small group discussions and the community participation may be quite enough to keep him happy and to give him a sense of rootedness and belonging and a belief that he understands the mechanism of the state and has a share in its control. Whether the average Soviet citizen will ever realize that these are delusions cannot be predicted. It is quite possible that the avoidance of the sharpest weaknesses of the mass society will leave him sufficiently satisfied to avoid questioning whether he has any voice that actually does reach through to the top of the Soviet hierarchy. The people of Russia also have roots in a pre-Communist folk society which was a highly integrated social organization, and this serves to give the Soviet society a stability based on the past stronger than would normally occur in a more modernized and industrialized society.

The purpose of considering the Soviet system of community participation and group discussion was to clarify the distinction between audience and public. Despite appearances to the contrary the Soviet system is not a true example of the public. The public can provide an antidote to the mass society, and the Soviet leaders have attempted to gain some of the advantages of the structure of the public as distinct from that of the audience. But the true public can exist only when there is diversity of opinions and backgrounds, when there are freedom and complexity, and when the sources of information are manifold. Yet it avoids isolation and confusion and puts people on the road toward resolution of mental and valuational conflicts.

The "public" is only a word, of course, and therefore it does not "do" any of these things. What is meant is that the conditions which create the social relationship known as the public are also the conditions which eliminate some of the characteristics of the social relationship known as the audience. The main condition is that of free and constant communication. If people can talk over their divergent points of view, and vicariously share their divergent experiences and sources of information, their confusion will diminish and they will have a clearer understanding of the forces that move society. If, through this communication, they can relate themselves to one another despite their initial differences, not only will they cease to feel isolated, but also they can develop a sense of participation in the political process. The achievement of a consensus in a political discussion usually results in a demand for expression of that consensus in some sort of political action.

Free discussion does not necessarily result in the elimination of divergence and the creation of uniformity. In the first place, diversity arises in our society naturally, and it would take a ruthless dictatorship to eliminate it. Secondly, discussion seldom results in unanimity of opinion (witness our presidential elections which involve a maximum of discussion but practically never a majority of more than 60 per cent). Thirdly, the deviation of minor groups in a society will be tolerated only if there is some understanding of the causes of deviation of those groups and of the exact nature of the deviation. Fourthly, if minor groups wish to participate in the processes which affect the society as a whole, and to see that their point of view and interests get represented, they must relate themselves to other groups and work cooperatively with them. Finally, the existence of minor groups with divergent ideas and culture forms depends on the preservation of democratic government, and democratic government requires at least a minimum of understanding and cooperation among its citizenry. Diversity thus fosters intellectual and cultural development only if there is adequate communication through most of the society.

Let us assume that this hypothesis is correct, that the solution for the difficulties created by mass society is the attainment of a "public" state of social relationships in which discussion is free and constant, and that no major issue is settled without a public opinion having been formed about it. How then can this social condition be achieved? Until further studies are made, no one can say. But some hypotheses may be offered which have a basis in general sociological knowledge:

1. A major block to communication from the standpoint of the individual is a feeling of insecurity. All efforts to promote security,

especially job security, will reduce these paranoid tendencies in people which block their communication with others.

2. Discussions take place most freely and constantly if people are in groups which have a definite purpose and time for discussion. Devices should be found for encouraging people to join functional groups —such as civic improvement organizations, political clubs, unions, and recreational associations. New kinds of voluntary interest associations could possibly be developed.

3. Attachment to neighborhood could be stimulated. Recently, city planning has taken the line of developing neighborhood units with all necessary facilities and space for recreation. More attention needs to be given to the social side of these "housing projects." Also, people in the older city blocks might be encouraged to take advantage of the benefits of cooperation to get advantages for themselves which they could not afford as individuals. All such activities would promote group attachment on a neighborhood basis and would also help to eliminate some of the major "evils" of city life.

4. On many important issues, people do not have access to the facts, or to the arguments for different points of view. Newspapers in many localities do not provide this information or see the need for providing it. Provision of basic information regarding important issues, in readable and easily accessible form, would seem to be an aid to discussion.

5. New ways of disseminating information need to be devised. Adult educators have been working on this problem for a long time but have not yet found enough ways to make adult education interesting.

6. Civic groups need to put pressure on newspapers to gain more adequate representation of issues. At present, newspaper adequacy and point of view seem to be determined almost solely by owners and advertisers.

7. There is too much cynicism about the possibility of making contact with differing groups. One of the characteristics of a leader is that he is not cynical regarding possibilities. Some group leaders have worked out effective techniques for making contacts between their group and members of other social classes and races.

8. Training in public speaking could be made available to members of functional groups who feel they need it. One of the most popular courses in most labor education programs is public speaking. The major reason the class members give for selecting the course is that

they sometimes feel the urge to express themselves at a union meeting but are afraid they will make fools of themselves.

These are simply suggestions for promoting more effective communication. Any of the suggestions may be wrong, and together they may be ineffective, as future experimentation would show. But they represent the sort of thing about which we must think and be inventive if we are to solve the problems created by the mass society. The alternatives seem to be either to continue to drift in a mass society, with its pain for the individual and its danger to culture, or to turn to some form of totalitarianism, with its loss of liberty for the individual and its placing of culture in rigid molds. Since the mass society is inherently unstable, if there are no efforts to combat the alienation of modern man, totalitarianism is our destiny. Unfortunately, too many seem to be willing to give up and accept totalitarianism as the way out of the mass society.

3

A Theory of the Function of
Voluntary Associations in Contemporary
Social Structure

THE *last chapter presented a description of the problems arising from the character of contemporary society. The following one describes some of the readjustments that contemporary society has made to the problems previously considered. The hypothesis presented here is that voluntary associations have three important functions in supporting political democracy in the United States: (1) They distribute power among a great many citizens. (2) They provide a sense of satisfaction with modern democratic processes. (3) They provide a social mechanism for continually instituting social change. If the hypothesis is correct, the voluntary association is a most important institution and deserves more research attention.*

STATEMENT OF THE THEORY

AMERICANS take their voluntary associations for granted, as an understood manifestation of democratic social life. There has never been a full-scale published study of voluntary associations in the United States, and what partial studies there are do not take up their role in relationship to political democracy.[1] Among intellectuals, there is even a bit of snobbishness in the attitude toward voluntary associations: They are assumed to be either groups of ladies (à la Helen Hokinson) who have little to do but chatter to one another, or groups of neurotic fanatics who want to reform the world by preachments. The hypothesis of this chapter, to the contrary, is that voluntary associations—at least those that are organized to accomplish some

---

[1] A major exception is the trade-union, which has been well studied. Since the trade-union requires special consideration it will be given little attention in this chapter. References to the literature on voluntary associations are made elsewhere in this and the following chapters.

goal outside the direct satisfaction of expressive needs of the members—play a major role in American democracy.

More specifically, the hypothesis is that the voluntary associations have three important functions in supporting political democracy in the United States: (1) They *distribute power over social life* among a very large proportion of the citizenry, instead of allowing it to be concentrated in the elected representatives alone, so that the United States has a little of the character of the ancient Greek democratic city-state, as well as of the modern European centralized republic. (2) The voluntary associations *provide a sense of satisfaction with modern democratic processes* because they help the ordinary citizen to see how the processes function in limited circumstances, of direct interest to himself, rather than as they grind away in a distant, impersonal, and incomprehensible fashion. (3) The voluntary associations *provide a social mechanism for continually instituting social changes,* so that the United States is a society in flux, constantly seeking (not always successfully, but seeking nevertheless) to solve long-standing problems and to satisfy new needs of groups of citizens as these needs arise. Data have not yet been collected to test these hypotheses; the purpose of this paper is to examine some of their implications and to take a look at some of the facts that are, in general, relevant to the hypotheses.

The thesis stated, it is necessary immediately to place some qualifications on it: (1) Certain other democratic nations—Switzerland, the Scandinavian countries, and Great Britain—use the same mechanism of voluntary associations to achieve the same functions. Even those democratic nations like France, which do not have a large part of their citizenry active in voluntary associations, nevertheless tolerate the associations. Thus, the thesis is in no sense unique to the United States. (2) Other democratic nations have other social mechanisms for achieving the same purposes that voluntary associations work toward in the United States. The French, for example, have other means of gaining understanding of, and satisfaction with, democratic processes, and other means of instituting social change. (3) The voluntary association is a far from perfect institution, in the United States, in achieving the social functions listed above. Many people— especially in the lower-income groups—are not active in associations, and many associations are frustrated in their efforts to leave their mark on social life. (4) There are numerous other mechanisms for instituting social, political, and economic changes in the United States; interest is here restricted to one mechanism without in the least denying the importance of the others. These qualifications should be understood as intrinsic parts of the thesis, so that there will be no misunderstanding that virtues are claimed for the United States or for voluntary associations which are not particularly unique or not particularly virtues.

A more careful definition of voluntary associations is now needed. A small group of people, finding they have a certain interest (or purpose) in common, agree to meet and to act together in order to try to satisfy that interest or achieve that purpose. Frequently their action requires that they urge other like-minded persons to join them, so that the associations may become very large and extend throughout the whole country.[2] They have absolutely no formal contact with the government (unless, of course, they commit an offense against the general criminal law, which is naturally extremely rare). As social structures they have distinct features of formal leadership, specialized activity, rules for operating, place and time of meeting, and so on. An important distinction among them must be specified: Some associations act only to express or satisfy the interests of their members in relation to themselves—these include the recreational and sports associations, the social and hobby clubs, and the scientific societies, which may be especially numerous in the United States but which are also found in large numbers in all literate societies. Other associations are directed outward; they wish to achieve some condition or change in some limited segment of the society as a whole. The former may be called "expressive" groups and the latter "social influence" groups. It is with the latter type that we are primarily concerned in this chapter.

Since the social influence groups have a specific and limited purpose, they also tend to have a limited life: When the purpose is accomplished, or the need which gave rise to the association changes, the association usually dies. Since change is rapid in the United States, and many social problems get solved while new ones continually arise, the turnover in voluntary associations of the social influence type is

[2] Fox has compiled a list of five thousand national associations in the United States but makes no claim that it is complete. Sherwood Dean Fox, "Voluntary Associations and Social Structure," unpublished Ph.D. thesis, Harvard University, 1952.

great. Even when an association continues in full vigor, there can be a large turnover in its membership. Members join and leave an association for a great variety of personal reasons, including a belief that the purpose of the association needs, or does not need, to be accomplished.

Voluntary associations are to be distinguished from "groupings" along class, age, sex, or ethnic lines, and from social structures into which persons are born (such as the family, the church, the state, and the community). In this narrow sense it can be observed that voluntary associations, at least in Western civilization,[3] are primarily to be found in communities that are urban and democratic in general character. Under the medieval synthesis, to exemplify an alternative, when the church and state had resolved their differences, few individuals could be members of any formal organization other than the church and state; and these were coterminous both with each other and with the community.[4] One of the most characteristic features of

[3] The generalization probably holds true for the preliterate societies also, although such societies vary so drastically among themselves that any generalization is hazardous. The number of voluntary associations in a given society is at least a function of the number of people and of the number of subcultures, among other variables, and no preliterate society has as many people or as many subcultures as ours. The anthropological literature suggests that there is a range from societies which have no voluntary associations to societies which have several, although no society has nearly as many as does contemporary Western society.

In many preliterate societies, the political, religious, and economic organizations seem to be coterminous, although this is by no means universal. When we examine the specific voluntary associations in those societies which have them, we find that most of them are for expressive or status-securing purposes (religious, recreational, sociable, etc.) rather than for the achievement of specialized and diverse interests (such as social reform, civic welfare, occupational protection, or politics). Since the latter kinds of voluntary associations are the major object of interest in this chapter the generalization in the text seems to hold largely even for non-Western cultures.

Scholars who specifically discuss the "paucity" of associations in preliterate societies include Robert Redfield, "The Folk Society," *American Journal of Sociology*, 52 (1947), 293–308; and R. M. MacIver, "Interests," *Encyclopedia of the Social Sciences* (New York: Macmillan, 1935), VIII, 144–148. Also see Robert H. Lowie, *Primitive Society* (New York: Boni and Liveright, 1925), Chaps. X and XI; Hutton Webster, *Primitive Secret Societies* (New York: Macmillan, 1932); Alexander Goldenweiser, *Anthropology* (New York: Crofts, 1937), Chaps. XIX and XX; E. D. Chapple and C. S. Coon, *Principles of Anthropology* (New York: Holt, 1942), Chap. 17.

[4] There were religious and knightly orders, of course, but these had the same characteristic tendency to be at once a community, governmental unit, and a religious unit. In the late Middle Ages, the guilds developed, but they did so in response to the urbanization and differentiation of society—which I hold to be among the characteristic conditions for the rise of voluntary associations. See Louis D. Hartson, "A Study of Voluntary Associations, Educational and Social, in Europe during the Period from 1100 to 1700," *Pedagogical Seminary*, 18 (1911), 10–31.

the shift from medieval to modern times is the rise of groups with specialized interests and divergent activities *within* the community. But not even in all modern communities is there a significant number of voluntary associations. Strictly speaking, in a modern totalitarian society there are no groups but the state (or, more precisely, the party or social movement that controls the state).[5] All the individual's affiliations are determined in some way by the state, and these affiliations exist ultimately to carry out the purposes of the state.

Even within our primarily urban and democratic society we may note wide variations in the complexity and diversity of group structure in any given community. In a relatively homogeneous rural community, at one extreme, most people tend to go to the same church, to be members of the same occupational organization, to participate in the same sociable activities, and to send their children to the same schools. While there are different organizations for the various activities, and while there is some differential participation in the groups according to age and sex, there is still no large number of groups distinguishable as to membership and interest in a homogeneous rural community. There is not likely to be much divergence of interest and attitude among the groups where all the members of the community belong to the same groups.

While we need to hear much more from the historian regarding the conditions under which group differentiation develops, we may take it as a close approximation to the facts that the discussion of intergroup processes in the community, at least in Western culture, concerns primarily the modern urban democratic society. The term "urban" is to be understood in its sociological sense, not in terms of the census definition. Many villages in the United States are urban, and there is a trend toward their becoming more urban. To put these observations in general terms, the existence of a significant number of groups in the community seems to require that the population be somewhat heterogeneous in background and interests and that no one institution like the church or state be successful in dominating the entire life of most individuals.

[5] The establishment of modern totalitarian regimes has regularly been attended by the destruction or "integration" of voluntary associations, especially those that were based on divergent interests—less so those that were purely expressive, sociable, or recreational in character. The church, which represents a loyalty alien to the state, is likely to become a problem for the totalitarian state and may even be a source of resistance unless it is assimilated into the state's interest in some way.

CHARACTERISTICS OF AMERICAN VOLUNTARY ASSOCIATIONS

No one knows how many associations there are in the United States. But the number is known for some local communities where special studies have been made. The most complete and representative study of voluntary associations is that for the city of Detroit, where 63 per cent of the population belonged, in 1951, to some organization other than a church. About half of those belonging to nonchurch organizations were members of two or more. The types of organizations the people of Detroit joined were as follows: [6]

	Per Cent
Occupational associations	37
Fraternal and social clubs	21
Church-connected groups	9
Athletic and other recreational associations	8
Youth-serving groups	8
Welfare organizations	7
Neighborhood improvement associations	5
Women's clubs	2
Political clubs	2
Community centers	1
Nationality groups	1
Other groups	3

A count of the voluntary associations—exclusive of the governmental, the specifically church affiliated, and the strictly occupational—in the Twin Cities (Minneapolis and St. Paul), by the Minnesota Council of Adult Education, turned up some 3000 organizations, of which about 450 were engaged in an effort to influence or educate the adult population. A list of organizations in a small New England city (50,000 inhabitants), prepared by the local council of social agencies, included some 300 associations.[7] In 1924, there were almost 3000 voluntary organizations in a group of 140 rural villages.[8] Warner's "Yankee City" (population 17,000) had 357 associations when it was studied in the early thirties.[9] Boulder, Colorado, a city of 12,000, had

[6] Detroit Area Study of the University of Michigan, *A Social Profile of Detroit* (Ann Arbor: University of Michigan, 1952), pp. 13–16.

[7] Arnold M. Rose, "Communication and Participation in a Small City as Viewed by Its Leaders," *International Journal of Opinion and Attitude Research*, 5 (Autumn 1951), 367–390.

[8] Edmund de S. Brunner and J. H. Kolb, *Rural Social Trends* (New York: McGraw-Hill, 1933), pp. 102, 244, 372.

[9] W. Lloyd Warner and Paul S. Lunt, *The Social Life of a Modern Community*, Yankee City Series (New Haven, Conn.: Yale University Press, 1941), Vol. I.

245 associations in the early forties.[10] In 1935, there were 200 associations among the 7500 Negroes of Natchez, and 4000 associations among the 275,000 Negroes in Chicago.[11]

While the number of associations in a community naturally appears to be a function of the number of inhabitants of that community, this is not entirely the case, for many of the associations are regional or national and have affiliates in small communities as well as large ones, thus raising the relative number of associations in the small communities. Even when the association is national or regional, there tends to be a great deal of local autonomy, with some exceptions, because of the voluntary nature of the membership. The officers of the central or parent body, usually elected by a congress of representatives from the local associations, secure a minimum degree of similarity among the local associations by demanding conformity to a small list of "basic principles." The major exception to this structural principle of complete democracy and local variation is found among the trade-unions. The greater degree of centralization and uniformity among trade-unions is made necessary by the fact that these associations engage in conflict with a common outside opponent, but even here the deviation from principle is not great, and the European observer is often surprised to see the great degree of local autonomy in the American trade-unions.

While the relationships of the local affiliates of a national association with one another tend to be democratic, democracy is not always the governing principle *within* the local association. The reason is easy to understand. Some people have more interest, more time, more drive, more ability than others, and they tend easily to take over control. Any person who wishes to, however, can usually join the leadership of most voluntary associations, if he is willing to spend the time and assume the responsibilities. And those who do not wish to become leaders exert an ultimate control over the latter by voting against them at the annual elections—or simply by resigning from the association, which, if done by sufficiently large numbers, kills the organization and permits the formation of a new one with the same purpose but with new leaders.

[10] Frederick A. Bushee, "Social Organization in a Small City," *American Journal of Sociology,* 51 (1945), 217–226.

[11] Gunnar Myrdal, with the assistance of Richard Sterner and Arnold M. Rose, *An American Dilemma* (New York: Harper, 1944), pp. 952–955.

While only a small proportion of the population are very *active* in the associations, a very large proportion—at least in the towns and cities—are *members* of the associations. Several studies show, however, that people of middle and higher incomes are more likely to join associations than people of lower income.[12] Lower-income people are, however, more likely to be attached to a trade-union, to a church, and to informal but fairly stable friendship groups (including kin groups) for recreation, and these perform some of the same functions that the more typical voluntary associations perform for the other classes.[13] To a certain extent, an association tends to draw members from a limited class range, and from a given religious, ethnic, or racial group, so that a given community will have several associations with the same function but with a different composition of membership.[14] Participation normally means attendance at general meetings (perhaps once a month except during the summer), payment of dues, attendance at committee meetings (which convene irregularly depending on the amount of activity), and the performance of the activity prescribed by the association. Membership in a single association can take as little or as much of one's time as one wishes to devote to it. The association has sources of income other than dues, and each has its effect on the psychological involvement of the contributors:

1. Solicitation of voluntary contributions from both members and nonmembers is usually moderately successful in a culture where "philanthropy" is an accepted cultural trait, even among poor people,[15] and

[12] Robert S. and Helen M. Lynd, *Middletown* (New York: Harcourt, Brace, 1929); W. Lloyd Warner and Paul S. Lunt, *op. cit.*; W. C. Mather, "Income and Social Participation," *American Sociological Review*, 6 (June 1941), 380–384; Herbert Goldhamer, "Some Factors Affecting Participation in Voluntary Associations," unpublished Ph.D. thesis, University of Chicago, 1942; Frederick A. Bushee, *op. cit.*; Mirra Komarovsky, "The Voluntary Associations of Urban Dwellers," *American Sociological Review*, 11 (December 1946), 686–698; Ira de A. Reid and Emily L. Ehle, "Leadership Selection in Urban Locality Areas," *Public Opinion Quarterly*, 14 (Summer 1950), 262–284; Floyd Dotson, "Patterns of Voluntary Association among Urban Working-Class Families," *American Sociological Review*, 16 (October 1951), 687–693; Walter T. Martin, "A Consideration of the Differences in the Extent and Location of the Formal Associational Activities of Rural-Urban Fringe Residents," *American Sociological Review*, 17 (December 1952), 687–694.

[13] F. Dotson, *op. cit.*

[14] Mhyra S. Minnis, "The Relationship of Women's Organizations to the Social Structure of a City," unpublished Ph.D. thesis, Yale University, 1951; August B. Hollingshead, "Trends in Social Stratification: A Case Study," *American Sociological Review*, 17 (December 1952), 679–686.

[15] An extensive study by the Russell Sage Foundation in 1950 revealed that contributions to voluntary associations and philanthropic causes of all sorts was part of

where most contributions can be deducted in calculating income taxes. Practically all American communities also have a "Community Fund," which is a voluntary association whose purpose is to collect contributions once a year, from as many citizens as want to contribute or can be pressured to contribute, for the purpose of distributing these funds to "worthy" associations of many types.

2. Legacies and special gifts are sometimes given by interested wealthy people.

3. Money-raising events are likely to produce funds even in hard times. These operate on the principle of *quid pro quo*: An association will give a dinner, or sell all sorts of objects at a bazaar (where the merchandise—especially cakes and other prepared foods—is provided gratis by members), or offer amusement at a card party or carnival. The labor and materials are donated by the members, and the money earned goes into the treasury of the association to carry on its regular work. Some of the bigger associations, and this includes practically all the national ones, have enough money to hire professional workers to help carry on the functions of the association and, incidentally, to help in the money raising.

The purposes of associations are as diverse as can be imagined. The only thing they have in common is that the purposes are limited, and almost never will an association act for a purpose different from the original one which brought the members together. The reason is easy to understand: People who have one interest in common will not necessarily have another interest in common, and any effort to act on a second purpose is likely to split the association. Thus, the association is the opposite of all-encompassing; it does not seek to involve the individual in all his interests or in all aspects of his life. It is thus quite the opposite of a family, of the Catholic Church, or of the Communist party. The specific nature of the purposes of voluntary associations gives to American culture a characteristic which was originally known as "cultural pluralism" (although that term has recently been distorted to refer solely to religious and nationality diversity). In its original usage—as stated by Dewey, Cooley, and Kallen—cultural pluralism meant the encouragement of all kinds of group differences characteristic of American life and especially the

nearly every family's expenditures, and that the lower-income groups devoted as large a proportion to this purpose as did the middle- and upper-income groups.

encouragement of those group differences that one voluntarily chooses to cultivate. Most individuals were encouraged to be "culturally plural" as they were encouraged to belong to several associations, with quite different purposes and often with different memberships.

In order to determine some of the social-psychological bases for the formation of voluntary associations, we may pose the question as to what other means have been used historically to satisfy the two needs for self-expression and satisfaction of interests through collective action. Again, we have to turn to the historian for a complete answer, but an impressionistic observation would suggest that historically societies have relied on the family—either the immediate family or the extended family (*grosse familie*)—on the church, or on the community as a whole for the satisfaction of these needs. This leads us to the observation often made by sociologists that in contemporary American urban society the extended family, the church, and the community are relatively weak social structures and that many people do not belong to them at all. The hypothesis is, then, that because the American extended family, church, and community are weak, each individual feels a need to turn relatively frequently to voluntary associations for self-expression and satisfaction of his interests, if these two functions are to be fulfilled at all.[16] If this is the case, the voluntary association would tend to contribute to the democratic character of American society, since strong family systems, churches, and communities tend to be totalitarian in their influence over the individual, whereas voluntary associations distribute and diversify power and influence.

If this hypothesis is correct, it is likely that another psychological satisfaction, served in other societies mainly by the immediate family, and secondarily by the extended family, church, and community, is also being inadequately provided by them in our society. This is the provision of a sense of security, which may be thought of as the defense of the individual against reduction of his need satisfaction by outside forces, as distinguished from attainment of satisfaction in a positive sense. That this social-psychological analysis of the motives for joining groups is on the right track has been suggested by several

[16] Of course, there exist those victims of the mass society who do not get their needs for self-expression and achievement of interests satisfied. For them, the family, church, and community are weak or otherwise unsatisfactory, but they have not joined voluntary associations.

studies of trade-unions, reform groups, fraternal organizations, and even churches.[17]

Certain students of the labor movement have attempted to explain the reasons for the rise and rapid development of trade-unions in such a way that their analysis has relevance as a hypothesis for explaining the historical proliferation of all kinds of voluntary associations in contemporary society. Polanyi,[18] the economic historian, starts by pointing out that the free enterprise system gives the producer a higher standard of living and lower degree of job security than any other known to either the historian or the anthropologist. The combination of modern technology and competition has produced such a high level of efficiency in production that the ordinary worker can afford to purchase the full range of necessities and some luxuries as well, and the owners and managers of industry can look forward to accumulations of wealth formerly possessed only by kings and the highest of nobles. At the same time the worker can suddenly lose his job, and the businessman lose his business, because of a technological change or a business depression, so that neither has a great deal of certainty about the future.

In premodern times the serf might exist on a pittance and not even be a free man, but he could not be removed from the land which provided him a basic sustenance (except by disease or crop destruction, which were regarded as acts of God and thus not subject to man's control anyway). The feudal lord might have a bare castle and be fairly restricted in the activities he might engage in or the distance he might safely travel, but he had a self-sustaining village to guarantee his support. The industrial artisan might have to work many years as an apprentice without pay, but his guild protected his occupation

[17] A by no means exhaustive list of such studies would include Arnold M. Rose, *Union Solidarity* (Minneapolis: University of Minnesota Press, 1952), Chap. III, Sec. D; Albert Blumenthal, *Small Town Stuff* (Chicago: University of Chicago Press, 1932); William Gellerman, *The American Legion as Educator* (New York: Teachers College, Columbia University, 1938); C. F. Marsden, *Rotary and Its Brothers* (Princeton, N. J.: Princeton University Press, 1935); E. Wight Bakke and C. Kerr, *Unions, Management, and the Public* (New York: Harcourt, Brace, 1948); Charles W. Ferguson, *Fifty Million Brothers* (New York: Farrar and Rinehart, 1937); Noel P. Gist, "Structure and Process in Secret Societies," *Social Forces*, 16 (March 1938), 349–357; Edward D. Starbuck, *The Psychology of Religion* (New York: Scribner, 1908), pp. 28ff; G. A. Lundberg, M. Komarovsky, and M. A. McInerny, *Leisure: A Suburban Study* (New York: Columbia University Press, 1934); E. Wight Bakke, "Why Workers Join Unions," *Personnel*, 22 (July 1945), 37–46.

[18] Karl Polanyi, *The Great Transformation* (New York: Farrar and Rinehart, 1944).

from competitors and assured him of a market. Neither lord nor serf nor artisan was subject to the whims of a competitive market, nor could he be threatened by inventions. He had economic security.

The Industrial Revolution and the free market system changed all that. Few men could now be sure of their economic futures; unemployment and business failure were possibilities for everyone. The average rewards were greater, but the occasional penalties were more severe. Furthermore, labor was regarded as a commodity, as a "factor in production." Under these circumstances it was natural for men to try to protect themselves, to reduce the risks, and to increase their power by collective action. The businessmen formed combines to control the market, created corporations to limit their liability in case of failure, entered into agreements to prevent the free use of inventions, distributed their investments so that all would not be likely to go bad at the same time, and paid politicians so that control of natural resources and transportation routes could be assured. Sometime afterward, the workers formed or joined unions, set restrictions on the number and qualifications of those entering the occupation, and pressured politicians into voting for minimum-wage laws and for old age and unemployment insurance laws.

In the light of history, then, unions can be viewed to some extent as a means of regaining the security, recognition, and self-expression for the worker which had been lost because of the growth of modern capitalism and the Industrial Revolution. Tannenbaum [19] goes one step further than does Polanyi. He holds that the union movement grew up in reaction to the segmentalization as well as to the insecurity of modern life to re-establish the "sense of community" which prevailed in preindustrial times. This approach to economic organizations could be applied to other kinds of voluntary associations; the declining influence of the community (and the extended family and the church) resulted in psychological insecurity, segmentalization of personal relations reducing intimacy, and alienation from once powerful values. The voluntary association is a new structure crescively established to meet these structural needs. The Kluckhohns have suggested this in a succinct passage:

Mass economic upheaval following upon unprecedented economic growth; lack of attention to the human problems of an industrial

19 Frank Tannenbaum, *A Philosophy of Labor* (New York: Knopf, 1951).

civilization; the impersonality of the social organization of cities; the
melting pot, transitory geographic residence, social mobility, weakening of religious faith—all of these trends have contributed to make
Americans feel unanchored, adrift upon a meaningless voyage. . . .
Why are Americans a nation of joiners? In part this is a defense
mechanism against the excessive fluidity of our social structure. Because of the tension of continual struggle for social place, people have
tried to gain a degree of routinized and recognized fixity by allying
themselves with others in voluntary associations.[20]

To bring into focus how the voluntary association relates an individual to the general society, let us enumerate some of the associations to which an ordinary American man and woman in a moderate-
sized city might belong. The man might belong to a sports club or
hobby club, which helps its members organize teams for playing base-
ball or basketball, or which provides materials for the hobby. The
sports club also has the purpose of putting pressure on the local government to provide fields and houses where these games can be played.
If he is a war veteran, the man might belong to one of the big veterans' organizations, which provides many types of nonathletic recreation and entertainment for him. The veterans' organizations also
put pressure on government to obtain special privileges for soldiers
and veterans, and occasionally the leaders speak on general political
subjects. Whether he is a member of a veterans' organization or not,
the average middle-income man may belong to a very similar organization known as a lodge or fraternal association. This group
provides recreation, entertainment, and fellowship, and occasionally
does a "good deed" for the community as a whole, but seldom puts
pressure on government. The fraternal associations are declining, but
a smaller, less formal type of social club seems to be taking their place.

Our average man also probably belongs to an occupational group—
to a labor union if he is a factory worker, to a trade association if he
is a businessman, to a farmers' organization if he is a farmer, or to a
professional association if he is in one of the professions. These groups
seek to defend the occupational interests and improve the occupational status of their members. In doing so, they combat each other
and even the society as a whole, since they occasionally stop the
functioning of the whole occupational group and often put pressure

[20] Clyde and Florence Kluckhohn, "American Culture: Generalized Orientations and
Class Patterns," Chap. XX of L. Bryson, L. Finkelstein, and R. M. MacIver (eds.),
Conflicts of Power in Modern Culture (New York: Harper, 1947), pp. 249–250.

on government to get laws or administration of laws favorable to the occupation. Only recently have some of them—mainly the unions—expressed any interest in government in general, but this is still very rare; their main concern with government is primarily in relation to improving conditions of work in their particular occupation.

The average man is also likely to belong to some kind of benevolent, social improvement, or "charitable" association. For people in the lower-income classes, this association is usually connected with the church. In the middle- and upper-income classes, people also tend to belong to one or more such associations organized independently for social welfare purposes. The activities of the voluntary associations for social welfare are supplementary to those of government. These functions are too numerous to describe adequately, but a few examples will give their general character. One association exists to collect money to subsidize intelligent but poor boys and girls at a university. Another collects money to subsidize scientific research on cancer. Another has its members help blind children in after-school hours. Another directs a neighborhood recreational house for children. Another sews sheets for the public hospital. Another works to integrate recent immigrants into American community life. And so on—for each "underprivileged" group in nearly every community there is at least one voluntary association to help it. Almost anyone may become a member of such an association, sometimes including the "underprivileged" themselves. Each of these functions is carried on by the government (federal, state, or local), but the association also helps in a supplementary and personal way.

Some of these social improvement associations shade over into "social reform" [21] associations. One of the latter has as its purpose the distribution of propaganda advocating a better law on the adoption of orphan children. Another gives out information about the United Nations and about other organizations for the betterment of international understanding. Another collects money to send a public school teacher to an annual institute for the modernization of teaching techniques. Another watches the local government to see that tax money is not "wasted." And so on—for every way in which a dozen

[21] I use the term "social reform" to refer to any kind of social change, regardless of direction or value. While most social reform associations in the United States would be judged to have mildly "liberal" purposes, some could be said to have "conservative," "reactionary," or "revolutionary" purposes.

or more people in the community think the community should be changed, one or more associations are working in some manner for that change. While there are hundreds of thousands of "social reform" associations across the country, only a minority of the population belong to even one, although some individuals belong to several. In general there is a connection between one's income level and one's membership in "social reform" associations; poor people usually belong to none, and rich people tend to belong to many.

Women belong to much the same types of associations as men do, but there are some differences. Only a third of the women have occupations other than housewife and so are not as likely as men to belong to occupational associations. Very few women belong to sports clubs, veterans' associations, or lodges, although feminine counterparts of the men's fraternal associations do exist. Women, however, tend to participate more than men in the informal social clubs, the "social improvement" associations, and some kinds of "social reform" associations. There is one type of association that many women but few men join—the "self-improvement" or "educational" association. Specific examples are a club that invites speakers to talk on various subjects, a music appreciation club, a book reviewing club, or a "recent political events discussion club." Men have something of this in their "service clubs"—Rotary, Kiwanis, Lions—but these groups also have the function of integrating the business and professional interests of a community. In many cities, a few men and women form musical societies (orchestras, choruses, chamber music sections, etc.). The participants in all these "self-improvement" associations come almost entirely from the middle-income groups, and only a minority of even this class is involved.

Young people belong to many types of associations, and these exist for children eight years of age and upward, of all socioeconomic classes. Many are connected with school life, but many others are outgrowths of the church, the local community, or any other institution to which young people may be attached. Children of high school age belong to sports groups, scout groups, religious groups, self-educational groups (for example, nearly every high school has its French Club), sociable or fraternal groups, hobby groups, or school or community improvement groups. College students have an even broader range of associations, for these include many of the adult types, many of the children's types, and still others peculiar to American university life.

In addition to the general types of associations mentioned, there are special types to which only a small segment of the population belong. College graduates, for example, may belong to their college alumni association, which exists for the purpose of supporting the old university. Scientists may belong to scientific societies, which have some of the characteristics of other occupational associations but which, like scientific societies in other parts of the world, are also devoted to the discovery of new knowledge. Last, but not least, those particularly interested in politics may belong to a local club of their political party. Even though only a small proportion of these persons ever run for political office, they provide much of the direction in politics—especially locally—and management of election campaigns.

Examination of some of the small but growing quantity of literature [22] on differential participation in community organizations and activities seems to point to important differentials along sex, age, class, and ethnic lines. Sex and age differentials are universal to all cultures although their specific forms vary considerably from culture to culture. In our society age and sex differentials in groups are not particularly important for the power relations among those groups. Class and ethnic differences, on the other hand, are very important for power relations. Classes and ethnic groups are not, of course, formally organized in our society, and the exercise of power usually requires formal organization.

The formal organizations in our society having a concentration of power are political groups, occupational or industrial groups, and what might generically be called "reform" groups. There was formerly a very high degree of linear correlation between the holding of power and class and/or ethnic position. As a matter of fact, the so-called "majority" grouping—as distinguished from various "minority" peoples—is not to be defined in terms of numbers but largely in terms of control over power. The upper class and the dominant ethnic group

[22] Herbert Goldhamer, op. cit., p. 19; Ira de A. Reid and Emily L. Ehle, op. cit., pp. 161–184; Mirra Komarovsky, op. cit., pp. 686–698; Lundberg, Komarovsky, and McInerny, op. cit., pp. 128, 135ff; P. F. Lazarsfeld, B. Berelson, and H. Gaudet, The Peoples' Choice (New York: Duell, Sloan and Pearce, 1944), p. 145; Warner and Lunt, op. cit., pp. 323, 339; Bushee, op. cit.; Bernard Barber, "Participation and Mass Apathy in Associations," in Alvin W. Gouldner (ed.), Studies in Leadership (New York: Harper, 1950), pp. 483–484.

secured their great power through a high degree of organization in political and management groups. Over the last two decades or so the situation has changed, and the correlation has broken down to a certain extent. Now, a significant proportion of the lower classes have organized into labor unions, and a significant proportion of ethnic minorities have organized into reform groups; and both groups are participating in political organizations. Thus, both the lower classes and the ethnic minorities today have a significant measure of power.

There is still, however, differential participation by class and ethnic status that needs further investigation. Let us first consider the class differential. The upper classes are in control of management, and the lower classes are in control of the unions (although observers since Marx's time have pointed out that people with the very lowest income are not active even in labor organizations, and economists since Ripley's time [23] have been aware that the top-income people are generally not in the managerial class). The upper classes also used to be in control of the political groups, but that is no longer nearly so true because of the larger number of political offices filled by popular election, because of the entrance of the unions into the political field, and because of the gradual disappearance of immigrants in the lower-class population.

It is, however, in the voluntary associations that the greatest changes are currently taking place. Up to and including the present, the low-income working population has not participated to any significant extent in voluntary associations. Many of these voluntary associations are pressure groups or reform groups and therefore have power over the community as a whole. There are groups like the Farm Bureau Federation, which are part of the intrinsic structure of government; there are groups like the League of Women Voters, which—by informing their members on a variety of issues—exercise a great deal of influence on members' political attitudes; there are specialized action groups like the National Association for the Advancement of Colored People, which bring cases before the courts or act as pressure groups in the formation of legislation. Groups that attract members

[23] William Z. Ripley, *Main Street and Wall Street* (Boston: Little, Brown, 1927). Also see Adolph A. Berle and Gardner C. Means, *The Modern Corporation and Private Property* (New York: Macmillan, 1936); James Burnham, *The Managerial Revolution* (New York: Day, 1949).

mainly for sociable or recreational purposes, like the American Legion, also openly function as political pressure groups. Even the fraternal organizations, which are predominantly sociable in their function, provide an avenue of influence for members who have political interests. In a largely decentralized democracy, such as ours, many political activities—in the broad sense of that phrase—take place in nongovernmental groups.

Very few of the great number of organizations having informal political power in our society have been able to attract membership from the lower-income classes. Lower-income people have been too poor to pay membership fees, too ignorant to know how to conduct themselves in group settings, or too apathetic to have any interest in organized group activities. As a consequence, members of the lower-income population have not had the power and influence which goes with membership in these groups. The pattern of nonparticipation has not changed significantly in recent years, nor is there any immediate prospect of its changing. Even the rising educational level of lower-income persons, the increasing leisure time available to workers, and the disappearance from the American scene of unassimilated immigrants have not yet resulted in appreciable increases in participation in those voluntary associations that have informal political power.

What is happening, however, is that a new class of middle-income persons, corresponding to the managerial class in the upper-income population, is rising.[24] This class is composed of union leaders, who have largely come out of the lower-income population and seek to represent it in the various power groups in the community. For example, when a group is formed to improve the street-lighting system of a city, to work for more adequate housing, or to make certain that legal rights are protected, it is now frequently considered necessary that "labor" be represented. Labor leaders find themselves increasingly requested to participate on boards and committees of both voluntary and official organizations. While occasionally the person invited is not a functioning labor leader but merely a figurehead, while some labor leaders are not democratically elected as heads of their organizations, and while by no means all workers are organized

---

[24] James B. McKee, "Status and Power in the Industrial Community," *American Journal of Sociology*, 58 (January 1953), 364–370.

into unions, when labor leaders become representatives in community-wide groups, they usually—in fact, almost invariably—express the workers' point of view.

Thus there are the beginnings of representation of the lower-income classes in a large number of the organizations which together make up the informal government of our society. But this is the mere beginning of a trend. The most important observation is still that the large proportion of lower-income people in our society do not participate in voluntary associations and that they therefore have little contact with persons of other classes and little power in the community as a whole. The lower-income person is effectively, although not legally, segregated in his neighborhood, his church, and possibly his labor union. The situation has hitherto unexamined weaknesses, not only because a large section of the population is not getting the power and personal satisfaction obtainable from social participation, but also because this very class is trying to centralize formal political power in itself as a mass through the entrance of its formal associations—unions and farmers' organizations—into political parties. What might happen, at the extreme, is that the lower-income classes, who are not active in the many voluntary associations (outside of unions and farmers' organizations) that *distribute* informal power in the community will, by virtue of their large numbers, create a formal government out of contact with—and therefore hostile to—these voluntary associations. Such a government, even though democratically selected by universal suffrage, might become so centralized as to be semitotalitarian.

CONCLUSION

To consider what the numerous, diverse facts about American voluntary associations might mean, we should return to the three functions in the hypothesis stated at the beginning of this chapter:

1. Through the voluntary association the ordinary citizen can acquire as much power in the community or the nation as his free time, ability, and inclinations permit him to, without actually going into the government service, provided he accepts the competition for power of other like-minded citizens. A consideration of the varied activities of the "social improvement" and "social influence" types of associations would support this. Political power, or influence, in

the United States is not concentrated in the government but is distributed over as many citizens, working through their associations, as want to take the responsibility for power. As Goldhamer says: "It is precisely this function of expressing and enforcing the wishes of its members that has characterized the activities of many American organizations. In this way these organizations appear to revive once more, in varying degrees, the participation of citizens in the governmental process." [25]

2. Those who thus participate become aware of how processes function in their society; they learn how things are done in at least the limited sphere in which they operate. The voluntary association informs its members on matters occurring in the society at large that affect the association's purpose. This does not make the members satisfied in the sense that they always like what they learn, but it makes them satisfied in the sense that they understand some of the complex social mechanisms that control them. As society grows more and more complex, the average citizen is usually less and less able to understand the devious controls within it, and this creates dissatisfaction. The voluntary association provides him an avenue for understanding some of the controls and thus a degree of social satisfaction. By working in voluntary associations, he also learns exactly what is wrong with the power structure of the society, and this gives him something definite to work toward, rather than leaving him with a vague and delusive feeling that because "something" is wrong, only a complete revolution can change it.

In like measure, the opportunity to engage in something creative, even if only in a hobby association, provides a compensation for the deadening effect of working on a simple, repetitive task on the modern production line.[26] The association which does most about this is the trade-union, which seems to the worker to provide him with a significant measure of control over his working conditions, to give him the leisure time outside the factory to engage in many creative activities formerly not available to him because of lack of time, and even to provide him directly with some recreations, "social reform" activities, and other "creative" opportunities. Many intellectuals overlook

[25] Goldhamer, op. cit., p. 509.
[26] No one has described this so well as the French sociologist Georges Friedmann in Problèmes Humaines du Machinisme Industriel (Paris: Gallimard, 1946); and in Où Va le Travail Humain (Paris: Gallimard, 1950).

the fact that there are many compensations for, controls over, and satisfactory adjustments to, the monotony of work on the factory production line. Not the least of these is participation in voluntary associations. The present difficulty—which has certainly not been solved in the United States—is that many people do not take advantage of their opportunities, because they do not see that their need for understanding the "mysterious" social mechanisms and their need for creative activity can be satisfied by participation in the associations. While they are constantly propagandized to join, the propaganda is far from being always successful.

3. The voluntary associations offer a powerful mechanism of social change; they are an important factor in making the United States what European observers call "dynamic." As soon as a felt need for some social change arises, one or more voluntary associations immediately spring up to try to secure the change. Not only do they operate directly on the problem, but their attention to it also makes the government concerned about the problem, as a democratic government has to pay attention to the interests of alert voters. It may take decades to effect the change completely, but movement toward that change is likely to occur in gradual steps all along the way. Sometimes the change is never completely achieved because the needs behind it disappear or are converted into other needs, but it would be hard to find a need for a specific social change that existed as long ago as a hundred years in the United States and that still exists today substantially unsatisfied. The associations and the other mechanisms of change are thus usually successful in the long run.

A final word about this often ignored aspect of American social life: The voluntary association is characteristically a voluntary activity, and to make it anything but voluntary would destroy its basic functions as listed above. It is true that informal community pressures occasionally push people into associations that they have no desire to join. Such people, with the exception of the few who change their minds once they are in the association, are seldom satisfied with, or effective workers in, the association. They do not share the power, understand it, or effect social change. They are the "paper" members, from whom dues cannot be collected, and they almost invariably drop out of the association.

This leads us to a broader observation: There is no value in participation per se; it is only when the individual spontaneously feels the need for participation that it does him or the society as a whole any good. This implies, further, that the effective voluntary association is one in which not only membership is voluntary but the type of activity is also voluntary, in that the members choose their goals and the means for obtaining the goals. Few things would do more harm to associations than to give them a coordinated goal and an identical means of action. In other words, pluralism is a necessary component of voluntarism in democracy.

Even worse than to force participation would be to encourage the individual to participate in a group activity which could not possibly have any effect, because the sources of power in the society were beyond the influence of that association's activity. If, say, all political power were lodged in a government, and the individual citizens were encouraged to be active in associations that were not allowed to influence that government, the individual's frustrations and lack of understanding of the power processes would be compounded. Fortunately for the United States, participation in associations is voluntary and the associations are able to compete for their share of real power in the society.

4

Voluntary Associations in France

THE *sociological hypotheses mentioned earlier formed the basis for the research to be reported in the present chapter. This is the only research study to be incorporated into this book, and it has been included here because of its intimate relation to the theory formulated in the preceding chapters. Based primarily on history and law, the study attempts to discover why there are so few voluntary associations in France and why they play such a minor role in French communities. The chapter then offers a theory of the functions of associations in modern social life now that certain social structures of the Middle Ages no longer perform such functions.*

THE RESEARCH PROBLEM

MANY of the great foreign observers of the United States have challenged sociologists with a problem for research which we have been slow to take up: Why are there so many voluntary associations in the United States and why do they play such an important role in the American community and nation? Tocqueville, Bryce, Weber, and Myrdal each raised this question but did not consider it within their province to attempt to answer it.[1] Nor shall the question be answered directly in this study, for the present problem is the logical complement of theirs: Why are there so few voluntary associations

NOTE: This study was prepared while I was a Fulbright Research Scholar in France (1951–1952). Additional aid for this year of study was provided by a grant from the Penrose Fund of the American Philosophical Society. I wish to express appreciation for both sources of aid. I also wish to thank Michel Crozier for a critical reading of this chapter.

[1] Alexis de Tocqueville, *Democracy in America*, translated by Henry Reeve (New York: Colonial Press, 1899, 1st ed., 1835), pp. 114–118; James Bryce, *The American Commonwealth* (New York: Macmillan, 1910, 1st ed., 1893), p. 294; Max Weber, "Geschäftsbericht," *Verhandlungen des Ersten Deutschen Sociologentages vom 19–22 Oktober, 1910 in Frankfurt a. M.* (1911), translated for private use by E. C. Hughes (1940), pp. 52–60; Gunnar Myrdal, with the assistance of Richard Sterner and Arnold Rose, *An American Dilemma* (New York: Harper, 1944), p. 952.

in some countries of Europe, and why do they play such a minor role in these European communities and nations? The procedure here will be first to present the facts and consider the causes and then to consider the theoretical significance and practical importance of the question, which I believe to be very great.

Several definitions, qualifications to the hypothesis, and limitations of the data must first be specified. By voluntary associations is meant those social structures of the community which have very limited but clearly specified purposes (excluding the pursuit of private profit), to which people belong deliberately and from which they may resign. It is the same definition which is in the French law (of July 1, 1901) on associations: "L'association est la convention par laquelle deux ou plusiers personnes mettent en commun d'une façon permanente leurs connaissances ou leur activité dans un but autre que de partager des bénéfices." [2] This definition implies a very important classification of associations into two groups: (1) those for the sociable or expressive purposes of the members themselves (such as sports groups or literary societies); and (2) those actively directed toward an outside purpose (such as social welfare or social reform groups). We may call the former "expressive associations" and the latter "social influence" associations.

Certain restrictions are an essential part of the question posed for research: (1) The study is limited to France. No specific information for other countries is offered but the general literature indicates that in Switzerland and certain northern European countries the voluntary associations play an important role.[3] (2) The hypothesis of the weak role of voluntary associations applies primarily to the

[2] "The association is the convention by which two or more persons place in common, in a permanent manner, their acquaintanceship or their activity for a purpose other than personal gain." All translations from the French in this chapter, whether the original is quoted or not, have been made by me, unless some other source is specifically indicated. Translations of this and other laws are made from the daily official journal. Its precise title changed under the various regimes, but shortly after the beginning of the Third Republic in 1871 it adopted the title it has since had: *Journal Officiel de la République Française*. It will be referred to here as the *Journal Officiel*.

[3] For Scandinavia generally, see Henning Friis (ed.), *Scandinavia, between East and West* (Ithaca, N.Y.: Cornell University Press, 1950). For each of the Scandinavian countries, the short guidebooks—"Facts about Norway," "Facts about Sweden," and "Facts about Denmark"—are valuable. For Sweden particularly, an unpublished study by Torgny Segerstedt and Agne Lundquist shows the high proportion of factory workers affiliated with voluntary associations. Also see Gunnar Heckscher, "Pluralist

social influence type of associations, less to the expressive type. (3) The basic social and psychological functions that voluntary associations have in the United States may be assumed by other types of social institutions in France. This question will be examined later in this chapter, but at the outset it is necessary to make clear that the hypothesis does *not* state that France does not have the values which voluntary associations provide for the United States.

MEMBERSHIP IN ASSOCIATIONS

The data to be presented are of the sort that provide strong evidence for the hypothesis; they do not *prove* it in a scientifically adequate sense. The reason is simple: While most associations in France are registered with the police, there has never been a complete statistical summary of their numbers.[4] For the United States we have reports only for the scattered communities which have been studied by those sociologists who happened to be interested in voluntary associations.[5]

Our best source of statistical information for France comes from incidental data secured in the course of a market-research study in December 1951 of a representative cross section of the French population by the *Service de Sondages et Statistiques*.[6] The data show that only 41 per cent of French adults belong to any kind of association, including the political parties, the semi-official veterans' organizations, and the trade-unions and other occupational associations.[7] (The figures in the accompanying tabulation total more than the 41

Democracy," *Social Research* 15 (December 1948), 417–461. Sample studies for England, showing a proportion of affiliation between that of France and Scandinavia, may be found in Mass Observation, *Puzzled People* (London: Victor Gollancz, 1947), pp. 119–122. For Switzerland, see Antony Babel, *Freedom of Association in Switzerland* (Geneva: International Labor Office, 1927).

[4] According to information provided by an assistant to the Préfet de Police, Paris (February 15, 1952), who has charge of registering all associations in the Department of the Seine.

[5] See Chapter 3, pp. 55–57.

[6] These statistical data were made available through the kindness of M. Max Barioux, directeur, *Service de Sondages et Statistiques*, Paris.

[7] The figure of 41 per cent is based on answers to the following question: "Etes-vous membre d'un groupement quelconque, tel que syndicat, club, parti politique, amicale, etc.?" The type of group was also asked, and the answers were classified into the categories shown in the tabulation. Since the classification had to be somewhat arbitrary, and since a person belonging to several groups might answer in terms of only one or two of his affiliations, the figures should be considered as only a rough indication of the distribution of members by types of groups. The figures are, however, the only ones of their kind available in France.

per cent belonging to all associations because some persons belonged to more than one type.) As in the United States, most of the memberships seem to be casual and passive. What is especially noteworthy is the small proportion of social influence associations among those listed, except for those of the occupational type and the political parties.

	Per Cent		Per Cent
Occupational associations.....	30	Fraternal and social clubs	
Athletic and other recreational		(*amicales*)	4
associations	9	Veterans' associations........	3
"Cultural" associations.......	6	Religious associations........	2
Political parties............	5	Others	2

Another indication of the role of associations in French life is provided by the only published systematic community study in France— that by Charles Bettleheim and Suzanne Frère on Auxerre.[8] Auxerre is a city of some 24,000 inhabitants near the geographic center of France. In the 265-page, closely-packed description of this city in all its aspects, six pages are devoted to associations. While the authors make a strong case that Auxerre is typical of small French cities, they believe that associations may be weaker here than elsewhere. They state at several points that associations are not important in Auxerre:

Associations are numerous and varied, but are generally not very important . . . these associations have not developed an *esprit de corps* among their members. . . . The activity of these groups seems to cut into the lives of their members very little. Although most of them have existed for a long time and function with a fair degree of regularity, they do not play any particular role in social cohesion. Their main role is to provide occasions for meeting or for presenting information to persons who, without the associations, would live in almost complete isolation.[9]

The authors list the specific associations: associations of businessmen, workers, farmers, or civil servants, ranging from purely social clubs (*amicales*) to unions for the defense of group interests; religious associations, except for Catholic Action grouped around the specific church bodies; youth groups, either for sports or scouting or for religious instruction; cultural associations (to which 13 per cent of adult men,

[8] *Une Ville Française Moyenne: Auxerre en 1950: Etude de Structure Sociale et Urbaine,* Cahiers de la Fondation Nationale des Sciences Politiques, No. 17 (Paris: Librairie Armand Colin, 1950).
[9] *Ibid.,* pp. 247, 252.

largely in the liberal professions, and 7 per cent of adult women, largely without gainful occupation, belong) for lectures, educational films, musical performances, or hobbies (stamps, photos); sports and tourist groups, some private, some state-supported; associations of former students at the Lycée and Industrial School which occasionally hold banquets or balls and raise money for scholarships, sports equipment, and a scientific library; associations of former servicemen for sociability and mutual aid (one group erected a monument); regional or neighborhood associations for sociable affairs.

Reading the authors' descriptions of these associations, one can understand what they mean by saying that, while a significant number of persons belong to one or more of these associations (no total figures are presented), only two or three of the groups provide a strong social link among their members. More important to us as outside observers is a fact which is apparently not noticed by the authors: Very few of the associations (the exception noted being the one veterans' group that erected a public monument to political deportees) are of the "social improvement" type; few are of the group-defense type (exceptions being some of the occupational groups and perhaps one or two of the veterans' groups); and few are of the philanthropic or "social welfare" type (exceptions being a few of the religious and veterans' groups and the one association of former students at the Lycée that raised money for scholarships, sports equipment, and a scientific library for Lycée students). These types are much more frequent and much more active in the United States and certain other countries.

Two other relevant studies give us an impression of the very minor role of associations in provincial France. One is an unpublished study of Vienne, a small city near Lyons, made by Clément and Xidias for UNESCO. Despite the broad scope of the authors' interests, the only reference to associations in the entire report is a brief description of certain business and occupational groups. The other is an excellent two-volume work by Abbé Elie Gautier devoted to answering the question of why Bretons move away from Brittany. In the course of providing an answer, the author takes up every aspect of social life in Brittany, but the only associations mentioned are some church and sports groups, which seem to be the only associations there are for these rural people. The author describes the use of leisure time thus: "The peasants have very little leisure time; in summer even siesta time and evenings are for work and only Sunday afternoons are free. There is more leisure time in the winter, but not much. The peasants are usually at a loss as to how they should spend their leisure time. One young adult stated: 'The proportion of young people who do not know how to occupy their leisure time is about 7 out of 10. . . . Many pass their leisure time doing absolutely nothing. One sees them passing their winter evenings warming themselves without occupying themselves with anything—never opening a book or a newspaper or doing a little work. On Sunday the young people hang around the *bistro*; often they ask one another where there may be a public dance.'" [10]

Interviews with French sociologists and other persons apparently informed about French social life provide the almost uniform impression that what social influence associations there are in France are largely "paper" organizations and that even if they claim a large membership they do not involve the members' interests and emotions very deeply. An exception here and there—of a church group, a welfare association, or an alumni association, as shown in the Bettleheim-Frère study—may be indicated, but even these exceptions are given rarely. The general impression is that associations play but a small role, both in the functioning of the community or nation and in the lives of the average citizens.

THE WEAK TRADITION OF ASSOCIATIONS

Another kind of evidence that voluntary associations play only a minor role in French social life takes us through the first stage of an analysis of the reasons for this fact. What will be shown, in some detail, is that France has no strong historical *tradition* of voluntary association. This is an important culture trait, fully as important for understanding contemporary France as is her multiparty system, her low birth rate, and her emphasis on agriculture and small industry at the expense of mass-production industry, all of which have been stressed so much by the many students and observers of France.

Before the Industrial Revolution there were few voluntary asso-

---

[10] Abbé Elie Gautier, *Pourquoi les Bretons s'en Vont* (Paris: Les editions ouvrières, 1950), II, 158.

ciations in France,[11] unless one includes the religious "congregations" (convents and monasteries), foreign exploitation companies, or guild corporations under that heading. The religious congregations are not to be regarded as voluntary associations, since they incorporated the whole lives of their members rather than a single aspect and since the members were not free to give up their membership; the guilds or trading companies are not to be regarded as voluntary associations because they were formed to secure private profit through trade monopoly and, in the case of the guilds, one could not disassociate oneself without giving up one's occupation.

The *confrèries* and the *compagnonnages* of the sixteenth to nineteenth centuries were the nearest approach to preindustrial voluntary associations.[12] A *confrèrie* was a religious brotherhood for laymen. Corporations—composed of persons working in specific occupations—belonged to certain *confrèries* which, under the aegis of a patron saint, aided the poor in those occupations and came to act as a pressure group to protect the occupations. *Confrèries* were abolished by the law of August 18, 1792, after a gradual decline. The *compagnonnage,* developing a little later but also composed of persons in a single occupation, dropped the religious function and extended the protective one; it aided its poor and traveling members, maintained trade secrets, and fought other occupations. The *ancien régime* persecuted *compagnonnages* and the Revolution's law of June 14, 1791, abolished them. They revived again with the restoration of the Bourbon monarchy but did not survive the onset of the Industrial Revolution because it created a sharp separation of masters and workers. Both *confrèries* and *compagnonnages* made little distinction between employers and workmen in including as members all persons in a given occupation. It is to be noted that these voluntary associations developed in an area of life where modern conditions of rapid social change and personal insecurity manifested themselves before the Industrial Revolution.

With the Industrial Revolution came a tendency, in all countries, to develop voluntary associations of all types. In the new cities, peo-

[11] Henri Pirenne, *Economic and Social History of Medieval Europe* (London: Kegan Paul, Trench, Trubner, 1936). Also see "Association," in *Larousse du XX* *Siècle* (Paris: Librairie Larousse, 1928), I, 396.
[12] *Ibid.*, II, 376, 407.

ple's interests became segmentalized and pluralistic, and rapid change required association for the defense or extension of one's interests. But, as we shall now see, this tendency in France, while continuously and spontaneously springing from the people, was stifled by the government. Before 1789 the absolute monarchy might have been expected to oppose independent formations as dispersions of its power and as potential sources of opposition. This may well have been especially true because of the unusually strong centralizing tendency of its government. But the French Revolution might also have been expected to release the barriers against free associations. Indeed, there was a decree (October 21–November 19, 1790) which granted the right of persons in a given occupation to form "free societies." However, the philosophy behind the Revolution was opposed to this development, and the opportunity was abused by the immediate transformation of the societies, ostensibly formed for occupational reasons, into political clubs in violent opposition to the government and employers.[13]

The Declaration of the Rights of Man—otherwise systematically liberal—contains no reference to freedom of association. The law of June 14, 1791, known as the Le Chapelier law after its author, was a more typical expression of the philosophy of the French Revolution; it called for the complete suppression of all occupational groupings, even temporary ones. With some modifications in 1803, 1834, 1848, and 1864, it remained the legal source of suppression fitted into the liberal thinking of the period. Observing the religious congregations and the guilds, the Enlightenment philosophers believed that associations restricted the rights of individuals and hampered good government.[14] An opinion of Voltaire's may be used to illustrate this highly individualistic philosophy: "When society is well governed, there is no need for private associations."[15] The physiocrats supported this opinion in their drive for freedom of trade as opposed to the monopolistic restrictions of the guilds. Le Chapelier, in presenting his bill—not openly opposed by any other legislator—before the Constituent Assembly, expressed succinctly the position of French liberalism in

[13] Bureau International du Travail, *La Liberté Syndicale*, Etudes et Documents, Série A, No. 29 (Geneva: Bureau International du Travail, 1927), II, 106.

[14] *Dalloz Nouveau Répertoire de Droit*, publié sous la direction d'Emmanuel Vergé et Georges Ripert (Paris: Jurisprudence Générale Dalloz, 1946), I, 244–251.

[15] *Larousse, op. cit.*, p. 396.

regard to associations: "There will be no more private associations
[*corporations*] within the state; there will be only the private interest
of each individual and the general interest. No one is permitted to
inspire in citizens an intermediary interest, to separate them from
public matters by an associational interest." [16] Eighteenth-century
liberalism did not oppose direct participation in political parties, but
rather encouraged it, and this may be one reason why party membership is relatively high in France today.

The principle first directed against economic associations was
quickly extended to prohibit all other associations. The law of the
7th of Thermidor of the year V declared illicit "the formation of all
associations occupying themselves with political questions." Finally,
the *Code Civile* of Napoleon, Article 291, prohibited—except by government authorization—"any associations of more than twenty persons with the intention of meeting every day or on certain specified
days in order to occupy themselves with religious, literary, political,
or other matters." This legislation, with slight modification, remained
in force until 1901—a whole century—and successfully stifled the
development of associations for any purpose (except occupational,
which will be examined separately) at a time when a tradition of
associations was being built in certain other countries.

This should not be taken to mean either that there were absolutely
no associations in France in the nineteenth century or that the law
was completely static. In the first place, associations of businessmen
and mutual-aid societies began to spring up illicitly in the early
nineteenth century, and they were followed, about 1830, by several
embryonic trade-unions: ". . . a regime of fact was juxtaposed to the
regime of law, permitting occupational associations to form and to
function in spite of the prohibition." [17] Secondly, the law permitted
associations of fewer than twenty persons, and that apparently opened
a loophole for associations to form that divided their membership into
sections with no more than twenty persons. The law of April 10, 1834,
however, took care of the legal loopholes; it prohibited associations
"even when these associations were divided into sections of fewer than
twenty members apiece and even when they did not meet every day
or on certain specified days."

[16] From the official journal, *Le Moniteur*, June 15, 1791.
[17] Etienne Villey, *L'Organisation Professionelle des Employeurs dans l'Industrie Française* (Paris: Alcan, 1923), p. 8.

The law further indicated that authorization given by the government to form certain specific associations could be revoked by the government. This points up another characteristic of the status of associations in the nineteenth century: While the laws were generally repressive, at some times they were more repressive than at other times. Associated with this variation was a variation in the enforcement of laws. Napoleon's regime was generally repressive—as the earlier reference to the civil code indicates—but it still authorized various associations if their purposes were in no way adverse to the government and if they did not stray from their purposes.[18] Authorized associations under Napoleon acquired a legal personality when a decree of the Council of State declared them to be of "public utility."

Freemasonry was an example of a voluntary association that managed to exist all during the nineteenth century despite the changing attitude of the government toward it. It was introduced in France by an Englishman as early as 1725. It started largely as a literary, debating, and philanthropic organization, oriented against the Catholic Church. Until the establishment of the Third Republic (when it became a direct force in government and was protected by the government) it was "sometimes feared and persecuted, sometimes considered inoffensive and neglected." [19] Thus it had periods of repression, when it was truly a "secret" society, and periods of formal recognition. Its continued existence and power is quite an exception, however, to the position of the typical voluntary association in France. Another powerful secret society of the nineteenth century was the Carbonari, introduced from Italy. It was terroristic and not as respectable as Masonry, and was ultimately completely repressed by the government.

The only recorded increases in legal repressiveness under the restoration of the Bourbon kings were the law of July 5–8, 1820, which abolished all student associations, and the law of May 24, 1825 (Article 2, Paragraph 2), which placed some restrictions on religious congregations. But the regime of Louis Philippe, beginning in 1830, saw a new wave of repressiveness, which is best expressed in the law of April 10, 1834, already referred to. The reason for this seems obvious. The Industrial Revolution was getting under way in France by 1830, and the "July Revolution" itself was a revolt led by the new bour-

---

[18] *Dalloz Nouveau Répertoire de Droit, op. cit.*
[19] *Nouveau Larousse Illustré* (Paris: Librairie Larousse, 1920), IV, 665.

geoisie against the old aristocracy. The new dominant class was no more tolerant of opposition than was the old. This time the opposition was directed primarily against the industrial workers who began to form embryonic unions after 1830 to protect themselves against the harsh conditions under which they worked and lived.

The bias that existed against workers may be seen in two ways: (1) The legal penalty for association was greater for workers than for employers; beginning with Napoleon's time the jail sentence was one to three months for ordinary labor union members and two to five years for leaders as opposed to six days to one month, plus a fine, for employers. (2) The differential application of the law against workers and employers was marked. While there were about the same number of employers' associations as workers' associations, legal charges against them in Louis Philippe's regime were in the ratio of 1 to 8.[20] Further, of all persons brought to trial for violation of the law against association between 1830 and 1848, 40 per cent of the employers were acquitted as compared with only 5 per cent of the workers. An interesting case of this discrimination and how it could be used to break a strike is cited by Dolléans.[21] A committee of employer-tailors denounced a group of worker-tailors, on strike, as political conspirators. Under the laws prohibiting associations without government permission, the leader of the union was sentenced to five years in prison, two others received sentences of three years each, and several others were incarcerated for a month. The employers' committee was exempted from punishment on the ground that it was formed solely to combat, by legal means, an illegal group.

Workers' groups were smashed time after time in this and similar ways, but still they existed because the new industrial system made it essential for occupational groups to organize for self-protection. Employers' groups were relatively unhampered by the government, and workers' groups went underground. Tchernoff records that "at Lyon, secret societies took the form of reading circles where one amused and instructed oneself at the same time. There were meetings to discuss socialism and politics and, when the police appeared, the

[20] Charles Gide, *Le Droit de Grève*, p. 12, as cited in Bureau International du Travail, *op. cit.*, p. 110.

[21] Edouard Dolléans, *Histoire du Mouvement Ouvrier*: 1830–1871 (3rd ed.; Paris: Librairie Armand Colin, 1947), p. 83.

participants played at innocent games."[22] The police had not learned techniques of repression developed by our contemporary dictatorships. Workers and republican groups flourished under the guise of authorized mutual-aid societies, cooperative associations, or societies for training apprentices, or they simply went underground.[23]

The long-range effect of the police repression of associations was not an elimination of the threat to the government (the Revolution of 1848 was accomplished largely by the secret societies). Rather, the repression caused the disappearance of nonpolitical and otherwise not highly motivated associations, so that France could not develop the wide range of associations which it normally would have had.[24] Repression also rapidly brought the workers to the realization that they would have to make political changes (that is, to secure a republican form of government) before they could effectively fight for their economic aims, and so they formed revolutionary groups rather than trade-unions of the Anglo-American-Scandinavian type.[25] Thus was begun a tradition of workers organizing to fight the government (with general strikes, *coups de main,* one-day strikes) rather than to fight the employers directly (with strikes of unlimited duration and intensity leading up to collective agreements with employers that bettered working conditions). This tradition has remained in France, to a considerable extent, up to the present day—long after the workers could have secured control of the government by political and democratic means (by use of the ballot and by political compromise with other

[22] J. Tchernoff, *Le Parti Republicain sous la Monarchie de Juillet* (Paris: Pedone, 1905), p. 398.

[23] Dolléans, *op. cit.,* pp. 171–172.

[24] A thorough social history, like that of Duveau on the Second Empire, mentions no organized sports or other recreations for workers, for example, when a whole chapter is devoted to the use of leisure time. See Georges Duveau, *La vie ouvrière en France sous le Second Empire* (Paris: Gallimard, 1946), esp. pp. 463–522.

[25] Prior to 1830, there were associations to promote a republican form of government, but without much support from the workers, they were very weak. In Paris in 1832, when the *Société des Amis du Peuple* changed its name to *Société des Droits de l'Homme et du Citoyen,* it was claimed that the membership in that year went up from 300 to 750. By July 1833, *L'Association Libre pour L'Education du Peuple* had 2,500 workers following its forty-six courses. *L'Association pour la Liberté de la Presse* was able to distribute six million brochures in three months in 1833 with the aid of workers and other republican groups. The secret societies that formed after the bloody repression of workers' groups in 1834, known under such names as *Familles, Saisons, Bannis,* and *Justes,* were composed not only of workers but also of bourgeois republicans, political refugees from other repressive countries, employees of stores, the self-employed, artisans, students, and soldiers. The immediate goals of the societies were more political than economic (Dolléans, *op. cit.,* pp. 79–81, 171–176).

segments of the population, as has occurred in Britain, Scandinavia, and the United States). This tradition has not only kept the French trade-union movement weak, since it has seldom gained the small but continual successes that help to build a strong movement, but has also made union activity ultimately self-destructive, since it has been directed at sabotaging a democratic government that could have been made, by political means, to promote the workers' goals.

The general effect, even among nonworkers, of the repression of associations working for mild reform was to drive those interested in social change into purely political, often revolutionary, groups. This may be a reason for the high rate of affiliation, relative to participation in other associations, with political parties in contemporary France, with each party desiring to transform the government to conform to its own ideology.

The Revolution of 1848 was one of workers, other republicans, and other socialists, and one of the first acts of the new republic was to decree freedom of association (decree of February 27, 1848). But before the year was over, reaction had set in (secret societies were abolished by a decree of July 28, 1848), and very soon thereafter the new freedom was suppressed altogether (law of November 27, 1849). The net contribution to associations of the short-lived Second Republic was the encouragement of mutual-aid insurance societies by government credits.[26] Napoleon III carried on the strong repression of associations, especially during the first eight years of his regime, when he was supported by the big business and financial interests. The ratio of his prosecutions of workers' groups to employers' groups was the same as under Louis Philippe (8 to 1), but the acquittal rate was more equitable (17 per cent of workers acquitted; 27 per cent of employers acquitted).[27] Between 1848 and 1864, 1,164 associations of all types, but mostly workers' groups, were brought to justice, implicating 6,812 persons, of whom 1,034 were acquitted, 80 condemned

---

[26] The philosophic liberals of the first Revolution were against mutual-aid activities by virtue of their suspicion of all associations and of their belief that protection of the individual against poverty in old age was a function either of the individual himself or of the government. The law of June 14, 1791, forbade mutual-aid societies as well as occupational associations. Nevertheless, they began to spring up in the early nineteenth century and none of the regimes wholeheartedly attempted to suppress them, except when they served as fronts for trade-unions. Most of the societies failed because they did not have experienced managers and because they had no steady union movement to back them (Bureau International du Travail, *op. cit.*, p. 111).

[27] Gide, *op. cit.*, p. 12.

to more than one year in prison, 4,765 to less than one year, and 933 to a fine.[28] In 1860, Napoleon III began a somewhat less repressive policy against workers' groups, since he had lost much of his big business support and was trying to compensate with support from the workers. In 1862 he sent a workers' delegation to London to study the powerful English trade-union movement, and on May 25, 1864, he passed a law that removed the sanction against trade-unions as such, unless they made efforts to stop work, to interfere with freedom of labor, or to engage in violence.[29] The overthrow of Napoleon III in 1871, however, saw another wave of repression against organized workers. The first government of the Third Republic, dominated by Thiers and not at all devoted to democratic concepts, repressed the Paris Commune with great and unnecessary bloodshed. It also passed another repressive law (March 14, 1872) against unions, especially those affiliated with the First International: "Any association which has as its purpose to provoke the suspension of work, or the abolition of the right of property, family, country, religion, or free worship, constitutes by the mere fact of its existence and of its activities on French territory a violation against the public peace." This law made the republic just as hostile to unions as had been the earlier empire and monarchy. The law, and the memory of the unnecessary killing of some twenty thousand Parisian workers and their families by the army and police under Thiers in 1871, further fixed the orientation of the unions against the government and toward revolution.

In 1879, a more democratic government in favor of maintaining the Third Republic came to power and did not attempt to repress unions. In 1881, in Paris alone there were 130 associations of employers with some 15,000 members, and 150 associations of workers with some 60,000 members, and in the provinces it was estimated that there were 350 occupational associations.[30]

Finally, on March 21, 1884, France passed a law guaranteeing the

[28] Bureau International du Travail, *op. cit.*, p. 112. Dolléans (p. 252) reports higher figures.

[29] Dolléans, *op. cit.*, pp. 282–283. The law of 1864, however, set up no positive conditions under which trade-unions could form, as did the law of 1884. In a country like France, with Roman law and a centralized government, a positive statement in law is almost essential before an organized activity of any sort can successfully develop, since people become used to asking the conditions under which they may organize and carry on the activity.

[30] Bureau International du Travail, *op. cit.*, p. 115.

right to form occupational associations.[31] This law, slightly modified by numerous special statutes and a general revision law of March 12, 1920, has remained, except during the Vichy period, the basic French law governing workers' and employers' associations to this day. It is a liberal law—the only relation with the government that is required is the filing of a statement of aims, bylaws, and officers; and it sets few crippling restrictions, such as the financial ones applying to non-occupational associations.

There are, however, some restrictions which make the French law different from the ones applying in the northern European or North American countries:

1. The right to join or to resign from a trade-union or employers' association is reserved completely to the individual. This provision prevents the "closed shop" or "union shop" from being established since these require that all workers in a given plant join the union.

2. Children under sixteen cannot join a union, and until the age of twenty-one they cannot be officers of the association. Until 1920, married women could not legally join a union unless they secured the consent of their husbands (although this provision seems to have been seldom enforced). Only persons of French nationality can hold office in an occupational association. Officers must not be persons deprived of civil rights because of some penal offense. Only persons working in the occupation can be members of the association in that occupation (in 1920, this was somewhat modified to permit persons who *had* worked in the occupation for one year to be members, but the 1920 revision did not specify whether the person had to be a member of the association at the time of his retirement from the occupation). These restrictions limit somewhat the freedom and strength of unions (not to speak of legally discriminating against married women until 1920).

[31] Carlton Hayes gave a seriously wrong impression to his readers when he stated that the 1884 law granted the right to organize and operate associations freely, and that after this there was a tremendous development of strong associations. (Carlton J. H. Hayes, *France, A Nation of Patriots* [New York: Columbia University Press, 1930], pp. 196ff.) The 1884 law was a liberal law, but it applied to *occupational* associations only. The law establishing "freedom of association" generally was not passed until 1901, and the latter law placed several important restrictions on associations, which will be examined later in this chapter. Largely as a consequence of these restrictions, few strong associations, except occupational ones, have developed in France even up to the present day, even though their formal membership lists occasionally appear large.

3. Occupational associations are exclusively limited to the defense of economic interests. Thus they are not supposed to engage in political or religious action, work for any *individual*, or go into business (the restriction on forming producers' cooperatives was later modified). That this provision of the law has seldom been enforced does not limit the potential friction between government and occupational associations that it permits.

4. After World War I, and especially during the period of the pro-labor governments of the 1930s, the government helped to set the contract between union and employers or otherwise limited the conditions under which unions could bargain with employers.[32] Its aim was to improve wages and working conditions, but its effect was to take over the bargaining relationship between unions and employers, and it thereby prevented unions from becoming strong by performing this important function for their own members. Despite these weakening limitations, unions and other occupational associations have had the freedom to collect dues and fines from members; to receive gifts; to act as legal personalities in court (even against their members); to set requirements for membership and to eject members; to acquire property and spend their money as they wish; to establish institutions of welfare (including those for credit, employment, and retirement insurance), publicity, and education; to subsidize housing and garden plots for members; to take legal action against employers who fail to follow laws for the protection of workers; to put union labels on products; to make collective agreements that bind nonmembers as well as members who are in the same occupation; to advise the government when asked; and to place their representatives on government boards (e.g., to administer tariffs, social security, research) when asked.

Following the passage of the 1884 law, occupational associations had a very rapid growth in numbers and membership, as shown in the accompanying table. The table presents data up to 1925, which is sufficient to show the growth of occupational associations. Never very reliable, the data become especially unreliable after 1925, according to information given to me by the Paris office of the Bureau

---

[32] An excellent description and analysis of this, noting especially its long-run debilitating effects on the labor movement, has been prepared by Adolph Sturmthal, "Collective Bargaining in France," *Industrial and Labor Relations Review*, 4 (January 1951), 236–248.

International du Travail and by Michel Crozier, one of the better known students of the labor movement. The latter informs me that the membership of *syndicats* was alleged to have risen to six million, after a slump in the early 1930s, and to six million again in 1946, after being driven underground by the Germans and the Vichy government. No one seems to have the slightest reliable estimate of what the membership of the *syndicats* is today, because of the political implications of such figures and because membership is difficult to define at present.

GROWTH OF OCCUPATIONAL ASSOCIATIONS FROM 1884 TO 1925

Year	Industrial and Commercial Associations			Agricultural Associations	Total
	Employers	Workers	Mixed		
Number of Associations					
1884	101	68	1	5	175
1905	3,291	4,857	140	3,553	11,841
1920	5,078	5,283	175	6,519	17,055
1925	6,596	7,072	196	9,041	22,905
Number of Federations of Associations					
1884	10	10	0	0	20
1905	107	167	10	52	336
1920	195	208	6	99	508
1925	309	392	7	176	884
Number of Members in Associations					
1890	93,411	132,692	14,096	234,234	474,433
1905	268,036	836,134	28,178	677,150	1,809,271
1920	379,855	1,580,967	31,806	1,083,957	3,076,585
1925	496,360	1,846,047	32,331	1,222,534	3,597,272

SOURCE: Bulletins of the Ministry of Labor, compiled in Bureau International du Travail, *La Liberté Syndicale,* Etudes et Documents, Serie A., No. 29 (Geneva, 1927), II, 133.

The latter half of the nineteenth century also saw a lessening of the legal repressions on associations other than occupational, although they have never achieved the freedom which occupational associations have had since 1884. A decree-law of January 31, 1852, permitted certain religious congregations of women (the law of May 24, 1825, had legally repressed all "congregations," that is, convents and monasteries). A law of July 12, 1875, permitted the formation of associations whose purpose was to develop higher education. The law of April 1, 1898, gave full legal status to mutual-aid societies. However, it was not until the law of July 1, 1901, that France recognized freedom of association as a legal principle. This important law, with minor modifications during the succeeding years, governs all noneconomic associations at the present time. It provides for three legal categories of associations:

1. *Nondeclared associations.* These have absolutely no relation to the government except that they are subject to all the legal restrictions on the other types of associations. They have no legal status, cannot sue or be sued, and cannot acquire property. They can, however, collect limited dues. Because the officers are individually responsible for the activities of the association, and hence suable and taxable, there are apparently few associations of this type, although no one has presumed to make an estimate of their number. They correspond more to the informal social club of the United States than they do to the regular voluntary association.

2. *Declared associations.* This is by far the most important type of association, in terms of numbers and variety of purposes. The declared association has a legal status in that it may sue or be sued in court, federate with other associations, collect and administer dues of members (up to an amount fixed by law), go into debt, and acquire property by purchase which is necessary for carrying out the declared purpose of the association. It is not taxable on income (though taxable on capital growth), since its activities cannot be for individual profit. It may sue any of its members to secure conformity to regulations (members may resign freely, and so avoid suit), and it may exclude members after a hearing in which the offending member is given a chance to defend himself. To gain the status of a declared association, a group of individuals has to register with the local prefect a copy of its constitution, which must contain, as a minimum, a title, a statement of purpose, a location, and a list of the names, dates and places of birth, occupations, and residences of their officers. Information on manner of election, times of meeting, power and procedure of officers, affiliations, and conditions of dissolution is encouraged by the Paris prefect but is not required by law. Each time there is a change of constitution, or purchase or sale of real property, or a change of officers, this must also be registered. A small fee is charged for each registration. The title, purpose, and location, and any changes therein, must be published in the *Journal Officiel.*

3. *Associations recognized to be of public utility.* After a certain num-

ber of years (now three) following declaration, an association of at least one hundred members, with a treasury of a certain minimum size, may petition the government to recognize it as an association for "public utility"—that is, of value to the community or nation and not simply to the members. Such associations are comparable to the "social welfare" type of associations found in great numbers in the United States. But the French government gives this recognition sparingly and provides for a yearly inspection of the activities and finances of all such recognized associations. Why, then, does an association apply for recognition? Because this permits an association to acquire funds by means other than the collection of dues (that is, by gifts, legacies, charity sales, charity performances), and thereby to administer funds beyond the low limit on dues set by law. Further, a recognized association may petition the government for a grant of state money, and many philanthropic, welfare, "cultural," and research associations in France thus operate primarily on government money.

There are several restrictions on associations other than those already indicated:

1. Each gift or legacy to an association for "public utility" must have the approval of the government. (In this case as in most others, the government's function is discharged by a council of higher civil servants in the central government—the Council of State; in only a few minor matters can the local prefect act for the government.) As we have seen, associations not formally recognized as having public utility cannot receive gifts or legacies under any circumstances.

2. Associations which are formed for illicit purposes (that is, for purposes contrary to regular criminal laws), or which threaten the territorial integrity or the republican form of government in France, or which act contrary to good custom (*bonnes moeurs*) are illegal. Needless to say, the latter part of this provision is rarely enforced except in time of political upheaval (as from 1938 to 1940).

3. Any member may leave an association at any time provided his dues are paid up.

4. "Public utility" associations receiving real property by way of gift or legacy must immediately sell such property unless it is used in direct furtherance of the purpose of the association; an association

may hold its funds only in the form of cash, bank deposit, or bonds and must never run a profit-making business.

5. Associations which have a majority of members who are foreigners, or which have a foreign director or a foreign seat of operation, or which affect foreign exchange or national security may be dissolved without specified cause by the government, through decree of the president of the republic.

6. No religious congregation (that is, a monastery or convent) may be formed without a special law to determine the conditions of its operation (many congregations, for example, educate children). This may be revoked and the congregation dissolved by government decree. Each congregation must give the prefect upon request a list of names of its members, their "pseudonyms" (that is, religious titles), their nationality, age, place of birth, and date of entry into the congregation; it must also file an annual financial report showing all receipts and expenditures. Property in illegal possession of a congregation may be confiscated for the national treasury.

7. Violations of the law, including failure to file changes in officers or statutes of the association, are punishable by fine or by imprisonment of the officers for up to one year.

FURTHER DATA ON LEGAL FUNCTIONS AND LIMITATIONS
OF ASSOCIATIONS

The following decisions of the courts and the Council of State involving associations reveal a good deal about their legal functions and limitations.[33]

1. Property owners and taxpayers of a district may form an association to promote the interests of the district by way of improving streets, sanitation, and attractiveness. (Court decision of December 21, 1906.)

2. An association may not aid only one section of its members, even if the section not aided is willing, since this would be for individual profit instead of mutual profit. The case involved advantages for

[33] Summaries of all court decisions involving associations from 1901 to 1950 were read, although not all are reported here. These summaries were taken from *Recueil Général des Lois et des Arrets, Fondé par J. B. Sirey* (Paris: Recueil Sirey), quinquennial volumes up to 1920, annual volumes from 1920 to 1950. All decisions under the rubric "Associations" were read, and to these were added all decisions after 1940 under other rubrics cross-referenced under "Associations." Reference will be made to this source hereafter as *Recueil Sirey*.

curés only when all types of priests were members. (Court decision of May 29, 1908.)

3. While civil servants may not form occupational associations under the law of March 21, 1884, to defend their interests against the state, they may form a nonoccupational association under the law of July 1, 1901, to defend their interests against detractors. The case involved public school teachers who were the objects of a pastoral letter, signed by the bishops of France, stating that public schools imperiled the faith and virtue of their pupils. Since the letter involved an attack, not only on the state, but also on the teaching profession, teachers could form an association to sue the bishops and thus defend their professional honor and careers. (Council decision of May 17, 1911.) This decision has been superseded by a law permitting *syndicats* of civil servants.

4. Fathers of children in public schools may form an association to encourage the maintenance of respect for the Catholic faith and Christian morality in the schools. The association, like any individual father, may write a letter to a teacher promoting its views, provided it does not use any indirect pressures on the teacher. (Court decision of July 23, 1918.)

5. An association of coal dealers, who had made an agreement with a government bureau during the war to expedite the delivery of coal in a certain way, could exclude a member who had violated the agreement. (Court decision of December 22, 1920.)

6. A teachers' association, not having the status of a union under the 1884 law, cannot represent *all* teachers in court, but only the members of one association. (Court decision of June 15, 1923.) This decision is presumably also superseded by the law permitting *syndicats* of civil servants.

7. An association of consumers of gas and electricity may sue an electric company for failing to provide electricity to its members when it has agreed to do so. (Court decision of December 28, 1925.)

8. A founder of a "national republican league" to assure internal and external peace for France cannot sue the league for supporting a royalist candidate for public office instead of himself. (Court decision of November 13, 1925.)

9. The minister of war has the authority to prohibit soldiers from forming an association. (Council decision of December 28, 1928.)

10. An association may sue in the interests of its members only to the same degree that individual members may. An association of tenants, evicted by a landlord who says that he wishes to occupy the premises, but who then does not, cannot sue for damages to the "moral interest" of the association when the tenants have already been financially reimbursed for losses sustained as a result of moving. (Court decision of February 13, 1930.)

11. Persons are permitted to form an association to watch butchers who sell meat under the designation "kosher" and to sue butchers when they sell meat that has not been prepared according to the forms of the Israelite religion. (Court decision of March 5, 1931.)

12. A chamber of commerce has the right to exclude temporarily a member who disturbs order in the meetings. The Council of State may review the case to determine whether the exclusion was justified. (Council decision of June 30, 1933.)

13. An association recognized to be of public utility, which runs a hotel-restaurant in direct pursuit of its disinterested purpose, still has to pay taxes on this enterprise. (Council decision of November 9, 1933.)

14. Members of a nondeclared association who make a contract with an outside party are individually responsible for the engagements to which they have subscribed in the name of the association and must be sued personally. (Court decision of January 3, 1935.)

15. A declared association, but one not recognized to be of public utility, cannot make a gift to an individual for whatever purpose. (Court decision of February 19, 1935.)

16. A member excluded from an association by the general meeting of the association may demand reinstatement, if there was no prior announcement that the exclusion would be considered, and he did not know that he would be called on to defend himself. But if there was prior notice that a hearing was to be held, and the member did not appear, on grounds of inconvenience, or formally seek a delay of the hearing, the member may be excluded. (Court decisions of May 21, 1935, and January 24, 1936.)

17. An association whose purpose is the protection of animals (horses, in this case) cannot be recognized as having public utility since its purpose cannot be called philanthropic or social. (Council decision of June 13, 1937.)

18. A political party that sponsors a military group whose purpose is to undermine republican institutions must dissolve. (Council decision of November 27, 1936.)

19. The law of January 10, 1936, prohibiting militarized associations, does not apply to a group of boys (with members under seventeen years) who wear uniforms, even when they are led by young men, unless the latter are numerous enough to form a combat unit. (Court decision of May 24, 1937.)

20. A producers' cooperative has to pay the same taxes as a private company, even though all profit is made by sales to its own members. (Council decisions of 1941.)

The general impression one gathers from reading the decisions of the courts and the Council of State is that these bodies follow the law carefully in developing the conception of an association as a contractual relationship among individuals for the purpose of carrying on collectively such functions as already inhere in them individually. Most of the cases concern associations of the social influence type, which is one of the rarest types in France, and the decisions seem to declare that such associations may exist and function within the framework of the law. This observation suggests the ambiguity in the minds of the French as to the legality of associations of the social influence type. The numerous restrictions of the laws apparently do not serve to clarify the popular ambiguity.

Besides the numerous decisions of the courts and the Council of State, there are many laws, decrees, and ordinances made by the legislature or by the executive to govern associations. During the trying ten years after the outbreak of World War II, through the fall of France, the Vichy period, and the reconstruction period (1939–1949), thirty-four such laws, decrees, and ordinances were recorded in the annual volumes of the *Recueil Sirey*. Only the seemingly most important provisions of these will be summarized here, again to provide an indication of the status, functions, and limitations of associations in France during a period of national crisis and reconstruction.

1. Three separate decrees of 1939 set more rigid restrictions on associations of foreigners.

2. A decree of September 26, 1939, dissolved all Communist organizations and a later decree distributed their property to communal welfare bureaus. This was shortly after the outbreak of war and the announcement of the Russo-German Pact, which turned all Communists into temporary pacifists.

3. One of the first Vichy decrees (August 13, 1940) abolished all secret societies and all associations that refused to furnish information on their rules, internal organization, membership, and purposes of specific meetings. All property of such an association was confiscated and officers were punished with a fine and jail sentence. No one might be a functionary of the state in any way unless he declared that he did not belong to a secret society and never would if an interdicted association were secretly reconstituted. A commission was formed later to advise the Chief of State on punishment of officials, former officials, and dignitaries of Masonic societies.

4. A Vichy decree of November 9, 1940, dissolved all trade-unions and many employers' associations.

5. A Vichy law of February 5, 1941, permitted associations to change

location and operate without new elections (to adjust to the disruption of the nation).

6. A Vichy law of July 11, 1941, permitted the Council of State to dissolve all associations whose acts were "contrary to the general interest of the country."

7. A Vichy law of February 2, 1942, subjected each act and each officer of an association for public assistance or public health to the approval of the Secretary of State for Family and Health.

8. A Vichy law of April 8, 1942, gave legal status to religious congregations and permitted them to receive donations. A law of December 31, 1942, required congregations to register all their property and state its purpose.

9. A decree of the "French Committee of National Liberation" operating in North Africa (October 21, 1943) abolished all Vichy-created associations (especially for youth and sports); dissolved associations for commercial purposes, for antirepublicanism, and for opposition to freedom of religion; and prohibited collaborationists from being officers in any association.

10. An ordinance of May 6, 1944, restored Communist property.

11. An ordinance of August 9, 1944, repealed the laws of August 13, 1940, and July 11, 1941.

12. An ordinance of May 14, 1945, created "L'union française des combattants" as the sole organization for war veterans and victims which may represent these persons before the government and the sole association of this type to receive state subventions. Property of Vichyite veterans' associations was transferred to this association.

13. A decree of October 29, 1946, finally abolished all Vichy laws governing associations.

14. A law of January 26, 1949, facilitated borrowing by associations and congregations for reconstruction and getting new equipment.

15. A decree of April 1, 1949, permitted prefects, instead of the Council of State of the central government in all cases, to approve small sums donated to congregations and associations recognized to be of public utility. The Council of State remained the authority for larger sums.

Still another kind of evidence of the close relation between the state and associations can be provided by a brief description of some types of associations in France for which there are special laws:

1. *Farmers' associations.* There are four kinds of farmers' associations: (a) *Syndicats agricoles* are associations of farmers, like employers' associations, which must limit their activities to construction and maintenance of agricultural improvements, serve as intermediaries in the sale of products, furnish expert advice, and otherwise aid in the

business of farming. (b) *Associations agricoles* may engage in any action—including putting pressure on government—to protect the interests of farmers, but, like all declared associations, may not acquire funds except through the limited dues of members. (c) *Associations autorisées* result from a request of a group of farmers to the prefect to conduct an inquiry to determine whether an association should be formed to make a certain agricultural improvement. (d) *Associations obligatoires,* to which all farmers of a district must belong by order of the Council of State, make agricultural improvements considered to be of public utility and hence usually receive a state subsidy.[34]

2. *Family associations.* These groups were started by the Vichy government but are now considered as declared associations of public utility under a special ordinance of March 3, 1945. Families of a district may unite to defend their common interests, develop a liaison with one another, and engage in propaganda. They federate by departments and nationally into the *Union Nationale des Associations Familiales.* This organization gives advice to public authorities on present and future legislation and on the administration of laws relating to family life, sends delegates to any conference where family welfare is discussed, performs some administrative services for the state, and otherwise acts like any association of public utility. The existence of this semiofficial association does not preclude any other association, which has been formed in the past or which might be formed in the future, from concerning itself with special groups of families, with teaching problems, with religious questions, etc., but none of these other groups may gain recognition as being of public utility—that is, they may never acquire funds except through the dues of their members. A number of the latter type of associations do exist in various parts of the country; many of them are concerned with the teaching of religion in the public schools.[35]

3. *Mutual-aid societies.* We have already noted the long history in France of mutual-aid societies to absorb the risks of old age, illness, health, maternity, etc. Though seldom hampered by government repression, they did not have a clear legal status until the law of April 1, 1898 (superseded by the ordinance of October 19, 1945). The law is very detailed concerning them; they must conform to numerous pre-

[34] *Larousse du XXe Siècle, op. cit.,* p. 397.
[35] *Dalloz Nouveau Répertoire de Droit, op. cit.,* II, 514–515.

scriptions and be regularly inspected. Besides providing insurance, they may have *oeuvres sociales,* such as dispensaries, maternity hospitals, rest homes, pharmacies, medical and dental clinics, parks or gardens for working members, activities for the prevention of disease. Most funds are secured through the dues of members, but the government aids them by providing meeting places, free registration forms, remission of two thirds of the taxes on funerals, and certain other tax exemptions; and they may apply for state aid like any other associations recognized to be of public utility.[36]

4. *Producers' cooperatives (Associations ouvrières de production).* While a few of these associations were founded in 1848, they had no legal status until the law of July 24, 1867. They were allowed to operate like other business enterprises, except that the profits could be distributed among all workers (even those not members of the association) if they were distributed in the form of certain benefits (pensions, for example) rather than dividends. The producers' cooperatives had difficulty in securing capital, since few workers had accumulations of savings. A credit corporation—*Société du Credit au Travail* —was created in Paris in 1863, following a German model, to provide capital for producers' cooperatives, but this and successive credit cooperatives did not have much success.[37] Consumers' cooperatives provided another source of capital. (These groups began in the latter half of the nineteenth century, following an English model, but they have also not had much success in France.) Nevertheless, some producers' cooperatives did manage to succeed, usually those developed through the devoted efforts of a few leaders and sustained by an anarchist or socialist philosophy.[38]

[36] *Ibid.,* III, 179ff.

[37] Armand Cuvillier, *Manuel de Sociologie* (Paris: Presses Universitaires de France, 1950), II, 415.

[38] For example, the *Associations des Ouvriers en Instruments de Precision* (AOIP) now claiming to be the largest producers' cooperative in France with some 1,100 workers, was founded in 1896 by 60 anarchist members of a trade-union. It started as a modest workshop, employing only three of the most devoted members, and knew several years of struggle before it began to succeed as a manufacturer of telephone equipment and later of electrical measuring equipment. Today it has a modern plant and is able to compete very well with private capital producers. It has deviated from ordinary manufacturers by allowing its workers to set their own working hours (provided they meet a minimum standard over the week); formerly requiring its workers to belong to a union; formerly paying all its workers the same wage; leading French industry in the introduction of the eight-hour day, five-day week, and paid vacations; providing pensions for its retired workers (and their widows) and a school for its

An over-all impression gathered from reading the laws and the decisions of courts and Council is that the government restricts and directs a great deal of the activity of associations in France.[39] This tends to weaken the associations, although there have been many individual associations, and even types of associations, that have played an important role in the lives of their members and in community life in general. The economic associations—comprising trade-unions, employers' and professional men's associations, farmers' groups, mutual-aid societies, and consumers' and producers' cooperatives—have sometimes been very strong and important and have always played a significant role. (It should be recalled, however, that they are governed by the relatively liberal law of 1884, or by various special laws, equally liberal, rather than by the law of 1901 which governs noneconomic associations.) The "nationalist associations," especially during the period between the two world wars, were often very powerful, and so have been a few of the pacifist groups.[40] Their power, however, has been directed mainly toward the influencing of general government policy, rather than toward seeking very limited and specific reforms. Thus several of them were practically political parties (generally of a fascist orientation),[41] rather than voluntary associations. Many of the recreational groups—especially sports and hobby groups—have succeeded in capturing the wholehearted interest of their members, but this has less often happened to the social improvement and social welfare types of associations.

THE CAUSES OF THE WEAK TRADITION OF ASSOCIATIONS

The question of causes of the weakness of associations in France has already been touched on in our brief historical survey of associations and the laws governing them. There is no long tradition of free

workers; developing programs of insurance for sick or injured workers; and providing a library and recreational activities for its members. (This brief description of AOIP was kindly provided by MM. Pouderoux and Hug, two of AOIP's current managers.)

[39] By way of contrast, it may be noted that associations in the United States have no governmental restrictions on them, except those of the general criminal and civil law. They may, if they wish, however, secure "incorporation" under state law. This restricts their activities in no way, but merely limits the financial liability of the members for the debts or lawsuits of the association. Of course, a certain amount of red tape is involved in incorporation.

[40] Hayes, op. cit., pp. 196–228, 318–340.

[41] For a description of the fascist nature of some of the pre-World War II "nationalist associations," and their tie-up with the international fascist movement, see Heinz Pol, *Suicide of a Democracy* (New York: Reynal and Hitchcock, 1940), Chap. I.

association, and even today there are numerous minor but significant legal restrictions on associations. The reasons we have observed thus far are that the government, especially under the monarchy and the empire, feared associations as opposed to the power of the state and that many liberal thinkers considered associations as restrictive of the rights of individuals.[42] The author of the legal analysis of "Associations" in the important *Dalloz Encyclopedia of Law* [43] succinctly summarizes these fears:

1. that powerful associations are groups too important always to bow docilely to the laws and regulations of public authorities, too irresponsible to be effectively reprimanded when they are led astray, and too careless of the public welfare.
2. that powerful associations might become tyrannical over the right of their members and even of nonmembers.

And he adds a third important historical fear as a cause of repression of associations:

3. The government fears . . . the accumulation of property in the hands of legal persons, property that does not circulate and constitutes immobile wealth that is not susceptible to taxation exacted by the state in the course of the circulation of wealth.

The latter is a reasonable economic argument against *mainmort,* or the accumulation of wealth that damages the public welfare because it does not circulate and is therefore deflationary and untaxable.[44] Such a problem was actually faced in France in the centuries preceding the French Revolution because of the huge accumulation of wealth in the church, especially by the religious congregations.[45] It helps to explain why even the restored Bourbon monarchy (1815–1830) was so repressive toward the congregations and why the government today, which theoretically supports freedom of association, strictly limits

[42] It is perhaps outside the concern of a scholar to observe that neither of these fears has proved justified since the 1901 law permitted a large measure of freedom of association. Legal safeguards have prevented a revolutionary type of association from developing too far, and the exercise of the right of association has only enhanced, not restricted, the freedom of the individual.

[43] *Dalloz Nouveau Répertoire de Droit, op. cit.,* p. 244.

[44] This problem has hardly been discussed or adjusted to in the United States.

[45] The argument against *mainmort* was also, to a certain extent, a rationalization for the bourgeoisie, dominant in the nineteenth century, in their antagonism against the church. The confiscations of church property during and after the 1789 Revolution paralleled the much earlier confiscation of church property by the bourgeoisie in Protestant countries.

the total wealth, the sources of wealth, and the uses of wealth of all associations.

Several French authors have provided explanations of the weak tradition of free association in terms of the three factors mentioned above. A cross-cultural comparison allows us to speculate about some other causes. One is led first to think of the "Protestant ethic," since democratic nations with strong "low church" Protestant traditions (the United States, Switzerland, the Scandinavian countries, and perhaps others about which I have no direct information) have tended to have a strong development of voluntary associations.

This hypothesis gains strength from the following facts: (1) Many American associations were started in the Protestant churches, or by Protestant leaders acting outside the church proper. (2) The Protestant churches, in contradistinction to the Catholic Church, made no attempt to encompass all of their members' activities, and in fact encouraged a separation of religious from nonreligious activities—a distinction which the Catholic Church has not encouraged. Philanthropy, for example, has been almost forcibly channeled through the church in Catholic countries, whereas in Protestant countries it was frequently thought of as a secular activity even by religious leaders. (3) The Protestant religion encouraged a close attention to the individual conscience—which some critics have called a "sense of guilt" —which is the basis of many of the reform and social improvement associations. Some Catholic writers have distinguished between the passive acceptance of faith in their church and the active searching for unattainable values in the Protestant Church.[46] (4) Scattered evidence suggests that American Catholics are less inclined to be "joiners" than are American Protestants, even when income differences are held constant.[47]

While the Catholic Church historically did not encourage voluntary associations, at least to the same extent as did the Protestant churches, today in France it does stand for "free" movements and associations as distinguished from those dominated by the state. Major examples

[46] See, for example, Sebastian de Grazia, *The Political Community* (Chicago: University of Chicago Press, 1948).

[47] Detroit Area Study of the University of Michigan, *Factors Affecting Group Membership in the Detroit Metropolitan Area* (Ann Arbor: University of Michigan, 1953); Arnold M. Rose, "Communication and Participation in a Small City as Viewed by Its Leaders," *International Journal of Opinion and Attitude Research*, 5 (Autumn 1951), 367–390.

would be the "free" schools, hospitals, charitable organizations, and such associations as the scouts, parents' organizations for the promotion of Catholic teaching in the public schools, the *Confédération Française des Travailleurs Chrétiens* (the Catholic trade-union organization), and various Catholic "pressure groups" to influence legislation. This change has come about apparently because of the changed relations between church and state in France during the past two hundred years. Whereas formerly they were closely linked and aided each other's purposes, under the republic the church has usually found itself in opposition to the state, and certainly separated from it by law.

The particular circumstances of American community life seem to have encouraged the American propensity for forming voluntary associations. The weakness of government on the frontier forced the association of citizens for the carrying on of activities that would normally be governmental under more developed conditions. The tradition of distrust for government—born out of the unhappy relation with England in colonial days and out of a dominant laissez-faire economic philosophy—encouraged the citizen to take action that would forestall the entrance of government, and this often required the association of like-minded persons. The greater mobility of a new and rapidly developing nation weakened the ties of the extended family, and there was need of a substitute institution that could provide affection and sociability. The social club and fraternal organization, as well as perhaps the increasing intimacy of the small family, provided the substitute. The more rapid change in American life—consisting of such factors as greater mobility, greater openness to capitalist initiative, and the unusual juxtaposition of people with diverse cultural backgrounds—created a greater need for social mechanisms of individual and group adjustment, and the voluntary associations were among the most important of these mechanisms.

Still another cultural difference that seems to have a relationship to the degree of formation of voluntary associations, especially of the social influence type, is the importance of local government. For well-known historical reasons, France developed a strong central government with practically no local government, whereas the United States, at least until 1933, had more functions reserved to the local governments than to the federal government. The Scandinavian countries and Switzerland, with many associations, also have strong traditions of local government, whereas Spain and Portugal, with few associations, also have little local government. While there are probably several common historical factors underlying the development of both local government and voluntary associations, there would seem also to be a direct causal influence of local government on the development of associations. It is fairly easy to organize some neighbors and other like-minded people of a given community to put effective pressure on an accessible local government. It requires considerably more organizing skill, and much money, to form a movement in many different communities that could effectively put pressure on a national government, simply because of the difference in physical proximity. In France, the lack of strong local government adds to the weakness of private associations in putting the individual citizen directly under the power of the national government.[48]

Considering the relatively costly activities of many associations in countries where associations play an important role, it would seem that the French legal restriction on the acquisition of funds is an especially repressive force on French associations today. The dues that declared and nondeclared associations in France are permitted to collect would not permit the great range and intensity of programs engaged in by American associations. Only associations recognized by the Council of State as having public utility have recourse to gifts and legacies of any type, or to the use of bazaars, concerts, tags, or any other means of raising money (France has no equivalent of the Community Fund). Recognition is given sparingly and then only to associations whose activities are clearly for the benefit of "the public"—that is, associations of the "welfare" type. On top of that comes the fact that each gift or legacy must be approved by the Council of State and then published in the *Journal Officiel*. A perusal of the *Journal Officiel* for the years 1947–1950 gives strong support for the common observation that there is little development of the tradition of philanthropy in France (except possibly through the church, since a certain amount of leeway is legally permitted in making contributions to the church). The nonfinancial restrictions on associations, consisting of the limita-

---

[48] It may be of interest to observe that the resistance in France to the German occupation in World War II was organized largely around the Communist party, one of the few strong "voluntary associations." In Norway, also, the organization of the resistance was immeasurably aided by the existence of the many voluntary associations.

tion on activities to those declared and of large amounts of "red tape," may also have a repressive effect on associations today.

A THEORY OF THE FUNCTION OF VOLUNTARY ASSOCIATIONS

The final sections of this chapter will consist of the statement of a theory of the function of voluntary associations in contemporary society and an assessment of the significance of the weakness of voluntary associations in France in the light of this theory. The formulation of this theory has involved something of the historical and comparative methods, although a great deal more comparative and historical data must be gathered before the theory can be regarded as substantiated. The formulation of the theory has also involved something akin to a method employed by theoretical economists—that is, the method of conceptually removing one element from the situation and imagining what the consequences are likely to be. The theory postulates certain psychological needs—for human fellowship, for a sense of personal security, and for a satisfying "explanation" of the forces controlling the perceived world (in this context we are interested only in the immediate social world, not in the metaphysical explanations of the ultimate natural world). These needs are not necessarily biological in origin; they may be developed out of infantile experience in the manner which Cooley described,[49] or simply out of the vacuum left when social institutions change and no longer perform the function within a culture that they once performed.

The theory has two parts: (1) Prior to the Industrial Revolution, the community, the church, and the extended family were able, in large measure, to satisfy whatever felt needs there were for human fellowship, personal security, and "explanation" of the forces controlling the perceived world. The Industrial Revolution was the strongest of a series of major social changes that drastically weakened the all-encompassing community, church, and extended family. These changes exerted their influence through a rise in geographic mobility, urbanization, and secularization, and through the elimination of "rights" to a plot of ground, a trade, and a "just price." (2) The reaction of people to these drastic social changes was different in different countries. In the United States and several other Western countries, it largely

---

[49] Charles H. Cooley, *Human Nature and the Social Order* (New York: Scribner, 1902). See particularly his discussion of the sentiments constituting human nature.

took the form of forming associations. Associations of all types provide human fellowship. Economic associations—trade-unions (including professional societies), businessmen's associations for "restraint of trade," mutual-aid societies, consumers' and producers' cooperatives—all aim at achieving personal security. Several types of associations, including economic associations but especially social influence associations, not only provide a large measure of understanding of social forces but also provide some control over them.

THE SOCIAL SITUATION OF FRANCE RELEVANT TO THE THEORY

The drive for forming associations since the Industrial Revolution can easily be seen in the United States. This study has provided evidence of this drive in France in considering the nineteenth-century history of the economic associations. But in France the drive for association was repressed, as we have seen. Even when the "liberating" laws of 1884 and 1901 were passed, they did not release all the forces that were finding expression in associations in other countries. Trade-unions in France have never provided personal security for their members, since the functions of the unions are primarily political rather than economic. (Other economic associations in France do provide a large measure of personal security for their members.) Noneconomic associations multiplied after 1901, but as we have seen, they seldom were of the social influence type that satisfied the need for an explanation of forces controlling the perceived world.

Two complementary questions now need to be raised: (1) Did France experience the full degree of breakdown of the preindustrial community, church, and extended family that other Western countries did? (2) Did France develop institutions other than the voluntary association to satisfy needs for fellowship, security, and an explanation of the forces controlling the perceived world? These are questions demanding a great deal of future research. Only a few rough sketches of the directions the answers might take can be given here.[50]

Almost half (47 per cent) of the population of France is still rural.[51] Furthermore, it is the impression of two French sociologists, who are familiar with the American scene as well as that of France, that urban

[50] The data consist of all the relevant facts that were found available in already collected form; I could not attempt an independent field investigation.

[51] From the national Census of 1946. "Rural" is defined as a community containing fewer than two thousand inhabitants.

people in France—especially those in the provincial cities—have closer ties to some rural community than do American urbanites.[52] A study by the *Institut Français d'Opinion Publique* shows that 18 per cent of Parisians have parents living in the provinces, 49 per cent have brothers, sisters, or cousins there, and 24 per cent have close friends in the provinces.[53] Only 19 per cent of Parisians have neither relatives nor friends in the provinces. Fully 88 per cent of Parisians have visited other cities in France, and 45 per cent have lived for a significant period in other French cities.[54] Among persons living outside of Paris, 8 per cent once lived in Paris and 47 per cent have visited there several times. Yet the total internal migration rate in France is not very high; in 1936, only 25.5 per cent of the French population were living outside the *département* in which they were born, and most of these were in the Paris area.[55] Further, the *quartier* (neighborhood) in the French city is quite generally alleged to be a social as well as a geographic unit.

What associations there are in France are largely of the sociable type (including sports groups, *amicales*, fraternal groups, etc.), and throughout France the *café* serves as an informal neighborhood club for a large part of the population, especially for the men. Women have a good deal of neighborhood social life in the numerous small shops, which have never been replaced in France by the supermarket. In the village and small towns, the *place* in front of the church is a general meeting place on Sunday, even for those who do not attend the mass. The *café*, the *boutique*, and the *sortie de la messe* have only limited equivalents in the United States. If facts like these were found, on further research, to be typical and reliable, it would seem that the French community is still a relatively stable unit and thus probably satisfies much of the need for human fellowship. But this is a statement of conditions in France relative to those in the United States; an examination of the same facts would also lead us to the

[52] Georges Friedmann and Raymond Aron, from personal interviews (October 1, 1951, and December 17, 1951, respectively). These observations were made spontaneously by the two sociologists, and I would agree with them from my more limited observation.

[53] *Sondages*, 1951, No. 2, p. 10.

[54] *Ibid.*, p. 14.

[55] Calculated from the 1936 Census, in *Sondages*, 1951, No. 2, p. 8. For the three *départements* including and bordering Paris (Seine-et-Oise, Seine, and Seine-et-Marne) the figures for those born outside the *départements* were, in 1936, 65.1, 53.3, and 45.2 per cent respectively.

conclusion that the community has much less hold over its members in France today than it did in preindustrial times. Geographic mobility, for example, has been steadily rising [56] and there has been a good deal of concern over it in terms of its effect in breaking up the small community. Between 1823 and 1906, at least thirty studies were published on this subject,[57] and even today there are some alarmists among social scientists who are studying the breakup of the community.[58]

If the community has been moderately stable, the church in France has lost much of the hold over the average Frenchman that it had in the Middle Ages. During the French Revolution many areas exiled their priests and smashed the material symbols of religion.[59] Throughout the nineteenth century—especially during republican periods— and at least until World War II, a very large proportion of the French were anticlerical in politics [60] and did not allow themselves to be greatly influenced by the church in other ways—in such a matter as birth control, for example. A map of religious influence in France, prepared in 1947 by two sociologists sympathetic to the Catholic Church, shows that the larger part of even rural France consists of "parishes indifferent to Christian traditions" and that there are some "mission areas" which do not even have parishes.[61] In November 1947

[56] *Ibid.*

[57] The list is taken from the bibliography of Louis Chevalier's excellent study, *La Formation de la Population Parisienne au XIXᵉ Siecle*, Institut National d'Etudes Demographiques, Travaux et Documents, cahier no. 10 (Paris: Presses Universitaires de France, 1950). For a survey of the historical literature, see also Joseph J. Spengler, *France Faces Depopulation* (Durham, N.C.: Duke University Press, 1938).

[58] See, for example, the scholarly two-volume study of Abbé Elie Gautier, *op. cit.*; also, Jean F. Gravier, *Paris et le Désert Français* (Paris: Le Portulan, 1947). An amusing example of this concern is the reaction of the labor historian Edouard Dolléans, *op. cit.*, pp. 254–255, against the beautification of Paris beginning in 1853. For this author, such beautification meant the breakup of the *quartier*, since old houses were torn down and new and wide streets built. Dolléans says: "Mais, en touchant aux vieilles pierres, c'est aussi au coeur de l'ouvrier parisien qu'on touche!" ("But, in disturbing the old stones, it is also the heart of the Parisian worker that is wrenched!")

[59] Georges Le Febvre, *La Revolution Française* (Paris: Presses Universitaires de France, 1951).

[60] L. Arthur Minnich, Jr., *Modern France*, E. M. Earle (ed.) (Princeton, N.J.: Princeton University Press, 1951), pp. 109–123.

[61] The map was prepared by Fernand Brulard from his own researches and those of Gabriel Le Bras. It was originally published in the *Cahiers du Clergé Rurale*, No. 84 (November 1947), and has been reprinted in Jean Bourgeois-Pichat, "Un Nouvel Indice de Mesure de la Fecondité," *Population*, vol. 3, no. 2 (April–June 1948), pp. 310–311.

a public opinion poll of a representative cross section of Frenchmen asked: "Do you believe in God?" Only 66 per cent said they did believe in God; 20 per cent flatly stated that they did not; and the remaining 14 per cent did not answer.[62] Of course, many of those who stated that they did believe in God were not active churchgoers. Questions about whether the respondent went to mass habitually (or on the preceding two Sundays) revealed that 55 per cent did not, only 33 per cent did (4 per cent belonged to a non-Catholic religion, and 8 per cent did not answer).

The evidence is clear that the church does not have much hold over a majority of the French today, although there are many active movements within the French Catholic Church to regain the relationship.[63] Even for the minority of loyal Catholics, and the relatively small proportion of persons adhering to other religious faiths, it is doubtful whether the religious doctrines provide a completely satisfactory explanation of forces that control the social world (an equivalent statement might be made for most other countries). The Catholic Church does, however, offer a significant partial ideology for its adherents, and it provides a place for community meeting after the religious service.

It is difficult to determine to what extent the extended family[64] still exists in France since the Census does not inquire about the relationship of persons living in the same household. It is likely that the extended family has broken down somewhat since the Middle Ages—when practically all persons had close contact with, and dependence on, collateral relatives—but that the process of breakdown has not developed as far as in the United States.

The following evidence supports this statement: (1) The data already presented on geographic mobility reflect the degree to which it is possible for the extended family to maintain itself in France. (2) A

[62] Figures on belief in God and church attendance are from studies of the *Institut Français d'Opinion Publique*, whose files were generously made available to me by Professeur Jean Stoetzel.

[63] For an excellent summary of researches comparing communities where the church has a strong relationship to the people and where it does not, see Gabriel Le Bras, "Mesure de la vitalité sociale du Catholicisme en France," *Cahiers Internationaux de Sociologie*, 8 (1950), 3–39.

[64] By "extended family" I mean the conjugal family (father, mother, and children) plus any other relatives (grandparents, uncles, aunts, cousins) who live with them or are in close contact with them.

public opinion study, made in July 1946, of a cross section of retired
and pensioned persons in France revealed that 39 per cent were living
with their children; 40 per cent were living alone (or with their
spouses); and among the remaining 21 per cent who did not answer
some may have been living with other relatives.[65] Among those actively engaged in their occupations, 23 per cent expressed the intention
of living with their children, but this, of course, is not a reliable
measure of actual behavior. (3) Another public opinion study, made
in July 1949, showed that of the 43 per cent of the adult French population planning to leave home for a vacation that summer, 47 per
cent planned to stay in the home of some relative.[66] (4) Several holi-
days were found, in *Institut Français d'Opinion Publique* polls, to be
occasions for family reunions. For All Saints' Day, 1947, 38 per cent
of a cross section of French adults reported such a family reunion;
for Christmas Eve of that same year, 39 per cent reported some sort
of reunion without specifying whether it was for family members
alone or not, and the same was true for 25 per cent at New Year's Eve.
(5) An unpublished study by Jesse Pitts [67] reveals a great dependence
on the extended family in France for social status and vertical mobility, a dependence which is much less common in the United States.

While the French seem to maintain contacts with their family and
to see their friends often in *cafés* and at meetings or entertainments,
they do not seem to have as much home visiting as do Americans.
To receive friends at home or visit them at their homes ranked fourth
in distractions preferred (after reading, listening to the radio, and
going to the theater or movies) according to an *Institut Français
d'Opinion Publique* survey; and on the evening before the poll was
taken, in January 1948, only 7 per cent had received guests or paid
visits to homes of others, including relatives. In Auxerre, only 59 per
cent of the cross section of adult population said they ever received
guests or paid visits to others' homes.[68] Alfred Sauvy, the eminent
sociologist and demographer, believes that there is a tendency to avoid

---

[65] Alain Girard, supplement to Jean Daric, *Vieillissement de la Population et Pro-
longation de la Vie Active,* Institut National d'Etudes Démographiques, Travaux et
Documents, cahier no. 7 (Paris: Presses Universitaires de France, 1948), p. 191.

[66] *Institut Français d'Opinion Publique* study. The figure was slightly higher in
previous years—up to 54 per cent in 1946.

[67] Forthcoming Ph.D. dissertation at Harvard University.

[68] Suzanne Frère, "Les Loisirs à Auxerre," *Cahiers Internationaux de Sociologie,* VII
(1949), 107.

the home, and to go to the *café* for social life, because of the poor housing conditions of the average Frenchman.[69]

One other measure of social attachment will be referred to briefly— attachment to the occupation. In the Middle Ages it was practically impossible to change one's occupation. Today fully 77 per cent of retired Frenchmen have always exercised the same trade, and 19 per cent have changed their occupation only one time.[70] The difference is not only a matter of percentages; it is also a matter of a major change of social structure. In the Middle Ages, one inherited an economic position and had a right to it, and the position had a claim on the individual so that it was practically unthinkable that one would leave it. Today, no such mutual claim exists. As I have had occasion to observe in another context,[71] the combination of modern technology and competition have produced such a high level of productive efficiency that the ordinary worker can afford to purchase the full range of necessities and some luxuries as well, and the owners and managers of industry can look forward to accumulations of wealth formerly possessed only by kings and the highest of nobles. At the same time, the worker can suddenly lose his job and the businessman his business—because of a technological change or a business depression—so that neither has a great deal of security. Thus, following the Industrial Revolution, the average rewards became greater, but the occasional penalties became more severe. The French historian Charles Morazé has made the same type of observation. In speaking of the rural French after the passage of the "liberalizing" laws of the first French Revolution, he observes: "Many regretted [the passing of] the ancient traditional usages, which assured them a condition that was mediocre but certain." [72]

We turn now to the question of whether France has developed new

[69] "Logement et Population," *Population*, vol. I, no. 3 (July–September 1946), pp. 448–449.

[70] Girard, *op. cit.*, p. 184. Among Frenchmen still actively working, 74 per cent have always exercised the same trade, and 24 per cent have changed their occupation once. Among the retired, businessmen have changed their occupation most frequently (31 per cent with one or more changes); civil servants and professional men have changed their occupation least frequently (11 and 13 per cent respectively). Civil servants and white-collar workers are increasing their rate of change of occupation most rapidly now. For civil servants, the proportion with one or more changes among the retired is 11 per cent, but among the actively working it is 24 per cent; for other white-collar workers, the equivalent figures are 26 and 34 per cent.

[71] See Chapter 2, esp. pp. 31–33.

[72] Charles Morazé, *La France bourgeoise* (Paris: Librairie Armand Colin, 1946), p. 81.

institutions to substitute for the preindustrial community, church, and family in satisfying needs for fellowship, security, and an explanation of, and influence on, the forces controlling the social world. We have already observed that there has been a certain development of associations for fellowship, but that few of the occupational or other associations provide security or "explanation" and control. Several other institutions worthy of note are the *café*, the political party, the conjugal family, and the public parks.

1. The *café* has not been studied but is highly worthy of study as an informal social club. As early as 1868, Leroy-Beaulieu could point to the important new role of the *café* in the life of French workers: "The *café* holds for the working classes in the present society the place of the church in the past society." [73] The American tavern or soda fountain is hardly comparable to the French *café*; probably only such establishments as the Greek coffeehouse or the British pub would be comparable. While some of the trade at the *café* is transient, a good part is regular, and the men, and often the women, of an urban *quartier* can count on meeting a good number of their neighbors there at certain hours of the day (before going to work in the morning, just before and just after lunch, and especially just before dinner and in the evening). Much more time is spent in talking than in drinking, and the proprietor—who transmits messages, news, and gossip—provides a certain continuity for the fairly formless group. The *café* satisfies much of the need for human fellowship.

2. The *political party* has been extensively studied [74] in France for its political functions but rarely for its relationship to the ordinary citizen. In the major election of June 1951 for the Chamber of Deputies only 19.8 per cent of the eligible voters abstained, and these were mostly women who received the suffrage only in 1945. The proportional representation system of voting, the pre-eminent importance of the deputy among elected officials, the relatively small size of the deputy's electoral district, the character of many French newspapers as organs of a party, [75] and the multiparty system help to permit the

[73] Paul Leroy-Beaulieu, *De l'Etat Moral et Intellectuel des Populations Ouvrières et de Son Influence sur le Taux des Salaires* (Paris: Librairie Guillaumin, 1868), p. 74; quoted in Duveau, *op. cit.*, p. 499.

[74] See, for example, the series *Cahiers de la Fondation Nationale des Sciences Politiques.*

[75] That Frenchmen are great readers of newspapers is illustrated by the Bettleheim-Frère study of Auxerre. In that small provincial city, 93 per cent of married men, 81

ordinary French citizen to have a closer relationship to his political party than is the case in the United States. The greater role of the government in relation to the citizen encourages the French to pay closer attention to politics.

The trade-union or other occupational association (*syndicat*) also serves as a source of close political affiliation, since the trade-union in France is more a branch of a political party than an organization to gain advantages from employers for workers.[76] In the case of the Communist party—which claimed 27 per cent of the voters, or 20 per cent of all French persons eligible to vote, at the 1951 election—the relationship of the party member to his cell is very close indeed. (Of course, only a small proportion of Communist voters are actual party members.) Yet the evidence does not show that the Frenchman is so attached to his party that he does not change it. New political parties are formed in France relatively frequently and old ones die. An *Institut Français d'Opinion Publique* survey shows that party fidelity, between the elections of November 1946 and June 1951, was 81, 70, 41, 61, and 46 per cent for the five leading parties that were in existence in 1946.[77] When asked, "Do you think it would make much difference whether one party or another were in power?" 39 per cent of the French answered negatively and 12 per cent more were without opinions. In this respect, the French were less concerned about which party was in power than were the British, the Norwegians, the Swedes, or the Danes. Only the Americans were still less concerned than the French among national groups of whom this question was asked, and this was probably for entirely different reasons.

Except for the Communist party, the political party in France does not satisfy the needs for fellowship or security, but it might possibly have some effect in satisfying the need for understanding the forces that control the social world. That it gives the ordinary citizen a sense of control over these forces is highly questionable, however, since the multiparty system in France gives no party the opportunity

per cent of married women, 82 per cent of unmarried men, and 62 per cent of unmarried women read a daily newspaper. (Suzanne Frère, *op. cit.*, p. 106.)

[76] This characterization has been made in private conversation, by a prominent American trade-union official who is thoroughly familiar with the French trade-unions. There are twelve federations of *syndicats* for workers (excluding those for employers) and often four or five or more will operate in the same plants. The major distinction between them is affiliation with different political parties, although the smaller federations are also limited to specialized categories of occupations.

[77] *Sondages*, 1951, No. 2.

to have stable control over the government, and since there is little local government in France and the central government is naturally distant from ordinary people. A special word should be given to the partisan newspaper in France. Since its emphasis is on explanation rather than information, it does attempt to satisfy the need for understanding the forces controlling the social world. Its success is only partial, however, as many of the French seem to be skeptical of the veracity of mass media.

3. The *conjugal family* is not particularly a modern institution, of course, but the French seem to have maintained a higher degree of integration and intimacy in it than is true in the United States, and thus it has always provided a higher degree of satisfaction of the need for human fellowship. This may be due to some of the following factors: The French family has had, for at least a century, a small number of children; the disintegrating force of the automobile has never been great; there has never been much difference in social outlook between successive generations within the family; and the French divorce rate has never been high (103 divorces per 100,000 population in 1931, as compared to 320 in the United States).[78]

4. The *public parks,* while also not entirely a modern institution, have greatly expanded in number and attractiveness since the Middle Ages. During warm weather, especially, it is a meeting place for a neighborhood, particularly for the women and children.

Summing up the evidence of the latter section of this chapter, we gather the impression that the average Frenchman's need for human fellowship is probably satisfied, despite the changes in social structure since the Middle Ages, but that his needs for security and "explanation" and "control" of forces determining his social world are not satisfied. Studies of the *Institut Français d'Opinion Publique* provide some direct evidence on the lack of satisfaction of the latter two needs. The *Institut* periodically asked the question: "What is the most important problem for you and your family at present?" Each time the

[78] Jacques Desforges, *Le Divorce en France* (Paris: Editions Familiales de France, 1947). The data for the year 1931 are presented because that is the latest year for which there are good international comparative statistics. France legally repressed divorce until 1884 and then permitted it fairly freely. Thus in 1931 France had a much higher rate than England (19 per 100,000), where divorce was still legally repressed, but lower than the United States, Japan (155), Switzerland (144), and Germany (127), where divorce was fairly freely allowed by law. Countries like Belgium (62), Sweden (77), and others had even lower rates than France.

question was asked, between 1946 and 1950, a majority of the responses were in terms of problems of economic insecurity. In the latest survey (September 1951), with both an international crisis and a French governmental crisis in progress, still only 6 per cent of the respondents mentioned the war or the political situation, and only 12 per cent mentioned personal problems.[79]

Some indication of whether people feel satisfied with the explanation they have of forces controlling social life is given indirectly by answers to the question, "Do you believe that the radio gives you adequate or inadequate information on what is presently happening in France?" Radio news reports in France are much like those in Great Britain or the United States, but fully 40 per cent of the French believed the radio badly informed them (December 1947) and 33 per cent more did not venture to give an opinion (probably many of them did not have access to a radio). Only 27 per cent felt that the radio was a good source of information. The fact, too, that the French newspapers on any given day are so different in content, and so prone to "interpretations" of events from different angles, helps to give the average Frenchman the impression that much more is going on "behind the scenes" than he can find out about. Whether this is a justifiable skepticism or not, or whether it is "healthy" or not, is not important in this context. What it reveals of importance is that the French are not satisfied with the explanations they are given of forces controlling their social world.

Another, somewhat less direct, evidence of the Frenchman's failure to get an adequate sense of explanation of, and influence over, the forces controlling his social world is provided by a poll taken by the *Service de Sondages et Statistiques* in June 1951.[80] Despite the high rate of voting and newspaper readership, in answer to the question, "Do questions concerning politics interest you?" only 10 per cent indicated a great interest, 39 per cent expressed a little interest, and 51 per cent said they had no interest at all. The high percentage saying that politics interests them "not at all" is startling.

CONCLUSION

This study has shown that the voluntary association, especially of the social influence type, is of lesser social significance in France than

[79] *Sondages*, 1951, No. 3, p. 4.
[80] *Sondages de l'Opinion Publique Française*, No. 53, Mars 1952, p. 758.

in the United States, both in terms of its role in the community and national life and in terms of involving the interests and concerns of the average individual. The popular explanation for this usually refers to the greater "individualism" of the French, but this is merely using a symptom to explain a cause. Causes of social phenomena have to be stated in institutional and historic terms.

The reasons given for the weak tradition of voluntary associations in France have been these: (1) the deliberate repression of associations by government, fearful of nonconforming and revolutionary forces; (2) the liberal tradition concerned with the freedom of the individual (and, to a minor extent in the late eighteenth century, with freedom of trade); (3) the general concern over the economic consequences of *mainmort* (that is, the hoarding of wealth by associations so that it does not circulate and cannot be taxed); (4) the Catholic tradition of attempting to encompass the individual within the church and of having priests, rather than laymen, active in the welfare and improvement activities of the community; and (5) the strong central government—as opposed to decentralized and even frontier conditions of the United States—which performs many functions left in the United States to local governments, which are closer to the people, or to the citizens themselves.

The major structural restriction on associations in France today is the rigid limitation on the amount of money it can function with and the limitation of its source of income to dues, although it is likely that the weak tradition of associations is more important in inhibiting them than this structural fact.

An exception to the pattern of nonparticipation in social influence groups was noted for the regular political parties, which together claim about 5 per cent of the adult French population as members. The tentative explanation offered for this was in terms of (1) the eighteenth-century liberal philosophy's encouragement of direct political participation, and (2) the nineteenth-century repression of associations, forcing those interested in reform into revolutionary political action.

The chapter then offered a theory of the function of associations in modern social life, in terms of satisfying needs for human fellowship, personal security, and explanation of the forces controlling the perceived social world, when certain social structures of the Middle Ages

—the all-encompassing community, church, and extended family, and the certainty of occupation—no longer performed these functions. For France today evidence was presented that the community, the extended family, and the certainty of occupation have probably not disintegrated as much as in the United States but that they are considerably weaker than they were in the Middle Ages. For the majority of the French today, the church has disintegrated even more than it has for most Americans. It is possible that in France the modern *café*, the political party, the conjugal family, and the public park have taken over some of the functions formerly performed adequately by the community, church, and extended family.

On the whole, it appears that the average Frenchman's need for human fellowship is being satisfied, but that his needs for security and explanation of the forces controlling his social world are not. The functional weakness in French society that this involves is a major source of instability in French social life. It is perhaps one reason for the fact that dissatisfied groups of persons—unionized workers, for example—turn to revolutionary political activity rather than to reform within a democratic political system. It is probably a reason for the widespread feeling in France that ordinary news channels—the radio, for example—is concealing the most important facts. It is possibly one factor among many in the type of dissatisfaction that leads to personal disorganization. The relation between such possible consequences and the functional weakness analyzed here needs further investigation. The greatest of French sociologists, Durkheim, was even more certain than I am that France's lack of voluntary associations would have dire consequences, when he wrote in 1893: "A nation can be maintained only if, between the state and the individual, there is intercalated a whole series of secondary groups near enough to the individuals to attract them strongly in their sphere of action and drag them, in this way, into the general torrent of social life." [81]

[81] Emile Durkheim, *The Division of Labor in Society* (1st ed.; Paris: Felix Alcan, 1893; 1st American ed., translated by G. Simpson; New York, 1933), p. 28.

5

Some Suggestions for Research on Race and Culture Conflict

IN MANY *areas of social science research, specific investigations have been so diversified and so unintegrated that the subject matters are not ready for systematic theory construction. In the following series of suggestions for research in the field of race and culture relations no effort is made at integration; instead the specific current research needs of the field are outlined. Much of the contents of the chapter was assembled for presentation at a conference on behavioral research called by the Rockefeller Foundation in February 1953.*

THE STUDY of race and culture conflict is both one of the oldest and one of the currently most popular among sociologists, and it has recently been taken up by a significant number of psychologists as well. The bibliography of research reports on the subject, not to speak of essays, is huge and seems to be growing at an irregularly accelerating rate. Yet, as in the case of so many other research areas in sociology and social psychology, the studies do not have a cumulative character; that is, most of the recent studies have not built on earlier ones but have started out afresh as though no previous research on the topic had ever been done. I do not know the reasons for this, but I believe it would be enlightening to ascertain them. At any rate, it is not appropriate to speak of *trends* in research on race and culture conflict but of the *current characteristics* of this research. An examination of such current characteristics of research, in the light of what has been done before, will suggest certain problems to which research can usefully be extended.

One of the current characteristics of research on race and culture relations is a renewed interest in studying them in societies other than our own. This comparative study has again turned up situations in which two or more racial or cultural groups dwell side by side without

116

noticeable group conflict.[1] This fact, which should act as a corrective on those who hold that conflict is inevitable whenever groups with "observable" differences live in the same society, has sometimes been inappropriately used to urge that we should no longer study the *problem* of intergroup *conflict,* and its manifestations in prejudice and discrimination, but simply the *fact* of group *relations,* as another among many kinds of human relations. There is nothing inherently inappropriate about studying conflict in general, or race and culture conflict specifically, for its own sake. While the description of group relations in general is a legitimate study, so is the study of group conflict as a specific dynamic process. The value of these studies in other societies to a more general study of the problem of conflict is that they will permit a comparison that will lend some of the characteristics of a controlled experiment to our search for the causes of intergroup conflict.

It would be worth while, in studying group conflict, to plan a large table in which degrees of intergroup conflict are arranged in order along the vertical axis and significant characteristics of the culture of both dominant and subordinated groups, and of their relations, are classified and subclassified along the horizontal axis. The units entered into the body of this projected table should, of course, be all studied cases of group relations. The patterns revealed by such a table would both increase our knowledge of the causes of intergroup conflict and suggest where our categories of analysis (along the horizontal axis) are faulty and need revision in future research.

Another advantage of planning research in this way is that it would bring us back to an initial interest among sociologists in discovering the social conditions under which intergroup conflict arises and continues. Much of the research in this field in recent years has taken the form of ascertaining the individual personality characteristics of those most prone to manifest intergroup antagonism. While there is much of value in this research, it has significant defects and it leads to a neglect of social factors in intergroup conflict. It is of interest that among the studies recently published under the auspices of the American Jewish Committee,[2] the one that stressed social rather than psy-

---

[1] See Everett C. and Helen M. Hughes, *When Peoples Meet* (Glencoe, Ill.: Free Press, 1952); Paul A. F. Walter, *Race and Culture Relations* (New York: McGraw-Hill, 1952).

[2] Dynamics of Prejudice series (New York: Harper, 1950).

chological determinants of prejudice, and that presented the most unequivocal information about a most significant manifestation of prejudice, was the one that attracted least attention.[3]

One of the difficulties of trying to explain intergroup conflict in terms of the personality characteristics of the most prejudiced, in a society where group antagonism is an important cultural value or norm, is gradually coming to light as this type of study is extended. In an as yet unpublished study by Adelson and Sullivan,[4] the persons found to score the highest on the prejudice scale were also found to score the highest on a misanthropy scale. It seems that the "authoritarian personality" (the term popularized by the California psychologists [5]) hates not only Negroes, Jews, Orientals, and so on, but he tends to hate everybody. This seems to be a reliable finding, and it indicates how valuable the research initiated by the California psychologists can be. But it also reveals that researchers have been distracted from their original significant question: How does it come about that certain categories of people in a society—in American society these are primarily racial and cultural groups—are singled out as objects of significant prejudice and discrimination?

Another difficulty of the "personality" approach to the study of intergroup conflict is that it poses too unrealistic a hurdle for social change. The practical implication of the California study, based as it is on psychoanalytic theory, is that prejudice is to be eliminated only by individually psychoanalyzing "authoritarian personalities" and by giving their children a nonauthoritarian upbringing. Without denying in the least that such therapy might be socially valuable, we may note that significant reductions in race prejudice have been achieved without such character reformation.[6] We are living in an era of rapid reduction of the kinds of group antagonisms that dominated the United States during the century preceding World War II, and

[3] I refer to Paul Massing's *Rehearsal for Destruction*.

[4] For a brief summary, see Joseph Adelson and Patrick L. Sullivan, "Ethnocentrism and Misanthropy," address to the 1952 Convention of the American Psychological Association. This address is briefly mentioned in *American Psychologist*, 7 (July 1952), p. 330.

[5] T. W. Adorno *et al.*, *The Authoritarian Personality* (New York: Harper, 1950).

[6] For reports of experimentally induced changes in prejudice, see Robin M. Williams, Jr., *The Reduction of Intergroup Tensions* (New York: Social Science Research Council, 1947); Arnold M. Rose, *Studies in Reduction of Prejudice* (New York: American Council on Race Relations, 1947). Numerous other relevant research reports have been published since these summaries appeared.

yet there has been no extensive psychoanalytic reformation of the character of the prejudiced.

Numerous researches have shown that intergroup *contact,* under certain conditions, has had a significant effect in reducing prejudice.[7] What happens to personality under conditions of intergroup contact? This has been the subject of two studies, which, unfortunately, come to diametrically opposite conclusions; these are the studies by Paul Mussen[8] and by the Cornell group of researchers. Mussen studied boys in an interracial camp and found that those who became more prejudiced toward Negroes during their interracial experience had some of the characteristics of the "authoritarian personality" as described by Adorno and his colleagues. Those who became less prejudiced showed the opposite personality characteristics. On the other hand, the Cornell studies in two small cities showed that interracial contact was more likely to lead to favorable changes on the part of individuals who gave "authoritarian" responses in a number of F-scale items than on the part of those who gave "nonauthoritarian" responses.[9] Even though the two studies have opposing conclusions both show that "authoritarian personalities" do change their attitudes under certain social conditions.

Other kinds of problems which the personality approach to the study of prejudice fails to consider are the practical absence of prejudice among authoritarian types of personality in other societies and the frequent appearance of prejudice in nonauthoritarian types in our own society, especially at times and places where prejudiced behavior has been a cultural norm. It is doubtful whether there has been a larger proportion of "authoritarian personalities" among southerners than among northerners, and yet it has been in the South that race prejudice has been most virulent. My guess is that what the California group calls "authoritarian personalities" is none other, in the United States, than what the literary people have long been calling "Puritans" or "fundamentalists." As the general course of social change has been

---

[7] See the summary and analysis of these researches by Stuart W. Cook, "Contact and Intergroup Attitudes: Some Theoretical Considerations," SPSSI presidential address, September 1952, mimeographed.

[8] Paul H. Mussen, "Some Personality and Social Factors Related to Changes in Children's Attitudes toward Negroes," *Journal of Abnormal and Social Psychology,* 45 (1950), 423–441.

[9] According to a personal communication from John Dean, as reported by Stuart W. Cook, *op. cit.,* p. 24.

making inroads both on Puritanism and on race prejudice, it is natural that those who have been least affected by change would be both the most puritanical and the most prejudiced.

If a personality approach to the study of prejudice is to extend either theoretical or practical knowledge, it must be fitted into an experimental research design. Many of the recent studies on the effects of various social conditions on prejudice have had the character of being field experiments, and while they have faced many technical obstacles, they have produced findings that *work* when applied practically and that fit into our general knowledge of the history of intergroup conflict.

Our major opportunity in research on race and culture conflict at the present time is to take advantage of the rapid changes now going on in this sphere in a variety of social circumstances. Studies of interracial contacts in housing projects,[10] of membership in a trade-union that has an equalitarian race policy,[11] of efficient Negro sales personnel in a leading department store,[12] and of interracial military units [13] have not only given us information as to the conditions under which prejudice and discrimination may be reduced in our society but have also extended our knowledge of the psychological and social dynamics of prejudice as a cultural phenomenon. The Saenger study of the effect on customers of Negro sales personnel extended theoretical knowledge of the nature of psychological rationalization. The Minard and Rose studies of the effect on union members of an equalitarian union policy show how a significant and clear-cut change of attitude in the work situation does not carry over into the social situation for most people.

While we have begun to exploit the field experiment to gain new

---

[10] Morton Deutsch and Mary E. Collins, *Interracial Housing: A Psychological Evaluation of a Social Experiment* (Minneapolis: University of Minnesota Press, 1951); D. M. Wilner, R. P. Walkley, and S. W. Cook, "Residential Proximity and Intergroup Relations in Public Housing Projects," *Journal of Social Issues*, vol. 8, no. 1 (1952), pp. 45–69.

[11] Ira N. Brophy, "The Luxury of Anti-Negro Prejudice," *Public Opinion Quarterly*, 9 (1945), 456–466; Arnold M. Rose, *Union Solidarity* (Minneapolis: University of Minnesota Press, 1952), Chap. V; Ralph D. Minard, "Race Relationships in the Pocahontas Coal Field," *Journal of Social Issues*, vol. 8, no. 1 (1952), pp. 29–44.

[12] Gerhart Saenger and Emily Gilbert, "Customer Reactions to the Integration of Negro Sales Personnel," *International Journal of Opinion and Attitude Research*, vol. 4, no. 1 (1950), pp. 57–76.

[13] Dean Manheimer and Robin M. Williams, Jr., "A Note on Negro Troops in Combat," in S. A. Stouffer *et al.*, *The American Soldier* (Princeton, N.J.: Princeton University Press, 1950), Vol. I, Chap. 10.

information about the effects of social and psychological variables, we have not yet begun to exploit the laboratory experiment, except to test the effects of certain kinds of propaganda. The potential use of the laboratory experiment in this area may not be very great, but it deserves more effort than has thus far been devoted to it. Careful planning can make the inductions realistic and the measures valid. Two research problems especially amenable to laboratory experiment may be mentioned for purposes of illustration:

1. We have become aware of the important role of inconsistency of attitudes in the area of race prejudice.[14] The laboratory experiment would probably be the only way in which we could confront a prejudiced person with his inconsistent and ambivalent attitudes and observe his reactions. By varying the circumstances under which this confrontation takes place, we could learn something about the social-psychological function of inconsistency.

2. Another valuable laboratory experiment would be to create a primary group situation in which the participants are highly prejudiced people and members of the racial or cultural groups against which they are prejudiced. In real-life situations prejudiced persons are seldom brought into intimate face-to-face relations with those against whom they are prejudiced, and the few occasions when this does occur are difficult to anticipate and observe. A clever experimenter can show the prejudiced in specific form the consequences of their prejudice and can observe their reactions under a variety of controlled conditions. The same type of experimental situation can be used to study the reactions of minority persons to manifestations of prejudice and their resistances to social contact with the prejudiced.

Much recent research in this field has been directed toward answering the question, "What is the effect on prejudice of certain planned actions intended to reduce prejudice?" Much of this research is conducted in the form of an oversimplified experiment involving mere stimulus and response: A measurement of prejudice is taken on a group of people, the action is induced, and a measurement is taken again (perhaps there is also a control group to hold constant the effect of the measurement and of extraneous influences). A more complete answer to this question of effect may be had by breaking up one question into the following components:

[14] Earlier investigators like LaPiere and Myrdal first brought this to our attention. For a recent statement, see the *Journal of Social Issues*, vol. 5, no. 3 (1949).

1. Prerequisites of effect: Regarding the social action, is it
   a. attention-getting? attention-holding? [15]
   b. liked or disliked?
   c. readily recalled?
   d. comprehended?
2. The change itself: Is there change in
   a. information and skill?
   b. interest in the problem?
   c. attitude toward the problem?
   d. objective action with regard to the problem?

These research questions can be raised for the techniques of social action that are in current use in efforts to improve intergroup relations, such as specific mass propaganda, discussion groups, catharsis sessions, community self-survey, rumor refuting, mass demonstration or picketing, or several of these or other techniques taken together. The list of questions above points to the need for clarifying what the action program is trying to do, or what counterpropaganda it is trying to combat. It indicates that "effect" is a very complicated thing—that there are certain "prerequisites" of it as well as different levels on which it is manifested. There remains the question for further research, of course, as to whether the so-called "prerequisites" are really prerequisite to effect. It might be, for example, that a piece of antidiscrimination propaganda which apparently is not liked, or which apparently is hard to recall, still has an effect on people. A study needs to be done to correlate the prerequisites with the effects.

Certain other important considerations, which too often are lost sight of, should always be kept in mind whenever studies of this sort are carried out:

1. A study is always carried out in a certain *situation* and with a

---

[15] Attention-getting and attention-holding studies frequently use different bases of measurement, and must therefore be separated for our purposes. However, an attention-holding study can hardly be done unless it is preceded by an attention-getting study, since attention-holding is generally expressed as a proportion of the original amount of attention secured. Neither attention-getting nor attention-holding should be measured simply in terms of the number of people being attentive, since some of the people are attentive against their will. For example, when a short movie is shown or a commercial is inserted in a full-length entertainment program, people are watching or listening to these things frequently because they are interested solely in the larger program. The attention-drawing power of the technique itself must be sought. More important, the effect of the involuntary attentiveness must be examined.

certain *population,* and the findings apply only to that situation and population. Too often there is an unstated, and perhaps unconscious, generalization beyond the data. If it is necessary to estimate to what extent the findings derived from a study of one situation and population apply to others, such extrapolation should be done openly and consciously. In general, the degree of success of a given technique should be specified in terms of the physical, social, and psychological characteristics of a particular population and situation. Also, care must be taken not to generalize from a conclusion regarding one kind of prejudice to another kind of prejudice.

2. A single technique is often employed as part of different strategies. It may have one value when used with one strategy, but a different value, or no value, when used with another strategy. Our findings should specify the strategy as part of the "situation" in which the test of the technique is carried out. For example, propaganda or discussion groups are one technique when used with community leaders, and another when used with the ordinary people of a community.

3. Almost never can it be said that a technique aiming to reduce prejudice has no effect on anyone. What can be said is that technique *A* has an effect on people of type *M* only, in situation *X*, but that type *M* and situation *X* are so rare or unimportant that the technique has little use. If findings are reported in this way, they are likely to be not only nearer to the truth but also more useful for the action people.

4. When we consider effect, we should think of it not only in terms of reducing prejudice or converting prejudiced people but also in terms of reinforcing the attitudes of the nonprejudiced and activating neutrals to work against prejudice.

5. When an effect study is being done, it should measure, or at least consider, long-run as well as short-run effects.

6. Content analysis is a necessary first step in a study of effect in that there must be a precise specification of the induced cause.

As sociologists and psychologists learn more about the specific factors that increase and diminish prejudice, and the manner of their operation, those who are skilled in making the kinds of observations usually made by the historian and the political scientist can begin to study how these factors have been utilized, or can be utilized, to create a given concrete social situation. We must not forget that any social situation arises as a result of the interplay of broad impersonal social forces and the deliberate manipulation of social power. There have been a few excellent recent studies of the development of what might be called the politics of group antagonism,[16] but studies are needed that are oriented more to questions about the precise mechanics of social change. We are just beginning to acquire a realistic conception of the role of social structure—including that which is created by the law and the judicial decision—in creating patterns of discrimination regardless of the personality characteristics of those engaging in the discriminatory behavior. Not to be ignored in this analysis is a consideration of social forces emanating from the minority group itself.

The minority group, under certain circumstances,[17] develops a strong sense of group identification in the face of prejudice and discrimination from the dominant group. While there have been descriptions of this group identification among minorities in the United States,[18] more specific and systematic studies are needed. The following are suggested as relevant topics of research among American Negroes:

1. Which manifestations of protest against discrimination promote high morale and which are simply frustrating and so make for low group morale? (E.g., cheating whites in petty ways vs. organization for protest.)

2. Which manifestations of group identification promote high morale but later hinder most effective use of resources? (E.g., avoidance of high technical education in favor of academic; strongly nationalist activities.)

3. What are the first effects on group identification of leaving a terror-ridden but simple existence (the rural South) and coming to a free but anomic city? The later effects?

[16] One of the first American studies of this type is that by Donald S. Strong, *Organized Anti-Semitism in America* (Washington, D.C.: American Council on Public Affairs, 1941). More recent analyses are those by Massing, *op. cit.;* Robert F. Byrnes, *Anti-Semitism in Modern France* (New Brunswick, N.J.: Rutgers University Press, 1950); J. D. Lohman and D. C. Reitzes, "Note on Race Relations in Mass Society," *American Journal of Sociology,* 58 (November 1952), 240–246.

[17] These circumstances are listed tentatively in Arnold and Caroline Rose, *America Divided* (New York: Knopf, 1948), Chap. 7.

[18] S. Frank Miyamoto, *Social Solidarity among the Japanese in Seattle* (Seattle: University of Washington, 1939); Kurt Lewin, "Self-Hatred among Jews," *Contemporary Jewish Record,* 4 (June 1941), 219–232; Arnold M. Rose, *The Negro's Morale* (Minneapolis: University of Minnesota Press, 1949). The list of research topics is taken from this last-named source, pp. 145–146. Also see the selections in Arnold M. Rose, *Race Prejudice and Discrimination* (New York: Knopf, 1951), Part III.

4. What individual psychological motives are called into play by group pride?
5. When an individual Negro is converted to a predominantly white movement (Catholicism, Communism) which is making a bid for Negro membership by working against discrimination, what is the nature of the new attachment and how does Negro group identification affect it?
6. How does Negro group identification affect a situation in which Negroes and whites are working together (for a range of situations)?
7. What are the relative effects of a major setback to Negroes, or of a major gain for Negroes, on Negroes who have high group identification as compared to Negroes who have low group identification?
8. What is the effect on Negro group identification when individual Negroes are thoroughly accepted in white society (Communists, intellectuals, seamen, miners, artists, etc.)?
9. What is the interrelation between anomie and group identification? (That is, find some individuals who are anomic and see what effect it has on their group identification, and vice versa.)
10. What is the effect on group identification of economic success? (Compare professionals and businessmen.)
11. What is the "incidence" of group identification, by class, age, educational level, region, rural-urban residence?
12. What personality disturbances, if any, accompany group self-hatred?
13. What is the etiology of group self-hatred in the individual?
14. How do Negroes with high group identification act toward whites as compared to Negroes with group self-hatred?
15. What are the attitudes toward other minority groups of: (1) Negroes with high group identification based on concern with protest; (2) Negroes with high group identification based on nationalistic race pride; (3) Negroes with group self-hatred?
16. What are the motives for Negroes' voting, and voting for particular candidates?
17. What are Negroes' attitudes toward various race leaders?
18. What are the reasons for nonparticipation in protest organizations?
19. What is the factual knowledge of national and international politics on the part of Negroes with high and with low group identification?
20. To what extent is there cynicism, negativism, and "tiredness with protest" on the part of Negroes with high group identification? In general, what is the relation between an individual's group morale and his personal morale?

As several students of race and culture conflict have suggested, there is much to be gained by studying the problem in a broad context of group conflict generally, and by considering the processes involved in intergroup relations as characteristic sociological processes that apply in all sorts of human situations. Any such theoretical effort is bound to produce hypotheses and other ideas for research, and it should aid in the ultimate integration of science. But such an effort is subject to some of the same defects to which attention was called in the earlier consideration of the personality approach to the study of prejudice: namely, that a consideration of race and culture conflict as just another kind of conflict may cause us to neglect the very problems we intended to do our research on. We still want to know, for example, why at this stage of American history there are race and culture conflicts between certain groups and not others. The integration of the sciences will not come about by by-passing significant research problems but by exploring them all relatively fully and determining at what points the findings mesh. In any study of race and culture conflict, the distinctive characteristics of this kind of conflict must be kept in mind, if only as variables to be held constant; and the application of findings from studies of other types of conflict—say, labor-management conflict or international conflict—must be considered to be mere analogy until tested within the field of race and culture itself.

Finally, a word should be said about theory in this field. Lasting and fruitful theory builds up slowly, in intimate contact with empirical research. After decades of research we are just now becoming able to formulate soundly based theory. The recent essay of Stuart Cook on "Contact and Intergroup Attitudes" is an example of real theory, and this type of effort now needs to be encouraged. The earlier essays that have passed for theory were in the nature of intelligent guesses and have had the function of provoking research.[19] Unfortunately, not all of these ideas have been tested empirically, and most of them deserve to be.[20] So many of the researches in the field of race and culture conflict have consisted of pointless description or of description to

[19] My essay, "Anti-Semitism's Root in City-Hatred," *Commentary*, 6 (October 1948), 374–378, had such a tentative and limited "theoretical" character.

[20] See, for example, the list of untested hypotheses with broad theoretical implications in my *Race Prejudice and Discrimination* (New York: Knopf, 1951), pp. 425–432.

refute stereotypes and other false popular ideas that there has not been enough time available to specialists to test many of the seminal ideas that could lead to the development of real theory. Perhaps the changing popular attitudes toward minority groups and the new opportunities for conducting research in the social sciences will allow an increased emphasis on research with broader theoretical implications.

6

Group Conflict and Its Mediation: Hypotheses for Research

AMONG *the various broader areas into which the conflict aspects of race and culture relations may be placed is a field of study that is just beginning to get integration: the subject of conflict and mediation. In this chapter are suggested some systematic possibilities for research not only on race and culture conflict but also on management-labor conflict, international conflict, and possibly others that do not receive adequate consideration. Interest in conflict is herein directed toward hypotheses concerning the possibilities for its reduction. The chapter was prepared as my contribution to the section on conflict and mediation of the International Sociological Congress held in Liège, Belgium, in August 1953.*

TYPES OF GROUP CONFLICT

WHILE various scholars have sought to claim that intergroup conflict [1] has a single source—such as in a struggle for control over the means of production (Marx) or in an inevitable opposition because of racial differences (Gumplowicz)—a survey of actual cases in history reveals that there are several distinct types of intergroup conflict with correspondingly distinct etiologies. To insist that there is but one source of motivation for group conflict is to distort the facts and to misdirect the search for cures. A survey of historical and contemporary group conflicts suggests the following working classification: power, or conflict over scarce values; ideological, or conflict over ways of life; and racist, or conflict over biological dominance. Further investigation might suggest the need for further classes of group conflict, so that

[1] In this chapter, the term "conflict" is used in the generally accepted sense, but interest in conflict-avoidance and conflict-reduction extends to all relevant actions with such purposes, even though primary consideration will be given to mediation, defined as the employment of a third party to try to stop or prevent the spread of conflict between two contending parties.

this classification should by no means be considered exhaustive; but it may serve to give us leads for an initial program of research. In a given conflict situation more than one of the motivations may be present, although historical data would seem to indicate that only one is a dominant motivation in a given conflict situation. A secondary factor in a given conflict situation should not be overlooked when it comes to formulating a practical plan of mediation, however, as it will often be a stumbling block when the basic issue seems to be resolvable.

Let us start with a brief exposition of the three-fold classification of types of intergroup conflict. Power conflict has been defined as the struggle for control of scarce values. If the scarce values are economic, they can refer either to the means of production, the channels of distribution, or the economic product. Class conflict such as Marx envisioned referred solely to the control over the means of production, which may be either natural resources and capital equipment as in our society, or slaves as in a less advanced economy. Much of modern economic conflict, however, both between nations and between classes, is not on the direct level of competition for means of production but on the indirect level of seeking control over channels of distribution. This kind of conflict calls for more indirect, more sophisticated, techniques and hence is less overt. Also, we must recognize that there has always been conflict simply over the economic product itself, as in the case of organized crime, racketeering, and piracy. Piracy, which historically has sometimes taken the form of national warfare,[2] seems never to involve the means of production or channels of trade but merely the wealth carried by the vehicles of transportation. Organized crime and racketeering have thus far been studied in a criminological context, but it might also be valuable to analyze them in terms of conflict between highly organized, powerful small groups and poorly organized, dispersed, but ultimately more powerful, large groupings.

Scarce values need not be solely economic, although this type is probably the most important. Influence and prestige are values in their own right, and in groups from nations down to the smallest segments of society can be found a struggle for these values. Most of the struggles we see in university faculties and professional societies are not struggles over economic values but over influence and prestige.

---

[2] For example, the English-Spanish "war" of Elizabethan times, and the Tripolitan-American war of the last years of the eighteenth century.

There are other kinds of power conflict over other scarce values that may merely be mentioned to illustrate their diversity. At the present time there is conflict between the Catholic Church, the state of Israel, and the Moslem world over possession of the city of Jerusalem. This is not so much for the economic value of that city or even its prestige, but rather, primarily, for its symbolic value, at least in the case of the Catholic Church. The so-called "conflict of generations" emphasized by many child-psychologists, to take an entirely different example, is not over economics or power but primarily over the value of independence (although here we border on the second major category).

Ideological conflicts have been defined as struggles for the maintenance or supremacy of different ways of life. Perhaps the term "cultural" would be more adequate than "ideological" except that that term has been used in so many diverse ways that it would not aid communication. In ideological conflict, groups oppose two distinct sets of values, each of which is believed to contain the only right and good and even necessary values. Historically, most ideological group conflicts have been between organized religions. In recent centuries the ideological conflicts have been less religious and metaphysical, more political and economic, in the specific content of the values contested.

Conflict over political and economic ideologies is to be sharply distinguished from conflict for the possession of scarce political and economic values. Whereas the aim of the power type of conflict is to assume possession of the scarce values, the aim of ideological conflict is to annihilate or convert those who do not accept what the group considers to be true or necessary values; or, if victory is out of the question, the aim is to avoid annihilation or conversion. Whereas the former is selfishly motivated, the latter is selfless and even self-sacrificing. In religious conflict the true values are supposed to emanate from a supernatural source, and the motivation to superimpose these values on nonbelievers is considered to be service for this supernatural power. A group which denies the true God is insulting to this highest good, and therefore must be destroyed or converted.

Groups engaged in ideological conflict which is not religious in nature have substituted such forces as history or the true happiness of mankind for God. If history is believed to decree that the bourgeoisie must disappear then the bourgeoisie must be annihilated or converted to a proletarian way of life; or if the perfect Utopia does not have a class of employers, then present employers must be convinced that they should not continue to perform their current role. Ideologies which are the source of ideological conflict invariably are absolutistic. The values and forces of God, history, or Utopia are in some way transcendent over all others.

The third major type of motivation for intergroup conflict that has been noted is the racist one. It rests on the desire to maintain what is believed to be biological purity and caste separation. While the goal of power conflict is the seizure of scarce values and the goal of ideological conflict is annihilation or conversion of nonbelievers, the goal of racist conflict is complete separation, and the strongest demands are for the avoidance of personal contact. One group, members of which consider themselves to be a biological unit or race, takes positive steps to segregate all other groups in the society from all spheres of life where they may come in contact with the active group. The segregation is on the basis of physical distance where possible without interference with economic exploitation; otherwise it is on the basis of symbolic separation. Since such segregation inevitably involves material deprivations for some groups, conflict frequently is the result. The terminology usually employed refers to the active group as the "dominant" one and the segregated groups as "minorities," although it must be clearly recognized that these terms refer not at all to numerical proportions within the society but to the control over power to segregate in a certain fashion.

In its efforts to segregate the minorities, the dominant group—since it does not wish to reduce its own power or restrict its control over scarce values which it currently holds in the society—is obliged to subordinate the minorities in a great variety of ways. While discrimination may not be the intention behind segregation, it is the inevitable result.[3] Some members of the dominant group may sincerely hold to a doctrine of "equal but separate," but since any movement on the part of minority persons toward the achievement of equal values necessarily involves strains on the barriers of segregation, efforts to

[3] Marxist writers, in their efforts to explain all conflict in economic terms, insist that there is always *intention* to discriminate behind all efforts to segregate. See, for example, Carey McWilliams, *A Mask for Privilege* (Boston: Little, Brown, 1948); Oliver C. Cox, *Caste, Class and Race: A Study in Social Dynamics* (New York: Doubleday, 1948).

reinforce segregation also serve as efforts to maintain the existing distribution of scarce values.[4]

The motives of minorities in such a situation might very well be power seeking rather than racist—that is, in becoming the opposing group in a conflict situation the motives of the minorities may not be the desire to maintain racial purity, but rather to gain some control over scarce values. On the other hand it is also possible for nondominant numerical minorities to have racist motives and to initiate conflict. In such cases, the nondominant numerical minorities generally segregate themselves to keep their biological condition uncontaminated, and conflicts set in when out-groups find the self-segregating activities of the minorities a nuisance obstructing the maintenance of the functions of the society. Groups with racist beliefs regard themselves as biologically superior, and any publicity given to that belief encourages bad relations.

Since concern over the biological composition of a population is primarily a modern phenomenon, the racists' motivation to conflict is also primarily modern. However, the "chosen people" concept of the Hebrews since ancient times, the ancient Greeks' concept of their distinctiveness from barbarians (which included all non-Greeks), and a tendency found among members of many primitive societies to consider themselves as the only true "people," to be distinguished from the semi-animals, suggest that the racist basis of conflict is not exclusively a phenomenon of modern Western culture.

SUGGESTED TECHNIQUES FOR REDUCING CONFLICT

In formulating hypotheses about the techniques most likely to be effective in reducing conflict, it is important to keep these categories of conflict distinct. This is not to say that the techniques for reducing conflict must always be directed at its causes, but merely that constructive efforts to reduce conflict must take cognizance of the goals of the groups engaged in conflict. It is an oversimplification to say that eradication or control of a phenomenon requires an attack on its sources; it might just as successfully be directed at its symptoms or its carriers. To use analogies from the control of physical disease, we may

---

[4] See "The Effects of Segregation and the Consequences of Desegregation: A Social Science Statement," Appendix to Appellants' Briefs, School Segregation Cases Nos. 8, 101, and 191 in the Supreme Court of the United States, October term, 1952, by 32 social scientists.

observe that the practical eradication of malaria does not involve any attack on the protozoon that "causes" it but simply on the mosquito that carries the protozoon to humans, and that control of diabetes does not involve remedying the defective pancreas but simply requires periodic injection of insulin. "Symptom treatment" is not universally ineffective.

Coming back to group conflict, we may observe that it will never be possible to reduce motivation to seize scarce values; still it may be quite feasible to prevent that motivation from inspiring group conflict. Nevertheless, it is important to know which motivation is causing the conflict, since then a more appropriate deflecting technique can be fashioned. Medical scientists do not grope for cures at random, even when they cannot control the causes of a disease, but seek some technique that will satisfactorily "adjust" the patient to his disease. I would thus take a position opposed both to the pessimist who states that it is impossible to stop group conflict because the human motivations leading to it are ineradicable and to the optimist who blithely treats symptoms without considering the causes.

Before we turn to the specific techniques, let us recognize that there are certain limits to this discussion, outside of which these hypotheses would be irrelevant. The first is that a superpower which can impose itself on conflicting groups can suppress conflicts even without mediation and that no technique can stop the deliberate bullying by a superpower which no other power can successfully oppose. Only rarely, however, are powers that strong without some other power, or combination of powers, being almost as strong.

A second limitation is something of an antithesis to the first. Mediation cannot occur in a condition of absolute anarchy, when the conflicting groups communicate neither with each other nor with third parties. This is known to have occurred temporarily, but is usually not a permanent condition of group conflict.

Thirdly, certain psychological assumptions must be made even if all the available evidence cannot be brought in at this point to support them. For example, it must be assumed that man does not have an ever-present and uncontrollable instinct of pugnacity. If man had such an instinct, conflict—by definition—could not be eliminated or even reduced. Few informed persons today hold that the instinct of pugnacity is the root of intergroup conflicts, although frequently we do hear such a cause assigned by uninformed persons. An allied assumption is, however, still made by certain social scientists, and its implication is that conflict is uncontrollable. This assumption is that man has an inherent dislike of differences and that conflict generally follows upon recognition of differences.[5] Since differences in physical appearance, behavior patterns, dress, or beliefs are constantly found among strangers, and since strangers are always present in our society, antagonism and conflict are inevitable and frequent. It is unquestionably true that there must be some differences between two groups for them to define each other as antagonists, and it is probably true that two groups in conflict seize upon and emphasize their differences. Since no two groups are alike, the dislike of differences must come after the fact of conflict, and probably serves as a rationalization, justification, and morale builder for conflict. We can thus consider dislike of differences as a "necessary cause" of conflict—because it is invariably present—but not as a "sufficient cause" in the sense that it is an effective stimulator of conflict.

Certain hypotheses about mediation can be formulated by considering the different goals of conflicting groups outlined above. Power conflict over scarce values tends to be both the most frequent kind of group conflict and also the type most amenable to mediation, since it is based on rational motives. The mediation process, which gets the conflicting groups to communicate with each other and to bring the best available information to bear on the values under conflict, may be able to persuade the conflicting parties to compromise—that is, to share the scarce values in certain proportions. Shares might be divided according to several principles, such as the relative strength of the group, the need of the group, or the abstract justice involved in the claims of the group. Mediation is especially successful in getting conflicting groups to compromise when it can be demonstrated to them that they are sacrificing other values in order to continue the conflict over certain values. A systematic study needs to be made by the mediator to determine what these other values that are being sacrificed are. Certainly the conflict itself involves a certain sacrifice of values;

---

[5] Earlier writers making this assumption include Nathaniel Shaler, *The Neighbor: The Natural History of Human Contact* (Boston: Houghton Mifflin, 1904); Bernard Lazare, *Anti-Semitism, Its History and Causes* (New York: International Library Publishing Company, 1903). A recent acceptance of the assumption has been stated by George A. Lundberg in an unpublished paper, "The Survival of the Moralistic-Legalistic Orientation in Sociology" (1952).

conflict is always costly in some way. Even nations at war have been induced to call an armistice when it has been demonstrated to both sides that they have more to lose by continuation of the war than by its cessation.[6]

When the conflict involves a violation of law, sometimes the mere agreement to cease further conflict and ignore prosecution for the illegal quality of the conflict activity will serve to stop it. There have been times in history when pirates and racketeers have been only too happy to stop their predatory activities upon the promise of immunity from punishment by government, and the government has been willing to accede because it was too weak to devise any effective means of stopping the conflict by physical or legal force. On the other hand, such a procedure is sometimes regarded as destructive of the prestige of the law.

Clarification of the aims of the conflicting parties will often aid in the resolution of conflict. Even though the conflict may basically be carried on for rational and selfish purposes, groups often add a whole series of secondary claims to justify and rationalize their conflict activity in order to maintain group solidarity and morale. These aid the group in carrying on the conflict but are impediments to mediation of the conflict. If the mediator can determine what the basic goals of the conflict groups are, he can, by adroit maneuvers which will be considered in greater detail later, readily persuade the group to slough off its secondary demands.

For example, some trade-unions in France, Germany, Italy, and perhaps other countries claim to desire nothing less than the complete expropriation of the means of production from the employer class and sometimes make even more extreme demands, such as the complete physical elimination of the employer class. Actually it is quite possible that these trade-unions, or at least the workers who form their membership and strength, would be willing to accept an equitable distribution of an increased economic product instead of persisting in the more drastic demands, especially if it could be shown that a less destructive and more institutionalized conflict process would permit an increase of the total economic product for the workers as well as for the employers. Such a compromise has actually been

[6] Most wars between the religious wars of the sixteenth century and World War I were stopped by such compromise; "unconditional surrender" was never their goal or their achievement.

achieved in Sweden, and to a lesser extent in the other Scandinavian countries, and it seems to be on its way in Great Britain and even the United States. While the threat of strike remains as an ultimate possibility, in effect strikes are eliminated and the conflict takes place over a bargaining table at which a resolution is always achieved by compromise.

These observations suggest a further one. Some political conflict, especially that between labor and management, may arise basically out of a desire to satisfy a rational need. It has been suggested by many sociologists, at least as far back as Durkheim,[7] that modern industrialized society disrupts satisfying social relations and creates an alienation from cultural values. Subjectively this is felt as a deep sense of personal insecurity. Studies of suicide,[8] mental disorder,[9] family disruption,[10] and industrial relations[11] give empirical support to this thesis.

Other writers have suggested that the modern development of formal and informal associations, especially those intended to take some action in the society, are correctives for this.[12] A specific and important example would be the case of workers with a sense of personal insecurity banding together into a trade-union to set some limits on the impersonal social forces that control them and to regain personal security through power conflicts with those who are perceived to create the insecurity (i.e., the employers).[13] Conflict of this type thus rests ultimately on certain socially created needs, according to this theory. If the theory is correct, conflict could be avoided by satisfying the needs as completely and expeditiously as possible. The solution would have to be worked out by further research and by trial

[7] Emile Durkheim, *The Division of Labor in Society* (1st French ed., Paris: Felix Alcan, 1893; latest American ed., Glencoe, Ill.: Free Press, 1947).

[8] For example, Emile Durkheim, *Suicide* (1st French ed., Paris: Felix Alcan, 1897; American ed., Glencoe, Ill.: Free Press, 1951).

[9] For example, Robert E. L. Faris and H. Warren Dunham, *Mental Disorders in Urban Areas* (Chicago: University of Chicago Press, 1939).

[10] For example, Robert C. Angell, *The Family Encounters the Depression* (New York: Scribner, 1936).

[11] For example, Elton Mayo, *The Social Problems of an Industrial Civilization* (Cambridge, Mass.: Harvard Business School, 1945); Karl Polanyi, *The Great Transformation* (New York: Farrar and Rinehart, 1944); W. Lloyd Warner and J. O. Low, *The Social System of the Modern Factory. The Strike: A Social Analysis* (New Haven, Conn.: Yale University Press, 1947).

[12] See chapters 2, 3, and 4 of this volume.

[13] Frank Tannenbaum, *A Philosophy of Labor* (New York: Knopf, 1951); Arnold M. Rose, *Union Solidarity* (Minneapolis: University of Minnesota Press, 1952).

and error, but in general it would take the form of increasing personal security and social participation. In industrial relations this would involve concessions, mostly by employers to workers but some by unions to individual employers, at the expense of free competition. The theory and the suggested solution for conflict have relevance for ethnic conflicts as well as for industrial conflicts.[14]

Still another kind of compromise can occur, although rarely, where it is possible to demonstrate that both parties stand to gain their full goals if they cease the conflict. This actually occurred in the cessation of conflict between Great Britain and India when Great Britain got fuller economic cooperation from a free India than it did from a controlled India and the Indians got their independent government. Such might be the basis of resolution in the conflict now pending among the three great Western religions over the use of the city of Jerusalem. A free Jerusalem—open to members of all three religious faiths alike and under the control of no one government—might serve the interests of all the faiths better than the exclusive control by one of them over the Holy City.

Whatever means are employed to accommodate conflicts of the power type, the mediator must use great skill to overcome the non-rational psychological barriers to accommodation. The "face" of each party must be saved, and the hostile emotions generated must, like steam, be allowed to vent themselves harmlessly (perhaps against third parties, such as the mediator himself).

Before turning from the power type of conflict, we should give brief attention to an issue that has divided experts in international relations for a long time[15] and that is relevant to conflict in other spheres as well. The issue is whether consensus is needed between potential contenders as a precondition to the cessation of conflict between them. One aspect of the matter can be dealt with summarily, even though it still divides specialists in the international relations field. This involves the question as to whether an essential prerequisite to peace is consensus on the value of not resorting to violence to settle differences of interests. Such a value is not found among all subgroups in

[14] Arnold M. Rose, "Intergroup Anxieties in a Mass Society," *Phylon,* 12 (Fourth Quarter 1951), 305–318.

[15] Richard W. Van Wagenen, *Research in the International Organization Field,* Publication No. 1 of the Center for Research on World Political Institutions (Princeton, N.J.: Princeton University, 1952).

any society, since crime with violence is found in all societies. Even though it is possible to instill this value in many of the subgroups, there is no certainty that new subgroups will not arise that will be willing to resort to violence to gain their ends. Thus other groups can hold a value of nonviolence only if there is a superior authority which can forcibly suppress violence and isolate its perpetrators for at least a while. The practice of nonviolence in the absence of such authority leads to death; Gandhian nonviolence is no exception, since the British government was a legal authority suppressing violence at the same time that it used violence on occasion against the Indians.

Much the same can be said against the prerequisite of a general consensus (outside of the specific value of nonviolence) for the maintenance of international peace. There is no great amount of consensus within large and culturally heterogeneous nations; it is the presence of a powerful legal authority in them which keeps conflict within bounds. What is probably true in the consensus theory is that there must be enough common culture between contenders for them to communicate with and understand each other. While this is probably true within most nations—thus permitting conversations that lead to compromise—a serious question can be raised as to whether it is true between nations at present. Perhaps this degree of consensus must be reached before effective international compromises can be attained. This is the only element of validity a sociologist can find in the theory that consensus must be developed before wars can be abolished. This is not to say that wars are inevitable; the development of legal forces superior in power to any single potential contender and of conflict-preventive machinery could greatly reduce the possibility of war. In fact, we may have already reached such a point with the invention of hydrogen and atomic bombs, controlled not only by the United States and the Soviet Union but also partly by a large international public opinion to which both nations for different reasons are sensitive. International public opinion is a new force that seems to be more powerful than any single nation. While mutual understanding may be a prerequisite for mediation, it is not a sure cure for conflict. The fact that understanding the real motives of an opponent may increase, rather than decrease, tensions should not be lost sight of.

Ideological conflict is the most difficult type to resolve, since both groups have the goal of either annihilating or converting the other,

and since to compromise is to betray one's highest ideals. Policing
by a powerful third force has been the only historical way in which
satisfactory control has been established to prevent the victory of
one side over another. This was the basis, of course, of the Pax
Romana and to a lesser extent of the Pax Britannica and is, of course,
now the goal of those who seek a strong United Nations as a force
superior to any single nation that might wish to eliminate, on the most
ferocious of ideological grounds, any other nation. But this goal has
not yet been achieved in the contemporary world, and even if it were
it would involve the use of force to prevent other kinds of force,
especially when one of the contending parties is so fanatic as to prefer
death to compromise of any of its principles.

Direct argument against an idealistic contender or suggestions for
compromise only serve to irritate him further. The means of change
must come from fairly indirect procedures. Sometimes it can be shown
that the ideologies of the contending groups themselves are opposed
to force. This has always been a partially effective technique in dis-
suading religious Christians from annihilating Jews. It is conceivable,
although I would not be too sanguine about the method, that zealous
Communists could be persuaded that their ideology encourages them
to wait until the capitalist enemy is ripe for self-destruction rather
than to take up the sword to force his demise. Sometimes diversion
of the contenders is also a means of at least delaying or postponing
conflict on an ideological basis.

Ideological contenders usually have many enemies, including internal ones, against which they may direct their antagonism. Thus the
specific serious conflict in which ideological contenders are engaged
is, in one sense, a matter of mere historical accident. A wise mediator
might be able to encourage the deflection of the antagonism from a
serious channel to a relatively harmless one. The advantage of this is
that, like all other social institutions and behaviors, ideological fervor
does change and sometimes even disappears through forces inherent
in it—although we would not want to make this an inevitable law
of history.

Racist motivations to conflict have something of the ideological
quality of resistance to mediation, but certain techniques developed
out of understanding of the psychological basis of racist conflict have
alleviated, moderated, and reduced motivations behind this kind of

conflict. Whereas ideological conflict is based upon a positive desire
to serve the highest good, racist conflict is ultimately based upon
fear. Those promoting racist conflict are afraid that their progeny will
degenerate if there is amalgamation, and hence that their civilization
will decline. (Of course, in ideological conflict too, nondominant groups
may also have fear—fear of forced conversion rather than of amalgamation.) Activities which alleviate the fear will tend to alleviate the
motivation for racist conflict. Scientific information that racism is
based upon a biological fallacy will have its effects on a significant
number—although not on all types—of racists. Demonstration to the
dominant group that the minority group is not interested in biological
penetration—i.e., intermarriage—but rather in equal civil rights, will
have its effect on still others. From my own experience I have seen
how the mere demonstration that "racial" minorities were present in
only small numbers and that they were not growing in numbers served
to alleviate substantially the fears of some hostile racists.[16] Still other
techniques to reduce the motivation to racist conflict have been suggested by an understanding of the psychological basis of this motivation, to which we may now turn.

Hypotheses concerning the effective mediation of conflict are suggested by psychological theories that seek to explain the motivation
for aggressive behavior. At least two difficulties present themselves
in translating these theories so that they have a practical value for
the mediator. One is that the theories have been developed in an
effort to explain individual behavior, whereas the conflicts we are
concerned with are group conflicts. Insofar as a psychological theory
claims to explain all of individual aggressiveness, however, it must be
relevant to a consideration of group conflict since a group cannot
engage in conflict unless a sufficient proportion of its members, or at
least its leaders, are individually motivated to engage in that conflict. To apply a psychological theory of individual aggression to the
explanation of group conflict we must assume and seek a social situa-

---

[16] A few investigators have demonstrated the relationship between prejudice and
exaggeration of the numbers of minority persons. In South Africa, for example, a
group of Public Service Examination candidates were asked to "underline the percentage that you think Jews constitute of the whole population of South Africa:
1 per cent, 5..., 10..., 15..., 20..., 25..., 30 per cent." The mode of their estimates
was 20 per cent, whereas the true figure was slightly over 1 per cent. E. G. Malherbe,
Race Attitudes and Education (Johannesburg, South Africa: Institute of Race Relations, 1946).

tion common to the members of the group which activates the psychological mechanisms. A caution must be observed, however: It is possible to have conflict without hostility (as in certain labor-management disputes), and it is possible to have hostility without conflict (as when a worker hates his employer but can do nothing but resign his job or bear with it, because there is no union in his shop). Conflict is a sociological phenomenon, whereas hostility (or aggressiveness) is a psychological phenomenon, and while there is a correlation in their manifestations, there is not necessarily a perfect relation or equivalence between them.

A second drawback in applying psychological theories to the formulation of hypotheses concerning the possibilities of mediation of group conflict arises from the fact that while there have been numerous excellent researches supporting the psychological theories, each of the theories is independent of the others and fails to indicate the social circumstances under which the psychological mechanism posited would be activated. None of the evidence supporting one theory limits its applicability nor does it disprove any of the other theories. We are thus faced with a number of unintegrated theories concerning the psychological motivation of aggressiveness, each well supported by the evidence and each purporting to explain all of individual aggressiveness, and in that sense to be mutually exclusive. As a result, one who is concerned with concrete conflicts is as yet obliged to use his imagination to determine when each of the mechanisms might be operating, thus limiting their usefulness from the scientific standpoint. The next stage of research in the social psychology of aggressiveness and conflict needs to be a delimitation of the social situations under which the psychological mechanisms come into operation.[17]

PSYCHOLOGICAL THEORIES OF AGGRESSION

One theory, first formulated by certain psychiatrists and later supported and partially verified in research by psychologists, is that tendencies to conflict are a manifestation of a troubled and insecure personality.[18] The insecurity is held to have its roots in improper care

[17] I have suggested some hypotheses for this delimitation in an essay, "Intergroup Anxieties in a Mass Society," *Phylon*, 12 (Fourth Quarter 1951), 305–318.

[18] T. W. Adorno *et al.*, *The Authoritarian Personality* (New York: Harper, 1950); Nathan W. Ackerman and Marie Jahoda, *Anti-Semitism and Emotional Disorder* (New York: Harper, 1950); B. Bettleheim and M. Janowitz, *Dynamics of Prejudice* (New York: Harper, 1950).

and training of the person during his infancy. Ernst Simmel, for example, developed the theory that the person with tendencies toward strong racial antagonisms is one who has never learned to love, and that hatred must therefore govern all his environmental relationships.[19] Other psychiatrists have looked to more specific, buried traumatic experiences. Direct mediation cannot, of course, eliminate these deep-seated tendencies to aggression. Only psychiatric therapy would suffice, and if the tendency is so widespread as to be a source of a major group conflict, such a procedure obviously demands too much time to be practical. *Preventive* psychiatry is in order, however, as a means of avoiding the development of hostility drives in the younger generation, and short therapy sessions may be used with the leaders of group conflict even without the active compliance or awareness of the individuals involved. Experienced mediators have actually employed this approach, often without being aware of the psychiatric nature of the technique. By offering unceasing affection and personal generosity to the leaders of the contending groups, mediators are sometimes able to build up a sense of personal confidence and to satisfy a "need for love" which retards individual motivation toward aggression.

Another suggestion for the reduction of intergroup conflicts offered indirectly by the theory that tendencies toward aggression have their motivation in individual personality malformations is that the object of aggression can be transferred from one group to another. This is a procedure involving a change in social definition, a technique which is rapidly being developed by public relations experts. In the United States, for example, organized campaigns have changed the social definitions of such politically significant terms as "isolationism" and "price control." Even in the group-conflict area we may note how the social definition of "Japanese" changed partly from that describing a weak and foolish little people before Pearl Harbor to a sly, clever, and fanatic race during World War II and to an easily led and gullible people under General MacArthur's guidance after the war. The purpose of the public relations campaign is not to eliminate the motivation to group antagonism but to deflect its expression from one object to another.

This practice may seem like eliminating one problem at the expense

[19] Ernst Simmel, *Anti-Semitism: A Social Disease* (New York: International Universities Press, 1946), pp. 33–78.

of creating another, much in the pattern of psychiatrists who eliminate one psychopathic symptom by repressing its motivation so that the motivation seeks outlet in the formation of another symptom. Such a situation may be the unfortunate outcome of a public relations program which merely redefines the object of aggression, when the antagonism has its root in personality malformation. On the other hand, the antagonistic tendencies may be made to express themselves toward harmless objects or may even be directed to real sources of social difficulties for the antagonistic persons. The mediator has a large enough job, to say the least, in helping to prevent the outbreak of, or in helping to bring an end to, a specific war, a specific race conflict, or a specific strike. He cannot be expected to solve all the problems of a nation, of a racial group, or of organized labor, even though he has a general moral obligation to avoid creating new problems for the groups with whom he is dealing in his efforts to stop an immediate conflict problem.

The process of socially redefining a group which is the object of antagonism of another group may also have some effect on what has already been referred to as one of the "necessary causes" of group conflict—namely, a sense of antipathy toward certain differences. The actual observable differences between dominant and minority groups, for example, are not nearly as great as the differences between the stereotypes which each group has of the other. Propaganda could both bring people's stereotypes closer to reality and make what differences do exist appear less significant. Much of the propaganda put out by organizations seeking to improve race relations is now exactly of this sort. It seeks to minimize people's distortions of racial and cultural differences and to interpret what differences there are in such a way that they will not be regarded as dangerous or distasteful.

A second type of psychological theory offering a possible explanation of the individual motivation to aggression holds that a group against which there is apparent hatred is not really hated for itself but because it serves as a symbolic substitute for another object which is *really* hated but against which hate cannot be admitted. One cannot express antagonism against certain objects because it is socially taboo to do so, because it would seem foolish to do so, or because one has ambivalent attitudes and really likes as well as hates the object. Under such circumstances, according to the theory, one seeks a symbolic substitute object, which is psychologically identified with the real hated object, toward which to exhibit overt and conscious antagonism. Variations of this theory have been advanced by psychoanalysts, historians, and sociologists, but it cannot yet be said that the theory has had any but presumptive evidence supporting it.[20]

Insofar as symbolic substitution is a psychological motivation for group conflict, the motivation could be reduced if the symbolic identification could be revealed to the antagonistic persons. People who repress one hatred and substitute another for it resist having the unconscious identification made conscious for them. They then have to face the facts of their basic hatred or seek a new symbolic identification, but the old prejudice would have to disappear. Another technique open to the mediator faced with symbolic antagonisms is to show the antagonistic persons how the substitute symbolism—that is, the group against which there is antagonism—is really an unsatisfactory substitute for the real underlying hatred. Objective facts can make a psychological identification seem unsatisfactory. For example, members of the hated group can be shown in settings and engaged in behaviors which are completely out of accord with the hated object with which they are identified.

The third theory of psychological motivations behind aggression is based upon classic theory and research in psychology. It holds that group antagonisms are learned by a process similar to the learning of any other behavior. The motivation to group conflict can thus be transmitted from parent to child, generation after generation. Insofar as psychologists have learned the mechanisms underlying learning,[21] they are also familiar with the process of unlearning or relearning. These theories and processes have been but infrequently applied to group antagonisms.

[20] Sigmund Freud, *Moses and Monotheism* (New York: Knopf, 1939); Maurice Samuel, *The Great Hatred* (New York: Knopf, 1940); Carl J. Friedrich in I. Graeber and S. Britt (eds.), *Jews in a Gentile World* (New York: Macmillan, 1942), pp. 8, 18; Jacques Maritain, *A Christian Looks at the Jewish Question* (New York: Longmans, Green, 1939), p. 41; Joshua Trachtenberg, *The Devil and the Jews* (New Haven, Conn.: Yale University Press, 1943); Lewis Browne, *How Odd of God: An Introduction to the Jews* (New York: Macmillan, 1934), esp. pp. 225–238; Arnold M. Rose, "Anti-Semitism's Root in City Hatred," *Commentary*, 6 (October 1948), 374–378; Margaret Halsey, *Color Blind* (New York: Simon and Schuster, 1946); Helen V. McLean, "Psychodynamic Factors in Racial Relations," *Annals of the American Academy*, 244 (March 1946), 159–166.

[21] E. R. Hilgard, *Theories of Learning* (New York: Appleton-Century-Crofts, 1948).

The final theory of psychological motivation to individual aggression to be mentioned here is the much publicized frustration-aggression or displacement theory.[22] The theory states, in simplified terms, that when people do not, or cannot, hit back directly at the frustrations of daily life, they are inclined to be generally aggressive. The persons toward whom they are aggressive are those who are weak and cannot retaliate or those who have been traditionally defined as safe objects of aggression. The theory does not require that these "scapegoats" be the objects of aggression. In fact the theory holds that if the original frustrating conditions are clarified and if the frustrated persons can engage in action directed against these conditions, displacement can be avoided completely. If the original frustrating circumstances are such that no direct action can be taken in relation to them, some other insignificant thing which aggression cannot hurt can be substituted as the object of displaced antagonism. There may even be displacement of aggression onto oneself. In labor-management conflict, mediators, even without specific knowledge of the frustration-aggression theory, occasionally seek to displace aggression directed toward the opposing parties onto third parties, such as the government, competing businessmen or labor groups, a church organization, or even the mediator himself.

SOME FURTHER SOCIAL FACTORS IN MEDIATION

Turning now to the social role of conflict and mediation, we note the paucity of information concerning the historical circumstances under which conflict has developed and become intensified and under which mediation has been successful in being called into operation and in resolving the conflict. In addition to a historical study, a comparative cross-cultural study needs to be conducted, to specify the social conditions under which conflict has been most prevalent and mediation has been most successful. We know, in a vague way, that intergroup conflicts are not equally frequent under all forms of social structure, and that within a given society conflicts have periods of increase and periods of decrease, but we have no systematic knowledge as to the social conditions accompanying these variations. To have

---

[22] This theory is best expounded in John Dollard et al., Frustration and Aggression (New Haven, Conn.: Yale University Press, 1939), esp. p. 31. In terms of displacement the theory is well expressed by David W. Petegorsky, "The Strategy of Hatred," Antioch Review, 1 (September 1941), 377.

the greatest value, this historical and comparative research should be guided by carefully framed hypotheses. To illustrate the character of the hypotheses a few examples with respect to mediation will be mentioned.

Perhaps the most important hypothesis is that if social structures are set up in anticipation of group conflict, and techniques developed to reduce friction, mediate opposed interests, and otherwise seek to prevent the rise and spread of conflict, they can often make a greater contribution than can efforts made *ad hoc* after a conflict situation is fully developed. This is at least true if the contenders are not both overwhelmingly powerful. Levi has made this point, with a great deal of support from history, in regard to international conflict.[23] In race and ethnic conflict, the point was widely made after it was discovered that a government survey anticipated the 1943 race riot in Detroit but that there was no agency, private or public, which could take action to prevent the outbreak of the riot. Since 1943, hundreds of local public organizations, and over a thousand private ones, have been set up in the United States, and have as one of their functions the foreseeing and avoidance of overt race conflict. While several cities have had incipient riots—Chicago alone has had a dozen incipient riots in the years following World War II—these agencies, with the cooperation of a great variety of other community organizations whose aid they enlisted, have prevented the outbreak of full-scale race riots such as occurred fairly frequently before the war.

The possibilities for success in mediation do not depend solely on understanding and doing something about the causes of conflict. There are conditions relative to the mediation itself which affect the likelihood of its success or failure. Hypotheses concerning the conditions under which conflict-prevention machinery is likely to be formed and utilized can be formulated from common experience. If mediation is a voluntary matter, a party that considers itself the stronger in the dispute will request or permit mediation only if it has good public relations or a more permanent reconciliation as one of its aims.

Another hypothesis is that mediation is avoided when one side to a dispute believes that there are advantages—either intrinsic or in terms of maintaining the current favorable distribution of power

<hr />

[23] Werner Levi, *Fundamentals of World Organization* (Minneapolis: University of Minnesota Press, 1950).

between the two sides—to maintaining the conflict situation. For example, leaders of a labor union may avoid mediation of a strike if they believe that the strike is "educating" the membership of the union in some desired way, or if they have reason to believe that the balance of power is turning in the direction of the union's ultimate victory in the dispute.

A third hypothesis is that mediation will be sought and have possible success only when the parties to the dispute have a common framework of definitions and values so that they can communicate with each other, and when there is a belief on the part of each party that the other will abide by the terms of any agreement reached in the mediation. This hypothesis gains support from the observation of the failure of "third-force" countries like India in their efforts to mediate between the United States and Russia in current international disputes.

Logically, it would seem that the likelihood of a mediation's being successful after it is underway is a function of (1) the attitudes with which the parties enter the mediation; (2) the intrinsic difficulty of solving the conflict—that is, the number and the complexity of the changes in the objective situation that have to occur before a resolution can be reached; (3) the perception during the mediation process of a compromise, adoption of which will give both parties greater advantages—material or psychological—than a continuation of overt conflict; and (4) the ability of the mediator to discern such compromises, to help the parties to perceive the merit of such compromises, to transform conflicts on the unconscious level into conflict on the communicable level, and to communicate viewpoints of one party so that they are understandable to the other party.

The role of the mediator as a "third person" needs to be investigated. He may be regarded as a "stranger"[24] who has wisdom and objectivity. He may be regarded as a friend who is trying to help out, or as a benevolent father figure who is to show the quarreling boys how to make peace, or as a stern father figure who has no business entering a private quarrel. He may be regarded as an expert who may be relied on to give relevant and reliable advice, as a representative of a third interest who is in opposition to both of the contending parties, and so on. Some of these perceived roles may provide the

---

[24] Georg Simmel, *Soziologie* (Leipzig: Duncker und Humblot, 1908), pp. 685–691.

mediator with certain assets in an effort to resolve the conflict, whereas others may hinder his efforts. The possibilities for him to manipulate and change his role during the different stages of the mediation need to be studied. The specific powers of a mediator are usually very limited, but the powers that he has—to hold the parties in conversation, to speak to them privately, to determine the order in which they present their points of view—need to be investigated for their potentialities in reducing conflict.

Some of the possibilities in the mediation situation that deserve to be systematically studied and experimented with are these: the relative effectiveness of presentation of facts as compared to the presentation of value-arguments, the psychological consequences of taking a hypothetical position "for the sake of discussion," the effectiveness of presentation of false statements as facts, the psychological effects of digression and other tension-relieving devices, the value of reference to outside threats and outside interests, the possibility of substituting purely symbolic or "psychological" satisfactions for material ones, the usefulness of bringing all matters into the open as opposed to the suppression of certain sources of conflict either temporarily or permanently, the relative value of the creation of a primary group atmosphere during mediation versus the value of formality, the technique of getting the greatest psychological value out of minor concessions, the mentioning of values which are not under conflict in the original dispute but which are possibilities for future dispute, the uses of drama, emotional outbursts, delay, created "crises," and reference to comparable cases.

While it would be most valuable to make studies of these matters in actual conflict situations, the short cut of using artificially constructed "laboratory" conflicts might be feasible if care is taken to make the variables realistic and to select subjects to be contenders who really have something at stake in the induced conflict. In all the excellent research on dominant group–minority group conflict there has been practically no use of the laboratory experiment for such purposes as bringing bigoted members of the dominant group together with members of the minority group in an intimate conversational setting in which some of their differences could be directly communicated and some of the stereotypes aired and protested in terms of the facts available right in the room where the experiment was being observed.

Whether the "tool" for investigation is the experimental laboratory, the historical archives, direct observation, or systematic interviewing, the fruits for both theoretical and practical knowledge should be very great, for research on the subject of group conflict and its mediation is still in its infancy.

Values in Social Research

7

The Selection of Problems for Research

THE *first chapter of this section is a direct continuation of the line of methodological thinking presented in Appendix 2 of* An American Dilemma, *in the preparation of which I served as assistant to Gunnar Myrdal. It attempts two things: (1) to examine the methodological implications of the nature of social knowledge, and (2) to relate these implications to the bases of choice of problems for research. As in the earlier work, here too emphasis is given to the importance of making explicit the value premises in research, although now with special attention to the* selection *of research problems.*

THEORETICAL AND PRACTICAL RESEARCH

SOCIAL data are so infinitely numerous and diverse that any scientific study must select its facts in accordance with the needs of the problem and the method. Historians have long recognized that they do not present all history, and to do so would mean never to complete a work and never to see the major changes of history because of the mass of detail. The psychiatrists have always been aware that an individual can literally spend a lifetime telling his life history and that, therefore, what is significant is what he selects to tell.

While the proposition that the scientist must select his facts from the infinity of possible data appears to be trite, there are some sociologists who still insist that the sole function of scientists is to present all the facts. They cannot possibly do so, and, indeed, they actually make no effort to do so. Consequently, there is a good deal of confusion about what occurs in selecting problems and data for research. What this chapter proposes to do is to present systematically the logical consequences of the fact that scientific data must be selected, consequences which some sociologists have not yet faced.

If there is selection of data, there must be a purpose in the selection, either conscious or unconscious. Since only a small proportion of sociological authors present the criteria for their selection, that must mean either that they are unconscious of the basis of their selection or that they deliberately withhold the information. Probably most of the investigators who deliberately withhold a statement on the basis of their selection of data do so because they believe that this is not proper in a scientific document. Yet it is one of the basic canons of science that all steps in the collection and analysis of data be specified. This is necessary so that the reader can determine whether there are any flaws in the study and so that another investigator can check the results. This specification of all the stages in research is what the physicist P. W. Bridgman originally meant by "operationalism." However, when the term was adopted by some social scientists, it took on a much narrower meaning. As a matter of fact, those who call themselves "operationalists" in the social sciences today are the very ones who denounce as unscientific any specification of the bases of the selection of their data.

A study may aim at securing either theoretical or practical conclusions. There are theoretical conclusions which contribute to the general body of propositions relevant to the specific subject matter of a science, and there are theoretical conclusions which contribute to the methodology of the science. Methodological studies are undertaken presumably to increase the number and precision of the tools used to collect or analyze data relevant to specific subject matter. Their purpose is thus indirectly dependent on the specific content of the conclusions which they are ultimately designed to secure. The sole criterion in deciding whether or not a given methodological study should be undertaken is an estimation of the usefulness of the tool which is to be devised or improved. This proposition seems obvious, and there has been little or no quarrel with it; therefore, there is no controversy as to the purpose or value of a methodological study.

There is some controversy, however, over the possibility and/or value of theoretical and practical studies. Some sociologists hold that practical studies should not be the purpose of scientists. They believe, apparently, that they take this attitude from the natural scientists who scorn studies involving practical applications. This involves a misunderstanding of the attitude of the natural scientists. What the physicist dislikes is to take a known theoretical principle and apply it to a specific situation so that it can be utilized for practical ends.

This for him is not an extension of knowledge but a mere mechanical exercise. He does not, however, scorn to develop theoretical principles which have potential practical value. As a matter of fact, he assumes, on the basis of the past history of his science, that all his theoretical findings will have ultimate practical value. He is not, therefore, making a distinction between theoretical and practical conclusions in the collection and analysis of his data, but rather a distinction between science and engineering.

The sociologist takes quite another position when he raises objections to engaging in practical research. What he is opposing is collecting and analyzing new information which would lead to conclusions that have practical value. There are only a few people engaged in applying known sociological generalizations to specific social situations comparable to the engineer who applies known physical laws to specific physical situations. There are specialists, for example, who apply life tables, devised by demographers to a specific population of customers of life insurance companies. There are also statisticians employed by a few state prisons who, in order to recommend the best risks for parole, apply the findings of Burgess and others on the factors associated with success or failure on parole to the population of prisoners. These statisticians should not be called scientists, since they are not searching for new generalizations but are simply applying old ones.

Perhaps sociologists might compare themselves to physical scientists in an earlier stage of scientific development rather than to contemporary ones. Merton points out that in the seventeenth century between 30 and 60 per cent of the scientific discoveries were *directly* practical (most of them relating to navigation, mining, and military techniques), and that there was an intimate interweaving of pure and applied science. All the better known scientists "devoted themselves to the prosecution of both theory and practice. What is more important, scientists were uniformly confident of the practical points which their continued industry would ensure. It was this conviction, quite apart from the question of its validity, which influenced their choice of problems." [1]

The distinction between theoretical and practical conclusions in sociology remains to be clarified. Just as in physical science, there is

[1] Robert K. Merton, "Science and the Economy of Seventeenth Century England" (1939). Reprinted in *Social Theory and Social Structure* (Glencoe, Ill.: Free Press, 1949), pp. 347–363.

no fundamental distinction between practical and theoretical research. All theoretical propositions must hold good in certain specified situations, and therefore they have practical value in predicting the development of those situations and in indicating how the expected development can be changed. If a theory cannot be applied, it is not a correct theory. Similarly, there can be no general propositions that have practical value unless they also have implications for a general theory of human behavior. If practical predictions can be made on the basis of a principle derived from field or experimental research, this principle must be added to, or used to modify, the general body of theoretical propositions in social science. The fallacious distinction between theoretical and practical arises out of the misconception of the man in the street of the specificity of the predictions that can be made with theoretical propositions. Sometimes it also, unfortunately, arises out of his finding that the scientist's theoretical conclusion has no validity or relevance to any possible situation. (When this occurs the man in the street is a better theoretical sociologist than the man in the university.)

What is theoretical in sociology is a moot point. Many sociologists assume that ultimately they will evolve propositions that are universal in their application in the same sense that the laws of physics are universal. Other sociologists, of a statistical bent, have abandoned the search for universals and are seeking propositions which hold true in most, but not in all, cases. The predictions they make aim at only a certain degree of accuracy. There has been little discussion of the differences between these two points of view, and each group goes its own way in the search for its own favored type of conclusion. To proceed further in the analysis of the nature of the scientific sociological conclusion, it is necessary to examine both of these points of view and their implications.

Those who aim at universal propositions usually use descriptive and case-study data. One case is used to sharpen or qualify a conclusion derived from the analysis of another case, and the study proceeds to the point at which all cases under examination fit into the conclusion. Since there has been no effort to secure a representative sample of cases or to test the null hypothesis that the conclusion derived is due solely to the small number of cases, it is implicitly assumed that the conclusion applies to all cases of the specified type. If some future investigation should reveal a case that does not fit the conclusion, the conclusion may be modified in minor details so as to encompass the new case. Many of the advocates of this type of method and conclusion profess to be followers of the psychology of Dewey and Mead, but they neglect one of the cardinal principles of this psychology. If man's actions are not simply responses to external stimuli, at least in some cases, but are rather responses to man's interpretation and definition of the entire stimulating situation, then allowance must be made for diverse reactions to any given stimulus or situation. If this is true, we cannot arrive at generalizations of the sort "if *a*, then *b*," "if this situation, then this human action."

Of course, Dewey, Mead, and their followers did not hold that all human behavior had the possibility of mediating interpretation. Obviously, behavior with a biological basis—that is, purely reflexive behavior—allows for no mediating interpretation, and universal propositions can be made about it. To the extent that psychiatric and other studies of the psychogenetic personality are correct, there can also be no mediating interpretation in behavior that is determined unconsciously by the specific character of the psychogenetic personality.[2] Studies of the mentally diseased, for example, indicate that these people have no control over their actions and cannot change them from the course laid down by the interpretations determined by the psychogenetic personality. The psychotic is commonly defined as one who is incapable of self-control and incapable of accepting a new definition of a significant situation. Students of crowd behavior describe the crowd situation as one in which the individual feels that he has lost control over his own actions and is impelled by "possession" of the crowd spirit. Insofar as the individual responds directly and spontaneously to suggestions running through the crowd, there can be no mediating interpretation.

In these types of situations, in which there can be no mediating interpretation between stimulus and response, social scientists ought soon to arrive at universal propositions of the type "if *a*, then *b*." But in every type of human behavior where something in the experience of the individual can modify the influence of a situation

---

[2] The psychiatrists and some psychologists have long been aware of the different levels of ability to control one's own behavior and their relation to consciousness (see A. H. Maslow and Bela Mittelmann, *Principles of Abnormal Psychology* [New York: Harper, 1941], esp. pp. 79–88.)

on his behavior—where, to use W. I. Thomas' phrase, there can be a new "definition of the situation"—we shall be a long time in developing the concepts and techniques necessary to arrive at universal propositions, even though they are "theoretically" possible for all behavior. For such situations the statistician is right in saying that a representative sample must be taken with a sufficiently large number of cases to ensure reliability of the findings. The conclusion then takes the form: "If a, then in this culture at this time most people respond in b fashion."

This does not mean that human behavior is not "determined" by causal factors. Human behavior is determined on a neurological level, and theoretically there can be universal propositions about neurological connections. But as long as social science deals with social phenomena on the level at which they can be observed directly, it cannot find cause-and-effect laws that apply universally in all known and possible cultures. The explanation of this requires no metaphysics; it is simply based on the fact that one of the determinants of an individual's behavior, when it is of the mediating type, is his "apperceptive mass," the full range of experiences that he has had since birth and that is retained in his nervous system. To predict his physical movements at these times, the predictor would have to know everything that ever happened to him, and this is impossible. Further, no two individuals have had exactly the same past experiences, and therefore knowledge of how one individual acts is no sure guide to how another will act. This is to say that we may never be able to make perfectly accurate predictions about human behavior or to make propositions about human behavior that hold good universally, as we may be able to make for the behavior of turtles or rocks.[3] It is because he is the sole possessor of language that the human being is the sole object partly determined by an apperceptive mass, as has been shown in the writings of Mead and Cooley.

[3] In this sense human behavior is more complex than animal behavior or rock behavior. But sociologists should not take the position that the things they study are always more complicated than the things studied by the physical or biological scientists, for a different type of complexity may develop for the latter scientists. While the sociologist finds it impossible to observe the full life history of a human being and yet finds it necessary to do so in order to arrive at universal propositions, the astronomer finds it impossible to transcend space and yet finds it necessary to do so in order to make certain kinds of universal propositions about the movements of bodies. There are different types of complexity, but social scientists do not necessarily have a more complex subject.

Two major exceptions need to be made to the point above:

1. Certain very general "universal propositions," almost in the nature of methodological principles, can be validly stated. Such a proposition would be Durkheim's dictum that the group behaves in ways different from those of any of the individuals composing it. Another is Wirth's observation that social phenomena do not continue their existence for exactly the same reasons for which they began. But these principles can hardly be regarded as universal laws, permitting highly accurate predictions of specific behavior, in the sense in which that term is used in the natural sciences.

2. Sometimes propositions in social sciences are based upon logical relationships rather than upon empirically observed ones. If relationships are logically connected, they must inevitably occur together. Such propositions may best be called tautological propositions, but the usual derogatory connotation should not be attached to the word "tautological." They are called "tautological" because they take the form "if a, then a" when the two a's are identical but are expressed in different concepts or different units. Further examination of such tautological propositions and their use in sociology is left for another chapter.[4] The purpose in referring to them here is to indicate that universal propositions exist which are inevitably true because of their logical character but which are not based upon empirical observations. They therefore do not come under the category of theoretical propositions, which were considered previously. The point remains that if, and to the extent that, human beings are capable of responding not directly to stimuli but to their interpretations of stimuli, universal propositions about human behavior on the level at which they can be observed directly cannot be discovered by empirical research.

UNIFORMITIES IN BEHAVIOR

In their reaction against the naïve kind of behaviorism that was formerly dominant in psychology, some psychologists became aware of this problem and sought to resolve it by stating that a, the "cause," must always consist of at least two interacting variables, environment and organism. Lewin, for example, stated his now familiar formula, $B = F(P,E)$, or, behavior is a function of the person and of his environment. This does not get around the problem of attaining universals,

[4] See Chapter 22.

however, since the "person" is so indefinitely variant that it is not *practical*, in any specific proposition, to specify all the possibly relevant characteristics of the person. In the kind of social-psychological experiments at which Lewin and his followers have excelled, only superficial aspects of the "person" have been held constant while attempts were made to arrive at universal propositions about the effects of a given kind of situation on the behavior of that person.

For example, the early Lewinians discovered the Zeigarnik effect: "The tendency to recall interrupted activities should be greater than the tendency to recall finished ones."[5] The ratio between these two tendencies was found to be approximately 1.9 to 1, and this was in some vague way assumed to be "normal." The Lewinians went on to discover various specified conditions under which the ratio differed significantly and consistently from 1.9. But they never did systematically consider the fact that 1.9 was an average, that there was variation in the subjects making up that average, that these subjects were not chosen to be a representative sample of the population, that they would have no trouble finding persons whose ratio differed not only from the normal 1.9 but from all the deviant ratios their special conditions led them to expect (even if such deviant persons proved to be a small minority in current Western culture), and that other groups (especially in other cultures) could be constituted where the "normal ratio"—even holding constant the variables which the Lewinians found could change the ratio—would differ sharply from 1.9, even to the extent of going below unity.

Similar considerations hold also for the more recent "universal propositions" discovered by contemporary disciples of Lewin, such as Festinger's "cohesiveness-power theory":

The more cohesive the group, that is, the more friendship ties there are within the group, and the more active the process of communication which goes on within the group, the greater will be the effect of the process of communication in producing uniformity of attitudes, opinions, and behavior, and the stronger will be the resulting group standard, as indicated by the degree of uniformity among members of the group and the amount of deviation from the group standard allowed in members.[6]

[5] Kurt Lewin, *Field Theory in Social Science* (New York: Harper, 1951), p. 10.

[6] Leon Festinger, Stanley Schachter, and Kurt Back, *Social Pressures in Informal Groups* (New York: Harper, 1950), p. 175.

This is a valuable generalization for predictive purposes, and it is now buttressed by several field and laboratory experiments, but for the reasons indicated it cannot be regarded as a universal proposition. Under some conditions it will not hold, and these are not specified; the conditions under which it does hold are assumed to be "normal."

I do not mean to say that there are no uniformities in behavior. Sociologists and anthropologists have discovered thousands of uniformities, although to my knowledge all of them admit to certain exceptions. They are cultural uniformities, characteristic of the structure and functioning of a given society at a given time. Sociologists with a statistical bent have discovered this, although they have not reported the new character of their conclusions. They report their findings in the form "As x increases, y also *tends* to increase," or "If a, then we can expect b in 80 per cent of the cases." They realize implicitly that if the cultural situation were to change or the society to develop more of one type of person than of another the tendency or the percentage might change. Many anthropologists have also recognized a certain aspect of what they call "cultural relativity." They observe certain relationships between cultural traits or cultural complexes characteristic of a given society, and they find that these relationships are largely determined by the norms of that particular society.[7]

While the statistical sociologist and many cultural anthropologists have recognized the limited scope of their propositions, they have not fully faced the implications of the fact. To do so would mean that they would have to acknowledge that it is impossible to find universal laws respecting many phases of human action. To admit this seems to them an acknowledgment that social science can never be completely a science. If science is to be defined as the derivation of universal laws by empirical observation, then there can be no social science except perhaps in the limited fields of psychobiology, child development, mental pathology, and crowd behavior. But if science is defined as the accumulation of knowledge that can be used for predictions more accurate than chance alone would allow, it is already a science. It is

[7] This does not throw out the old idea of "the psychic unity of mankind," since it was pointed out earlier that human actions are not based solely on cultural or individual mediating interpretations but also on man's biological structure and on the unconscious development of his psychogenetic personality. Insofar as man's actions are based on these two things and do not allow for conscious and deliberate change, there is an element in man's behavior which is universal.

maintained that this is the only sense in which it can be a science, and the natural scientists are not likely to scorn this definition.

Some sociologists feel that the main reason that we have not yet secured universal propositions is that we do not use the experimental method. But the selection of the sample for an experimental study and the number of controls used help to determine the nature of the conclusions. If this is true, experiments in social science will lead us not to universal propositions but rather to generalizations about social change characteristic of a given group at a given time. This is not to say that experimentation is not a valuable method; it is simply to recognize the limitations of a method and the value of the conclusions derived by use of the method.

If a conclusion is not universally true but is limited to a given culture at a given time, a question must be raised as to the value of doing research to arrive at such conclusions. Our purpose as social scientists cannot be to find out what is true of all societies, because there would not be time, and cultures change anyway, so that what is true at one time may not be true fifty years later. Most of the sociological research that we call "scientific" today will be called "historical" fifty years from now, and it will be recognized as not applying to the then current conditions. This calls for a criterion of importance in selecting problems for empirical research. This criterion must originate outside the science itself and serve as a value premise in any piece of research.

THE CRITERIA OF SELECTION

If social science propositions are generally true only within limits of time and space, the criterion for selecting a research subject must have something to do with the contemporary social importance of the subject matter. If the population generally does not find the subject important and if the generalization derived from the research becomes dated, the only purpose of the research is the aesthetic satisfaction given the researcher. Personal and aesthetic satisfactions are not thought to be good criteria for selection of a research problem, although logically there is nothing wrong with such criteria. The remaining choice, consequently, for determining a criterion of selection of research problems is practical importance. If a research problem in the realm where universal propositions cannot yet be achieved does not have practical importance, it has no importance. I repeat that what is of practical importance may also be of theoretical importance and that methodological, tautological, and empirical studies that deal with behavior determined by biology, psychogenetic personality, or the crowd do not have to meet the criterion of practical importance, since they can arrive at universal propositions.

Actually sociologists and other social scientists have unconsciously recognized the validity of these considerations. Most sociologists doing empirical studies have chosen practical problems. In the last thirty years the most fruitful and more frequent empirical sociological research has dealt with such practical problems as the adjustment of immigrants, the effects of urbanization, the causes of crime and suicide, adjustment in marriage, the conflict of races, the opposition between labor and management. The conclusions of all these studies have aided materially in developing better understanding of important social situations, in predicting future trends, and in suggesting controlled social change. None has led to universal propositions, yet many have had theoretical and practical importance.

There have been some sociologists who have advocated the study of subject matter completely divorced from anything currently recognized as having practical importance or as developing practical importance in the foreseeable future. Unless this attitude is based on a conscious or unconscious opposition to social change, it is due to a misconception of the nature of propositions in social science and of the demands of science itself. Probably most of these sociologists have been deluded by the desire to attain universal propositions.

Certainly, every researcher should specify the goal that he is seeking in selecting any given problem for research. This specification, which Myrdal and I have elsewhere [8] called "making explicit the value premises behind the selection of research problems," is caused by the demand for objectivity in science. The use of value premises in this manner increases, rather than detracts from, the objectivity of a study. If a sociologist believes he can attain a universal proposition in doing a given study, he should certainly be encouraged to go ahead.[9]

[8] "Communication to the Editor," *American Sociological Review*, 10 (August 1945), 560–561. This is a restatement of a point made in Appen. 2 of Gunnar Myrdal, with the assistance of Richard Sterner and Arnold Rose, *An American Dilemma* (New York: Harper, 1944).

[9] Physical scientists have now recognized that the observer and his instruments affect the observations and that conclusions of probability rather than of universality result. If this is true in the physical realm, it must be all the more true in the social

But it is necessary that he specify that he is seeking this universal proposition so that his readers can judge whether he has done so. I suspect that if this were done, sociological research would be much more practical than it now is.

Some of the same considerations apply to the selection of data. There is an indefinitely large amount of data relevant to any given research problem (although it may not be possible to collect all of it), and the type of conclusion desired can determine what data shall be selected. Scientific conclusions can take several forms, among which are the following: (1) what is, (2) what will be (or what is likely to be), (3) what can be, and (4) what should be done to achieve a given goal (if the goal is considered desirable). Propositions of the last-named type are scientific propositions rather than ethical ones only when there is specification of a goal developed outside the scientific process.

As an illustration of how value premises are involved in the selection of the type of conclusion aimed at, the first two of the four types mentioned above give no information about inducing social change, and the first type gives no clue even to whether social change is possible or not. The third and fourth types require further value premises which specify the conditions under which the scientist is to determine what can be done and the goal for which the scientist is to determine what should be done. All these value premises arise outside the scientific process itself except in one limited respect, to be considered in the following paragraph. The type of conclusion selected will determine the type of data sought and may even determine the method. For example, straight observations, whether handled statistically or not, will procure information for the first type of conclusion. But it frequently requires experimentation to secure data for conclusions of the third type.

The limited respect in which value premises arise within the scientific process itself stems from the nature of theory. If we consider that theory is valuable in science, and it is a fact that theory can point to certain research problems as more likely to extend its own development than do other research problems, then we are guided by

realm. Since the observer's set of social values is one of the most important parts of himself, with which he affects his observations, he ought—as a good scientist—to specify his values and try to point out their possible influence on the observations. Also, we seek to know more about the objects we are studying. This gives more room for the play of the observer's values in the social sciences.

theory in the selection of our research problems. In this respect as in many others, of course, the role of value premises is no greater in the social sciences than in the natural sciences. "Art" and cultural values play a role in the choice of problems that might be suggested by theory, as is indicated in the following quotation:

In discussing the nature of genius with my classes I sometimes raise this question: Would Marie Curie still have been considered a genius if radium had turned out not to have the remarkable properties which it did turn out to have? There is usually some discussion, and then one student makes the remark that the question is misleading, that she showed her genius in selecting for study an element that did have remarkable properties. In other words, scientific genius reveals itself in the choice of problems that it makes as well as in the technical brilliance which it shows in tackling them. And this ability to see and to formulate meaningful scientific problems is an artistic gift.[10]

MISUNDERSTANDINGS

Among the several misconceptions of the methodological viewpoints stated in *An American Dilemma* by Myrdal, Sterner, and myself is the one which holds that we are advocating the introduction of value premises in social research.[11] We do not say that social scientists *should* have value premises in research; rather, we point out that they *do* and inevitably *must* have value premises. The basis of selection of the subject for research is a value premise; a statement of the type of conclusion sought is a value premise. These and other value premises are found in all research, whether or not they are explicitly recognized to be there. What was advocated was not that social scientists should use value premises but that social scientists should make explicit their value premises. This is an implication of one of the canons of science, which requires that all steps in research be specified. It is probable that some sociologists would change their value premises if they made them explicit, because they really do not intend to advocate what they are, in effect, advocating. Although several sociologists still seem to misunderstand this point, others have become aware of it.[12]

[10] Jessie Bernard, "The Art of Science," *American Journal of Sociology*, 55 (July 1949), 1-9.

[11] This incorrect interpretation is given, for example, by Gwynne Nettler, "Toward a Definition of the Sociologist," *American Sociological Review*, 12 (October 1947), 553-560.

[12] An example is the following statement by Leonard S. Cottrell: "Social scientists have contended that they should avoid value judgments like poison. Actually, they

Another misconception about the methodological portion of *An American Dilemma* is that it claims that by rendering value premises explicit bias could be eliminated.[13] This is not true. The purpose of rendering explicit the value premises is not to eliminate bias but to allow the readers to recognize it so that it can be accepted, changed, or discounted. Talcott Parsons expressed an equivalent point of view in his paper read before the meeting of the American Sociological Society on December 28, 1947.[14] The point of view herein expounded does not mean that certain facts ought to be used to buttress a point and that no contrary evidence should be presented. Just the opposite. All evidence, pro and con, must be brought to bear on those points which the set of explicit value premises indicates to be important. The value premises thus help the scientist to make more sure that he is not overlooking any important facts.

A further misconception of the methodological portion of *An American Dilemma* is that it holds that social scientists should advocate that people should do certain things. Actually, the position is that social scientists should emphasize more conclusions which tell us that if people wish to achieve certain goals then they should do certain things. This is conceded to be a scientific type of statement, even by our critics.[15] Unfortunately, many social scientists, without realizing that they are doing so, advocate that people should act in

constantly make value judgments, although they frequently make themselves believe that they do not. In my opinion, it is very important to recognize the value judgments we make and thus avoid the errors of hidden and uncontrolled unconscious bias." ("New Directions for Research on the American Family," *Social Casework*, 34 [February 1953], 58–59.)

[13] An example of this misunderstanding, even on the part of one who read this statement when it was first published, appears in the following excerpt from a review by Ellsworth Faris of Talcott Parsons' *The Social System* (*American Sociological Review*, 18 [February 1953], 103): "The reader is impressed throughout by the truly scientific character of this book. The disciples of the Swede who holds that, since all sociology is written by prejudiced writers, the only recourse is to confess the bias, will find no support for their practice in this volume. Nor will the knowledge-for-what school find here any warrant for their views. The book is characterized by disinterestedness, objectivity, and rationality without which no work is truly scientific."

[14] Talcott Parsons, "The Position of Sociological Theory," *American Sociological Review*, 13 (April 1948), 156–171.

[15] A critic of *An American Dilemma* who condemns us for advocating that people should act in such and such a way admits in a footnote that it is properly scientific to have propositions of the form "if you wish Goal *x*, then you should do so and so." It is noteworthy that this statement is put in a footnote and dismissed forthwith. Propositions of this type, which are the main kind advocated in *An American Dilemma*, are exactly the sort which prevent concealing and ignoring value premises (Nettler, *op. cit.*).

such and such a way. If they stated all their value premises explicitly, they would realize that their conclusions stem from these value premises as well as from the facts that are gathered.

An example may be taken from the use of the concept "mores." Sumner observed that societies developed rules for human action which people believed were so essential to the welfare of the society that violating or even mildly criticizing them would lead to violent reaction and emotional revulsion. These rules were the mores, and they determined what people thought was right. This is a proposition based on empirical observation and takes the form of a statement of what is. But Sumner went beyond his observation and changed his proposition to the form of what can be without indicating that he was adding a new value premise. He says, for example:

Acts of legislation come out of the mores. . . . Legislation, however, has to seek standing ground on the existing mores, and it soon becomes apparent that legislation, to be strong, must be consistent with the mores. Things which have been in the mores are put under police regulation and later under positive law. It is sometimes said that "public opinion" must ratify and approve police regulations, but this statement rests on an imperfect analysis. The regulations must conform to the mores, so that the public will not think them too lax or too strict. . . .

[The mores] never contain any provision for their own amendment. . . .

The combination in the mores of persistency and variability determines the extent to which it is possible to modify them by arbitrary action. It is not possible to change them, by any artifice or device, to a great extent, or suddenly, or in any essential element; it is possible to modify them by slow and long-continued effort if the ritual is changed by minute variations.[16]

The new value premise that Sumner implicitly introduced might read, "It isn't worth the effort to change the mores." One can still recognize the existence of folkways and mores but start out with the different value premise that one is interested in changing a certain practice in the mores in a certain direction. He would then collect data about historical changes in all kinds of mores, paying close attention to the conditions under which change took place. He might even experiment, on a limited scale, with trying to break down people's con-

[16] William Graham Sumner, *Folkways* (Boston: Ginn, 1906), pp. 55, 79, 87.

ceptions about certain practices which they felt were essential to moral welfare. He would look for apparent exceptions to the mores in question and would observe which groups of people held more strongly to the mores than others. He would look for situations which make it difficult to carry out the mores, so that people, if placed in these situations, strain at the mores themselves. When all this information was gathered, our scientist would have a great deal of information on how to change these certain mores, if he wanted to. His conclusions would be quite opposed to Sumner's, quoted above, and far more scientific. For what happened was that Sumner inserted a new value premise, which required new data that he did not possess, and by changing the form of his conclusion, he reduced its validity.

Sumner had a startlingly erroneous conception of the nature of scientific law, and his error has had an unfortunate influence on many contemporary sociologists. Sumner said, "The truth is that the social order is fixed by laws of nature precisely analogous to those of the physical order. The most that man can do . . . by his ignorance and conceit [is] to mar the operation of the social laws." [17] Fortunately, man cannot mar the operation of the laws of nature, which include the social laws. The laws of nature apply under all known circumstances, even when man manipulates them.

We have seen how the selection of problems for research, the type of conclusion sought, and even the use of terms in certain ways all involve the use of value premises. Science demands that these value premises be made explicit, since only by specification of all steps in research can another scientist estimate the validity and relevance of the conclusions and duplicate the study if he wishes to see whether he will arrive at the same conclusions.

[17] Quoted by Merle Curti, *The Growth of American Thought* (New York: Harper, 1951), p. 638.

8

Where Social Action and Social Research Meet

SOME *of the abstract considerations mentioned in the previous chapter are given more concrete consideration in the following one. This chapter is a statement of the role of, and possibilities for, what has come to be known as "action research." Particular stress is given to the possibility of evaluation by means of research. Although the illustrative examples have been chosen from experiments conducted in connection with only two subjects of study—workers' education and intergroup relations—the research is, of course, applicable to a wide variety of action programs.*

THE PHRASE "action research" seems to have been coined by the late psychologist Kurt Lewin.[1] He thought of it as applying primarily to experimental research in ongoing social situations, although it was quickly extended to all practical social research. If the term was new, the idea was not. Chapin published a paper on experimentation in realistic social situations in 1917,[2] and in subsequent years he and his students carried out such experiments. The idea is even older; whenever man has had the idea of experimenting with social relations or social structures and observing the changed results, there has been action research.

An ancient example is provided by the Bible's Gideon, a general with insight. Military principles of his time specified that the basic operating unit (a "century") should consist of one hundred men. Each such century included a trumpet player and, at night, a torch-carrier. Gideon had just one century, but one crucial night he gave each of his soldiers a torch and a trumpet and told them to spread out widely

[1] For a history of the term "action research," see the exchange of letters between Z. Toeman and Laura Thompson in *Scientific Monthly*, 70 (May 1950), 345–346.
[2] F. Stuart Chapin, "The Experimental Method and Sociology," *Scientific Monthly*, February–March 1917; reprinted in modified form in Chapin's *Experimental Designs in Sociological Research* (New York: Harper, 1947), pp. 1–28.

before operating these devices. Each soldier thus represented himself as a whole century when he lit his torch, blew his trumpet, and began to march toward the enemy. On the basis of the social definition of torch and trumpet, the enemy expected that there were one hundred times one hundred, or ten thousand, men advancing on them, and they fled in fear and confusion. No "measurement" of effect was necessary; the enemy was panicked and dispersed, and that was easily seen.

The effects of most modern social action are not so readily apparent. When the social action organizations—government, business, trade-unions, pressure groups, advertising agencies, etc.—carry out a policy, they often wonder what kind of effect it is having, if any. Very occasionally they call in a social scientist to help give them the answer to that question. The social scientist may use the type of action research known in some circles as "evaluation." He has some measuring device—a questionnaire to be filled in by persons to whom the program is directed or a scale to be filled in by a trained observer. He uses "objective" indices such as the number of persons attending a meeting, the amount of discussion from the floor, or the extent of volunteering for committee assignments; or he uses "subjective" indices, such as statements of attitude, expressions of feeling toward others, or indications of knowledge or ignorance. He takes a measurement before the program begins and another one after the program has been in operation for some time; and he may, and should, use a control group to see whether any change noted is due to the program or to other forces which affect all groups simultaneously. That is his experiment, and insofar as he has employed it on a significant social program, it is action research. A not insignificant amount of such research is now going on, and more is being discussed for the future.

Such evaluation can be, and frequently is, disturbing to the action person. The program he works on so hard is held up for inspection and is frequently pronounced to be seriously deficient or absolutely useless. This is damaging to his ego and almost useless for his purpose, as it tells him only what he should *not* do rather than what he *should* do. Two other principles need, therefore, to be introduced into evaluation. One is that the action person himself should be encouraged to adopt an experimental attitude. He should constantly vary his techniques and approaches, noting the strengths and weaknesses of each, and never stop experimenting until he is absolutely certain that his techniques work. Social action, which is here understood to be any sort of activity designed to get a portion of the public to change its behavior in some way, should be conceived as a sort of game, in which the action person plays *several* roles, rather than following an administrative routine where there is no deviation from one policy. Then, when the research person comes in to evaluate, his problem becomes one of determining which of the various techniques that might be employed is the generally most effective one, and which best fits the needs of each type of social situation. This information is useful to the action person and is likely not to be damaging to his ego. A simple example of how to vary techniques is to take the same message and couch it alternately in terms of rational objective arguments, emotional exhortation, self-interest, and questionings to promote catharsis. Each of these techniques should be used with distinct groups and the varying results, if any, carefully noted.

The second principle that needs to be introduced into evaluation research is that it should be incorporated into the action process rather than regarded as something above and beyond it. What has frequently happened in the past is that the research person is not called in to evaluate until the action program is well under way. He has no choice then but to evaluate what there is. It is much simpler for him, and much more useful to the action person, if the research is incorporated into the action program from the beginning. The following are two examples of evaluation research:

1. In one education course for technical workers, a questionnaire was designed whose stated purpose was "to evaluate all phases of the work. This questionnaire was given at the first meeting of the course, as a way of indicating to the students what they would discuss in the course and as a means of determining which phases of the course would need more stress than others. A similar questionnaire, covering the same points in other terms, was administered at the end of the course." [3]

2. A report of the course on grievance procedure for shop stewards [4] indicated that "a teaching device called 'role-playing' was used. Cer-

[3] From an unpublished memorandum prepared by Mrs. Myrna Bordelon, C.I.O. staff representative, Council of Social Agencies, who was the organizer of the course.
[4] The course was under the direction of George Brooks, director, Department of Research and Education, International Brotherhood of Pulp, Sulphite, and Paper Mill Workers.

tain members of the class were told to act the parts of a union member with a grievance, a shop steward handling the grievance, and a foreman to whom the shop steward came with the grievance. Limited information was given each of the three players, but the rest of the class was given all the facts about the grievance. The class criticized the steward's handling of the case, and their criticisms guided the teacher into an understanding of what the particular lacks and needs of the class were. In the last session of the course, the teacher could repeat the role-playing session and note to what extent the criticisms had improved."

From these examples, it can be seen that evaluation research not only evaluates but also helps to guide the action process. Evaluation puts the action person into closer contact with the people he is trying to influence and serves as a critical mirror which he holds up to himself constantly so he can learn where his blemishes are. The role of the research scientist in this kind of evaluation is simply to act as a consultant in showing the action person how he can be more experimental and more critical. If necessary, the research person can also formally measure the effectiveness of the action.

When the action is to take place in an entire community, the research scientist has some special functions that he can perform along with the evaluation. One is what may be called the "obstacles and possibilities" plan of research.[5] In assaying the "before action" state of mind of the population, he can answer questions such as the following:

1. What kinds of people, especially in the community's leadership, will be the most cooperative with the action program?

2. What kinds of people are most in need of the action program, in terms of the value premises of the action person?

3. What existing groups and organizations are there in the community, with purposes similar or sympathetic to the action program, whose institutional facilities and channels of communication can be used?

4. What vested interests will be challenged by the action program?

5. What persons and organizations are there in the community from whom it is advisable to seek clearance, even though some of them are not likely to have any interest whatsoever in the action program?

[5] An example occurs in an unpublished study by Helen S. Dinerman, Dean Manheimer, and Arnold M. Rose of a small city in New England, with its possibilities and obstacles for a group discussion program.

6. What are the most effective channels of communication in the community?

7. To what extent can potential leadership become actual leadership? Can some of the unused potential leadership be drawn into the action program?

8. What are some of the felt needs of the community? Can any of these needs be joined in some way to the action program, so that it is identified with the satisfaction of a felt need?

The list could be extended almost indefinitely. The purpose of the questions is to find out as much as possible about the possibilities for, and obstacles to, the action program before it is put into operation. Many of the questions can be repeated after the action program has been under way for some time to see whether it is having any effect (notably questions 1, 2, 3, 7, and 8; other questions not on the list will also have to be asked, of course).

A second type of community survey that is useful to an action program, although not intended to be evaluative of the program, is the community self-survey. This survey fits the traditional pattern of surveys [6] in content but not in method. It is purely descriptive, and its only innovation is that the research work is carried on by participant members of the community rather than by trained research people. The idea has probably been used casually for decades, but the first systematic use of it as part of an action research program seems to have been due to the stimulation of Dr. Charles S. Johnson, director of the Race Relations Division of the American Missionary Association and chairman of the Social Science Department at Fisk University. He and his assistants organized self-surveys of discriminatory practices in Minneapolis, Pittsburgh, and San Francisco. Their work was observed, improved upon, and made more rigorously scientific by staff members of the Commission on Community Interrelations of the American Jewish Congress. [7] The latter group chose "Northtown," a small city in New Jersey, as a testing ground for their work, and out of this experience developed techniques and tools which, with only the slightest of guidance from a trained research scientist, can be used

[6] Pauline V. Young, *Scientific Social Surveys and Research* (New York: Prentice-Hall, 1949), Chaps. I and II.

[7] For further information on the method, see the following unpublished reports of the CCI-AJC: (1) "How to Conduct a Community Self-Survey of Civil Rights"; (2) "Northtown Survey on Human Relations: 1947."

anywhere for a community self-survey of discriminatory practices. Another town, Montclair, New Jersey, did its own community survey of discriminatory practices without the aid of any trained research persons.

The community surveys and most evaluation research are simple enough to be done by untrained persons with high general intelligence and knowledge, provided they use the proper research tools. Another kind of evaluation research, which seeks to get at repressed attitudes, must be done by the trained research person. Some attitudes are not considered respectable and so tend to be withheld, and some attitudes the respondent himself is not aware of. These can be probed only by the skilled interviewer.

An example of such an evaluation study is one conducted by Saenger and Gilbert on the effects of New York State's FEPC law.[8] Department stores in New York City were worried about whether hiring Negro sales clerks would drive away business. By interviewing customers observed buying from Negro clerks and from white clerks serving at the same counter as Negro clerks, Saenger and Gilbert reached the following significant conclusions: (1) Prejudice against Negro sales clerks does not inhibit a customer from going to one to be waited on. (2) Some who have been secretly observed going to a Negro sales clerk deny ever having seen such a person. (3) Customers rationalize their going to a Negro sales clerk, if they have been waited on by one in a food department, by saying it is all right in food departments but not in clothing departments; if they have just been served by a Negro in a clothing department, they say that it is all right to have Negro sales clerks in clothing departments but not in food departments. Saenger and Gilbert's study, although it was done on a small scale and so has limitations, shows that the FEPC law will not hurt the retail store and that it will, in the long run, improve attitudes toward Negroes. It is the sort of evaluation study that trained social scientists should spend more time on.

Action people have always seen another major use for research— specific fact gathering. Businesses, unions, government agencies, pressure groups, and the like, often have "research departments" whose major functions are to collect information which will make the operation more effective and to prepare annual reports on organizational

[8] Gerhart Saenger and Emily Gilbert, "Customer Reactions to the Integration of Negro Sales Personnel," *International Journal of Opinion and Attitude Research*, 4 (Spring 1950), 57–76.

achievements. Most research scientists refuse to call this kind of work research, and very few trained persons will be found in such departments. Granted that most of the work is picayunish, it need not necessarily be so. There is a dearth of imagination and useful tested knowledge available to these organizations—not least of all to the ones whose purposes are for the general welfare. The action people have very seldom become aware of what great value a practical-minded sociologist or psychologist would be to their operations, and the scientists have usually disdained to soil their hands with such mundane matters. Yet some of the possibilities for significant research in this field are thereby being overlooked. The following examples from the fields of intergroup relations and workers' education can be given:

1. One of the two remaining major *legal* barriers to full and equal citizenship for minority groups in the United States is the doctrine of "separate, but equal" (the other is the restrictions on aliens). This doctrine allows federal, state, and local governments to segregate minorities if they can succeed in maintaining that the facilities are equal. Actually the facilities are very seldom equal, and in extremely few other cases is there any intention of making them equal. So there is a plethora of court cases, which the minorities practically always win at great cost and great effort, to show how the specific facilities are not equal. What is needed is legal proof that segregation necessarily and inevitably implies inequality and discrimination.[9] The task is really one for the empirical social scientist, although only a few lawyers see that. The late Justice Brandeis, before he ascended the bench, was a lawyer who constantly used sociological evidence in court and thereby achieved his tremendous success and reputation. No other lawyer since Brandeis has had the understanding or ability to follow his example completely. But an imaginative sociologist or psychologist and a lawyer, working together, might equal a Brandeis.

2. One of the great current internal problems of the trade-unions, as they have expanded and become accepted as inevitable organizations on the American scene, is how to get themselves integrated with the rest of American society. The problem is really one for all Ameri-

[9] Since this was first written, 32 social scientists have prepared such a legal brief and have presented it to the U.S. Supreme Court: "The Effects of Segregation and the Consequences of Desegregation: A Social Science Statement," Appendix to Appellants' Briefs, School Segregation Cases Nos. 8, 101, and 191 in the Supreme Court of the United States, October term, 1952.

cans, not for the unions alone, since the growing political influence of the unions makes it dangerous to have the great bulk of union members estranged from most other community organizations. A sociologist is needed to discover the ways by which working people who feel shy and ill at ease with people of greater education and "poise" can be given the confidence to join them in responsible community functions. A sociologist is also needed to discover the ways in which the vested interests of the present community structure can be circumvented so that working people can take their rightful places as equal members of the community.

Most sociologists, and a good number of psychologists too, object to several of the points of view expressed in this paper. For good historical reasons there have been advantages to divorcing social science from social action. For these reasons, they fear action research as dangerous to the advancement of their discipline. But many of the historical reasons no longer hold good, and many of the kinds of research discussed on the preceding pages have value for the advancement not only of social action but also of social theory, if the scientist will but seek to apply action research to problems that have theoretical as well as practical importance. In fact, as has been shown in the preceding chapter, the attempt to divorce social research from practical social problems has resulted in sterile production and nonactivity. Nevertheless, many of the kinds of research mentioned thus far are of the sort that are dictated by the narrow, day-to-day needs of organizations that are primarily interested in action, not knowledge. On them alone, no science of sociology or psychology could be built.

However, there is one other area where science and action meet that avoids this objection. This is the area of theory. Social action needs good theory just as much as does social science. Every action organization has both strategy and tactics. The kinds of research discussed up to this point are aids in tactics, in the immediate techniques of taking specific forward steps toward achieving the goals. Good social theory, on the other hand, is fundamental to sound strategy, to the creation of a long-run plan to achieve reformulated goals in terms of the felt needs of the population. A social theory is obviously called for which can relate organizational goals to the needs of the population. In few fields have sociologists advanced far enough to provide tested theory. Where they have, it has usually been because they were given a practical problem to solve. We may note, for example, the relatively advanced condition of theory in the field of criminology, because sociologists have been faced for generations with the practical problem of what causes certain persons to become criminals. Let us take again our two fields of intergroup relations and workers' education to see to what stage theory has advanced and what the present needs are:

1. Much of the action intended to alleviate intergroup tension is based on the rationalistic theory current forty years ago in sociology (among Shaler, Thomas, etc.) that dislike of differences was the source of intergroup prejudice. The action consists largely of denying false charges (i.e., false accusations of group difference), showing how apparent differences are not really differences, and explaining how existing differences developed in a natural and understandable way. There has been a sufficient body of theoretical research to discredit this rationalistic approach, but no social scientist has yet offered a positive substitute to the action people. What relevant theoretical research there has been seems to point to the suggestion that intergroup hatreds are substitute responses (symbolic adjustments) to frustrating, depriving situations, where a specific group is unconsciously identified in the minds of the haters with the frustrating situation. This theory has not been proved either in its general formulation or in its specific identification of the symbolic meaning of any hatred group (although some good suggestive evidence exists[10]). If the theory *were* to be proved it would lead to such changes in action as the following: (a) encouragement of concrete action—taken preferably by the haters themselves—to eliminate the frustrating situation; and (b) disassociation of the unconscious mental identification of the hated group from the frustrating situation.

2. One of the basic internal problems of trade-unions is that a large portion of their membership has been uprooted by the Industrial Revolution from its integral position in an organized structure, and now does not know how to participate effectively in community organizations, often including the union itself. One of the manifestations of inability to participate is inability to communicate effectively, and workers are unable therefore to see their similarity of interests or to understand the operations of the union leaders. This is essentially

[10] See, for example, John Dollard *et al., Frustration and Aggression* (New Haven, Conn.: Yale University Press, 1939), esp. pp. 31ff; Arnold M. Rose, "Anti-Semitism's Root in City-Hatred," *Commentary,* 6 (October 1948), 374–378.

the problem of the mass character of modern society and the attendant psychology of alienation and irresponsibility. Sociologists and psychologists have all but neglected to develop a tenable theory of this situation, although many have recognized it to be of central importance to one aspect of their scientific interests.

It is obvious that some fundamental research has to be done by trained and imaginative sociologists and psychologists before these theoretical (and practical) problems can be solved. Many of the essential facts (for the most part "historical" in nature) for formulating basic theory on these subjects are only waiting to be integrated into a coherent form. The theory, once formulated, will probably be found to have gaps, and will need verification at most points. These are the places where empirical research will be essential. When research has substantiated a large portion of these theories, they will be found to form a very central part of general sociological theory. This is natural with action research that has a theoretical bent, since action research is group-oriented, rather than individual-oriented or culture-oriented, and since it has the generalizing character imparted to it by its concern for hypothesis and its experimental method. The theory, once developed and substantiated, will also have intense practical value, since it will be the best available guide to action people in intergroup relations and workers' education as to how they can formulate a realistic strategy for reaching their goals.

We see, then, that for some of the action research discussed, the action people have to rely heavily on the research people. Some of the dependence will be permanent and some of it is likely to be temporary, lasting only until the action people take over a few basic research attitudes and until they become acquainted with a few simple research tools. On the other hand, some of the action research will contribute just as heavily to the advancement of theoretical social science as it will to effective social action. There the scientists have something to gain which the history of our discipline suggests is not likely to be gained except by contact with these realistic social problems. Certainly there is likely to be mutual gain as research and action find a closer meeting ground.

9

The Social Responsibility of the Social Scientist

THE *following chapter moves outside the realm of social science proper and considers the relationship of social science to society. Its primary concern is the effect of social science on society but it also considers some of the implications of the influence of society on the social sciences. Although the subject matter in itself is not scientific, it should be of concern to the social scientist because it deals with possible new roles being imposed on him by history. The chapter was prepared as a paper for the 1953 annual meeting of the Society for the Study of Social Problems.*

THE INCREASE of knowledge about the control of the physical world has raised in the minds of informed citizens the question as to whether society will be able to control this knowledge. The problem has demanded a more immediate solution with the invention of the atomic and the hydrogen bombs. The question used to be raised as to how we could prevent the machine from enslaving man; the one now more frequently raised is how we can prevent atomic energy from destroying man and his civilization. How can our society gain the wisdom, the good will, and the commonness of purpose to control this and other inventions?

For many social scientists the question has become one of discovering enough about society so that society can, if it wishes to use this knowledge, control the use of physical knowledge. Hart, for example, poses the problem in these words: ". . . the fact of technological acceleration means that the problems of the future will keep on compounding and expanding until they wreck our world, or until organized intelligence applies science effectively to mastering the social problems which technological acceleration creates." [1]

[1] Hornell Hart, "Technological Acceleration and the Atomic Bomb," *American Sociological Review*, 11 (June 1946), 291.

The social scientist usually stops here and does not inquire further. He seldom raises what is logically the next question: Once the social scientists gain the social knowledge which can be used to control physical knowledge and to control society, how will this social knowledge be controlled? What is to prevent a social scientist from using social knowledge to expedite the enslavement or destruction of society? What is to prevent the social scientist from selling or giving his knowledge to one group in society for the purpose of controlling another group?

Of course, many social scientists feel that these questions are a little premature. After all, they say, the knowledge we produce is so trivial that it is no possible threat to society in the way that knowledge produced by physical scientists is. But the belief that social science knowledge has not yet developed to a point where it influences society is not correct, and the attitude that social scientists should not be concerned with their own influence on society is not consistent with their frequently expressed concern about developing social science knowledge that will aid in controlling physical science knowledge. If we are striving toward the control of physical science knowledge, should we not also consider the control of the potential social knowledge that is to control the physical knowledge?

There are evidences that we are acquiring some potentially dangerous social knowledge, that we are developing social "atomic energy," to speak figuratively.[2] First, we have witnessed the power of propaganda and other "mass persuasion" and mob-incitement techniques to control people, destroy political enemies, and seize power. Even though Hitler may have got his knowledge largely by brilliant intuition, social scientists can analyze the patterns of his successes and failures and from them draw conclusions as to how masses of people can be incited and controlled in the future. There have been books on the "governing of men," on "mass persuasion," and on a wide range of techniques of psychological warfare, all stating a number of tested

[2] It is, of course, logically quite appropriate to take an optimistic point of view toward the same kinds of developments that we are considering. John G. Darley, for example, considers that social scientists "are being asked to help society bring its human relations in line with the technological advances provided by the physical sciences. . . . We have been given the chance to produce our equivalent of the atomic bomb." (Preface to Harold Guetzkow [ed.], *Groups, Leadership and Men* [Pittsburgh, Pa.: Carnegie Press, 1951], p. 11.)

principles for controlling the minds of men.[3] Social scientists will soon know, with a small margin of error, how to turn ordinary citizens into a mass which follows its leaders' bidding.

Social scientists are already being paid large sums to develop knowledge about how to sell commercial products. The field of "market research" has boomed in the last decade or so, after starting out as a small subbranch of applied social science. Market research tells advertisers how to change their products to meet people's attitudes and how to change people's attitudes so they will buy the manufacturers' products. An example of a social scientist who has put his knowledge at the service of advertisers is Burleigh B. Gardner, who now runs a business enterprise for this and other commercial purposes. He is reported to have delivered a lecture to the American Marketing Association under the title "Putting Stereotypes and Prejudices to Work in Your Advertising Strategy." [4]

The creation of public opinion has expanded, upon the basis of study of public opinion, to uses other than that of market research. During World War II, orientation films were made by the Army, using the best of Hollywood talent, with the intention of making soldiers understand the causes of the war and thereby become better soldiers. These films were tested for their effects on the attitudes of the soldiers and a number of lessons were learned.[5] There have been many more recent studies on how to change people's attitudes by means of films and radio.[6] Studies have been conducted telling us how individuals may best be convinced to change their food habits,[7] their attitudes toward minority groups,[8] their attitudes toward political

[3] See, for example, Alexander Leighton, *The Governing of Men* (Princeton, N.J.: Princeton University Press, 1945); Paul M. A. Linebarger, *Psychological Warfare* (Washington, D.C.: Infantry Journal Press, 1948); Robert K. Merton, *Mass Persuasion* (New York: Harper, 1946); Dorwin Cartwright, "Some Principles of Mass Persuasion," *Human Relations*, vol. 2, no. 3 (1949), pp. 197–292.

[4] Ralph Goodman, "Freud and the Hucksters," *Nation*, 176 (February 14, 1953), 143–145.

[5] C. I. Hovland, A. A. Lumsdaine, and F. D. Sheffield, *Experiments on Mass Communication* (Princeton, N.J.: Princeton University Press, 1949).

[6] For a summary, see Joseph T. Klapper, *The Effects of Mass Media* (New York: Bureau of Applied Social Research, 1950).

[7] Kurt Lewin, "Forces behind Food Habits and Methods of Change," *The Problem of Changing Food Habits*, Report of the Committee on Food Habits, Bulletin of the National Research Council, 108 (Washington, D.C., 1943), pp. 35–65.

[8] Studies up through 1947 are summarized in Arnold M. Rose, *Studies in Reduction of Prejudice* (Chicago: American Council on Race Relations, 1948), Chap. I. An

issues,[9] and so on. The Yale psychologists have under way a vast program of carefully designed research in the changing of attitudes.[10] This happens to be well-motivated research; but cannot the question be raised as to what can happen to this knowledge once it is accumulated by social scientists? It might be utilized by those who do not have the general welfare at heart; it might be directed against certain groups; it might be used with good intentions but without the assent of those to whom it is directed.

Another area of social science research, which has developed largely within the last few decades and which has possibilities for modifying the power positions of groups within society, is the field of industrial relations research. One purpose of this research is to increase the happiness of workers in industry, which involves finding out what makes them dissatisfied and what techniques can be employed to reduce their dissatisfaction. Another purpose is to increase productivity.

These purposes give the research a noble and altruistic motivation in the minds of many of the social scientists engaged in this research. But the knowledge gained can be viewed in another light. It can be viewed as an increase of the power of the employers at the expense of the unions. Some employers regard employee research as a union-avoiding or union-breaking activity, and that is why they are willing to pay for it. Unions may go along with it if they feel strong, but their basic philosophy, ideally, is to increase the happiness of workers by giving them the power to *demand* improvements in working conditions and so control some part of their condition, rather than to let employers control workers by minimizing the dissatisfactions of everyday working relationships. Since the research is on the attitudes of workers alone, the knowledge gained increases the possibilities of control only over workers, and not over employers. As such, it is potentially dangerous research to the labor unions. In this context, a quotation from a book review by an industrial sociologist who is aware of the social implication of research in his field is relevant:

example of an important study since 1948 is Morton Deutsch and Mary E. Collins, *Interracial Housing* (Minneapolis: University of Minnesota Press, 1951).

[9] See for example, George W. Hartmann, "Field Experiment on the Comparative Effectiveness of Emotional and Rational Political Leaflets in Determining Election Results," *Journal of Abnormal and Social Psychology,* 31 (April 1936), 99–114.

[10] Carl I. Hovland, "Change in Attitudes through Communication," *Journal of Abnormal and Social Psychology,* 46 (July 1951), 424–437.

The author states in the Introduction and repeats in his conclusion that the aims of industrial psychology must be to further "democracy in industry" rather than to serve as a tool for any interest group. The fact that psychology has been employed almost exclusively by management to further its own goals is acknowledged, although very brief mention is made of its possible use by unions. The author apparently assumes that industrial psychology is neutral in the industrial scene because it is "scientific" and employs experimental methods. The fact that empirical techniques and empirically determined knowledge can be directed and used by one interest group to further its position in relation to another interest group does not seem to be recognized. "Democracy in industry" as used by the author seems to mean a recognition by management that workers think and feel as human beings. The ideal situation is one in which management successfully predicts and guides the reactions of employees. This can take place without regard to the social, economic, and legal relations of worker to management. Such a definition of "democracy" is meaningless, at least as far as sociology and political science are concerned.[11]

Another field of social science research potentially dangerous to society at large, or to certain groups in society, is that on economic control. Economists are learning more and more about the factors controlling prices. They are learning, for example, about stock market prices, and they are on the verge of testing predictions made about them.[12] The entrance of tested knowledge into operations on the stock market may increase the size of changes in market prices, with all the consequent changes in availability of loans for capital expansion or consumer purchases, the liquidity of funds, the attitudes toward risk taking on the part of businessmen, and so on.

Another example of the potentially dangerous effect of knowledge about the pricing process is in the field of price and monetary control. Price control under the Office of Price Administration helped to prevent a runaway inflation during World War II. A more thorough knowledge of the economics of prices and money might make it possible for an economist to gain a personal fortune by taking advantage of a price or monetary control program. There have already been cases of persons equipped with technical knowledge of international trade

[11] Review of Milton L. Blum's *Industrial Psychology and Its Social Foundations* (New York: Harper, 1949), by Donald E. Wray in *American Journal of Sociology, 55* (January 1950), 424–425.
[12] See, for example, Arnold M. Rose, "Rumor in the Stock Market," *Public Opinion Quarterly,* 15 (Fall 1951), 461–486.

who have been able legally to manipulate exchange rates in traveling from one country to another so as to make a profit for themselves. If this knowledge were applied on a larger scale it could wreck price control and the unstable balance of current international trade.

There are possibly other examples of social science's being on the verge of discovery of a body of knowledge that could be dangerous to society at large or to one segment of society. We can eliminate some value judgments from this conclusion by saying in a factual way that knowledge about society can be used by one group to enhance its power at the expense of another group. Expressed thus, we are simply restating the old truism that knowledge is power. At least one social scientist has projected a social system controlled completely by scientific psychological principles, directed toward what he conceived to be the happiness of men.[13] In the case of the social scientists' knowledge, it is political and economic power with which we are concerned. Wirth has stated the proposition in even more general terms: "Every assertion of a 'fact' about the social world touches the interests of some individual or group."[14]

Some questions are in order as to what kinds of persons these social scientists are who are acquiring this knowledge and potential power. Are they the sort of persons who will use their knowledge for their own gain or the gain of a minority within society whom they happen to favor? The answer to this question involves a systematic study of the social backgrounds, the personality traits, and the attitudes of the social scientists. Until such a study is made, we cannot begin to answer the fundamental question about what the social scientists will do with their knowledge. We can, however, give a partial answer to an allied question: Are there any tendencies observable among social scientists which might lead them to use their knowledge for ends dangerous to society as a whole or to large segments of society? Even a hasty examination of the processes by which social scientists are trained and do their research would lead one to answer tentatively in the affirmative.

In the first place, social scientists have a not too far from average number of human frailties, and there are none but the ordinary con-

<hr>

[13] See B. F. Skinner, *Walden Two* (New York: Macmillan, 1948).

[14] Louis Wirth, Preface to Karl Mannheim's *Ideology and Utopia* (New York: Harcourt, Brace, 1936), p. xvii.

trols prevalent in our society to prevent a social scientist's frailties from directing his knowledge toward ends dangerous to society. For instance, he may be selfish and callous of others. Such an attitude may have been stimulated by the shortage of opportunities available to satisfy his aspirations, especially during the depression, and by the multitude of special privileges available during the war boom. The pursuit of limited material advantages approaches its peak in countries beset by war within their borders. Whole nations have devoted much of their time and guile to procuring food and cigarettes and have demonstrated the demoralization that comes with such activity. While Americans are much more opulent, few would deny that some American social scientists have been "bought" when the purchase has been made under certain rules of "good taste." An economic depression which accentuates the competition among social scientists, or an increase in the monetary or prestige rewards to be striven for, could demoralize a significant proportion of social scientists.

A second fact to be noted is the low prestige of the social sciences and the consequent frustration of the social scientist. Intellectuals generally have never had high prestige in the United States, and education is far from being the most important determinant of social status. Social scientists have a lower status than do physical and biological scientists, not only in the minds of the general public, but frequently in their own minds as well. Quite a number of social scientists feel inferior to natural scientists in the possession of specialized knowledge and in the possession of techniques for acquiring new knowledge. The press campaign to discredit social scientists during the New Deal era, which was part of a larger political campaign, did not increase the self-respect of the social scientists. They do not hold their discipline in the highest esteem, and that results in a sense of personal insecurity for many of them. Outward evidences of this are seen in movements within the disciplines of psychology and sociology to ape the techniques of the physical sciences even at the sacrifice of some of the subject matter of their own disciplines. It is seen even more sharply in the large number of social scientists who escape academic life for business or government work when the opportunity offers itself. These people are not so devoted to the pursuit of knowledge as they claim to be. The statement of this fact should not be taken as an accusation, or an attempt to fix blame, but as an evidence of the relatively low prestige of the academic pursuit in the social sciences.

The implication of these remarks is that social scientists experience enough frustration in the pursuit of social knowledge that they might be willing to offer their services to anybody who could pay a high price for them. There is a deep desire in every social scientist to tell the world "I told you so" after all the questioning gibes about the value and significance of his work.

Even if the social scientist never sells his knowledge for personal profit or prestige, he has some tendencies which will allow him to give it away without regard to whom he gives it. Some social scientists believe that knowledge has no relation to social action, that conscious ideas and the possession of factual information cannot effect social change. This issue is too large to be debated here, but suffice it to say that *if* social scientists believe there is a lag between the invention of material objects and the invention of social wisdom to control these material objects, there is logically implied in this contention the belief that social knowledge can be used to change the course of society. However, if social scientists believe that their knowledge can have no social influence, they are likely to give away their knowledge without much concern as to where it is going.

It would be a mistake to give the impression that scientists have been completely unaware of the dangers they create for society. The natural scientists never had to worry too much prior to 1940 about the possibly harmful social effects of their discoveries, as the overwhelming proportion of their discoveries seemed to increase the health, standard of living, and opportunities of people. Of course, the broader social implications of certain discoveries were ignored—such as whether the creation of leisure time due to productive efficiency was really conducive to happiness—because there was unconscious acceptance of the notion that "progress" would eliminate these "cultural lags." When the few discoveries were made that seemed to have direct potentialities for human harm, the natural scientists were usually upset. Alfred Nobel, the inventor of dynamite, set up the Nobel Peace Prize, for example. David Lilienthal, former head of the Atomic Energy Commission, wrote:

. . . it is by no manner of means inevitable that scientific research and technology will work for good. It is equally possible that they may yield a harvest of bitter fruit. When those speak who imply that our problem is only one of securing more and more funds for more and more scientific workers in private or public research we need constantly to remind ourselves that, in terms of human happiness and freedom, such a conclusion is far from true. Unless research and technology are consciously related to a central purpose of human welfare, unless research is defined and directed by those who believe in and who have faith in people and in democratic ends and means, it may well be that the more money we spend on research the further we miss the mark. It is like trying to reach your destination in an automobile that is going in the wrong direction; the faster you drive the farther away from your goal you will be.[15]

My own guess would be that most physical scientists were shocked when, after the invention of the atomic bomb, several social scientists and philosophers claimed that science is amoral. Many physical scientists began to urge social scientists to develop social means of control over atomic energy and asked for effective techniques of communicating to the public some of the dangerous implications of the recent discoveries. The physical scientists themselves set up organizations to disseminate information on the potential social influence of the discovery of how to tap atomic energy.

Some social scientists have also expressed awareness of the possible harmful social implications of social science knowledge. Several studies have been made concerning how Hitler used social scientists to maintain his power. A distinguished mathematician and demographer, Lancelot Hogben, has the following to say of his colleagues: "No society is safe in the hands of its clever people. . . . Today economic tyranny has no more powerful friend than the calculating prodigy." [16]

A world-famous economist, Lord Keynes, makes a similar remark: ". . . the ideas of economists and political philosophers, both when they are right and when they are wrong, are more powerful than is commonly understood. Indeed, the world is ruled by little else. Practical men, who believe themselves to be quite exempt from any intellectual influences, are usually the slaves of some defunct economist.

[15] David E. Lilienthal, "Research Has a Moral Responsibility," *Christian Century*, 62 (July 4, 1945), 786–787.
[16] Lancelot Hogben, *Mathematics for the Millions* (New York: Norton, 1940), pp. 19, 24.

Madmen in authority, who hear voices in the air, are distilling their frenzy from some academic scribbler of a few years back." [17]

Another socially dangerous tendency is for educated people generally to identify themselves with the upper classes and to separate themselves from the poorly educated. The snobbery of family background in Europe is almost matched by the snobbery of education in America. A certain amount of separation, based on differences of interest, is natural. The problem is that the division is so complete that educated people, while retaining their respect for wealth, lose their respect for the more common values. The isolation is physical as well as social, since the universities, with their faculties, students, and hangers-on, frequently form distinct communities. It would be no more desirable for social scientists to ally themselves with the lower classes than with the upper classes. What is desirable for scientific purposes is for them to have the "free-floating" objectivity that Karl Mannheim spoke of and to have contact with all sectors of society.

Another danger stems from the tendency of some social scientists to carry over their attitudes from their role as scientists into their role as citizens. They have taken "objectivity" to mean that they are exempt from social responsibilities, and they have the tendency of educated persons generally to regard themselves as superior to the common herd. When social knowledge is discovered that can control the common herd, it can become dangerous to the common herd because of these attitudes of the holders of the social knowledge.

Also, there is possibly less use of rigorous procedure and less certainty of the reliability and validity of conclusions in the social sciences than in the natural sciences. The criteria of scientific method are much clearer and the tests for reliability and validity much simpler in the natural sciences than in the social sciences, and therefore it is much easier to be rigorous and unswerving in the former fields. A survey of replicated studies in the social sciences shows a high proportion that fail to reach the same conclusion as the original study.[18] Social scientists may thus be *unaware* that sometimes they are merely satisfying a propagandist's need rather than producing valid knowledge.

To the extent that the statements above are true, and admittedly they require further evidence before they can be regarded as of high

---

[17] John Maynard Keynes, *The General Theory of Employment, Interest and Money* (New York: Harcourt, Brace, 1936), p. 383.

[18] See Chapter 15 of this volume.

validity, certain actions are incumbent upon social scientists if they are not to be dangerous to our society. One approach is to demand that social scientists engage only in "pure science," as opposed to "applied science," and it is likely that one reason for the popularity of this demand is a deep-seated but inhibited concern about the social responsibility of the social scientist. Some of those who are engaged in the most utilitarian of studies, for business or government, are perhaps for that reason those who cry the loudest for "basic research" and "pure science." However, the points made in this chapter indicate that "pure science" and a profession which aims at "pure science" cannot avoid having some kind of social influence. Knowledge is power, and if we social scientists wish to avoid the misuse of the power we produce, we shall be obliged to take certain more positive steps. I cannot presume to offer a solution, as the problem is too difficult, and too little thought has thus far been concentrated on it. But I shall suggest tentatively a few partial steps.

One is to integrate the learned associations a little more so that membership in them confers some prestige. A more closely knit professional association tends to develop some standards and controls, even if informal, over its members. At present, anyone may join some of the social science associations upon payment of a nominal fee. There ought to be other criteria for selection of members than payment of low annual dues. One of the functions suggested for our professional associations is the minimization of frustration of the membership and the development of a sense of professional dignity. Any activity along these lines should enhance the integrity of the individual members.

Another suggestion is that we select our subject matter for study with some attention to its possible use by society. The selection of the problem should not prejudice our handling of it.[19] Nor should any individual social scientist be discouraged from following his own bent. But the usual influences which now direct selection of studies of one subject matter or another could include a recognition of social responsibility. The more we are made aware of the social implications of sociological knowledge, the more likely we are to choose problems for research that will produce knowledge that is not so usable for selfish or socially harmful purposes. As sociologists we know that the values

[19] Claire Selltiz and Stuart W. Cook, "Can Research in Social Science Be Both Socially Useful and Scientifically Meaningful?" *American Sociological Review,* 13 (August 1948), 454–459. See also Chapter 7 of this volume.

or standards of the groups we belong to help to determine our own individual values and standards. If our professional societies have standards directed toward the general social welfare, our professional behavior is more likely to be socially responsible than if the professional societies have no such standards.[20]

A change in attitudes of social scientists toward uneducated people might be suggested. Perhaps the only thing that is needed is more social contact. As for the masses of the people themselves, they could be brought a little closer to social science if social scientists made an effort to communicate their knowledge. If the results of a study might have some interest for persons outside of the discipline, they could be written in language understandable to outsiders. Some social science discoveries can be publicized by means of radio programs, newspaper reports, and other ways that physical and biological scientists have already begun to use. Stuart Chase, for example, seems to have made a successful venture of popularizing social science studies.[21]

Another way to get publicity for social science discoveries among educated persons who are not social scientists would be to publish annual summaries, in readable language, of some of the outstanding discoveries. Social scientists, representing their professions, might also offer their services more often to legislatures and other government agencies. All this contact with the public and its representatives would not only increase rapport with them but might also increase the prestige of the social scientist, and so reduce his frustrations. Of course, some social scientists are properly concerned about the repressions from power-holders that might come if we "tamper" with social affairs.[22]

Another activity, which is completely within the range of the usual activities of sociologists, would be to restore to the study of "Social Problems" its earlier level of prestige and attention. In previous decades some of the most fruitful sociological research was done on problems of public concern (e.g., Durkheim's *Suicide,* Thomas and Znaniecki's *Polish Peasant,* and several studies of crime). Many of our basic theoretical concepts, and the fashioning of several of our

---

[20] The psychologists have concerned themselves somewhat with the issues raised in this paper. See the August 1952 number of *American Psychologist* entitled "Ethics and the Profession of Psychology."

[21] Stuart Chase, *The Proper Study of Mankind* (New York: Harper, 1948).

[22] Talcott Parsons, "The Position and Prospects of Sociology as a Professional Field," speech delivered at the 1949 meeting of the Midwest Sociological Society, Madison, Wisconsin.

major research tools, were developed in connection with these studies. Today, the main theoretical and methodological work in sociology is carried on in connection with social psychology. Students and funds for research have also made this relative shift. The implication for social responsibility is this: The value premise involved in selecting problems for research in social problems is very simple, is comparable to that in psychiatry or physical pathology, and allows little "harm" to be done to society by use of its discoveries. This value premise is that it is desirable to find out the causes of human ills so that they may more effectively be eliminated. The value premise behind the selection of research problems in social psychology is more indirect and gives to that discipline a misleading appearance of value neutrality. Thus knowledge acquired in social psychology is often usable for selfish ends or for purposes harmful to society. Assuming that theoretical and methodological advance in sociology can just as well come out of properly planned studies of social problems as out of social-psychological studies, it would seem desirable to accord just as much research attention and prestige to the former as to the latter.

These suggestions, which could be multiplied, are logical extensions of the sociological principle that the ways to increase informal social control over an individual are to increase his integration into the society, to develop his sense of social responsibility toward the society, and to give the society a greater understanding of his activities. The individual in this case is the social scientist, and it is deemed necessary to increase informal social controls over him because he is on the verge of discovering knowledge that could lead to a redistribution of power relations in the society. Otherwise, either society as a whole or some sector of society might be hurt, or else society might check the redistribution of power in time by establishing formal social controls over the social scientist. Any of these prospects is dangerous to democratic society and to science. While science formerly thrived under monarchies, even absolute ones (possibly because the rulers were not concerned with science), the evidence is that modern *totalitarian* dictatorships distort science even as they exploit it.[23] Solutions must be

[23] Two studies of how Hitler's government turned scientists into propagandists and distorted science itself are Max Weinreich's *Hitler's Professors* (New York: Yiddish Scientific Institute, 1946) and H. L. Ansbacher's "Testing, Management and Reactions of Foreign Workers in Germany during World War II," *American Psychologist*, 5 (1950), 38–49. Similar reports about the Soviet Union are the following: Stuart A. Rice,

sought to increase the chances that the social scientist's activities are an asset to democratic society. Social scientists, either as individuals or as a group, are by no means in complete control of the situation, because knowledge produced for "its own sake" or for "good" purposes may be perverted to other purposes. But social scientists can make use of those degrees of freedom that the larger society permits.

"Methodology Conference of the Central Statistical Administration, USSR," *Scientific Monthly*, 75 (August 1952), 71–78; E. Ashby, "Marxism versus Science," *New York Times Magazine*, January 6, 1952, pp. 12ff; and Evsey D. Domar, "The Varga Controversy," *American Economic Review*, 40 (1950), 132–151.

SECTION III

The Contributions of Sociological Theory
to the Other Social Sciences

10

The Potential Contribution of Sociological
Theory and Research to Economics

WE *turn now to a section which considers the relationship of sociology to the other social sciences. The first chapter considers the possible relationship of sociology to economics—a field from which it secured some of its early nurture but from which it has been sharply divided during most of its later development. We are here concerned with the core problems of economics—those of economic theory, primarily—not the marginal areas, such as labor relations and institutional economics, which have traditionally retained a liaison with sociology.*

HISTORY AND POSSIBILITIES OF THE RELATIONSHIP BETWEEN
ECONOMICS AND SOCIOLOGY

HOWEVER economics is defined, it is considered to be a special social science that examines the interrelations of only a limited set of factors. At the same time, economists are interested in predicting *concrete* economic conditions and in making suggestions about economic *policy*. It can be demonstrated—and this chapter attempts to contribute to this demonstration—that, to a significant extent, concrete economic conditions are affected by factors that the economist has traditionally considered to be outside his purview, and that policies designed to achieve strictly economic goals *must* take into consideration noneconomic influences. Among the noneconomic factors and influences that enter into predictions about economic conditions and into policies to achieve economic goals are those that have traditionally been studied by sociologists. Thus sociologists should be able to make a contribution to economics.

Before sociology emerged as an independent discipline confined to

NOTE: I wish to express my appreciation to O. H. Brownlee and Leonid Hurwicz for a critical reading of this chapter.

the systematic study of a specific subject matter, some of those who were speculating about sociological phenomena were professional economists. Americans like William Graham Sumner and Thomas Nixon Carver retained chairs in economics departments when they shifted most of their academic duties to teaching courses in sociology. Europeans like Max Weber, Vilfredo Pareto, and Franz Oppenheimer were equally at home in both fields. Sociology was formerly a branch of economics at several universities, and still is so considered at Princeton. But the two fields began to separate sharply when students who had majored exclusively in sociology became the teachers of the emerging discipline, and when a body of research problems that did not interest the economists became the object of the sociologists' attention. In the United States, though not in Europe, one subfield of economics—demography—made the switch to sociology. As in the case of many developments of new disciplines from older ones—and sociology had roots in anthropology, history, and political science as well as in economics—the separation very soon became complete. Today very few sociologists know a significant amount of the researches, theories, and findings of economists, and vice versa. Each group maintains certain stereotyped derogatory attitudes toward the other,[1] and some economists have been known to use the term "sociologist" almost as an epithet to describe some of their colleagues—like Veblen and Commons—whose interests led them astray from orthodoxy.

Yet there is now a reverse movement, toward integration, under way in the social sciences; a liaison has already developed between psychology and anthropology and sociology and between psychology and economics.[2] Psychology, like sociology but unlike economics

[1] One of the better known exchanges of polemics involved an anthropologist rather than a sociologist, but the position taken could just as well have been stated by a sociologist. See Frank H. Knight, "Anthropology and Economics," and Melville J. Herskovits, "Economics and Anthropology: A Rejoinder," *Journal of Political Economy*, vol. 49 (April 1941); reprinted in Herskovits, *Economic Anthropology* (New York: Knopf, 1952). Also see the review of the latter by Murray E. Polakoff, "Economic Methodology and the Significance of the Knight-Herskovits Controversy," *American Journal of Economics and Sociology*, 12 (January 1953), 201–210.

[2] Leaders in the integration of economics and psychology include George Katona and his associates at the University of Michigan (see his "Contribution of Psychological Data to Economic Analysis," *Journal of the American Statistical Association*, 42 [September 1947], 449ff; see also his more recent *Psychological Analysis of Economic Behavior* [New York: McGraw-Hill, 1951]); Elmo Roper and his associates in the Fortune Poll; Franco Modigliani and others connected with the Merrill Project on Expectations and Business Fluctuations at the University of Illinois. On the general status

or political science, is a general science that seeks to explain the forms of human behavior in whatever setting or with whatever content they manifest themselves. If a knowledge of psychology has been found useful by economists it is likely that a knowledge of sociology soon will be. Psychology is concerned only with the characteristics of the individual as they affect his behavior, whereas sociology is concerned with the group structure and function as it affects human behavior. Both disciplines have equally valid and complementary contributions to make to economics.

Cross-fertilization between sociology and economics can develop in three logical directions:

1. Studies of the influence of economic factors on sociological phenomena. There have been numerous studies of the sociological and demographic consequences of changes in technology and economic structure,[3] of correlations between social variables and economic status where the latter is presumed to be causal,[4] and of the social consequences of business cycles.[5] This chapter will not be further concerned with studies of this type.

2. Borrowing of methods of research. The institutional economists learned many of their techniques of observation from the sociologists, and there are many tools of measurement which they could still learn. The sociologists have borrowed many statistical techniques from economic statisticians (especially in time-series analysis). Sociologists could probably make good use of the rigorous deductive type of analysis and the mathematical method, with which economists among all

of psychological studies of economic behavior, see Kurt Mayer, "Toward Understanding Economic Behavior," *American Journal of Economics and Sociology*, 8 (July 1949), 321–335; and Samuel P. Hayes, Jr., "Some Psychological Problems of Economics," *Psychological Bulletin*, 47 (July 1950), 289–330. For a critique of the psychological backwardness of economists, see Albert Lauterbach, "Psychological Assumptions of Economic Theory," *American Journal of Economics and Sociology*, 10 (October 1950), 27–38.

[3] Many of these studies have been conducted or stimulated by William F. Ogburn. For example, see his contributions to *Recent Social Changes in the United States* (New York: McGraw-Hill, 1933); *Technological Trends and National Policy*, report of the subcommittee on technology to the National Resources Committee (Washington, D.C.: Government Printing Office, 1937); *The Social Effects of Aviation* (Boston: Houghton Mifflin, 1946).

[4] See, for example, W. A. Bonger, *Criminality and Economic Conditions* (Boston: Little, Brown, 1916).

[5] See, for example, Dorothy S. Thomas, *Social Aspects of the Business Cycle* (New York: Knopf, 1927).

social scientists have been perhaps most familiar.[6] But these possibilities, too, are outside the scope of this chapter.

3. Studies of sociological factors in economic phenomena. Thus far, most of these studies have been undertaken by institutional economists, labor economists, and sociologists. The general economist has tended to shy away from such studies and to regard them as foreign to his interest. Most of the remainder of this chapter will be devoted to explaining and illustrating how sociological influences can contribute toward the development of the central interests of economists.

Let us start with an illustration of a very simple sort. Demography makes certain predictions that should concern the economists. Among these predictions is the one that most economically advanced countries show trends of an increasing population for a few generations and then a leveling off, accompanied by an increasing proportion of the aged in the population and by the simultaneous consequence that in a generation or so the labor force will be a relatively small segment of the population. The economic consequences of these trends need to be investigated, notably to see whether a stable or decreasing population is associated with pressure toward deflation and to learn how the changes in the age distribution shift the relationship between monetary rewards for production and the monetary pressures on consumers' goods. Changes in population put as much pressure on the price level as do changes in the amount of money in circulation. The shifting relationship between the productive portion of the population and those whose economic role is limited to consumption probably means that any change in the wage level has a decreasing influence on the circulation of money and hence a decreasing influence on the price level.

For a second example let us consider an influence closer to the heart of sociology—that of status differentiation and the phenomena of class and caste. Sociology here suggests that society is not a homogeneous unit but is composed of partially noncompeting subsocieties. The facts of status, class, and caste may possibly have such effects as (1) causing the demand curve for certain products to exhibit discontinuities; (2) giving the supply curve for labor a positive slope at certain points rather than a consistently negative, even if changing, slope; and (3) creating situations in which saving is higher at lower interest rates

---

[6] The usefulness of these methods for sociologists is discussed in Chapter 22 of this volume.

than at higher ones. The economic consequences of these and similar possibilities need closer theoretical examination.

The point I am trying to make is that the economist oriented toward theory could consider certain facts about social life provided by the sociologist, develop a truly economic theory around them, and then test the new theory on available data or make deductive predictions from it which could be tested by subsequent events. Economists have already used such a procedure in developing a theory of monopoly, for example, but they have apparently ignored the social facts considered central by sociologists.

Economic theory had its birth and early development at a time, considerably before the birth of sociology, when social and psychological thought was generally grounded in associationism. This was an individualistic psychology which assumed that man's behavior was strictly a rational response to his external experiences. Such an assumption unconsciously guided much of the work of classical and neoclassical economists. Today the assumption that behavior is a direct response to associations of experiences is no longer regarded by sociologists and social psychologists as tenable. The newer assumptions underlying social-psychological research consider that behavior is a response to selected and interpreted experiences. An individual has an expectation as to how others will act under given circumstances, he has a conception of how others expect him to act, and he has a conception of himself as a conformist or deviant of one of a large number of types. From these conscious or unconscious expectations, conceptions, and "definitions of the situation," the individual guides his behavior. These assumptions are too broad to be proved or disproved directly, but they have been found most useful in explaining and predicting the widest range of observable facts about social life.

APPLICATION OF SOCIOLOGICAL KNOWLEDGE TO ECONOMIC ASSUMPTIONS

Some economists, more aware than others of the social-psychological assumptions underlying economic theory, have tried to bring newer economic theory into harmony with the newer social-psychological principles. Frank Knight, for example, says: "Economic analysis may be truly said to deal with 'conduct,' in the Spencerian sense of acts adapted to ends, or of the adaptation of acts to ends, in contrast with the broader category of 'behavior' in general. It assumes that men's acts are ruled by conscious motives; that, as it is more ordinarily expressed, they are directed toward the 'satisfaction of wants'." [7]

Since Knight is one of the sophisticated economists, from both the philosophical and social-psychological points of view, it might be well to analyze the assumptions which he has set forth as basic for economic theory. An interdisciplinary contribution can be made if sociology and social psychology are able to offer realistic and useful modifications and extensions of the assumptions. Knight and all other economists recognize that their assumptions are arbitrary abstractions found useful for analysis and prediction. But they also believe that the assumptions depart only in minor respects from real life and are the most useful of all possible sets of assumptions. Knight makes this amply clear at several points in his book. For example, he says: "The abstract conditions first enumerated in chapter III represented in part divergencies in degree only from real life, and were in part arbitrary abstractions from fundamental characteristics of the pecuniary organization made for the purpose of a separate study of the constituent elements." [8] It might be valuable now to examine the assumptions [9] one by one, from the standpoint of a sociologist, to see where modifications or extensions might make them both more realistic and more useful.

1. *The members of the society are supposed to be normal human beings in essential respects—a "random sample" of the population of the industrial nations of today.* The two parts of the assumption are somewhat inconsistent, as no random sample can be regarded as normal except in the tautological sense of "what is, is." Over 20 per cent of the American people spend some part of their lives under the observation of the psychiatrist and it is well known that only a small portion of the population does not manifest psychopathological symptoms at some time, even though they are not always disabling. It is questionable whether the presence of a certain amount of mental pathology significantly affects the economists' laws, since it does not

---

[7] Frank H. Knight, *Risk, Uncertainty, and Profit* (Boston: Houghton Mifflin, 1921), p. 52.

[8] *Ibid.*, p. 174.

[9] The statement of the assumptions are abbreviated paraphrases from Knight, *ibid.*, pp. 76–80. While other economists might prefer a slightly different statement, my indication of the possible sociological contributions to them is so broad that only a drastic modification of Knight's statement would make the discussion here irrelevant.

create a systematic bias but merely uncoordinated deviations from rationality which can be expected to balance out. Much more important is the failure of the assumption to recognize heterogeneity in the population. This has already been considered in analyzing the effects of class and caste. There is also the equally relevant heterogeneity on the basis of sex, age, ethnic group, etc., which may have effects on economic variables similar to those noted above for caste-class heterogeneity.

2. *It is assumed that the members of the society act with complete "rationality." They are supposed to "know what they want" and to seek it intelligently. They are supposed to know the consequences of their acts when they are performed and to perform them in the light of the consequences.* In the eighteenth and nineteenth centuries, rationality was considered a mechanical process of working out the rules of Aristotelian logic as they applied in any given situation. Today we know that a man can be rational—in the sense of making accurate predictions as to the consequences of his acts—without always being strictly logical. In Mead's terms, rational thought consists of "taking the role of the other," thereby guessing how "the other" will respond to one's own acts. "The other" may be a physical object, for which responses are uniform in any given situation, and a person can predict these responses accurately insofar as he has knowledge of the principles governing the object. The same may be said when "the other" is a person or group of persons. Here the principles include, besides those governing the physiological structure of the human animal, the characteristics of the nonmaterial culture and the particular personality of "the other." All are learned and usually permit a high degree of accuracy in prediction. Our ability to carry on a fairly well organized social existence from day to day depends on the ability of most members of a society to predict, with a sufficiently high degree of accuracy, what the others will do under given conditions. This is the character of rationality, and not conformity to strict rules of logic. From this principle, we may deduce the conditions under which men will not act rationally: when they have not learned the characteristics of the culture and of the specific personality with which they are interacting; when they fail to perceive the relevance of a specific culture or personality characteristic for a given situation; when they have some block (volitional or not) against using their knowledge in a given situa-

tion. Thus, rationality is a function of the condition of the society as well as of the condition of a person. To sum up: The economist who requires that people be rational, as a premise for his science, may find it satisfactory that people can make accurate predictions even if they do not follow the strict rules of logic. In this way the economist can find rationality in a primitive society, swayed by superstition and other forms of illogical practice, as well as in a modern society. He can examine the economic consequences of deviation from rationality relative to the degree of disorganization of the society and to the mental and emotional inadequacy or disturbance of the individual.

The contemporary economist finds that the assumption of rationality need be made only in regard to "transitivity," defined as the consistent ordering of choices such that, for example, a person choosing *a* in preference to *b* and *b* in preference to *c* must also choose *a* in preference to *c*. It is quite possible that what has previously been stated with respect to rationality in the broad sense has relevance for transitivity in the narrow sense. It would be worth while to examine the consequences for transitivity of the individual's (1) incorporating within himself two or more conflicting sets of cultural values; (2) incorporating within himself two or more conflicting roles, taking extreme form in what the psychiatrists refer to as the "dual personality"; (3) giving differential weighting to a given value when in combination with other values; (4) being relatively alienated from all cultural values; and (5) being "other-directed," as compared to the "inner-directed" individual characteristic of Western society before 1900.[10]

There has been a strong tradition among sociologists which leads them to assume that their special concern is the study of the non-rational and "extralogical" in human behavior. To a considerable extent this arises out of the economist's failure to explain all of human behavior with his assumption of rationality. Insofar as sociology grew up as a discipline dealing with the residua after the economist carved out the subject matter of his discipline, the division of labor between the fields was assumed to be that between the rational and the non-rational. The balance set up by Adam Smith between the "wealth of nations" and the "theory of moral sentiments" was followed by many

[10] These terms are taken from David Riesman, Reuel Denney, and Nathan Glazer, *The Lonely Crowd* (New Haven, Conn.: Yale University Press, 1950).

economists and sociologists.[11] Of course, there were some economists, such as Ricardo or Nassau Senior, who regarded all behavior as rational and thus left no room for sociology, or who considered the nonrational as random and therefore not subject to scientific study. On the other hand, there were institutional economists, such as Veblen, and sociologists, ranging from Sumner to Durkheim, who regarded all behavior as determined by nonrational factors and thus left no room for theoretical economics.

By all these students the rational was defined as the pursuit of self-interest, and self-interest was ethnocentrically defined as economic gain in the form of goods and money. The battle was joined whenever the theoretical economist found his predictions about human behavior to be accurate, or when the economic determinist found an economic factor motivating some ostensibly noneconomic aspect of life, or when, on the other hand, the sociologist or the institutional economist seemed to demonstrate that important behavior was nonrational or that economic phenomena had noneconomic sources or motivations. It is the fashion today for economists and sociologists to attempt to be "interdisciplinary" and to avoid open conflict, but they have never resolved this issue or bridged the "division of labor" between them and this is one reason why they have not yet been mutually helpful on concrete research problems.

As noted in a later chapter,[12] the sociologist need not take the position that man's behavior is often nonlogical, which is what the economist means by "irrationality." The point of view can be taken that practically all human behavior is logical in the sense that it is consistent and deducible from certain premises, even if these premises have not been made explicit. If this proposition is true, the *framework* of the theoretical economist's model can be used to study any behavior. But the specific assumption that every individual seeks to maximize only material wealth can be partially discarded (where it does not lead to accurate predictions), not only because it is an ethnocentric assumption, but also because it does not apply even within our own culture much of the time. What can be substituted is that the

[11] Pareto, for example, distinguished between "logical thought" and behavior on the basis of "residues." See Vilfredo Pareto, *Traité de sociologie générale* (Paris: Librairie Payot, 1919).

[12] See Chapter 21. In the terminology in this paragraph and in Chapter 21, the word "logical" is equivalent to the economist's term "rational."

individual seeks to maximize *satisfactions*, which are, on the one hand, the values of his culture or subculture and, on the other hand, the unique desires of his personality. Values and desires are ascertainable and even measurable; they have considerable stability; and sociologists and psychologists have regularly studied them and can contribute knowledge of them to the economist who can thereupon insert them into his model. In other words, the sociologist and psychologist need not assume that human behavior is nonlogical and that their job is to study this nonlogical behavior. They can rather assume with the economist that practically all deliberate behavior is logical, but derived from premises that are by no means entirely materialistic, and that it is their job to specify and measure these premises. This approach would promise a more fruitful relation between the economist and the sociologist.

3. *People are free to act as their motives prompt in the production, exchange, and consumption of goods. Every person is the final and absolute judge of his own welfare and interests.* The adoption by early economists of the free-will philosophy of the eighteenth and nineteenth centuries antedated the development of the rest of social science, which has, like all sciences, been discovering one determinism after the other. No analysis of individual behavior today could be regarded as realistic without taking into consideration the determinism of cultural tradition and power structures, for example. However, we now also know that free will can exist only because of these social determinisms. Without social organization, there would be chaos, and no one would be able to accomplish anything but a minimum of animal acts. Thus, free will exists and the economist may assume it, but he must recognize that it is relative to a certain type of social organization. This should be no restriction on economic theory, but rather should open new, more realistic possibilities to it.

4. *It is assumed that there is complete absence of physical obstacles to the making, executing, and changing of plans at will; that is, there must be "perfect mobility" in all economic adjustments and no costs involved in movements or changes.* Everyone is aware of the obstacles to the movement of capital and equipment, especially across international boundaries, although more studies are needed regarding the circumstances under which potential capitalists are willing to take

risks. As for the mobility of labor, social scientists have been studying migration for decades and much is now known of a fairly exact nature.

It is known, for example, that people will migrate when there are numerous job opportunities elsewhere and their present location is depressed, but not when their present area is simply more depressed than other depressed areas.[13] It is known that people prefer to accept job opportunities close to their present location rather than better job opportunities at greater distances.[14] It is known that Negroes, one of the chief sources of manpower during times of manpower shortage in the United States, tend to migrate first from southern rural areas to southern urban areas, then to the large northern cities where there are already large concentrations of Negroes, and then sometimes to outlying localities where there are job opportunities. There is a lag in this migration, and seldom is it reversed.[15] It is known that people migrate for rational but noneconomic reasons, and it is known that they rationally do not migrate when they believe that relative lack of job opportunities in the home community is temporary. These are just a few of the generalizations about habits of migration discovered by recent research. They represent modifications of the assumption of perfect mobility that can be integrated into economic theory. Further study needs to be given to the attitudes of workers as a limiting factor in the actions of management.

5. *There must be perfect, continuous, costless intercommunication among all individual members of the society.* The type of communication envisaged in the assumption is that which is achieved through what Mead called "significant symbols" — that is, sounds or gestures which allow the listener to ascertain what the speaker intends or pretends to mean.[16] Sociologists also study other forms of communication, and have found that communication through significant symbols has certain defects depending on the condition of the society. Another type of communication relevant to the interest of the economist is that

[13] Harry Jerome, *Migration and Business Cycles* (New York: National Bureau of Economic Research, 1926).

[14] Samuel A. Stouffer, "Intervening Opportunities: A Theory Relating Mobility and Distance," *American Sociological Review,* 5 (December 1941), 845–867.

[15] Gunnar Myrdal, with the assistance of Richard Sterner and Arnold Rose, *An American Dilemma* (New York: Harper, 1944), Chap. 8.

[16] George H. Mead, *Mind, Self and Society* (Chicago: University of Chicago Press, 1934).

which is achieved through "natural signs" — spontaneous and more or less unconscious reactions to internal or external stimuli which an observer can often correctly interpret. Everyone is familiar with the "poker face," although no one has yet studied the economic implications of it, but there is also the opposite phenomenon of unintentionally revealing one's motives or condition without intending to do so, and this likewise requires study. One kind of natural signs is known to be highly contagious, so that an observer has an impulse to imitate the one making the signs. These are the natural signs expressing excitement of all sorts, including that due to fear. History provides many examples of panic determining short-run economic behavior,[17] and if we would be frank about some of our current economic behavior, we should find numerous semipanics acting as partial determinants of it.[18]

If we turn our discussion to the more important communication through significant symbols, we find that there are numerous defects in it. Our society has an unusually large number of barriers to communication, resulting not only from geographic factors but also from such social factors as class and caste, group or clique affiliation, and ideology. Studies have been conducted under controlled conditions showing that in an ordinary lecture given in straightforward English only about 60 per cent of the content was understood by the average literate member of the audience. What communication there is, is not always accurate, of course, and it does not reach all interested persons simultaneously. One study has been conducted showing that rumor has an influence on that economically most perfect of markets, the stock market.[19]

6. *Every member of the society is to act as an individual only, in entire independence of all other persons. He must be free from social wants, prejudices, monopolies, or any other values which are not completely manifested in market dealing.* This is, of course, a statement of the impossible. As Park pointed out, "Man is not born human. It is

---

[17] See, for example, Michael Harrison, *Gambler's Glory: The Story of John Law of Lauriston* (London: Rich and Cowan, 1940).

[18] For example, the summer of 1949 saw many merchants drastically cutting inventories and many manufacturers cutting production because of a widespread "feeling" that a depression was due to appear, rather than because of any objective signs that economic conditions would deteriorate. The term "psycho-recession" has recently gained currency.

[19] Arnold M. Rose, "Rumor and the Stock Market," *Public Opinion Quarterly,* 15 (Fall 1951), 461–486.

only slowly and laboriously, in fruitful contact, cooperation, and conflict with his fellows, that he attains the distinctive qualities of human nature." [20]

In a recent writing, Knight has recognized fully the unreality of his earlier assumption:

From a sociological or culture-historical standpoint, the individual is not the basic reality, but is rather insignificant. He is the ephemeral carrier of a "culture," a complex of institutions, beliefs, feelings, and usages—something like the proverbial water-drop in a flowing river. Certainly the family is the real unit in what is called individualistic society, and many communities fill in between the family and the state and world-order. The family is the economic unit in consumption, and for the most part in production. And a productivity system of distribution, even if defensible for the individuals who are "producers," does not seem very ethical in relation to non-producing "dependents," a majority of the population. These facts do not invalidate the principle of individual liberty; but this needs to be considered in the light of the limitations which they set. [21]

But this fact does not limit "market dealing." A prejudice or a social want can operate on the market just as can an "individual want." One of the weaknesses of classical economics was in assuming that competition results only from individual operations and that monopoly is the inevitable result of cooperation. Actually, a social organization may promote competition, whereas an individual can maintain a monopoly. It is likely that some of the efforts of trade-unions have resulted in bringing wages up to the level of the marginal productivity of the worker, whereas economists have tended to concentrate only on those activities of trade-unions which place wages at a monopolistically high level. In Sweden, the entrance of the government and of cooperatives into manufacturing seems to have resulted in creating a competitive market in certain industries in which previously there had been only cartels.

Contemporary economists have become aware that group decisions are not equivalent logically, as well as behaviorally, to the sum of the decisions of the individuals making up the group. [22] As specialists on the characteristics of groups, sociologists might be able to make a con-

[20] Robert E. Park, *Principles of Human Behavior* (Chicago: Zalaz Corp., 1915), p. 9.
[21] Frank H. Knight, in Glenn E. Hoover (ed.), *Twentieth Century Economic Thought* (New York: Philosophical Library, 1950), pp. 509–510.
[22] Kenneth J. Arrow, *Social Choice and Individual Values* (New York: Wiley, 1951).

tribution to the economists' need to know in what ways group decisions differ from individual ones.

7. *There must be no preying of individuals upon one another. There must be no way of acquiring goods except through production and free exchange in the open market.* The free enterprise and market system itself has made necessary the development of certain institutions which violate the assumption, thus creating a certain instability within the system. One of these institutions is the securities exchange, which grew up as a necessary adjunct of the joint-stock company or corporation. Without it, there would be no way of having a free market for the purchase and sale of capital. But along with its capital-providing function, the stock market has taken on the character of a gambling establishment. This seldom restricts the primary function of providing capital, but it does allow one to acquire goods by means other than production and free exchange.

Another exception arises through the use of the gift. The gift is a universal phenomenon, but its use as an instrument of power has become refined in our civilization. One of the latest uses of the philanthropic gift, through the modern institution known as a "foundation," is to permit control of a producing corporation to remain in the hands of a single heir when estate taxes would ordinarily force him to liquidate his inheritance. The foundation gets the wealth and is tax-exempt, whereas the heir retains the power which the wealth represents. Not all foundations are of this type, of course.

Finally it should be pointed out that what Knight calls "preying" is not limited to a few professional or incidental robbers who have little total effect on the running of the economy. There are two other types of crime—that of the big rackets and gambling syndicates which are tied in with legitimate business and government, and that which is intrinsically a part of most businesses [23]—which have a marked and constant effect on the economy. Again, these factors and institutional activities are capable of being integrated into economic theory.

8. *The motives for division of labor and for exchange must be present and operative. The principal condition is diversification of wants associated with specialization of productive capacities or dispositions, or with physical restrictions on the range of productive activity.* This condition obtains in our society, although not in many other societies.

[23] Edwin H. Sutherland, *White Collar Crime* (New York: Dryden Press, 1949).

The many studies of consumer purchases,[24] however, show a wide differential in the variation of wants among the various subgroups of the population. And, of course, various productive jobs have different degrees of specialization. It would be valuable to explore the economic consequences of this differential in diversity.

The eight points reviewed are one eminent economist's formulation of the assumptions behind the theory of free enterprise economy. While he recognizes that all are fictitious, he believes that all but one —that on the immediate distribution of knowledge—are practically realized in everyday life.[25] It has been shown here that a sociologist would question the practical realization of most of them, but it has also been suggested that the modifications would not destroy the theory but rather would offer it opportunities to expand in new directions. There are laws governing the modifications as well as the original assumptions. Instead of clinging to a prescientific psychology and sociology under which it happened to grow up, economics would be benefited by adapting some of the findings of those sister disciplines for its own development. The procedure used here in suggesting how sociology might aid economics is simply one of many possible ways; other approaches could be and undoubtedly will be used when economists and sociologists come to work together on common research problems.

[24] The last large-scale study was conducted by the U.S. Departments of Labor and Agriculture in 1935–1936.

[25] Knight, *Risk, Uncertainty, and Profit* (Boston: Houghton Mifflin, 1921), pp. 86–87.

11

Public Opinion Research Techniques
Suggested by Sociological Theory

PUBLIC *opinion research has been a marginal field, straddling psychology, journalism, market research, and sociology. Research in this field has had a high technical quality, but it has been relatively weak on the side of theory, despite the fact that some early writers provided the beginnings of a framework of theory in public opinion. Theory, of course, has relevance to method as well as to subject matter. Method in the study of public opinion has been of the common-sense variety, subject only to the refinements of sampling theory, which developed outside the social sciences. This chapter shows the relevance of sociological theory to specific public opinion research techniques.*

PUBLIC opinion research got its start in the practical hands of market researchers, industrial engineers, and newspaper and magazine editors. Academic psychologists and sociologists had an early interest in attitude studies in small groups but did not participate significantly in public opinion polling until the mid-1930s. As a consequence, the research procedures were developed before social science theory could influence them very much. That lag has existed to the present time, although periodically psychologists and sociologists issue critiques of one or another aspect of public opinion research in terms of the knowledge built up in their specialized disciplines.[1] The lag is likely to continue far into the future, since public opinion polling faces its own dynamic problems, since the academic critics make their points didac-

[1] See, for example, Daniel Katz, "Three Criteria: Knowledge, Conviction, and Significance," *Public Opinion Quarterly*, vol. 4, no. 2 (1940), pp. 277–284; Quinn McNemar, "Opinion-Attitude Methodology," *Psychological Bulletin*, 43 (1946), 289–374; Alfred M. Lee, "Sociological Theory in Public Opinion and Attitude Studies," *American Sociological Review*, 12 (1947), 312–323; Alfred M. Lee, "Social Determinants of Public Opinion," *International Journal of Opinion and Attitude Research*, 1 (1947), 12–29; John Dollard, "Under What Conditions Do Opinions Predict Behavior?" *Public Opinion Quarterly*, vol. 12, no. 4 (1948), pp. 623–632.

tically without illustrating them with concrete research, and since inertia or expense provides a motive for the pollsters not to change their policies. Nevertheless, theoretical suggestions from the academic people will continue to flow into the public opinion literature and will probably gradually influence public opinion research as they have in the past.

This chapter will take up some general sociological principles which have relevance for public opinion research but which do not seem to have been adequately presented in the public opinion literature.

The first such general principle stems from a distinction made by Robert E. Park between a public and a mass.[2] The public is a social grouping in which all the members are actively in communication with one another, either directly or indirectly. A mass, on the other hand, is an agglomeration of people who are recipients of communication from a central source and who are not in communication with one another. An archetype of a public would be the informal group that meets at the village store when the mail comes in, and such a public might extend to a whole nation if there is some object of common interest about which people form chains of communication. An archetype of a mass would be a movie audience in which the participants—unaware of one another's identity—sit passively for several hours absorbing the communication from the screen, and such a mass might extend to a whole nation if a widely scattered poster attracts the attention of the mass but is not considered interesting enough to talk about. In a public all points of view are brought to bear on an issue; each member is made aware of the varying viewpoints and of other relevant facts, and he is encouraged to present his own point of view to members of his community who engage him in conversation. In a mass, however, the only communication is from a single source (a "propagandist" in the broadest sense of the term), and the only opposition to the passive acceptance of this communication by an individual as his own point of view depends on incidental experience he may have had with the subject of the communication.

The result for the opinion itself is that public opinion is rational

---

[2] First presented in Park's doctoral dissertation, *Masse und Publikum* (University of Bonn, 1904), and later restated in Robert E. Park and Ernest W. Burgess, *Introduction to the Science of Sociology* (Chicago: University of Chicago Press, 1921), Chaps. XII and XIII. For a recent statement, see Herbert Blumer, in Alfred M. Lee (ed.), *New Outline of the Principles of Sociology* (New York: Barnes and Noble, 1946), pp. 241–250.

or rationalized, whereas mass opinion is superficial. That is, public opinion—as a resultant of many communications, of conflicts of diverse viewpoints, of modifications arising from the need to integrate the opinion with heterogeneous experiences and cultural backgrounds —is a product of much thought and may therefore be said to be rational. It is not necessarily logical in the sense that all fact and value premises are made explicit, and all relevant facts may not be available. But public opinion is rational in the sense that it has been thought over and integrated into the framework of existing ideas and attitudes. Mass opinion, on the other hand, is simply the resultant of an experience that is added to, not integrated into, the mind. It has no support except that given to it by repetition.

The consequences for public opinion research are fairly obvious. If the opinion investigated meets the criteria of public opinion, it will come out without much probing (assuming there are no moral blocks to its expression), the individual respondent will have his mind fairly well made up and will not have to "hunt around" for an answer, and different wordings of the question should elicit the same answer. Sometimes the respondent will not find a check-list answer to the question sufficient to express his opinion fully and he will tend to inform the interviewer of conditions under which he would answer differently. If the opinion investigated is part of mass opinion, on the other hand, the respondent will have to search for an answer. He will always be satisfied with a brief answer to the question, and different wordings of the question may elicit different answers from him.

We might also distinguish public opinion from mass opinion in terms of the greater stability of the former, since it is less subject to modification by propaganda. But this may be a misleading distinction, since public opinion is flexible and will change when social conditions change. Public opinion can also be changed if new facts and new points of view are brought to public attention. The distinction might better be stated in terms of the greater reliability of public opinion, in the technical sense of the term "reliability." If an issue is talked over, thought over, and subjected to divergent points of view and varying considerations, then varying forms of a question, asked under varying circumstances, are much more likely to elicit the same results than if the issue is newly or superficially presented to the respondents. Public opinion is more stable than mass opinion also because propaganda which makes only an emotional appeal, and does not present new facts or new insights, is less able to influence it.

A second sociological principle which has implications for public opinion research is that in contemporary urbanized society an individual is likely to belong to a variety of unintegrated groups which make different demands on him.[3] The very heterogeneity of our society which creates the diverse viewpoints that we wish to measure by polling people also creates a lack of uniformity in attitudes within a single individual. Probably few people anywhere have a completely uniform and consistent attitude toward any significant social object, and probably least of all in our own society. Each social role we take requires that we have a somewhat different attitude toward a social object. Just as we are somewhat different persons in our offices, in our homes, in our churches, in our various clubs, on our vacations, on our business trips, in our contacts with close friends and with superficial acquaintances, so we frequently have and express different attitudes toward the same social object in these varying social roles. It would be a valuable study in public opinion if the same questions on such subjects as international policy, race relations, the role of women, or social security were to be asked of the same group of subjects in two diverse social situations.

Public opinion researchers are accustomed to controlling their sample on "background factors" such as economic status, rural-urban residence, etc., in order to make sure that each segment of the population receives its proper weight in the expression of public opinion. They may also have to learn to control their sample for the type of social situation in which the opinion is expressed. The man who voices one opinion toward the role of women at the front door of his home may express a quite different attitude as he leaves his lodge. The person who holds forth on his political attitudes while relaxing in a park may manifest different political attitudes when confronted with a ballot in the privacy of a polling booth. These diversities may not exist for all kinds of attitudes or for all kinds of persons, but we do not yet know the conditions under which we may expect a single individual to hold different attitudes toward the same social object. Social psy-

[3] See, for example, Charles H. Cooley, *Social Process* (New York: Scribner, 1918); Louis Wirth, "Urbanism as a Way of Life," *American Journal of Sociology,* 44 (1938), 1-24.

chologists have long observed that an individual's *behavior* is frequently not consistent; we must assume that his *attitudes* are also not consistent under varying circumstances. Since the public opinion researcher is concerned not with the attitudes of a single individual but with the net consequences of the attitudes of a whole population, he need not bother with all the possible variations. He must, however, if he is to present an accurate picture, weight his sample for the types of situations under which the opinion is expressed.

A third sociological principle is that different groups or social roles have different significances for those who participate in them.[4] It is a continuing interest of sociologists to determine what social groups do most to satisfy needs or confer status, and what social roles are perceived as most desirable or most important. We are as yet far from having satisfactory knowledge; degree or intensity of group loyalty is still analyzed in terms of the factors influencing it rather than measured for comparisons among groups. There are some studies that trace the declining influence of the family and nationality groups on adult attitudes and others that suggest the growing influence of the occupational group, but they are hardly in a form to be used systematically by public opinion researchers in assigning weights to opinions obtained from different groups or elicited in different situations. They can be used, however, for considerations such as the following: If a group known to have strong and growing value for its members begins to swing its weight to influence their attitudes in a certain direction, their attitudes are likely to move in that direction. This is probably one of the things that happened in the 1948 national elections, when the labor and farm organizations put more and more effort into their campaigns to get members to vote for certain candidates. The implication for the public opinion researcher, if he wishes to estimate trends, is to keep his eye on the activities of powerful social organizations as they increase or decrease their efforts to influence the opinions of their members.

A fourth sociological principle is that broad population divisions, such as those of class and caste, may have excellent communication within them but that informal communications will much less readily

---

[4] The sociologist who early contributed most to the understanding of social roles was Charles H. Cooley. See his *Human Nature and the Social Order* (New York: Scribner, 1902), and his *Social Organization* (New York: Scribner, 1909).

cross into another class or caste.[5] Since communication is the basis of public opinion formation, we should expect sharp divisions between classes and castes in both the content and trends of public opinion. In the past election or two, public opinion researchers were aware that factors considered important in making up the minds of whites had little influence among Negroes. We must be prepared for even more discoveries of that sort. It may be, for example, that as whites are more and more swayed by a fear of communism and Russia, Negroes will have little of that experience. If this should be, the two groups will react quite differently to propaganda put out by the two dominant political parties. The same might be true of class divisions. For example, increasing exposure to the Republican campaign against the "welfare state" may gain that party increasing support from the middle class but decreasing support from the lower class. The public opinion researcher cannot assume that no change in the proportion of the total population favoring a certain policy means that there is stability in public opinion on this issue. He must, as he frequently does, break down his total population into those groups within which different communications or varying interpretations of the same communication may be circulating.

Such broad social groupings as class and caste also embody culture differences which manifest themselves in public opinion research as differences in the connotations of words. Public opinion researchers have become aware of the need for changing both the form and wording of a question when they wish to secure comparable findings in two different countries. They need to adapt the same principle, although in lesser degree, when they move from one class to another. The procedure now widely used is to try to find words and question forms which transcend culture differences within our society. But this is not always possible, as Kinsey, for example, found in the study of the most common forms of sexual behavior. Variations in wording can be used to increase the comparability and generalizability of findings, if we recognize significant culture differences within the American population.

A familiar sociological concept is that of the mores. Its very popularity has lessened its scientific usefulness, since its extended use has

<hr>

[5] See, for example, Allison Davis, Burleigh B. Gardner, and Mary R. Gardner, *Deep South* (Chicago: University of Chicago Press, 1941).

changed the meaning which Sumner[6] originally gave it. Sumner used the concept "mores" to refer to those traditional ways of doing things from which no deviation could be tolerated, as any deviation was regarded as a threat to the existence of the group and all its moral standards. To most people who use the term "mores" today, it means simply "customs" without any connotation of necessity or social welfare. Although few practices in our society correspond to Sumner's use of the term, occasionally in the course of public opinion research we come across people who regard it as grossly indecent or socially dangerous to express certain attitudes. The question may then be raised as to whether we have encountered a true example of the mores and had better not ask questions on that subject of certain groups in the population. Subjects on which there have been such experiences include religion, sexual practices, certain kinds of race relations, and violent crimes. Since mores are never matters of public opinion, there can be no discussion of them or questions about them.

Before we reach the conclusion that we are up against the mores when we ask questions that elicit strong or violent resistances and that the subject under study cannot be explored by opinion research, we might examine the possibility that they are rather pseudomores. Pseudomores may be defined as those customs which people believe to be mores for other people but from which they personally deviate secretly. Occasionally good friends will exchange information about these deviations, but they would be afraid to speak about them publicly. The Kinsey study has, of course, revealed that several behavior patterns and attitudes which were previously thought to be mores actually are pseudomores. On the surface, the pseudomores are as difficult to investigate through public opinion research techniques as are the mores themselves, although for different reasons. However, by stating questions indirectly rather than directly, and by creating an assumption that the interviewer is aware and tolerant of deviant practices, the pseudomores can frequently be successfully studied in public opinion surveys. During World War II, such an approach revealed a surprisingly large proportion of persons (in a nonrepresentative sample) who admitted a hope that the war would continue for some time.

The whole matter of public versus private attitudes used to intrigue

[6] William Graham Sumner, *Folkways* (Boston: Ginn, 1906).

social psychologists,[7] but it has recently been ignored in the quest for practical and measurable results. In earlier decades, perhaps too much was made of the difference. It was then maintained that most people held both public and private attitudes about most subjects, and that it was impossible to learn about private attitudes simply by asking questions. Since it was later found that public opinion research techniques elicited much of what researchers and practical people wanted, the distinction gradually came to be ignored. The distinction might prove valuable, however, in studying opinions about certain subjects (even outside the pseudomores).

A number of recent sociological studies have indicated that subjects which involve the highest types of group ideals are probably the focus of at least two kinds of attitudes. Questions regarding the role of fairness and impartiality in behavior toward minority groups, for example, will usually elicit a large proportion of expressions of desire to be fair and yet of willingness to practice discrimination.[8] Both of these are public attitudes in response to two different kinds of questions— some of the general kind, others referring specifically to minority groups. The inconsistency suggests that there are private attitudes behind both of these public attitudes which can only be inferred and that behavior is predicated on private as well as public attitudes. People who express attitudes of prejudice toward a minority group do not manifest only discriminatory behavior patterns toward them; nor do people who express general principles of fairness and equalitarianism manifest only nondiscriminatory behavior patterns. This suggests to the public opinion researcher that he should try to elicit the entire gamut of public attitudes which might be relevant to a given behavior pattern, so that private attitudes might more readily be inferred. Or, better still, the public opinion researcher might try to experiment with the behavior of his respondents and then ask them questions as they respond in varying ways. The rationalized answers obtained under those circumstances are very revealing of private attitudes.

To illustrate, two findings will be cited from a fascinating study by

[7] See, for example, Richard L. Schanck, "A Study of a Community and Its Groups and Institutions Conceived of as Behaviors of Individuals," *Psychological Monographs*, vol. 43, no. 195 (1932), pp. 44ff; Ellsworth Faris, *The Nature of Human Nature* (New York: McGraw-Hill, 1937), pp. 144–154.

[8] Gunnar Myrdal, with the assistance of Richard Sterner and Arnold Rose, *An American Dilemma* (New York: Harper, 1944).

Gerhart Saenger,[9] throughout which he recognizes the need to plumb private attitudes as the basis for understanding actual behavior. Saenger interviewed persons who had just been waited on by Negro sales clerks in a large department store but who did not know they had been observed by the interviewers. He interviewed an equal number who had been waited on by white sales clerks at the same counters. The proportions opposing Negro sales clerks in department stores were about the same in both groups! He also found that some of those who had just been waited on by Negro sales clerks in food departments said they were not opposed to being waited on by Negroes in food departments but would be opposed to Negro clerks in clothing departments, while some of those who had just been waited on by Negro sales clerks in clothing departments said they were not opposed to Negroes in clothing departments but would be opposed to them in food departments. On the basis of these and similar findings he was able to predict that the department store would not lose customers by hiring Negro sales personnel—a prediction later verified as accurate by the manager. To have accepted the simple proportion of those opposed to Negro sales clerks as an indication that the new policy would hurt sales, without having observed the respondents' behavior, would have led to an error.

One other sociological theory may be called on for guidance to the public opinion researcher. This is Simmel's theory of the "stranger." [10] The public opinion interviewer, even though he identifies his purpose and indicates the organization for which he works, is a stranger to practically all his respondents. It is by virtue of his role as a stranger, and especially of the anonymity which he can allow the respondent to maintain toward him, that the interviewer can secure some of his most confidential and honest answers. Having a mistaken idea of rapport, some interviewers strive to establish their personal identity and a possible relation to the respondent. If the interviewer's effort is successful, the respondent can no longer answer the questions freely and with the sense of security that comes from the belief that his answers can never reflect back on him or be used against him. If he loses his anonymity, the respondent will answer in another social role—as an acquaintance

<hr>

[9] "Customer Reactions to the Integration of Negro Sales Personnel," paper read to the American Psychological Association, Boston, September 1948.

[10] Georg Simmel, *Soziologie* (Leipzig: Duncker und Humblot, 1908), pp. 685–691.

whose statements might be repeated to those who know him as a certain type of person. This may well serve to inhibit the fullness or accuracy of his answers.

It is necessary, of course, for the interviewer to establish his authenticity by indicating his innocent purpose and the legitimacy of his organization. He may also seek to establish confidence in himself as a person. But beyond that he should remain a stranger, for the purposes of most kinds of public opinion research. The suggestion is of greatest value in small towns, where the chances are large that the interviewer has an acquaintanceship with the respondent. In such a setting it is most often wise to import an interviewer from outside the town.

The sociological theories from which these suggestions for public opinion research are drawn have a long and respected tradition of thought and empirical research to support them. They are not completely verified, of course, and when transferred from one scientific setting to the new one of public opinion research they would need further testing; they are therefore presented in the form of suggestions. They are especially valuable, however, as they help to throw additional light on some problems which have long disturbed the more thoughtful public opinion researchers and on other matters which have never been questioned in public opinion research. The older and more theoretical disciplines need to be probed constantly for such suggestions if the new field of research is to have maximum validity.

12

The Hiatus between Sociology and Psychology

THE *relations between economics and sociology are so undeveloped that one can only put out tentative feelers to see whether there are possibly areas of common research interest. Differences in the historical roots of psychology and sociology—in the realms of assumption, theory, and method—have often prevented effective communication and collaboration between these two disciplines. For the most part, however, relations are so mature between them that one can make explicit some of the remaining gaps, as is done in the following chapter.*

PSYCHOLOGY and sociology have been very closely affiliated in the United States. Along with anthropology, they have sought to be "basic" social sciences—that is, to explain the fundamentals of human behavior. They share a common field, social psychology. There has always been communication between their respective practitioners, and this communication has been growing.[1] But there have been historical differences between them which have often prevented their intercommunications from being mutually intelligible and which have sometimes prevented effective research collaboration. The purpose of this chapter is to make explicit some of the underlying differences between the disciplines, in the hope that this may lead to more effective communication and research collaboration. There are considerable differences within the ranks of those specializing in each discipline in the degree to which they have made efforts to learn about the researches and points of view of the other discipline. This chapter is

[1] Sargent counted the number of references made to sociologists in textbooks on social psychology written by psychologists and the number of references made to psychologists in textbooks on social psychology written by sociologists and found a trend toward increasing mutual reference. See S. Stansfeld Sargent, "Interdisciplinary Contributions and Cooperation in the Development of Social Psychology," in J. E. Hulett, Jr., and Ross Stagner (eds.), *Problems in Social Psychology* (Urbana: University of Illinois, 1952), pp. 8–9.

primarily relevant to the work of those who have made the most effort to extend their information and thinking to the other discipline. The biases of a sociologist will be evident throughout the discussion.

From its earliest days as an independent discipline, sociology has had as its central problem the question of how individuals learn to act together and to adjust to one another. The basic question raised by psychologists about social factors is what effect they have on individual behavior. The assumptions underlying these two questions are different. The question raised by psychologists assumes that a human individual is biologically equipped with organized behavior patterns and that the influence from other people can be dealt with as a series of more or less specific factors that modify the inherited behavior patterns. The question raised by sociologists assumes that the human individual is born with no organized behavior patterns but rather with an indefinitely large number of biological potentialities ("random movements") which receive organization as a result of social definition and evaluation. The sociologist does not conceive of the "social influence" as so many factors which impinge on the individual as vectors to deflect his behavior from what it might "naturally" be, but as a sort of mold into which the formless individual is poured. The mold is such that in the very process of getting his behavior patterns organized the individual is learning to coordinate with, and adjust to, other individuals, even in conflict and competition. Stated in the unfortunately extreme, but basically representative, terms of F. H. Allport and G. H. Mead, society for the psychologist is *a number* of discrete individuals who can influence one another, while society for the sociologist *is* the mature ("socialized") individual ("me" = "the generalized other").

The methods of research early chosen by the psychologist and the sociologist for the study of human behavior were selected to conform to the assumptions and, in turn, reinforced the implicit acceptance of the assumptions. The psychologist, receiving his methodological training from the experimental natural sciences, adopted the experiment as his basic research tool. Typically, he measured the subjects' behavior in one certain respect before a social factor—the presence of a group, a group product such as a film, or a group characteristic such as cohesiveness—was introduced and then measured the same characteristic of behavior after that social factor was given an opportunity to make its impact on the subjects. He came out with a conclusion that such and such a factor did, or did not, have a measurable influence on human behavior. Sociologists had much less training in the experimental sciences, although they probably had more training in history, descriptive biology, and philosophy, and they chose observation—soon refined with diaries and other "personal documents," questionnaire responses, scales, etc.—as their basic research technique. They came out with descriptions of "functional interrelationships" and "the seamless web of life" (much as did Darwin in another realm of inquiry).

Both psychologists and sociologists have been concerned with the relative influence of heredity and environment in determining human behavior. While psychologists differ considerably among themselves in the relative weights they would assign these two sets of factors, most of them agree that the environmental influences are imposed on the hereditary ones. Most sociologists assume not only that any given behavior is a product of inseparable (even for research purposes) hereditary and environmental influences but also that in order to change any given behavior one must change the environment so that hitherto untapped biological potentialities can come into operation. It is no longer the fashion to debate the relative influences of "heredity versus environment," so psychologists and sociologists have made a formal peace on this issue. But they have never reached agreement on their assumptions in respect to the issue, so that there is still a block in certain kinds of communication between them.

The divergent approaches to "intelligence" may be taken as an example. While psychologists disagree among themselves as to whether it is a single capacity or several distinctive capacities, they consider it as approximately measurable through performance. Taking the psychologist's definition of intelligence as inherited capacity, the sociologist would say that it can never be measured through performance, although typical present performance can be measured and be predictive of future performance and although biological intelligence undoubtedly exists even if as yet it is unmeasurable. For the sociologist, intelligent behavior is an inseparable compound of hereditary and environmental influences, and no one has yet succeeded in holding environmental influences constant to measure the varying influence of differential heredity (although studies of identical twins allow control of heredity even if environment is not systematically varied in them).

Most sociologists are willing to leave the study of the learning process to the psychologists. They have been impressed by the careful and systematic researches on learning by conditioning, trial and error, the formation of Gestalts, and reinforcement. But many sociologists are concerned by the failure of the learning theorists to explain learning by communication of significant symbols. Most people can learn a significant amount by reading a book, listening to a lecture, engaging in a discussion. They must learn a good deal very rapidly in this way. For example, an item culled almost at random from the encyclopedia tells us that Tiberius was the second Roman emperor. Assuming presumptuously that most readers of this book did not know this fact before, I know that they can learn it now, just by reading it. Furthermore, a significant number will remember it for many months and years to come, and probably an even larger number would "recognize" it if it were brought to their attention again at some time in the distant future.

During the course of a year each of us must learn millions of meanings like this one, and none of the processes described by psychologists seems to explain this vast amount of extremely rapid learning satisfactorily. It is quite possible, on the other hand, that a slight modification in psychological theory will account for it. But until that modification is made, sociologists will feel a barrier between themselves and psychologists as they have to account for the socialized man's knowledge which permits him to adjust to millions of different expectations held by other people. Man is not born with a culture, but he learns one or more of them, material and nonmaterial, overt and covert, general and specialized, structured and diffuse, definitional and evaluative. This the psychologist has yet to explain.

Within the ranks of psychologists and of sociologists there are divergent views concerning the nature of personality, and it is probable that a considerable number from each discipline hold substantially the same views on this subject. But within each discipline there are some who hold a point of view concerning personality which would not be found at all in the other discipline. There are some psychologists—Sheldon and Cattell, for example—who consider personality to be a resultant of a number of inherited tendencies to behave in certain ways. On the other hand, some sociologists—Thomas and Faris, for example—have held that personality is the subjective aspect of culture. These two viewpoints are quite opposed and neither could be reconciled with the other, although it should be understood that many psychologists and sociologists do not agree with their colleagues named above.

One of the interesting recent developments in the gradual harmonization of sociology and psychology is the sociologist's acquisition of techniques of research from the psychologist and the psychologist's acquisition of theory and concepts from the sociologist. During this process, each side is somewhat amused at the naïveté of the other who is struggling to learn. For the sociologist the harmonization has had an advantage. Previously disturbed by inferiority feelings about his theory, as it was never subjected to rigorous testing, he can now recoup his self-esteem when he sees Asch demonstrating that group pressures will produce distortion in perception, Bruner showing how social status is related to patterns of perception, Sherif demonstrating that groups establish norms which determine the perceptions of their members, Cantril finding that previous experience selects cues from the environment for establishing adjustments of the individual to his environment, Mowrer discovering that when behavior is blocked a mental process occurs in which trial and error takes place imaginatively in the effort to overcome the block. The sociologist has been assuming these things to be true for the past thirty to fifty years because his observations of ongoing social behavior have led him to believe that such assumptions were the only ones that would square with the "facts" (although he has ignored the complexity and uncontrolled character of these facts). He has been mistaken in merely assuming these things without attempting to prove his assumptions, but he has not had to write books almost completely repudiating previous decades of theory and research, as has been done by such psychologists as Asch,[2] Cantril,[3] Mowrer,[4] and Snygg and Combs.[5] On the other hand, since the psychologist is catching up with the sociologist in theory, and using advanced methods of research to boot,

[2] S. A. Asch, *Social Psychology* (New York: Prentice-Hall, 1952).
[3] Hadley Cantril, *The 'Why' of Man's Experience* (New York: Macmillan, 1950).
[4] O. H. Mowrer, *Learning Theory and Personality Dynamics* (New York: Ronald Press, 1950).
[5] D. Snygg and A. W. Combs, *Individual Behavior* (New York: Harper, 1949).

the younger students—in sociology as well as in psychology departments—are inclined to attribute the "innovations" to the recent workers in psychology. The younger people are inclined to refer to "Newcomb's role theory," "Sherif's social norm theory," and "Hyman's reference group theory" as though Cooley and Mead had never expounded these concepts thirty to fifty years ago.

There are still several important concepts and observations developed by sociologists which the psychologists have not yet comprehended. Coutu[6] has pointed out that Newcomb and Sargent (as well as Lindesmith and Strauss, who are sociologists) have failed to distinguish between role-taking and role-playing. Newcomb[7] has correctly pointed out the antidemocratic value premise in Le Bon's *The Crowd* but has failed to observe the objective phenomenon of crowd behavior that Le Bon and dozens of his successors among sociologists have described. The California psychologists[8] have made a notable contribution to knowledge with their concept of, and researches on, the "authoritarian personality," but they have failed to consider the concepts of "racism" and "mass society" which provide necessary social contexts for the behavior of the "authoritarian personality" that they are considering.[9] The Yale group of psychologists[10] have made important theoretical and research contributions to the understanding of aggression but have failed to comprehend that aggressive impulses do not always lead to conflict (as some of their fellow psychologists have pointed out), and that group conflict need not always be attended by aggressive impulses—in some kinds of industrial and international warfare, for example. Similarly, from the standpoint of the psychologist, sociologists fail to understand contemporary learning and motivation theory and to realize how far it has advanced from the early work of Pavlov, Thorndike, and McDougall.

The main theoretical hiatus perceived by the sociologist between the psychologist and himself, however, is the previously referred to

[6] Walter Coutu, "Role-Playing vs. Role-Taking: An Appeal for Clarification," *American Sociological Review*, 16 (April 1951), 180–187.

[7] Theodore M. Newcomb, *Social Psychology* (New York: Dryden Press, 1950).

[8] T. W. Adorno *et al., The Authoritarian Personality* (New York: Harper, 1950).

[9] For partial critiques of the work on the "authoritarian personality" along these lines, see Chapter 5 of this volume and my "Intergroup Anxieties in a Mass Society," *Phylon*, 12 (Fourth Quarter 1951), 305–318.

[10] John Dollard *et al., Frustration and Aggression* (New Haven, Conn.: Yale University Press, 1939), and numerous subsequent researches.

misunderstanding as to the meaning of social group, society, and culture. This is serious, as these are core concepts in sociology. For the psychologist, a group is simply a number of interacting individuals; a society is the sum total of groups having some degree of contact within an area; and culture is the sum total of practices transmitted from generation to generation within a society. For the sociologist, a group is a number of persons who can take the role of each of the others in the group simultaneously and thereby predict more accurately than can outsiders the behavior of each of the others; a society is a number of interacting and interdependent groups such that any individual in it can predict the culturally influenced behavior of every other individual in it with reasonable accuracy; and a culture consists of all the meanings and values learned by individuals from others that give specificity and organization to behavior.

An example of a more specific hiatus in terminology may be found in the use of the term "cohesiveness." By "group cohesiveness," sociologists since Durkheim have meant a sense of solidarity or identification with an existing group into which the accidents of birth and/or life experience put them. Sociologists have used the term with respect to nations, classes, ethnic groups, families, and other "nonvoluntary" groups or categories, but seldom with respect to voluntary associations. In the last two decades, some psychologists have used the term "group cohesiveness" in their researches on voluntary associations and have measured it by asking such questions as how many close friends one has in the group, which persons one would like to associate with, how much prestige membership in the group is believed to confer on one. These variables indicate whether an individual will remain in a voluntary association but have little to do with his remaining in a nonvoluntary group, since he is already perforce in the group and cannot get out.

The sociologist would observe that a person may be low on all these variables and yet have a high group cohesiveness, in the sociologist's sense of the term, because he has a sense of identification with his "group" conceived of abstractly. For example, one might despise a large number of persons in his (lower) class and yet have a high sense of class solidarity. Obviously, there is nothing wrong scientifically with using the term "cohesiveness" in either way, but it should be recognized that sociologists and psychologists generally use the term in different ways. The hiatus arises from the fact that sociologists and psychologists generally do not realize that, in using the same word, "cohesiveness," they are employing two distinct concepts, usually with respect to two different kinds of "groups."

There are enough differences between the definitions of core concepts in the two disciplines to warrant further investigation of them if psychologists and sociologists are to engage in fruitful cooperation on common research problems.

13

Problems in the Sociology of Law and Law Enforcement

THE *concrete and historical qualities of the study of law, in the United States, have tended to place that field within the humanities rather than the social sciences. While many teachers and students of the law prefer to think of their discipline as a social science, there has been relatively little concrete effort to tie the field to the so-called basic social sciences of anthropology, psychology, and sociology. What is called the "sociology of law" interests the sociologist but seldom the student of law. This chapter offers some suggestions as to how sociology might contribute to the study of law and law enforcement as the student of law perceives it.*

THERE are at least four general areas of interest to students of law in which the types of research usually conducted by sociologists and social psychologists would be of great usefulness. These concern (1) the formulation of legislative measures, (2) the formulation of judicial decisions, (3) the consequences of laws and judicial decisions, and (4) the function of law.

THE FORMULATION OF LEGISLATIVE MEASURES AND JUDICIAL DECISIONS

When a bill is introduced into a legislature, certain social conditions are presumed to exist which need the correction or change which the bill is designed to effect. A legislative committee conducts hearings, of voluntary or subpoenaed witnesses, to ascertain whether the social conditions are what the bill assumes they are and whether the changes

NOTE: I am indebted to members of the University of Minnesota Law School—primarily Kenneth Davis, William Lockhart, and Monrad Paulsen—for ideas for, and criticisms of, this chapter. They should not be held responsible, however, for the opinion expressed herein.

supposed to be effected by the bill are likely to have the corrective effect desired. Occasionally the legislative committee hearings are a model of painstaking investigation, and several have turned out to be classic descriptions of some important phase of American social life. But there have been two general conditions which limit the effectiveness of the legislative committee hearings as a source of information about relevant social conditions.[1]

One of these conditions is the huge number of bills which the legislative committee is expected to investigate and report on competently to the legislature as a whole. Not only are members of legislatures greatly overworked at present, but they do not have the facilities to accomplish many of the tasks which are set before them. Secondly, there are inherent limitations in the hearing as a source of information about social conditions. The legislative committee has both formal and informal powers to bring a wide variety of witnesses before it and to compel the witnesses to answer honestly. Also, in recent years, congressional committees have added expert personnel to their staffs who operate as combined detectives and library research assistants, thus extending the scope of information brought to the consideration of the committee. Nevertheless these methods of accumulating social information do not exhaust by far the techniques now available to social scientists for adequate and accurate description of social conditions.

The social survey—both of a community as a whole and of some specific condition in a community—has been developing in England, France, and the United States for over a century. Statistical sampling of respondents, scales of measurement, interviewing approaches to secure frank answers, and measures of correlation are among the many techniques that have developed in a growing science to gain adequate description of social conditions but that naturally cannot often be used by an overworked legislative investigating committee or even by its paid assistants.

Occasionally a congressional committee will act to gain the services of experts in social description, such as when in the formulation of the

---

[1] I am here discussing only those legislative hearings which disinterestedly seek facts relevant to the legislation under consideration. It is recognized that there are others which are intended simply to serve as a sounding board for a certain viewpoint or to justify a bill already fully formulated. See, for example, Julius Cohen, "Hearing on a Bill: Legislative Folklore," *Minnesota Law Review*, 37 (December 1952), 34–45.

so-called G.I. Bill of Rights in 1944 the committee on veterans' affairs asked the War Department to conduct a survey among its troops to ascertain soldiers' expectations for going to school after the war and their planned use of other facilities envisaged in the bill. The War Department happened to have a facility, the Research Branch of the Information and Education Division, to conduct such a survey scientifically; but most government agencies do not have such research arms, and congressional committees seldom think of calling on those that do to make use of such research facilities. Yet sociologists and other social scientists are conducting investigations every day which have relevance, or might have relevance, for the kinds of questions which every legislative committee has to pose for itself in formulating or modifying a bill.[2] Great Britain and Sweden, which have far fewer social scientists than does the United States, have made extensive use of social scientists by means of "Royal Commissions" which are asked to prepare the groundwork for important social legislation. In the United States such commissions have been used less systematically, and usually by the executive rather than by Congress, but there have been the Wickersham commission on law enforcement during the 1930s and the President's Commission on Civil Rights during the 1940s, as well as others less well known.

There is another way in which social scientists can be useful in the formulation of legislation. The press of business in both the federal Congress and the state legislature is so great that few legislators do the original drafting of bills today. This work is done by experts, mainly lawyers, on the staffs of legislative committees, of individual legislators, of executive offices of the government, or of private organizations. The drafter of a bill has to know not only the legal technicalities involved, which he is well equipped to know, and the social conditions which the bill is designed to correct, which has already been discussed here, but he also must know the *intent* of a majority of the legislators. Unfortunately, in most cases the drafter of a bill is not in a position to ascertain the intent of the legislators. Generally he is in direct communication with one legislator and at best with a committee composed of perhaps up to a dozen members. Every language has a considerable amount of ambiguity in it, and perhaps

[2] Much of the work that social scientists do is for private "pressure groups," as in the area of race relations.

English has more than other languages, and there can be no doubt that various legislators read different things into the same bill. Courts are kept busy trying to make judgments about ambiguous phrases in legislation and they are frequently obliged to conduct historical investigations into the intent of important pieces of legislation.

Rather than to assume that it will continue to be necessary to conduct these difficult investigations, with inadequate data, into the intent of legislation of perhaps a generation before, it would be feasible to plan now for the future—to conduct investigations, at least for important pieces of legislation, into the intent of legislators while the legislation itself is being considered. Certainly not all the problems facing all future courts concerning a piece of legislation could be clarified by the sort of study proposed, but many ambiguities could be interpreted and there would be available more expressions of legislators' opinion from which future courts could make historical studies of legislative intent. Social psychologists have spent years in perfecting techniques for ascertaining attitudes and statements of intention on matters very similar to those of legislators' intent, and their techniques could readily be transferred to the service of legislatures. This would have two highly beneficial effects: (1) It would increase the likelihood of legislators' obtaining the kind of legislation which they think they are getting; and (2) it would aid the courts in many of their important decisions.

The second area of concern to students of the law on which sociologists could aid materially is very similar to the first area. Judicial decisions, especially those of the higher courts, often have the character of extending and clarifying the law—as many students have long been aware—and consequently the remarks made previously about the need for an understanding of social facts applies almost as much to the judge as it does to the legislator. That is, the judge has to make certain assumptions about the state of social reality in many of his decisions, and this is especially true when he is deciding on general principles that apply outside of the particular case which he happens to have at hand. The judge is much more handicapped than the legislator in ascertaining social conditions, since he does not have a staff or the legislators' extensive power to call witnesses. Thus it has become the function of the attorneys on both sides of every case to present the information to the court that would be relevant for the formulation of the judicial decision. The late Louis Brandeis was, of course, the one who made the most extensive use of the description of relevant social conditions in the briefs he presented as a lawyer to the courts at which he was serving.[3] While the Brandeis brief has received its due acclaim, it has not been extensively emulated or improved in the several decades since Brandeis was acting as a lawyer. Yet the techniques developed by social scientists for acquiring the kind of information which Brandeis used in his briefs have improved vastly during these decades. There seems to be something of a "cultural lag" in the practice of law as compared to the development of relevant social science.

Among the few attorneys practicing before the United States Supreme Court who have systematically used some of the more developed social science techniques and information have been the attorneys for the National Association for the Advancement of Colored People (NAACP). For many years the attorney was Charles Houston, and at present it is Thurgood Marshall. These attorneys have realized the need of the various courts to have specific information about the conditions under which Negroes live that are relevant to the case in question, and they have had an almost unbeaten record in obtaining decisions in their favor since they started practicing before the Supreme Court in 1915.

Their most recent case—that involving school segregation—can be used to illustrate how they make use of expert social science information. The keystone of the case involves the question as to whether state segregation of Negro children from white children in the public schools is illegal under the Fourteenth Amendment. Previous decisions have clearly established the principle that any form of discrimination against Negroes is clearly illegal, but in the case of *Plessy vs. Ferguson* in 1896 the Court established a subprinciple that it was not illegal to segregate Negroes from whites if there was substantially no discrimination or unequal opportunity involved. *Plessy vs. Ferguson* involved the question of separation on public vehicles, but it has been used since 1896 to provide the legal basis for all other forms of legally enforced segregation as well. The NAACP position in the case is that school segregation inevitably and inherently involves discrimination,

[3] See, for example, Muller vs. Oregon, 208 U.S. 412.

and since discrimination is illegal, segregation in the schools must therefore also be illegal.

At the request of the NAACP thirty-two social scientists formulated a brief *amicus curiae* which summarized social science studies relevant to this point.[4] A good deal of evidence was provided to show that school segregation induces in Negro children a sense of inferiority and a realization that they are likely to be handicapped economically, socially, and politically throughout their lives because they are Negroes. The brief cites a study of a representative sample of sociologists, psychologists, and anthropologists, all of whom had made studies of, or had taught courses on, race relations. Ninety per cent of the persons in this sample gave evidence to support the contention that segregation, even if physical facilities are substantially equal, has detrimental psychological effects on Negro children.[5] The brief referred to other studies which show that the impact of a school on a child is not to be measured solely in terms of the size of the school buildings, the number of books available, and the formal training of the teachers. Even here the states maintaining segregation admit that there has not been substantial equality even in some of these things, though they promise to rectify the inequalities within a limited number of years.

Other social science findings relevant to this case are the following conclusions from researches: (1) Segregation creates a false sense of personal superiority in white children which handicaps them in later life when they have to have equalitarian relationships with colored people for diplomatic or economic reasons. (2) The Court's judgment in 1896 that it could not fly in the face of established custom (and physical violence was then used extensively to uphold this "custom") is no longer supportive of segregation today, since custom has changed significantly and violence is much less used to uphold what is left of the old custom. (3) The intent of the Congress (and of the states) in proposing and ratifying the Fourteenth Amendment was clearly to prevent the states from passing discriminatory legislation, and there is some evidence that segregation was included in the legislators' con-

---

[4] "The Effects of Segregation and the Consequences of Desegregation: A Social Science Statement," Appendix to Appellants' Briefs, School Segregation Cases Nos. 8, 101, and 191, in the Supreme Court of the United States, October term, 1952, by 32 social scientists.

[5] M. Deutscher and I. Chein, "The Psychological Effects of Enforced Segregation: A Survey of Social Science Opinion," *Journal of Psychology,* 26 (1948), 259–287.

ception of discrimination. This information is directly relevant to the question which the court has to decide, and the court has always shown its appreciation for having this kind of information brought to its attention.

THE CONSEQUENCES OF LAWS AND JUDICIAL DECISIONS

The third general area in which sociologists may aid the student and practitioner of law is to assess for them the consequences of laws and judicial decisions. All branches of government, as well as many private organizations and individual citizens, seek to ascertain the consequences of specific laws. Besides the time-honored method of observing the historical course of change following the passage of a law, they use the social science techniques of systematic observation and public opinion polls. Not many sociologists, however, have brought their theory and research techniques to this type of study.[6]

One technique that seems to have been little used, except in an informal way, is the controlled experiment.[7] Such a technique is made possible in the United States by the fact that different states adopt substantially the same law at different times, or that some states never adopt a certain law while others do. The effect of the law can be abstracted from other influences operating in the society by systematically comparing the relevant changes, measured statistically, in the states that adopt the law with the comparable changes in the states that do not adopt the law. The date of adoption of the law is arbitrarily set at "year zero" so as to make the states comparable. For example, in my study of the effects of the compulsory mediation law on reducing strikes, the three states having this law—Michigan, 1939; Minnesota, 1939; and Connecticut, 1949—are compared, before and after adoption of the law, with all other states on two measures: workers involved in work stoppages, and man-days lost due to work

[6] European sociologists have been more interested in the study of the effects of specific laws than have American sociologists. An excellent study is that of Vilhelm Aubert, Torstein Eckhoff, and Kurt Sveri, *En lov i sokelyset* (Oslo, Norway: Akademisk forlag, 1952). This is a study of the development of a need for, and effects of, a law controlling the employment of housemaids when the older folk society broke down in Norway.

[7] For two different examples of its use, see Gunnar Myrdal, with the assistance of Richard Sterner and Arnold Rose, *An American Dilemma* (New York: Harper, 1944), pp. 482–483; Arnold M. Rose, "Needed Research on the Mediation of Labor Disputes," *Personnel Psychology*, 5 (Autumn 1952), 187–200.

stoppages. Many other state laws could be tested by the same technique.

The question "What are the effects of a given law?" may be too broad for research. The specific circumstances under which a law does or does not create social change have to be examined. It is equally significant to raise these questions: "What are the limitations of law as a means of inducing social change?" and "How does a law fit in with other social forces which enhance or diminish its influence?"

There has always been an assumption that a judicial decision has some social effect either on the persons involved in the case or on the public at large, whatever theory of law is accepted. The indeterminate sentence in criminal cases and the possibilities of compromise in civil suits have been written into the law partly so that the judge can make a decision within a considerable range of possibilities, depending upon his conception of what would achieve the most effective results for the maintenance of respect for, and the effectiveness of, the law. But again we note the "cultural lag" in the means available to the judge to determine what the effect of his decision is. Judges are busy people, and most of them do not get the opportunity to assess systematically the consequences of previous decisions they have made, which would guide them for future decisions. They often base what judgment they are obliged to make in this respect upon casual experiences and upon newspaper reports. Needless to say, these sources are often highly unreliable.

Social scientists unfortunately have been remiss in ascertaining and measuring the consequences of major court decisions even though they have the techniques to do this. However, even in those few areas where sociologists have measured the effects of certain kinds of judicial decisions there has been practically no communication of these findings to the judges who have to make decisions that are relevant to them. For example, in the area of punishment of juvenile delinquents a number of sociological studies have shown that the sentencing and incarceration of a juvenile delinquent is likely to have the effect of hardening him into more permanent criminal habits.[8] For a very significant number of juvenile first offenders, the mere fact of appearing in a courtroom seems to have the effect of defining them in their

[8] For a summary of such studies, see Paul Tappan, *Juvenile Delinquency* (New York: McGraw-Hill, 1949).

own minds as "criminals." Not only have many judges not been informed of these studies and so have not tried to counteract the effects of contact with the law, but, with the best intentions in the world, they have sought to extend their jurisdiction to nondelinquent children who in some ways did not seem to be receiving the full benefit of parental and community attention. There is some evidence that this well-meaning activity on the part of some judges is creating among children and youths who have not been accused of delinquency a propensity toward antisocial behavior.[9]

The effects of a judicial decision on the public as well as on the criminal need to be studied further. Does a harsh sentence in a criminal case increase respect for law or disrespect and antipathy? Does a light decision in the same kind of criminal case create friendly attitudes toward the court or disrespect for law? What kinds of decisions are most likely to deter potential criminals from engaging in overt criminal acts, especially in such kinds of cases as customs violation, income tax violation, and other "white-collar" crimes? What is the effect of a decision which is made largely on procedural grounds rather than on substantial grounds? In civil suits, what is the effect on the attitudes of the public of delay, court costs, and insufficient evidence to substantiate what the public believes to be an open-and-shut case?

We might extend this line of questioning to ask, irrespective of specific judicial decisions, What is the public image of the role of the courts and judicial process? A high-level committee was formed some years ago in the American Bar Association to inquire into the public conception of the role, the integrity, the motivations, the interrelationships of judges and lawyers, but nothing by way of careful research has come out of the efforts of this committee to date. The committee was properly concerned with the effects of movies, comic strips, magazine stories, and newspaper reports, as well as of specific popular and unpopular decisions, on the public's perception of the court and the legal process. The effect of a judicial decision on the public is not to be measured without regard to the pre-existing framework of attitudes held by the public. A large number of people have conceptions regarding their individual legal rights which are not the same as the actual rights conferred upon them by existing laws. The judge who is concerned with the educational, or crime- and lawsuit-preventing, effects

[9] Tappan, *op. cit.*

of a given judicial decision is not in a position to estimate these effects unless he has some conception as to what people in general think their legal rights are and what is morally considered to be a crime as distinguished from what is legally considered to be a crime.

In criminal law there is an assumption that the severity of punishment should be gauged approximately to the seriousness of the crime. There is nothing absolute about the severity of punishment or the seriousness of the crime, but rather these things are relative to cultural definition and to the current state of public opinion. Hence the assumption that the punishment should fit the crime is an assumption that implicitly measures cultural definition and public opinion. Yet there have been only tangential studies of public opinion concerning the hierarchy of severity of sanction and the hierarchy of seriousness of crimes.

When our society was highly integrated—prior to the Industrial Revolution—the law was, in most cases, probably a direct reflection of cultural definition, and the judge was probably thoroughly familiar with both his culture and current public opinion. Today, no one can be thoroughly familiar with our heterogeneous culture and diversified public opinion without reading thoroughly the social science literature and without making some special studies of how they relate to the types of cases with which he is concerned.[10] The difficulty in simply assuming without question that the law actively reflects current custom is revealed by the variation in sanctions for identical crimes among the various states and by the variation among judges in applying sanctions for identical crimes when leeway is given—as it generally is—under the law. Judges are obliged to make assumptions about the popular conceptions regarding the seriousness of crimes and of the severity of sanctions they are permitted to apply (within the limits set by law), especially in such rapidly developing areas as administrative and business law, and it is likely that they would appreciate some more accurate and systematic studies to guide them in formulating the assumptions they have to make. This is especially true, of course, in trials that excite great popular interest. Some careful surveys are needed of the effect of such trials on public opinion and of the influence of newspapers and other mass media in reporting

[10] Even this might not be sufficient since, unfortunately, social scientists do not conduct studies describing all aspects of contemporary culture.

these trials, both for the necessary interpretation of what is going on in the courtroom and for the benefit of the public.

Even if it is maintained that the law should not reflect current culture, but a more abstract justice, the suggestions offered here for engaging in studies to ascertain the public conception of the law and the public reaction to court decisions still have merit. For example, it might be that the public condones "mercy killings" when the laws and the courts do not, but it may be that a study would reveal that severe penalties for mercy killings have the effect of inhibiting other kinds of murders under the false guise of mercy killings.

It is quite possible that certain practices prevalent as a result of law, judicial practice, and police practice are currently encouraging violations of the law without persons responsible for the administration of the law being aware of this fact. The only way, of course, to find out whether this is true or not would be to make sociological studies on these matters. For example, is there a widespread belief among the public that laws are currently being violated without punishment of the lawbreaker? Does public opinion have an exaggerated notion of corruption among the police and judiciary? What is the effect of a manifestation of a "legal fiction" or a "legal loophole" on respect for the law? When the public observes variations in the application of sanctions in comparable cases between states, or between judges in one state, does this encourage disrespect for the law?

Criminologists have been discovering that prisoners often compare their crimes and sentences; and when, as frequently occurs, persons with relatively heavy sentences for relatively unimportant crimes find persons with light sentences for serious crimes, they become bitter. Coupled with the knowledge that most crime escapes punishment, either because the criminal avoids detection or has good "connections" or because his lawyer proves the inadequacy of evidence against him, this observation of the "arbitrariness" of sentence helps, according to leading criminologists, to create a disrespect for law among first offenders that encourages them to go into a career of crime when they are released from prison.[11] Studies of first offenders who serve

[11] For a study and discussion of variations among judges in sentencing behavior, see F. J. Gaudet, G. S. Harris, and C. W. St. John, "Individual Differences in the Sentencing Tendencies of Judges," *Journal of Criminal Law and Criminology*, 23 (January-February 1933), 811–818; F. J. Gaudet, "The Sentencing Behavior of the Judge," *Encyclopedia of Criminology* (New York: Philosophical Library, 1949), 449–461.

prison sentences show recidivism to be very high—around 70 per cent—whereas large sections of the general public commit "first offenses" but escape detection and never go on to a career of crime.[12]

The whole process of assigning sanction is deserving of considerable further study. What circumstances characteristic of a criminal or of the commitment of a crime leads a judge to assign a heavy sentence rather than a light one? What outside pressures of public opinion, lawyer contacts, personal friends of the convicted criminal, status of the criminal, and so on, impinge on the judge as he assigns a sanction?

The effects of laws and judicial decisions are not to be measured only in terms of public opinion in regard to the law and violations of the law. They are also to be considered in terms of their influence on social structure which guides behavior into certain channels. My study of the history of legislation against voluntary associations in France in the eighteenth and nineteenth centuries indicates that this legislation has at once helped to create a higher degree of "individualism" in France as compared to the relative "cooperation" found in the Scandinavian or Anglo-American countries and at the same time a greater dependence upon government as compared to individual or community action. These laws seem to have affected the whole character of French social life and have a significant influence on French politics.[13] This, of course, is historical interpretation of a *post hoc* order and cannot be considered adequate from a strictly scientific standpoint. To do an adequate social science study we should have to study current laws and current judicial decisions. An example of a problem which would be amenable to social science investigation and which would materially increase understanding of the effect of judicial decisions on significant social structure is the following: Under the Wagner Act and its successor, the Taft-Hartley Act, certain practices on the part of the employer are known as unfair labor practices. In deciding that a given employer has engaged in an unfair labor practice, say one involving discriminatory discharge, the court has a variety of sanctions which it may apply. For example, it may approve the Labor Board's cease and desist order which prohibits the continuation of the unfair labor practice, or it may approve an order for restitution

[12] Austin L. Porterfield, *Youth in Trouble* (Austin, Texas: Leo Potishman Foundation, 1946).

[13] See Chapter 4, "Voluntary Associations in France."

of back pay which has been accruing legally as long as the unfair practice has been in operation. The court, in making a judgment as to which type of sanction to approve in the various cases coming before it, has an effect on the future of union organization, since one decision may aid the union materially in its future organizational work as compared to the other decision. The court is usually aware of the financial implications of one decision as opposed to another, but it has little basis for estimating the implications for social structure and the future distribution of social power.

THE FUNCTION OF LAW

The fourth general area in which the social scientist through his investigations might aid the student of the law is in helping him to achieve a more complete understanding of the purpose and function of the law and of the legal process. The contribution of the social scientist can be only partial here, since there are philosophical and historical factors which are beyond the scope of the social scientist who studies contemporary phenomena. On the other hand, purpose and function cannot be understood wholly in philosophical and historical terms; they must also be studied in relation to contemporary effects on society.

There have been a certain number of studies by political scientists on how legislation actually gets passed, with the appropriate emphasis on pressure groups, letters to the legislator, newspaper campaigns, etc. These studies need to be greatly extended, and the conception of a pressure group should not be limited to a selfish vested interest but should be extended to any kind of organized group action, very often representing the very best and most unselfish concerns in the society. The pressures should be considered to be not only the direct and obvious ones of organized groups but also those resulting from the most subtle of individual communications and expectations.

There are pressures not only on legislators but also on judges, juries, and witnesses.[14] What, for example, is the effect on a judge of a "moral position" taken by the church to which he belongs toward the kinds of cases which come up in his court? Do Catholic judges apply more severe penalties to abortionists than do judges who have no religious

---

[14] A challenging statement from a lawyer's standpoint is Jerome Frank's *Courts on Trial* (Princeton, N.J.: Princeton University Press, 1950).

affiliation? Are Catholic judges less inclined to grant divorces and to look for expedients to avoid divorce decrees?

The variations in judicial decisions are not solely a matter of social pressures. Clinical psychologists have been doing some interesting studies on the relation of personality characteristics to attitudes and behavior [15] that have a good deal of relevance for understanding how the personality of the judge affects his decisions. Other psychologists, especially in Germany, have been conducting studies for many decades on psychological factors involved in the distortion of observation, which affect the reliability of testimony presented by witnesses in court. The social-psychological effect of witness performance and attorney performance on juries has not been adequately studied, and the judge who is responsible for the proper conduct of his court would benefit considerably from knowledge of these possible influences. What are the effects on the jury of hysteria and histrionics, for example? Are remarks by an attorney ordered by the judge to be "stricken from the record" actually stricken from the minds and evaluations of members of the jury? Lawyers could think up a large number of significant questions of this type which would be amenable to social science investigation and tests.

Rather than extend this list of suggestions indefinitely, I shall close by referring briefly to a study which I am currently conducting at the University of Minnesota. Students—who are, of course, future jury members and occasionally even future lawyers and judges—are being asked to "judge" the severity of punishment which is appropriate to different criminals coming from different class levels of the population. The preliminary results show significant differences in what is believed to be the seriousness of the crime and the appropriateness of different punishments according to the different socioeconomic classes from which the criminals are alleged to come. Further, the students, who represent a very wide range of backgrounds, show significant differences among themselves in their attitudes on these matters, depending upon whether they have a rural or urban background, whether their parents were wealthy or poor, and so on. The students' evaluations will be compared to actual penalties assigned

[15] See, for example, T. W. Adorno *et al.*, *The Authoritarian Personality* (New York: Harper, 1950); M. B. Smith, "The Personal Setting of Public Opinions: A Study of Attitudes toward Russia," *Public Opinion Quarterly*, 11 (Winter 1947–1948), 507–523.

by judges for similar offenses. A student population is obviously not the best kind for this study, but the technique will offer a model for future studies.

Assuming that all these suggestions for social science research which have been presented could be carried out efficiently and accurately, it should not be presumed that all of them would be useful for control or improvement of current legal practice, although certainly some of them would. The kinds of subject matter the sociologists and social psychologists study are only a small part of the total matter a legislator, a judge, an administrator of a law, or a lawyer should know in order to function effectively and justly. But whether directly "practical" or not, social science studies should extend materially the understanding of lawyers and judges as to the kinds of problems they face and permit them to make more realistic assumptions about the nature of man and society when they are obliged to make such assumptions in their actions.

In several European countries the study of law is considered to be an integral part of the social sciences, and there are many American students of the law who would also like to consider it in that light. Unfortunately there has been a sharp hiatus between the study of law in the United States and the development of research techniques and relevant content knowledge in the social sciences. There has been a certain amount of sermonizing that students of the law and the other social sciences ought to "get together," but there have been relatively few concrete suggestions as to the actual points at which there would be a mutual advantage in this relationship. Some law schools have encouraged their students to take courses in the social sciences, but seldom have the social science teachers been aware of the particular needs of these law students; hence the training is merely "interesting" rather than directly useful. If lawyers and others responsible for the administration of law are to make the best possible use of social science, and if social scientists in their quest for knowledge of the sources of human behavior are to take into consideration the very important legal sources, they must begin by collaborating on researches of a very concrete and specific character such as have been suggested in this chapter.

SECTION IV

Methodological Issues in Sociology

14

A Basic Methodological Issue in Sociology: Problem Orientation versus Method Orientation

SCIENTIFIC *method has not reached such a stage of detailed formulation and universality that no controversy remains about the specific procedures to be used in applying it to the social sciences. It may never do so. Certain discussions of method—including the ones in this section—therefore have a somewhat controversial character. My purpose in presenting these controversies is not to engage in polemics but to help clarify the logical and practical nature of methodological problems facing social scientists. The first chapter of this section considers a problem which periodically plagues the social scientist— the question of whether he should orient himself primarily toward a subject matter or toward techniques of research.*

A METHODOLOGICAL issue which besets sociology today, one which underlies so many of the other issues, is the argument over the primacy of subject matter or of method. Proponents of the primacy of subject matter hold that the topics for research [1] are set either by value premises external to science or by theoretical developments within science, that the selection of a topic is a very important step in scientific work even if the criteria for selection are not scientific, and that each topic makes its own unique selection of research techniques, which must be adapted to meet the particular requirements of the topic. Proponents of the primacy of method hold that there is but one scientific method, although many techniques can be employed in the concrete application of this method, and that scientists must choose topics which are practically researchable in terms of this method in order to obtain valid knowledge. The former accuse the

---

[1] The term "topics of research" is used to include both hypotheses and questions for research.

245

latter of being narrow and rigid and of trying to ape the natural sciences although the techniques of research in the natural sciences are not always applicable to the social sciences. The latter accuse the former of being philosophers and of lacking understanding of scientific rigor.

If we define science as the product of scientific method, as do some of the proponents of the primacy of method, we engage in question-begging, circular reasoning. But if we define science as a body of valid knowledge, where validity can be tested by making predictions from the knowledge that prove to have an accuracy that is beyond that which could be expected by chance alone, we have set up an independent criterion to which both schools could agree. The proponents of the primacy of method would then hold that the inductive, experimental method which they advocate would give the only body of knowledge from which valid predictions could be made. This is an assertion subject to empirical test, and it remains to be seen whether, for certain subject matters, other methods do not permit equally accurate prediction, methods such as the following: extrapolation of historical trends, structural analysis of the functionally related components of a society or a personality, logical deduction from truisms resting on empirically verified assumptions, comparisons from history or ethnology, applications of generalizations arrived at by analytic induction through modification of hypotheses by successive tests with exceptional cases, application of generalizations arrived at by statistical measures of correlation or significance.

Relative to the total number of studies, there have been few experiments—of either the laboratory or the field variety—in sociology, and it is questionable whether many of the research problems we have set for ourselves are amenable to the experimental method in the foreseeable future. It is, of course, desirable to use the experimental method whenever society permits its use and whenever it can answer the questions which our discipline raises, but it is not likely that the experimental method can meet these two tests sufficiently in the near future to make it the dominant method. Does this mean that sociology is not, and cannot be in the near future, a science? The proponents of the primacy of subject matter say that sociology is a science because other methods are available which will allow somewhat accurate predictions—perhaps not as accurate as those permitted by the experimental method, but significantly better than chance would permit. The proponents of the primacy of method also say that sociology is a science because they believe that certain statistical techniques, especially partial correlation and successive subclassification, are equivalents of the experiment. This belief is logically fallacious for most kinds of social data.[2]

Finally we note that the natural scientists have always defined their science in terms of its content rather than its method. While they have often found the experimental method a most successful way of attaining accurate predictions and while that method has often been practically feasible for them, they have on many occasions used other methods when the latter were more appropriate or feasible. Some natural sciences, such as astronomy and plant or animal ecology, make little or no use of the experimental method, and are still regarded as sciences. The *Encyclopaedia Britannica* offers a widely accepted definition of scientific method which does not restrict it to one proper process: "Scientific method is a collective term denoting the various processes by the aid of which the sciences are built up. In a wide sense, any mode of investigation by which scientific or other impartial and systematic knowledge is acquired is called a scientific method." [3]

For all of the above reasons, I would support the primacy of subject matter and hold that methods are mere tools to be chosen by the requirements of the research problem under consideration. This does not mean that the methodological sloppiness of many proponents of the primacy of subject matter is to be condoned. Nor does it mean that all problems in social science are researchable with our present techniques. It means simply that where there is good reason, either theoretical or practical, to study a certain topic, it is worth while to study it even when present techniques of research permit us to obtain only a low degree of validity for our conclusions. It also means that those who prefer to study a topic about which much valid information can be acquired, but which there is little practical or theoretical reason to study, are using a personal, esthetic reason for their choice and not a scientific one. While our thinking should be rigorous, our conclusions cannot always be "neat" because of the present difficulty in getting certain kinds of data and because of certain limitations in available techniques of research.

[2] See "A Weakness of Partial Correlation in Sociological Studies," Chapter 17.
[3] "Scientific Method," *Encyclopaedia Britannica* (1941), XX, 127–133.

The question may be raised as to why the issue over the primacy of subject matter or method developed among sociologists. A satisfactory answer to this question would require extensive historical research, and I do not intend to embark upon that. But I would like to offer a hypothesis which is one step beyond the usual observation that some social scientists felt the need to be rigorous and to copy the procedures of the natural scientists as much as possible. The hypothesis is that the proponents of the primacy of method have been affected by the general movement of our culture toward what is sometimes called mass society,[4] which involves, among other things, an emphasis on means rather than ends, a shift—to use Riesman's terms—from being inner-directed to being other-directed.[5] In lesser form, the movement manifested itself in the declining prestige of the fields of social problems and social theory and the heightened prestige of social psychology because the latter discipline seemed to arrive more readily at discrete, testable "basic" propositions that were "value-free." In its extreme form in American sociology, this movement took the form of such statements as the following by George Lundberg:

What price must we probably pay for a social science of a comprehensiveness and reliability comparable to some of the better developed sciences? . . . First of all, the advancement of the social sciences would probably deprive us in a large measure of the luxury of indignation in which we now indulge ourselves as regards social events. This country, for example, is enjoying at present a great emotional vapor-bath directed at certain European movements and leaders. We believe today apparently that the assassination of Hitler would quite solve the problems of Europe, just as we believed twenty years ago that hanging the Kaiser would achieve the same end. . . .

Closely related and indeed inseparably connected with the necessary abandonment, in science, of personalistic and moralistic types of explanations is the necessity of abandoning or redefining a large vocabulary to which we are deeply and emotionally attached. Concepts like freedom, democracy, liberty, independence, free speech, self-determination and a multitude of others have never been realistically analyzed by most people as to their actual content under changing conditions. . . .

Finally, the advancement of the social sciences will cost the abandonment not only of individual concepts carried with us from prescientific

[4] See "The Problem of a Mass Society," Chapter 2.
[5] David Riesman, Reuel Denney, and Norman Glazer, *The Lonely Crowd* (New Haven, Conn.: Yale University Press, 1950).

times. It will require us also to abandon deeply cherished ideologies, resembling in form if not in content their theological predecessors. . . . I know of no scientific evidence whatever to indicate that democracy, or any other single system of social or political organization, is the *sole* system under which science can prosper. All that I can find any *scientific* warrant for is that under some conditions, democracy, defined in any constant way you please, is compatible with a certain degree and type of intellectual freedom. . . . I am opposed to making science the tail of *any* political kite whatsoever. . . .

I have emphasized that physical scientists are indispensable to any political regime. Social scientists had better work toward a corresponding status. Already some of them have achieved it to a degree. I venture to believe, for example, that qualified social statisticians have not been and will not be greatly disturbed in their function by any political party. Their skill consists in the ability to draw relatively valid, unbiased and demonstrable conclusions from societal data. That technique is the same, regardless of social objectives. No regime can get along without it.

Thus the social sciences of the future will not pretend to dictate to men the ends of existence or the goals of striving. They will merely chart the possible alternatives, the consequences of each and the most efficient technique of arriving at *whatever* ends man shall from time to time consider it worth while to pursue. If the social sciences devote themselves effectively to this role, they have a future of unlimited possibilities and have nothing to fear from the changes that will doubtless occur in the future as they have occurred in the past.[6]

The major form taken currently by the controversy over the primacy of content or method comes close to putting the whole field of sociology into the camp of the proponents of the primacy of method. This is the argument that a body of disciplines known as the "behavioral sciences"—psychology, sociology, and social anthropology, plus a very small section of political science and economics [7]—is distinct from a body of disciplines known as "documentary sciences"—history, ethnology, political science, law, institutional and labor economics (the rest of economics is put in a class by itself). This distinction con-

---

[6] George A. Lundberg, "The Future of the Social Sciences," *Scientific Monthly*, 53 (October 1941), 356–359.

[7] Of published books in economics which would be considered in the behavioral sciences as currently defined, there are few besides George Katona's *Psychological Analysis of Economic Behavior* (New York: McGraw-Hill, 1951). In political science there are the earlier studies of Gosnell and Lasswell, and now a subfield is developing within political science called "political behavior." An example of the current work is the symposium "Research in Political Behavior," *American Political Science Review*, 46 (December 1952), 1003–1045.

fuses content (human behavior) with method (the study of documents). It implies that the former disciplines, including sociology, do not, or should not, use documents and that the latter disciplines do not study human behavior.

It is true that there are certain differences, on the average, between the two groups of disciplines. One generally seeks to verify general propositions, while the other generally seeks to explain unique events or situations. One relies heavily on statistical method, while the other makes practically no use of statistics but has cultivated techniques of careful observation or critical examination of documents. One tends to set up a system of carefully defined concepts with which to apprehend facts; the other seeks to convey meanings, equally carefully, with the common language. One aims to make predictions through deductions from inductively acquired generalizations; the other seeks to make predictions through comparison of cases and examination of all the relevant facts in a situation.[8]

There are these, and perhaps other, differences between these two sets of disciplines, on the average. But it cannot be said that the second group of social sciences is not interested in human behavior, or that it does not achieve valid information usable for making accurate predictions. Nor can it be said that the first group of social sciences is not interested in using documents, such as the protocols of projective and other tests, life histories, diaries, propaganda literature, questionnaires, census reports, etc.

The first group could learn much from the second about how to recognize a valid fact (the so-called rules of external and internal criticism), how to synthesize a wide variety of diverse facts, and how to take the perspective of cultural relativism. The second group could learn much from the first about the possibilities of survey techniques and the statistical method, especially techniques of sampling and summarization, and about the dynamics of individual personalities and groups. Each social science group could learn from the other, as each discipline within a group could learn from others within the same group, and while each has several failings, none is to be denounced as the pursuit of nonsense. Yet the latter kind of derogation is the order

---

[8] W. H. Walsh has called this the method of "colligation" and defines it as "explaining an event by tracing its intrinsic relations to other events and locating it in its historical context." (*An Introduction to Philosophy of History* [New York: Hutchinson's University Library, 1951], p. 59.)

of the day, because those who would urge the primacy of method are in the ascendancy in the so-called behavioral sciences.

It would be a great loss to sociology if it were separated from, and put in opposition to, history and ethnology. Besides learning from history the techniques of external and internal criticism and of synthesis of a variety of factors causing a given occurrence, sociologists have a series of uses for the *content* of history and ethnology which they neglect because of their current negativism toward those fields:

1. History and ethnology provide comparative data with which to test hypotheses. Durkheim's study of suicide and of religious behavior, and Weber's study of capitalism, made just this use of historical and ethnological data. While a few contemporary sociologists attempt to carry on in this tradition,[9] most sociologists neglect this rich source of data, highly relevant for testing certain hypotheses.[10] Comparative study must be systematic and representative to be scientifically useful; unfortunately many historians and sociologists are given merely to "those historical parallels so stimulating to oratory, so crippling to thought." [11]

2. History and ethnology provide descriptions of certain occurrences which occasionally can be used as "crucial tests" of certain theories. In physics we note that occasionally certain theories can be tested by a single crucial fact, provided certain assumptions—based on other tested facts—are accepted. The "ether" theory of the movement of light seemed plausible for many years and was used successfully to predict many characteristics of light. When an alternative theory was found to be equally successful, the famous "ether-drift" experiment was set up by Michelson and Morley. By means of a single measure, replicated a few times to make sure it was not the result of a defect in the measurement process, the ether theory was disproved (other facts were already "known" and accepted, of course). Unfortunately sociologists do not have their theories sharpened to such a fine point that a single observation could demonstrate one theory to be correct and another incorrect. But the kind of diversified observations, under

[9] For example, Don Martindale's unpublished study, "The Social Basis of Intellectual Productivity and Stereotypes."

[10] In Chapter 5 we suggested the use of a comparative study of intergroup relations to test certain hypotheses about the causes of race prejudice.

[11] D. W. Brogan, *France under the Republic: The Development of Modern France* (New York: Harper, 1940), p. 680.

unusual conditions, provided by history and ethnography could demonstrate the crucial weaknesses of many current sociological theories.

3. Sometimes in sociology it is important to understand the causation of a single important event, or series of events, as distinct from a generalization. History provides the only source of this understanding of what might be considered a unique pattern of nonunique events. For example, we know that the important racist ideology that has dominated and given a special quality to white-Negro relations in the United States was practically nonexistent before the year 1800. To find out how and why it developed, we must turn to history. The historical data I use to explain why there is little voluntary cooperation in secondary groups in contemporary France[12] provide a comparable example. Gordon Allport has made a significant contribution to our recognition of the need for life histories to understand adult personalities[13] and thus provides a case parallel to the recognition of the need to study culture history in order to understand contemporary society.

4. History and ethnography can be used to give a "realistic" basis to definitions, assumptions, and indices used to measure factors in formulating and testing social theory. In the next chapter the value of this is pointed out. This is the sort of thing Cooley had in mind when he said that a broad acquaintance with history and ethnology was extremely valuable for a sociologist.[14]

5. In the effort to "hold constant" numerous interfering conditions in field experiments, history can aid in the specification of many of the conditions held constant, since it describes the setting in which the experiment takes place.[15]

The advocacy of the primacy of method—and a narrow method at that—has tended to put other limitations on the sociologist. By examining the folkways of research method in contemporary sociology— even from the biased standpoint of an advocate of the primacy of content, and without data as to what the folkways are—we may be

---

[12] See Chapter 4.

[13] *The Use of Personal Documents in Psychological Science*, Social Science Research Council Bulletin No. 49 (New York, 1942).

[14] Charles H. Cooley, "The Roots of Social Knowledge," in *Sociological Theory and Social Research* (New York: Holt, 1930).

[15] For a partial illustration of this use of history in a sociological study, see Arnold M. Rose, "The Adequacy of Women's Expectations for Adult Roles," *Social Forces*, 30 (October 1951), 69–77.

able to suggest extensions of the means of collecting data. The study which gets the most praise is the one which carries through systematically and rigorously on a single, narrow point. This results in the neglect by some sociologists, to a certain extent, of studies which are based on data gathered from a wide variety of sources. Perhaps this tendency is in reaction to the earlier tendency of sociologists to over-generalize and spend a great deal of time in synthesizing alleged facts that were never too well established in the first place. Whatever the reason for the tendency to go deeper into narrower problems, it has resulted in a neglect of problems which require synthesis from a wide variety of sources.

An allied tendency is to distrust the evidence furnished by the investigator's own senses. A personal observation needs to be tested for reliability, but it need not be taken for granted that a personal observation has low reliability. Natural scientists often make their first observations with their unaided senses, and only later in a study, when they need to verify and be precise, do they use instruments for exact measurement. An effect of our current predilection is that sociologists neglect areas of study where most of the data would have to come from direct observation. When we do tackle such a study we tend to devise petty, roundabout techniques to provide sources—such as getting statements from interviewees to describe conditions which are observable by anyone, including ourselves. In some instances, untrained interviewees could not be expected to observe subtle relationships or unconscious manifestations. The study of group symbolisms, for example, has been all but overlooked by sociologists. So has the study of the relation between fear and desire in respect to such controversial matters as urban life, dictatorship, the treatment of minority groups. Thus, sociologists avoid areas of research where many observers have not gone before or where untrained laymen cannot be expected to make spontaneous observations.

This tendency among sociologists to separate themselves from their investigations goes even deeper. They seldom introduce new conditions into a social situation in order to observe changed reactions. This may be due to a feeling that the social situation is a natural product and that an effort to change it either would be fruitless or would lead to an unhealthy or unrealistic condition. Or, more simply, it may be that a controlled experiment is too expensive or not feasible in a social situation. Whatever the cause, it is fairly evident that sociologists avoid experimentation with the social situations they study. It is true that sociologists pay homage to the method of experimentation they see practiced by the natural scientists. But the concept of an experiment is of something that is carried on in a laboratory under strictly controlled conditions. Even should the laboratory be more desirable because it permits the use of controls, it does not follow that uncontrolled experiments in ordinary social situations give no knowledge at all.

This chapter is best closed with two quotations. The psychologist A. H. Maslow summarizes as follows what he believes are the consequences to psychology from the current preoccupation with techniques rather than problems, and the same points apply with only slight modification to sociology:

Overstress on and too exclusive concern with method, instrument, technique, or procedure foster the following mistakes:
1) Emphasis on polish and elegance rather than on vitality, significance and creativeness.
2) Giving the commanding positions in science to technicians rather than discoverers.
3) Over-valuation of quantification for its own sake.
4) Fitting problems to techniques rather than vice-versa.
5) Creation of a false and pernicious hierarchical system among the sciences.
6) Overstrong compartmentalization between the sciences.
7) Emphasis on the difference rather than the similarities between scientists and other truth-seekers (poets, novelists, artists, philosophers).
8) Creation of a scientific orthodoxy, which in turn a) tends to block the development of new methods, b) tends to exclude many problems from the jurisdiction of science and c) tends to make scientists "safe" rather than daring and
9) Neglect of the problem of values, with a consequent blurring of the criteria for judging the worth or importance of an experiment.[16]

The return to a recognition of the crucial role for science of the selection of research problems would put sociologists in accord with the dominant attitude of physical scientists. Einstein and Infeld express this clearly and give no support to those sociologists who con-

---

[16] A. H. Maslow, "Problem-Centering vs. Means-Centering in Science," *Philosopsy of Science*, 13 (October 1946), 326–331.

sider so casually the formulation of hypotheses for research: "The formulation of a problem is often more essential than its solution, which may be merely a matter of mathematical or experimental skill. To raise new questions, new possibilities, to regard old problems from a new angle, requires creative imagination and marks real advance in science."[17]

The advocacy of the primacy of method may have been a wholesome reaction to the antiempiricism and sloppy "theorizing" of the earlier sociologists, but to continue it at this stage of the development of our science is a mark of immaturity.

[17] Albert Einstein and Leopold Infeld, *The Evolution of Physics* (New York: Simon and Schuster, 1942), p. 95.

15

Generalizations in the Social Sciences

SINCE *one of the aims of science is generalization, sociologists and social psychologists, more so than their fellow social scientists, have striven for generalization. Looking at the results of the past thirty years of research, one can at least raise the question as to whether there has been considerably more striving than achievement. Replications often do not verify the original studies. Perhaps everyone knows that sociologists and social psychologists overgeneralize, but the implications of this for their research can be examined as well as some suggestions for what to do about it. These are the tasks of the following chapter.*

THE NEED FOR REPRESENTATIVE SAMPLES

MY concern in this chapter is to indicate something about the nature of the operations necessary to achieve generalizations in the inductive social sciences. There is a certain confusion among some social scientists between the conditions necessary for generalization, which might be called "generalizability," and the generalization itself. For example, there is an incorrect belief that by dealing with the "forms" or "processes" of human behavior, rather than the "content," one achieves generalizations regardless of the representativeness of the data used. Another phrase frequently used is that by "abstracting to a higher conceptual level" one achieves generalizations regardless of the representativeness of the data used.

When social scientists seek generalizations about all human beings, rather than, say, about members of a specific culture or a specific organization, their sample is invariably nonrepresentative. No one has

NOTE: This chapter was first prepared as a report to the Laboratory for Research in Social Relations, at the University of Minnesota. The laboratory is supported jointly by the College of Science, Literature, and the Arts and the Graduate School of the university and by the Carnegie Corporation of New York. None of the other members of the laboratory should be held responsible for my views.

yet studied a representative sample of persons or behaviors from all cultures at all periods. The nearest approach is that of some anthropologists who make cross-cultural surveys,[1] but even they neglect historical and subcultural variations. Most other social scientists, while they specify the limited universe of which their sample is representative, imply that their findings have generalizability beyond that universe without indicating why this should be true.[2] Consequently there is a growing *science by analogy*. The conclusion of many an excellent study based on a limited sample is couched in the form of a universal generalization, and there are otherwise well-conceived studies of "industrial productivity" or "psychological warfare" conducted on volunteer student subjects in a classroom.[3] While it may be desirable to eliminate "extraneous" variables in laboratory experiments, it does seem questionable whether it is legitimate to generalize about industrial productivity without the motive to produce being present or to generalize about psychological warfare when there is no war. The criticism being made is not that the laboratory experiment is not a method applicable to the study of human behavior, but that a conclusion about the relation between an independent and a dependent variable under one set of circumstances cannot automatically be generalized to apply to the relation between these same two variables under

[1] See, for example, G. P. Murdock, *Social Structure* (New York: Macmillan, 1949). Most of the findings in cross-cultural surveys are correlations considerably below unity. The universals claimed by Murdock are not in the form of associations among cultural variables but in the form of institutions alleged to be discovered in all cultures without exception. Concerning these universals, it is valuable to cite the comment of another anthropologist, Clyde Kluckhohn: "There are admittedly few genuine uniformities in culture content unless one states the content in extremely general form— e.g., clothing, shelter, incest taboos, and the like. The seventy-two items listed by Murdock (1945) 'which occur, so far as the author's knowledge goes, in every culture known to history or ethnography' are mainly blanket categories of 'the universal ground plan,' though a few such as 'modesty concerning natural functions' approach a certain kind of specificity." (Clyde Kluckhohn, "Anthropological Studies of Human Relations," address to Rockefeller Foundation Conference on Research in Human Relations, February 27–28, 1953, unpublished, p. 32.) The work of the cross-cultural anthropologists is challenging and promising, but it is doubtful whether they have achieved any but the most superficial and tentative of generalizations.

[2] The statement above specifically excepts those who seek generalizations only about particular nations, subgroups, institutions, etc. Those engaged in public opinion polling, for example, almost invariably specify the limited universe of which their sample is intended to be representative and are not concerned with anything outside that universe.

[3] Following the current folkways of social science, I am participating in this science by analogy, and the criticism applies to several of my own completed and ongoing studies.

another set of circumstances.[4] It is still an unverified assumption that "cohesiveness" (to take one concept frequently generalized about) in one situation, or induced by one means, is the same as cohesiveness in another situation, induced by another means—as some of the followers of Moreno seem to imply. This procedure seems to reify the concept.

Certain misconceptions concerning the nature of research procedure are the source of some overgeneralizations. In studies where one seeks to find characteristics differentiating two known groups—say happily-married and non-happily-married groups, or delinquent and nondelinquent groups—one can either begin with the hypothesis that certain specific characteristics will differentiate the groups or one can measure the subjects on a large number of personal characteristics and hope that some characteristics, without its being specified in advance which ones, will differentiate the groups. The former is a more advisable procedure because the investigator (1) has to have more prior knowledge about the characteristics being studied, (2) can work with a smaller number of variables, (3) might be better able to relate the findings to a general theory, and (4) can better do *future* studies which extend the generalization to other samples. There is, however, no difference between the two procedures in the extent to which one can generalize to other samples from the findings based on the study of one limited sample. The findings are still applicable only to the universe of which the sample of people studied is representative, despite a belief held in some quarters that the use of a hypothesis derived from theory makes generalization appropriate.

Another misconception also arises in connection with such studies when the investigator measures two known groups on a large number of variables in the hope of finding some which differentiate the two

[4] An illustration of the dangers of indulging in science by analogy is provided by the engaging study by Muzafer Sherif (reported in a preliminary way in *Social Psychology at the Crossroads,* edited by Rohrer and Sherif [New York: Harper, 1951], pp. 388–424). Sherif experimentally creates hostility between two artificially separated groups of boys and shows how the hostility was induced by separation and rivalry in sports and other camp activities. While the experiment is ingenious and fascinating, one is forced to raise the question as to whether the conclusion about separation and rivalry has any relevance—as Sherif seems to believe—for the study of relations between Negroes and whites in the United States. One reason why this question is raised is that an essential factor in Negro-white relations is a syndrome of culturally determined attitudes known as "racism" and this important factor is not present in the relations between two groups of white Protestant boys at a boys' camp.

so that he can use the differentiating variables in a predictive test. Apparently some sociologists believe that one should expect there to be a certain number of variables, in the large number tested, for which the difference should go beyond three standard errors and that if one eliminates these one can generalize the findings regardless of the representativeness of the samples. It is true that the 3σ test is arbitrary and that one can occasionally find some differences beyond 3 σs which could arise by chance (this would be proved by replications on different samples). But in a single study one cannot know *which* of the differences beyond 3 σs are occurring by chance, since each variable is presumably measuring something different from any other variable, and therefore one is not justified in eliminating any of them until the study has been replicated several times on other samples. (Then some variables which differentiated the first time can be expected to fail to differentiate again.) Certainly the elimination of some variables which differentiate beyond 3 σs does not help the generalizing power of the resultant test.

What rationale can be used to justify the procedure of generalizing beyond the universe of which the cases studied are selected to be a representative sample?

One rationale can be built around homogeneity. If there is no variation in the persons or behaviors to be studied, then any sample—no matter how it is drawn—is representative. Most natural scientists operate on this basis, and they almost never concern themselves with selecting a random or stratified sample before describing its characteristics or experimenting with it. A gram of pure magnesium is representative of all pure magnesium, and a healthy liver is representative of all healthy livers. The chemist has a definite concept of purity in a substance, and the biologist has a definite concept of a healthy and properly functioning organ or organism. While purity and homogeneity are certainly not identical concepts, they may be said to have the same methodological function in regard to the matter considered here. When observations or experiments are essayed, the scientist makes a considerable effort to secure pure or healthy specimens, but beyond that he has no need to select a random or stratified sample.[5]

[5] There are, of course, some types of natural science studies, particularly in certain fields of biology, where complicated causation and considerable variation necessitate the drawing of representative samples for experimentation.

The social scientist is in the same position when he is dealing with behavior that is unmodifiable, or practically unmodifiable, among all humans—so that one individual is, for the purpose at hand, like any other. We do not yet know all the categories of behavior which are unmodifiable, but future research will add to the list. In general, we can probably say that behavior which is determined almost completely by generic hereditary factors and behavior which is determined by universal experiences are practically unmodifiable. These probably include the reflexes, the learning process, the psychiatric mechanisms, perhaps many of the processes of socialization and of crowd behavior. Much more research, including that of an anthropological and historical character, is needed to determine what behaviors are unmodifiable. Such behaviors can then be studied almost without regard to how the sample is chosen, the only necessary precaution being that a defective or pathological specimen is not included in the sample.[6]

But much of what the social scientist studies is not unmodifiable among all mankind. Many social scientists—particularly political scientists, institutional economists, and certain categories of sociologists —deliberately limit their studies to our own culture. Their findings are in the nature of cultural or institutional generalizations. Most historians and many anthropologists do purely descriptive studies in which the issue of generalization is not raised. It is largely the social psychologists, sociologists, and social anthropologists who deal with variable human behavior that have to seek a rationale for generalizing from nonrepresentative samples. The problem of variation confronts them not only in the sense that they do not know whether their findings would hold under different cultural conditions but also in that not *all* their own cases conform to the generalization true for *most* of their cases. Their generalizations usually take the following form: When condition A was established, and C, D, E . . . N eliminated, B followed in *80 per cent* of the cases; *or*, in a group in which A was induced, as compared to a group in which A' was induced, and extraneous variables randomized, a *greater degree* of B was manifested. Such conclusions are never completely satisfactory, as there is varia-

[6] A more general way of stating the point of this paragraph is to say that if the bias in sampling is not related to the variables studied, then a lack of representativeness in the sample has no limiting influence on the generalizability of the conclusion. The difficulty is that we do not know what the specific biases in a nonrepresentative sample are, and much less do we know their relationship to the variables under study.

tion in the dependent variable which is not explainable by the variation in the independent variable despite the fact that extraneous variables have been held constant or randomized. Such a variation may represent differences in subcultures or in individual experience, although it may also be due simply to errors of measurement.[7]

The physical and biological sciences find some variations in their conclusions, but the variations are tiny in comparison to those found in social science, and upon repeated replications are found to distribute themselves normally. The variations in the conclusions of natural science studies may therefore be attributed to errors of measurement. These are the so-called "chance errors." The large size and

[7] At least two quite diverse metaphysical positions are held by contemporary social scientists regarding the nature of social laws. One is that all human behavior is determined by a finite number of causes, which—if known in their entirety, as universal laws—would allow for the prediction of every person's behavior under all circumstances. The other position is that human behavior is determined by the laws of probability so that at best we can make actuarial predictions that will ultimately have high, although not perfect, accuracy when applied to specified categories of people, but that will always be lacking a good deal when applied to any single individual. The differences between the two positions can be best illustrated by examining the forms which they hold generalizations should take:

I. Holding constant C, D, E . . . N, when situation A develops, then B will follow.
II. Holding constant C, D, E . . . N, when situation A develops, then B will follow 80 per cent of the time (eighty is, of course, an arbitrary figure).

I hold to the former position, which I believe to be the metaphysical position taken by natural scientists from Galileo through Einstein, with the discoveries of Bohr and Heisenberg representing no intrinsic exceptions but rather a technical inability to achieve as much knowledge about the movement of individual particles as is desired. I emphasize adherence to the first position because the statements in the text may *appear* to be predicated on the second position.

When some physicists say that science must abandon the quest for universals, what they have in mind is the discovery that the very process of measuring something disturbs the phenomenon being measured so that we can never hope to know exactly the "true" state of the physical universe except within a certain degree of probability. In other words, the physicists have not stated that there is no complete determinism in the universe; they have simply stated that we can never expect to learn the complete determinism because of the inevitable distortion of "errors of measurement." It should be needless to say that social science is a long way from discovering a relation with such a high degree of accuracy and thoroughness that its probability coefficient for prediction purposes is solely a tiny error of measurement.

The deviations from perfection in the probabilities we discover are more likely to be due to failure to hold constant disturbing variables and to the use of inadequate measuring devices. Practically speaking, it will probably be necessary for social scientists to be satisfied with predictions of low probability for some time, but this need not disturb our premise that there is complete determinism in the universe toward which our knowledge will gradually approach (except for errors in measurement). Certainly social scientists ought to be able to agree that there is no reason to expect greater error of measurement in the observation of one individual's behavior than in the observation of the behavior of a collection of individuals.

often irregular character of variations in social science conclusions suggest, not errors in measurement, but failure to control important variables and to use reliable and valid measuring devices.

THE NEED FOR REPLICATION OF STUDIES

Since American culture contains numerous subcultures, we would expect not only heterogeneity in the performance of the cases making up any one sample but also different results from different studies of the same variables. Unfortunately, there have not been replicative studies in most areas of the social sciences.[8]

The term "replication" has been used with at least two meanings. One is a repetition of a study of a given problem with research procedures and measuring devices as similar to the original ones as possible, but with a different sample of cases. In a broader sense, replication has meant any effort to test the conclusion of a previous study, using any scientifically proper research procedure and measuring devices with the new cases. Since this chapter considers the stability of the conclusion (or generalization) rather than the re-use of procedures and techniques, the term "replication" will be used in the broad sense. Thus we are concerned with all studies that state the observed relationship between what are purported to be the same pairs of variables, regardless of methods or measures used. Following this interest we find that on a few subjects there have been not only replicated studies but also systematic summaries of them. At the end of this chapter there is a list of all the replicated studies in sociology and social psychology that I could find in the published literature.

This annotated list reveals that there is little consistency in the conclusions of the studies reported. The differences might be due to one or more of several factors: (1) cultural variations in the composition of the different samples used; (2) different indices or measures of the major variables; (3) different personalities or approaches of the

---

[8] Donald Young has pointed out the implications of this lack of replicative studies for a developing science: "It is axiomatic that scientific knowledge is cumulative, that well-designed projects must be capable of repetition, that procedures must be convincing at least to fellow scientists. Yet only a very few research projects are designed to build directly on the results of previous studies; in most social fields few projects are capable of repetition and fewer still are ever repeated; and plausibility is almost as readily accepted as methodological integrity." (Donald Young, "Limiting Factors in the Development of the Social Sciences," in *Research Frontiers in Human Relations,* Proceedings of the American Philosophical Society, 92 [November 12, 1948], 330.)

experimenters or other data collectors; (4) different social conditions under which the data were collected; or (5) different factors measured under the same name. If we are to know which of the five sets of factors is responsible for the variation in findings, it will be necessary to control the last four much more carefully than has been done heretofore. The first set of factors—variation in the persons studied—is much too complicated to control readily.

With these observations in mind, we can specify at least some of the conditions necessary for securing more consistent replications in the social sciences.

1. While it is recognized that an isolated hypothesis can be scientifically proved or disproved, it would be more efficient if the proposition for which verification is sought were a logical part of a general theory.[9] This is true for at least three reasons:

a. An infinite number of hypotheses are capable of being tested scientifically, and an integrated body of propositions will aid in the selection of fruitful and significant hypotheses for investigation.

b. If the tested generalizations fit into each other, social science knowledge will gradually assume a structure rather than consist simply of a pile of discrete bits of knowledge.

c. If the hypotheses form a part of a structure, data collected for one study have a better chance of being utilizable in another study than they have if the hypotheses are developed and studied independently of one another.

An adequate system of general propositions is based on an internally consistent set of assumptions and definitions, such that each proposition is capable of being logically deduced from the assumptions and definitions (in the manner of a theorem). The building up of an adequate theory—the shorthand term for the framework of assumptions and definitions as well as the propositions deducible from them—requires a constant interplay between theory and data in which the theory is regularly modified and new deductions are derived from it and once more tested by crucial facts.[10]

[9] It is to be noted, however, that many of the better executed studies in sociology have completely ignored any sort of theory.

[10] An interesting variation of this procedure is that which allows the universalized hypothesis to be developed out of the data. Such a method was employed in A. R. Lindesmith's *Opiate Addiction* (Bloomington, Ind.: Principia Press, 1947), and D. R. Cressey's "The Criminal Violation of Financial Trust," *American Sociological Review*, 15 (December 1950), 738–743. Their method involves the formulation

2. The second proposal for achieving more consistent replications is that propositions be stated in terms capable of being generalized. If the categories or variables of a proposition are spatially or temporally localized, obviously the proposition cannot be generalized. Any body of data can be stated in terms of generalized or localized categories. For example, a number of facts about a sample of persons can be classified according to the residential location of the individuals, to their socioeconomic class, to their degree of perceived life satisfaction. If residential location is the variable used, the data can never be used to verify a proposition other than one referring to the specific locations involved. If socioeconomic class is the variable used, the data can be used to verify propositions that refer to the culture or subculture in which that class structure is prevalent. But if degree of perceived life satisfaction is the variable used, the data can be used to verify universal propositions since presumably all normal men evaluate their lives in terms of satisfaction or its converse. However, there is an extremely important matter to be recognized: simply by choosing categories that are capable of being generalized does not in itself generalize the proposition when verified. The verified proposition still has no validity beyond the universe from which the sample is drawn; hence the need for replications.

It is obviously impossible to secure a representative sample of all men, from all cultures, at all times. Most propositions will never claim validity beyond our current culture. Since this is so, propositions stated in terms of categories frankly limited to our culture should have as high a status in research as propositions whose variables are

of an initial hypothesis from cursory inspection of a few case histories and from suggestions arising from the general literature on their subject. This hypothesis is then tested on more cases, and as soon as it proves unsatisfactory, it is modified. After all the available cases in a given population are exhausted, the study is "temporarily" terminated, and the hypothesis is stated to be proved for *all* cases in that population. A criticism of the method is that it is unduly time consuming. If the initial hypothesis were *deduced* from a more general theory, and if a *range* of cases were selected from the start, the final conclusion would be arrived at more readily than if *all* cases are examined and re-examined with a progressively modified hypothesis. Still, these authors have probably come closer to universal conclusions than most others working in the social sciences, and their conclusions have characteristics interesting and instructive to other social scientists. For an early formulation of the procedure used by Lindesmith and Cressey, see F. Znaniecki, *Laws of Social Psychology* (Chicago: University of Chicago Press, 1925). Another early approximate application of the method is to be found in R. C. Angell's *The Family Encounters the Depression* (New York: Scribner, 1936). For a critique of the method, see W. S. Robinson, "The Logical Structure of Analytic Induction," *American Sociological Review*, 16 (December 1951), 812–818.

universal. They may have as much predictive value. Possibly a happy compromise between universal generalizations, desirable but unattainable, and generalizations that are frankly limited culturally is a proposition stated in universal terms and then restated with the variables specified for the culture or cultures to be studied. The restated proposition, when verified for the culture(s) studied, is highly amenable, of course, to reconversion into its universal form when other studies in other cultures or in different social situations later justify the universal form. In the specific study, the historical premise "in our culture" serves to hold constant numerous variables that could not otherwise feasibly be held constant in a strict experimental design.[11]

3. Even within our culture it is so difficult to secure a representative sample for research on most variables that it would be well to have some device that could be employed to obviate the need for representative samples. The purpose of securing representative samples for verifying general propositions is not the same as the purpose of securing representative samples for a survey or a public opinion poll. In the latter the purpose is to find out what the distribution of certain attributes is in the population. In the former it is simply to see whether the proposition will hold up to data in the entire *range* of the distribution. It is usually easier to estimate roughly where various points on a distribution are than to secure a representative sample of a large, complex, and widely distributed population. Replication should be done at various points, especially the extremes, of the distribution of the population studied. The distribution differs somewhat for each independent variable studied, since it covers the range of possible interpretations of, or reactions to, the independent variable.

It is often difficult to replicate a study on divergent populations with the same observer or experimenter, the same index or measure of the independent variable, and the same conditions of observation or experimentation. Making these things as simple as possible will, of course, aid in approximating them over and over again during replications. But a certain amount of variation is almost inevitable, and we must recognize that it will prevent exact replication. The terms of the proposition must be broad enough to cover the variation in replication.

---

[11] Anthropologists and historians, whether by design or by accident, have frequently utilized this happy compromise. An example of its use in sociology appears in my article, "The Adequacy of Women's Expectations for Adult Roles," *Social Forces*, 30 (October 1951), 69–77.

Replications, to be useful in the way that they have proved useful in the natural sciences, must be undertaken systematically. If one replication secures results consistent with the original finding, further replications should vary slightly the conditions of the original study. If one replication fails to secure results consistent with the original finding, further replications should approximate even more closely the conditions of the original study. The scientific function of replications, in addition to verification, is to set the limits under which the generalization is valid.

4. Just as an infinite number of discrete hypotheses can be advanced about social behavior, so can an indefinitely large number of different frameworks of assumptions and definitions. Rather than to proceed at random, and to find out only after a considerable amount of time has been spent in testing the proposition arising out of a certain framework that it is not particularly fruitful, it is preferable to develop some criteria for setting up a framework of definitions and assumptions. These criteria should also be used in selecting an isolated hypothesis, since a tremendous amount of time can be wasted in testing, disproving, and discarding hypotheses. I do not pretend to know what these criteria might turn out to be but merely offer the following thoughts as possible bases for setting criteria:

a. Definitions, assumptions, and variables in hypotheses which have proved valuable in previous research should be given special attention before these necessary constituents are created *de novo*. The result will then contribute to a cumulative product, rather than being an isolated conclusion, and it should have a better chance for verification and successful replication.

b. Definitions, assumptions, and variables should be relevant to experience. That is, they should bear some relation to observations made by the investigator, or to meanings perceived by the subjects, or at least to what psychiatrists claim are unconscious meanings. This may not be asking for much, but some researches have set up definitions, assumptions, and variables out of the imagination of the investigators. Any such items created out of thin air, so to speak, can hardly be expected to be relevant, manipulable, and productive of hypotheses likely to be verified. We do not need, of course, to go all the way back to the position of the old-line behaviorist and insist that all variables (stimuli and responses) be materially observable, but some relation to perceived reality, conscious or unconscious, is desirable. A person told to feel cohesive with strangers in a group may manifest more cohesiveness, when observed or tested, than a person not told to feel cohesive, but it is questionable whether this cohesiveness operates in the same way as cohesiveness developed through years of personal contact. Perhaps this approach will help to meet one of the criticisms, and weaknesses, of the laboratory experiment in the social sciences—namely, that it is "unrealistic." [12] It may not be necessary for the laboratory situation to be realistic, but it probably is necessary for the *variables* introduced into the experiment to be realistic. Of course, the test of a variable is not its apparent realism, but whether or not it has a consistent effect. What is suggested here is that, of all the myriad of variables which a strong imagination can dream up, only those which bear some relation to social or psychological reality, conscious or unconscious, are likely to have an effect. In the future, better trained observers, using more powerful tools, may be able to perceive more that is realistic than social scientists are able to do today.

c. One of the best ways of choosing, from among a large number of possible hypotheses, the one or few most likely to be verified after testing is to have an initial period of informal and unsystematic, but thoughtful and critical, observation, using whatever relevant descriptive studies and general information may be available. This kind of observation is especially important in the early stages of any science, before frameworks of assumptions, definitions, and tested propositions are known to be workable and fruitful. Too frequently in research today what is called a hypothesis is an arbitrary or fortuitous guess on the part of a social scientist whose experience is necessarily limited. This must be a wasteful procedure, even if the experimental design for the ensuing study is rigorous. If the researcher has a fairly good knowledge about a few selected, but relevant, cases, he has at least

[12] G. E. Swanson, in a very thoughtful paper, meets many of the usual objections against the use of the laboratory experiment in studying social behavior by showing that the criteria for validity in laboratory experiments are the same criteria for validity in field studies. He does seem, however, to fall into the error of assuming that generalizability is generalization. For example, in making a suggestion for the study of cultural factors in the laboratory, he says, "Suppose that we move from the particulars to a higher level of generalization." This may, of course, simply be an unfortunate choice of a word. (G. E. Swanson, "Some Problems of Laboratory Experiments with Small Populations," *American Sociological Review*, 16 [June 1951], 349–358, esp. pp. 355–356.)

some ground for hypothesizing a cause for the phenomenon he wishes to study.

Finally, we have to face the possibility that none of our proposals for the improvement of research design will lead to generalizations that will stand up under systematic replication, because our techniques of acquiring data may not be delicate and precise enough to isolate the basic elements of human behavior and social organization. In that case, we would have to undergo a long process of refinement of techniques before we could achieve any reliable and valid generalizations.

REPLICATED STUDIES

A. Summaries of replications

1. Karl F. Schuessler and Donald R. Cressey, "Personality Characteristics of Criminals," *American Journal of Sociology,* 55 (March 1950), 476–484. Survey of studies correlating personality traits and criminality. Conclusions not consistent.
2. Arnold M. Rose, *Studies in Reduction of Prejudice* (2nd ed.; Chicago: American Council on Race Relations, 1948), Chap. I. Survey of experimental studies on reducing intergroup prejudice. Conclusions not consistent. On the same material, Robin M. Williams, Jr., *The Reduction of Intergroup Tension* (New York: Social Science Research Council, 1947). Conclusions not consistent.
3. Robert R. Sears, *Survey of Studies of Psychoanalytic Concepts,* Social Science Research Council Bulletin, No. 51 (New York, 1943). Conclusions not consistent.
4. Dorothy S. Thomas, *Research Memorandum on Migration Differentials,* Social Science Research Council Bulletin, No. 43 (New York, 1943). Survey of studies on selective factors in migration. Conclusions not consistent.
5. Ralph M. Stogdill, "Personal Factors Associated with Leadership," *Journal of Psychology,* 25 (January 1948), 35–71. Survey of studies of physical and personality traits of leaders. Conclusions not consistent.
6. Raymond B. Cattell, "The Cultural Functions of Social Stratification: II. Regarding Individual and Group Dynamics," *Journal of Social Psychology,* 21 (February 1945), 25–55. Summary of studies of the effects of social stratification on the acquired characteristics of individuals. The summary includes studies on class mean differences in intelligence and character traits such as honesty, aggression, and maladjustment. Items pulled out of studies and interpreted to be consistent.
7. Allen Edwards, "The Retention of Affective Experiences—A Criticism and Restatement of the Problem," *Psychological Review,* 49 (January 1942), 43–53. Summary of studies dealing with the Freudian theory that unpleasant experiences and events are repressed (i.e., that forgetting is an active process). Conclusions not consistent.
8. Jerome D. Frank, "Recent Studies of the Level of Aspiration," *Psychological Bulletin,* 38 (April 1941), 218–226. Summary of level-of-aspiration studies. Frank is not concerned with a specific hypothesis but cites several studies on each of several determinants of levels, such as knowledge of group performance or personality traits. Consistent findings on some things, but not on others.
9. W. A. Kerr, "Correlates of Politico-Economic Liberalism-Conservatism," *Journal of Social Psychology,* 20 (August 1944), 61–77. Summary of studies on a series of factors which are supposedly related to liberalism-conservatism, such as parental attitudes and religion. Consistent findings on some things, but not on others.

10. Milton Metfessel and Constance Lovell, "Recent Literature on Individual Correlates of Crime," *Psychological Bulletin*, 39 (March 1942), 133–164. Summary of factors found to be associated with criminality in various studies. Also factors associated with different types of crime. Conclusions not consistent.

11. Alexander Mintz, "A Re-Examination of Correlations between Lynchings and Economic Indices," *Journal of Abnormal and Social Psychology*, 41 (April 1946), 154–160. Considers three studies—those by Hovland and Sears, Raper, and Thomas —which correlate lynching with economic variables. He criticizes the studies from the standpoint of statistical methodology. The three studies had the same general conclusions.

12. Llewellyn Queener, "The Development of Internationalist Attitudes: III. The Literature and a Point of View," *Journal of Social Psychology*, 30 (August 1949), 105–126. Summary of studies of the prestige factor as a determinant of international attitudes. Also concerned with "negative prestige," similar to the frustration-aggression hypothesis in attitude formation. Conclusions interpreted into a consistent framework.

13. H. M. Richardson, "Studies of Mental Resemblance between Husbands and Wives and between Friends," *Psychological Bulletin*, 36 (February 1939), 104–120. Summary of studies on question of whether "like" attracts "like" or "unlike." Deals with studies on selective mating where selection is based on physical resemblances and/or similarities in intelligence, attitudes, and personality traits. Some consistency in findings for intelligence, interests, and attitudes, but not for personality traits.

14. Julian B. Rotter, "Level of Aspiration as a Method of Studying Personality," *Psychological Review*, 49 (September 1942), 463–474. Summary of studies on the effect of success and failure on explicitly set goals. Concerned with the consistency of an individual's response and whether or not there is a relationship between the responses and personality traits. Conclusions not consistent.

15. Anselm L. Strauss, "The Literature on Panic," *Journal of Abnormal and Social Psychology*, 39 (July 1944), 317–328. Summary of descriptive features and causes of panic as cited by various authors. Not complete studies, but some consistency in descriptions, although less agreement on causes.

16. William W. Wattenberg, "Delinquency and Only Children: Study of a Category," *Journal of Abnormal and Social Psychology*, 44 (July 1949), 356–366. Studies of the relationship between delinquency and being an only child. The question is whether (1) being only children they become spoiled or (2) being exempted from the effects of sibling rivalry they have an advantage over other children. Conclusions not consistent.

B. Replicated studies in which comparison with the original study is made by the author of the replication

1. Walter Firey, *Land Use in Central Boston* (Cambridge, Mass.: Harvard University Press, 1947), pp. 76–86. Replicative of E. W. Burgess in R. E. Park and E. W. Burgess (eds.), *The City* (Chicago: University of Chicago Press, 1925), and of Maurice R. Davie, "The Pattern of Urban Growth," in *Studies in the Science of Society* (New Haven, Conn.: Yale University Press, 1937), pp. 142–161. See also Lloyd Rodwin, "The Theory of Residential Growth and Structure," *Appraisal Journal*, 18 (July 1950), 295–317. Studies of "typical" patterns of modern city growth. Conclusions not consistent.

2. Eleanor C. Isbell, "Internal Migration in Sweden and Intervening Opportunities," *American Sociological Review*, 9 (December 1944), 627–639. Replicative of Samuel A. Stouffer, "Intervening Opportunities: A Theory Relating Mobility and Distance," *American Sociological Review*, 5 (December 1940), 845–867; and of Margaret L. Bright and Dorothy S. Thomas, "Interstate Migration and Intervening Opportunities," *American Sociological Review*, 6 (December 1941), 773–783.

Studies of "intervening opportunities" as a determinant of distance of migration. Conclusions consistent.

3. Paul Wallin, "Cultural Contradictions and Sex Roles: A Repeat Study," *American Sociological Review*, 15 (April 1950), 288–293. Replicative of Mirra Komarovsky, "Cultural Contradictions and Sex Roles," *American Journal of Sociology*, 52 (November 1946), 184–189. Conclusions consistent.

4. Paul H. Landis, "Personality Differences of Girls from Farm, Town, and City," *Rural Sociology*, 14 (March 1949), 10–20. Replicative of A. R. Mangus, "Personality Adjustments of Rural and Urban Children," *American Sociological Review*, 13 (October 1948), 566–575. Studies of relative "adjustment" among rural and urban children. Conclusions not consistent.

5. G. S. Klein, H. J. Schlesinger, and D. E. Meister, "The Effect of Experimental Values on Perception: An Experimental Critique," *Psychological Review*, 58 (March 1951), 96–112. Replicative of J. S. Bruner and L. Postman, "Symbolic Value as an Organizing Factor in Perception," *Journal of Social Psychology*, 27 (May 1948), 203–208. Also of L. F. Carter and K. Schooler, "Value, Need and Other Factors in Perception," *Psychological Review*, 56 (July 1949), 200–207. Conclusions not consistent.

6. J. F. Rosenblith, "A Replication of 'Some Roots of Prejudice'," *Journal of Abnormal and Social Psychology*, 44 (October 1949), 470–489. Replication of G. W. Allport and B. Kramer, "Some Roots of Prejudice," *Journal of Psychology*, 22 (July 1946), 9–39. Conclusions consistent except in two minor respects.

7. Bradley Reynolds, "A Repetition of the Blodgett Experiment on 'Latent Learning'," *Journal of Experimental Psychology*, 35 (December 1945), 504–516. Replicative of H. C. Blodgett, "The Effect of the Introduction of Reward upon the Maze Performance of Rats," *University of California Publications in Psychology*, 31 (1928), 114–134. Conclusions partially consistent.

8. F. Stuart Chapin and Sheldon Stryker, "Confirmation of Results of an Ex Post Facto Experimental Design by Replication," *American Sociological Review*, 15 (October 1950), 670–672. Replicative of F. Stuart Chapin, Clarence A. Johanson, and Arthur L. Johnson, "Rental Rates and Crowding in Dwelling Units in Manhattan," *American Sociological Review*, 15 (February 1950), 95–97. Conclusions not consistent.

9. Georg Karlsson, *Adaptability and Communication in Marriage: A Swedish Predictive Study of Marital Satisfaction* (Uppsala, Sweden: Almquist and Wiksells Boktryckeri Aktiebolag, 1951). Replicative of Harvey J. Locke, *Predicting Adjustment in Marriage: A Comparison of a Divorced and a Happily Married Group* (New York: Holt, 1951). For a direct comparison, see Harvey J. Locke and Georg Karlsson, "Marital Adjustment and Prediction in Sweden and the United States," *American Sociological Review*, 17 (February 1952), 10–17. Most conclusions consistent.

10. Gerhart H. Saenger, "Social Status and Political Behavior," *American Journal of Sociology*, 51 (September 1945), 103–113. Replicative ot P. F. Lazarsfeld, B. Berelson, and H. Gaudet, *The People's Choice* (New York: Duell, Sloan and Pearce, 1944). Replicates only in parts, but these parts are consistent. Also consistent with one conclusion in the 1944 study is a finding by Alice S. Kitt and David B. Gleicher, "Determinants of Voting Behavior," *Public Opinion Quarterly*, 14 (Fall 1950), 393–412.

11. T. W. Adorno, E. Frenkel-Brunswik, D. J. Levinson, and R. N. Sanford, *The Authoritarian Personality* (New York: Harper, 1950); B. Bettleheim and M. Janowitz, *Dynamics of Prejudice* (New York: Harper, 1950); N. W. Ackerman and M. Jahoda, *Anti-Semitism and Emotional Disorder* (New York: Harper, 1950). Replicative of E. L. Hartley, *Problems in Prejudice* (New York: King's Crown Press, 1946). Results generally, but vaguely, consistent.

12. Virgil R. Carlson and Richard S. Lazarus, "A Repetition of Williams' Experiment

on Stress and Associated Rorschach Factors," *American Psychologist*, 7 (July 1952), 317. Replicative of Meyer Williams, "An Experimental Study of Intellectual Control under Stress and Associated Rorschach Factors," *Journal of Consulting Psychology*, 11 (January–February 1947), 21–29. Conclusions not consistent.

13. L. Festinger, S. Schachter, and K. Back, *Social Pressures in Informal Groups* (New York: Harper, 1950); and T. Caplow and R. Forman, "Neighborhood Interaction," *American Sociological Review*, 15 (June 1950), 357–366. Independent studies, both arriving at the conclusion that in a homogeneous neighborhood the frequency of association with different neighbors is a direct function of the proximity of the neighbor's front and back doors to one's own.

14. S. Schachter *et al.*, "An Experimental Study of Cohesiveness and Productivity," *Human Relations*, vol. 4, no. 3 (1951), pp. 229–238. Replicative of Kurt Back, "The Exertion of Influence through Social Communication," *Journal of Abnormal and Social Psychology*, 46 (1951), 9–23. Studies show that the more cohesive a group, the more influence it is able to exert on its individual members. Other laboratory experiments on this hypothesis have been conducted at the universities of Michigan, Texas, and Uppsala, Sweden, but are not yet published. Field studies verifying the same hypothesis are Festinger, Schachter, and Back, *op. cit.*; A. Rose, S. Schachter, and H. Zetterberg, "Social Responsibility as Affected by Group Standards and Cohesiveness," unpublished. All these studies support the hypothesis, but there are minor variations in results.

C. Replicated studies of attitude differentials

In studying a given attitude in various segments of the population, different investigators report differentials in certain background factors. Attitudes on race have frequently been studied, and I have summarized all empirical studies on this subject up to 1947.[13] The following is a brief summary, from this source, of the differentials reported in the scientific literature on race attitudes:

1. In seven studies, it is reported that northern white college students are more favorable to Negroes than are southern white college students. In four studies, it is reported that there is no significant difference in attitudes toward Negroes between northern and southern students or, in one study, that northern students are more anti-Negro than southern students.

2. In five studies, it is reported that girls or women have more liberal race attitudes than do males. In two studies, it is reported that males are more liberal than females. In two studies, significant sex differences are found, but they vary by type of attitude. In four studies, no significant differences in race attitudes were found between the sexes.

3. In three studies, students with higher IQ's were found to be more favorable toward minority groups than were the less intelligent students. In three other studies, no significant relationship was found between IQ and race attitudes.

4. Three studies report that rural or small town students have more liberal race attitudes than do urban students. Two studies report that urban students have more liberal race attitudes than do rural students. Two studies report no differences between urban and rural students.

D. Replicated studies, reported within a given publication, based on different samples or on the same sample at different times

1. Samuel A. Stouffer *et al.*, *The American Soldier* (4 vols.; Princeton, N.J.: Princeton University Press, 1949–1950). Conclusions consistent on some subjects but not on others.

---

[13] Arnold M. Rose, *Studies in Reduction of Prejudice* (2nd ed.; Chicago: American Council on Race Relations, 1948), Chap. III.

2. Clifford Kirkpatrick and John Cotton, "Physical Attractiveness, Age, and Marital Adjustment," *American Sociological Review*, 16 (February 1951), 81–86. Conclusions not consistent.

3. Louis Guttman, in Paul Horst *et al.*, *The Prediction of Personal Adjustment* (New York: Social Science Research Council, 1941), 360–362. A prediction of personal adjustment gave a coefficient of multiple correlation of +.73. The second one—using the same measures on a different sample—was +.04. Author attributes this to sampling error of insufficient cases and too many variables.

4. Arnold M. Rose, "Rumor in the Stock Market," *Public Opinion Quarterly*, 15 (Fall 1951), 461–486. Conclusions consistent.

16

Conditions of the Social Science Experiment

To *the extent that science is concerned with the relationship between cause and effect, the key method of science must be the experiment. It is the contention of the following chapter, however, that no technique developed to investigate one set of problems may be borrowed without modification and applied automatically without adjustment to another set of problems. The urge to use the experimental method developed in the natural sciences has now been properly fostered among social scientists. The conditions under which we can expect the experimental method to be useful and the adjustments that must be made when applying experimental techniques in the social sciences receive consideration in the following chapter.*

WHEN experiments are performed on social objects, special attention needs to be paid to certain features of the experiment which the experimenter on physical or biological objects can afford to overlook. It is not that the intrinsic characteristics of the experiment are different in the social and natural sciences, but that the characteristics of the social object and the social context of the experimenter are sufficiently different to warrant special consideration. Chapin,[1] Greenwood,[2] and others have performed an excellent service for sociologists by pointing out the ways in which the experimental method could be adapted to social science problems and by performing actual social science experiments to break the path for more extended use of that method. The experimental method is probably the most fruitful method of science generally, and its use in social science will no doubt extend knowledge markedly. While there is no intrinsic reason why the experiment cannot be applied to social science problems, there are differences between physical data and social data that should be taken

[1] F. Stuart Chapin, *Experimental Designs in Sociological Research* (New York: Harper, 1947).
[2] Ernest Greenwood, *Experimental Sociology, A Study in Method* (New York: King's Crown Press, 1945).

into consideration before the method is carried over from one science to the other. Before taking up these differences, some of the common characteristics of experiments will be restated.

An experiment consists simply of applying a stimulus to some object, holding constant other possible stimuli or conditions which might affect the object simultaneously, and noting the changes that occur in the object, presumably because of the application of the stimulus. The purpose of the experiment, then, is to discover cause-and-effect relationships applicable to certain classes of objects. The natural scientists regard the experiment as the major way of discovering, and probably the only way of proving, such cause-and-effect relationships. Most, but certainly not all, research in the natural sciences consists of experiments.

The holding constant of possibly interfering conditions takes place in one of two ways. First, such conditions are physically removed. For example, if the experiment would be affected by air, all air is removed from a jar or tube and the experiment is carried on in this vacuum. Second, a "control group" is used which is matched with the experimental object in all relevant respects except that of the experimental stimulus. This is done in order that interfering conditions will affect the control as well as the experimental object and allow the effect of the experimental stimulus to be subtracted.

There is a significant distinction between these two designs for holding constant possibly interfering conditions: In the former case the interfering conditions are removed so that the cause can have its effect *without interference,* whereas in the latter case the interfering conditions are equalized so that the cause has its effect *in the presence of the interfering conditions* but it is presumed that the influence of the interfering conditions can be measured and subtracted from the total effect. The physical scientist tries to follow the first type of design, and only occasionally is obliged to resort to the second, whereas the social scientist is practically always obliged to use the second type of design.

The matching in the second type of design takes place in one of two ways: (1) Pairs of individuals are selected who have certain identical traits, and one of each pair is placed in the experimental group while the other is placed in the control group. It is assumed that the traits on which the individuals are selected to be identical are the interfering conditions. Thus in this type of design it is assumed that all interfering conditions are known. (2) Individuals and conditions are "randomized" between the control and the experimental groups, so that which is true of one—before the application of the experimental stimulus—can be expected to be true of the other, except for chance deviations. In this type of design, the interfering conditions held constant need not be known.

There is an assumption behind the logic of determining causes by means of experimentation that the physical scientist—who devised the method of experimentation in the first place—never has to call into question. This is the uniformity of his experimental object. In early experiments on conductivity, for example, pure metals could be obtained through which electric charges could be sent and the conductivity of the metals measured. The metals were uniform, or deviated from uniformity by known, small amounts, and therefore a single experiment could determine, within narrow limits, the conductivity of a given metal.

When the biologists came to perform experiments, they discovered that they had more difficulty in finding "normal" organisms than the physicists had in finding "pure" metals. However, they developed their concept of normality and made an effort to include a range of specimens before performing an experiment on a living object. There was still no need to question, however, that an experimental finding derived from one group of organisms applied to any other organisms of the same species.

The social scientist faces a still more difficult problem when he uses the experimental method. Variability among people's minds is so great that a serious question can be raised as to whether the effect of an experimental stimulus applied to one group of individuals is the same effect that would be obtained if the same stimulus were applied to another group of individuals. The social scientist does not have the biologist's recourse to the concept of normality because for most social phenomena there is no norm except in terms of individual or group values. Who is to say what a normal attitude toward war is, or what the healthy organization of a social club may be? An individual's reaction to an experimental stimulus, his ability to "absorb" the stimulus, is based upon all his previous experiences with related objects—that is, upon his apperceptive mass. Since few people have identical apperceptive masses, an experimental finding for one group of people need not necessarily apply to another group.

The very variation within an experimental group in its response to an experimental stimulus should indicate to the social experimenter the nature of his problem. The physical or biological scientist seldom meets variant response, and when he does he always seeks its cause and reports on it along with his major experimental findings. The social science experiment, on the other hand, is usually reported solely in terms of a difference between two means, one for a group of people before the application of the stimulus, and the other one after the stimulus. The use of the average as a measure obscures the fact that the group was not uniform to begin with, and that the stimulus had differential effects on members of the group. A measure of variation may also be reported but an explanation of differential response is almost always regarded as beyond the scope of the experiment.

The result is that the experimental finding applies only to the group on which the experiment was performed—for example, to 329 seniors in 3 Chicago high schools. The addition of a dozen selected persons to the group would be expected to alter the experimental findings. If the experiment had been performed in a different type of high school, or in another city, the experimental finding would perhaps be different. This is a serious limitation on experimentation in the social sciences. It is the source of conflicting findings from similar experiments.

For example, a survey of experiments designed to measure the influence of certain stimuli on race attitudes revealed that there were greatly differing findings. This is demonstrated in the accompanying tabulation,[3] where the figures indicate the number of studies showing

Experimental Stimulus	Change	No Change	Indefinite
School or college course........	8	4	1
Specific propaganda...........	9	4	1
Personal contacts.............	4	3	3

change or absence of change in race attitudes as a result of specified influences. When findings like these occur, the experiments cannot be said to answer questions about cause-and-effect; they simply lead to further argument. The social scientist needs to realize that his findings apply only to that specific statistical universe of which his experi-

[3] This information appeared originally in Arnold M. Rose, *Studies in Reduction of Prejudice* (2nd ed.; Chicago: American Council on Race Relations, 1948), p. 27.

mental group is representative. If he makes his experimental group more broadly representative, he broadens the validity of his findings.

Another problem for the social science experimenter, and another source of conflict in his findings, is the difficulty in specifying his stimulus. The physical and biological scientists do not seem to have been faced with this problem to any extent. Heating a body to 200° C., or injecting a given chemical, served as a unitary stimulus, and there was never any difficulty in duplicating the stimulus. When the social scientist comes to perform his experiments, however, he frequently finds that his stimulus is a complex of elements, some of which he may have no control over, and each of which may have a different effect on, the experimental group. It may be difficult or impossible to reproduce the stimulus exactly for subsequent tests. For example, a movie is a frequently used type of stimulus in a social science experiment. Not only does a movie contain a large conglomeration of varying scenes, characters, and settings, but a movie has to be shown in a certain type of room, under a given context of events, by a given operator. Each of these elements may have a different influence on the experimental group, and it may be difficult to reproduce this concatenation of elements in order to perform the experiment a second time. Certainly this complexity of the stimulus reduces the possibility of generalizing about its influence. Yet the social science experimenter sometimes finds it difficult to specify a simpler stimulus than a movie without sacrificing the realism of the stimulus.

The social scientist is somewhat more handicapped than is the physical or biological scientist in holding extraneous influences constant, and he is quite aware of his difficulties in this respect. The social scientist is seldom in a position to remove the extraneous influences physically, although society sometimes creates situations in which such influences are physically held constant. The social scientist is usually obliged to use a control group, and his difficulties in matching individuals are somewhat greater than those of the biologist. It is difficult to find pairs of individuals who are alike in all respects that might influence their reactions to the experimental stimulus. Few social science experimenters who use the matching technique feel completely satisfied that their control groups are identical with their experimental groups in all relevant respects. This limitation does not apply in a laboratory experiment where experimental and control groups can be strictly randomized.

Even should perfectly matched controls be found by the social science experimenter, they would allow him only to *correct* for extraneous influences. The extraneous influences still operate on the experimental object; they are not "held constant" in the natural science experimenter's sense of the term. The correction process involves measuring changes in the control cases—changes which of course are not due to the experimental stimulus—and adding or subtracting these measured changes to the experimental change. This step raises two questions: (1) How good are our measurements? Are they sufficiently good to permit their addition to or subtraction from another set of measurements? (2) Does the existence of an extraneous influence, even when accounted for by the use of measured controls, sometimes change the nature of the experimental stimulus? For example, a piece of propaganda experimentally used to reduce race prejudice takes on an unusual significance if it is administered simultaneously with an endorsement of it by a powerful source of prestige—say, the Catholic Church.

The latter point can be stated more generally, in a form which indicates that it is a major methodological consideration for the social science experimenter. The control holds constant only *extraneous* influences, but it does not hold constant *internal* influences not part of the experimental stimulus. I was once given the assignment of setting up a social science field experiment in which excellent controls were available. These controls permitted the holding constant of those external influences which affected the control cases and experimental cases equally. But the experimental cases were social beings to whom things were happening completely beyond the control, and even beyond the experience, of the experimenter, and they were happening only to these cases and to no others in the world at that time. The social scientist cannot control his experimental cases as the natural scientist can control his. In this situation, the social scientist has to find out what is happening to his cases and seek to measure the influence of uncontrolled factors on them. This is not a completely satisfactory solution, but the social scientist is compelled to put up with an ongoing social process over which he has only limited control.

In the "laboratory" experiment, where experimental and control groups can be matched by randomization, the problem of control is much easier and the limitation cited above need not apply. But another problem arises in laboratory experiments which is not so likely to occur in field experiments. In laboratory experiments the experimental stimulus has to be "induced" under unrealistic or camouflaged conditions. Just exactly what is induced is not always clear, even though the cautious experimentalist measures the extent to which the induction has "caught." The difficulty is that the experimenter does not know what *else* has "caught." The experimental stimulus is supposed to be the independent variable, or cause, and the measured effect is supposed to be the dependent variable. But the experimenter may have inadvertently induced the effect itself, or a "suppressor variable" which inhibits the effect from appearing, or another causal variable which creates the expected effect rather than the intended experimental stimulus.

To obtain effective induction, the laboratory experimenter does not let the subjects know what he is inducing by way of independent variable. What would be the effect on them if some of them inadvertently guessed correctly what the intended induction was? As college students are used more and more frequently in social science laboratory experiments, their ability to guess correctly the intended induction may be expected to increase, and while they may still respond in the expected way (that is, the intended induction "catches"), another variable will have been introduced into the experiment that cannot be controlled.

Another aspect of the social science experiment can be called into question. When an experimental group is matched with a control group to hold extraneous factors constant, the situation is not the same as when the extraneous factors are physically held constant. The stimulus may have an effect at one level of control, but perhaps not at other levels. For example, holding ethnic status constant by selecting a control group with the same ethnic distribution as is found in the experimental group is different from eliminating ethnic status in the same way the physicist eliminates electric disturbance from his experimental setup. It does not preclude the stimulus from having an effect on some ethnic groups but not on others. Yet the social science experimenter frequently believes he can take any sort of experimental group provided he can match it with a control group.

Actually, conclusions can be made only for homogeneous groups, when homogeneity is defined as responding in the same way to the identical stimulus. Since the experimenter cannot know in advance how the members of his group are going to respond, he has to make some intelligent guesses, based on a great deal of general information, as to what factors identify a homogeneous group for his experiment. The determination of homogeneous groups and the use of the experimental method only on such homogeneous groups are major demands on the careful social science experimenter.

So much for the difficulties of the social scientist. There is another difference between the social scientist and the physical and biological scientists which is relevant to this discussion, however. One of the essential characteristics of modern science, as compared to the science of the ancient world, is that it assumes that all objects are constantly in motion and that they are constantly changing. The experimental method supports this point of view, since the experiment requires induced change. The natural scientist's knowledge of cause-and-effect relationships is based on his ability to change the world, and his success in attaining knowledge has led him to assume automatically that the world is highly susceptible to induced change. The social scientist, on the other hand, because of his difficulties in performing experiments, has had to do research on relatively static phases of his subject matter. Even when the social scientist studies trends or social change, he does not get the sense of mutability in society that he would get if he were inducing the change himself.

Psychology, a discipline with roots in biological science as well as in social science, has employed the experimental method on social science subjects to a much greater extent than has sociology (and probably to a much greater extent than have any of the other social sciences). One of the distinct impressions I got while surveying the experiments of psychologists in the psychology of prejudice is that they conceive the social world to be much less stable than the sociologists conceive it to be. The psychologists do not analyze prejudice and race relations in terms of folkways, mores, traditions, caste, in-groups, categoric contacts, and other common sociological concepts, but in terms of frustration and aggression, projection, displacement, catharsis, mental conflict, ambiguous attitudes, propaganda, conditioning, interests, and so on. The psychologists' concepts, regardless of what "school" they belong to, usually imply a more dynamic view of society and the individual than do the sociologists' concepts.

This observation does not involve a judgment of which set of terms is more correct or more realistic; it simply analyzes an implicit assumption contained in those tools of research known as concepts. It is not likely that the reliance on one set of concepts is related to political conservatism or radicalism. It is not likely that the prevalence of a certain assumption in the concepts of a discipline selects individuals with a congenial temperament to go into that discipline (that is, the personal motives which lead a person to go into social psychology are not likely to be different from those which lead a person to go into sociology). Nevertheless, sociologists have a more static picture of society than do psychologists. This is partly due to the fact that psychologists make extensive use of the experimental method and sociologists do not. The experimental method, in sum, involves certain problems and certain assumptions which are more significant for the social scientist than for the physical or biological scientist. The social scientist cannot properly take over the experimental method from the older sciences without examining it for its problems and assumptions in relation to his specific topic for research.

17

A Weakness of Partial Correlation
in Sociological Studies

IN view of the difficulty of applying the full experimental method to their subject matter, sociologists have tried to use certain statistical substitutes— developed primarily in agricultural and genetic research—for the natural science experiment. The following chapter shows that these substitutes meet the logical requirements of the experimental method only when applied to a few limited areas of social science research. Again we see the tendency on the part of sociologists to overgeneralize, this time in the area of method. That techniques of partial correlation are appropriate in biological research does not prove that they are applicable, without drastic changes which have not yet been made, to the usual sociological investigations.

THE SIMPLE correlation—a measure of the extent to which changes in one variable are associated with changes in another variable—has frequently been deprecated by statisticians. It is said to be of minor value because it seldom gives knowledge of scientific cause-and-effect relationships. Partial correlation, on the other hand, has been praised since it is thought to approximate the scientific experiment in which the concomitant variation between two factors can be noted when irrelevancies are held constant. It is the thesis of this chapter that for most kinds of social data the partial correlation comes no closer to the type of cause-and-effect knowledge yielded by experiment than does the simple correlation. Further, the simple correlation has what might be called an administrative value that is seldom had by the partial correlation. For the purposes of this paper, "partial correlation" will be used to refer to any form of measuring association when one or more factors are held constant. It thus includes standardized rates,

NOTE: I wish to thank Dr. Jane Loevinger, the psychologist-statistician, for a helpful reading of this chapter.

compared percentages, and cross-classifications of higher than first order, as well as the partial correlation proper.

When it is known from sources of knowledge outside of the data being correlated that one factor has a direct causal effect on another factor, it is proper to hold the first factor constant when studying the second. This is frequently the case with data on physical and biological phenomena, but seldom with data on social phenomena. An example of the valid use of partial correlation when applied to social phenomena occurs in the usual technique of comparing the birth rates of two regions. It is known from biology that women can have children only between certain ages. If one region has a disproportionate share of women in this age period, it would not be "fair" to compare the birth rate of the two regions without holding the age distribution constant. More complicated examples could be given of the valid use of "holding constant" some factors when comparing or noting associations between others, but they all involve a premise that a definite causal relation is independently known between the factor held constant and one of the factors compared or associated. "Cause" here means a "sufficient" cause, which is the common meaning of the term, not a "necessary but not sufficient" cause which is commonly spoken of as a *condition* which must occur for a cause to have its effect." It is never logically legitimate to hold the latter constant by means of partial correlation.

Most sociological or psychological studies using correlation are not based on such outside knowledge.[1] The usual procedure in such research is to associate two variables, holding constant another variable —education, for example. Now it is *not* known that there is an independent and "sufficient" causal relation between education and most of the other social variables studied. Education might be correlated with these other social factors and still not be the cause of their variation. Therefore it might be that in holding education constant we are holding constant part of the association, between the other social factors, that we wish to measure. Needless to say, this procedure is invalid. This objection to the misuse of partial correlation cannot be met by stating that the formula for partial correlation involves a subtraction of the intercorrelations between the factor held constant

[1] The major fields in the social sciences that use partial correlation with outside knowledge from other disciplines are economics and demography.

(education, in our example) and the factors being studied. Education may be correlated with the latter factors because (1) it has an indirect causal connection—that is, it is interconnected with other causal factors; (2) it has a fortuitous connection;[2] or (3) it is an effect of them, rather than because it has a direct causal connection with them. It is quite proper to subtract the intercorrelation when the factor held constant stands solely as a direct cause of one or both of the other variables, but the situation is quite different when one of the other three conditions prevails.

To illustrate the dangers of using partial correlation without outside knowledge, let us take a hypothetical example.[3] Let us say that in the year 1936 positive simple correlations were noted (1) between educational status and knowledge about the new social security laws, and (2) between economic status and knowledge about the social security laws. The investigator had a general theory that educated people keep themselves informed about current affairs to a greater extent than do uneducated people, and so he assumed that education was the basic factor. He then calculated a partial correlation coefficient between economic status and knowledge about social security laws, holding education constant, and found—sure enough—that the original zero-order correlation between economic status and knowledge dropped considerably. Similar partial correlations were done between several other factors and knowledge, with education held constant, and in every case they were low. The investigator then felt that his theory was correct and came to the conclusion that there was nothing unusual about lack of knowledge about social security laws. Only a rise in the general educational level would, in that situation, have resulted in a higher level of knowledge about the social security laws.

Four years later—after the social security laws had been in operation for some time—new data on this same subject were gathered, and it was found that less-educated people knew more about the social security laws than better-educated people did. This was explained in terms of the greater degree of contact with the operation of these laws that less-educated people had. But why should less-

---

[2] An example of a fortuitous connection would be such a situation as presidential election years being identical with leap years. That is, the two things are started off at the same time and keep pace with each other because of rules inherent in each of them independently, but not because there is any causal connection between them.

[3] This hypothetical example is based on an actual study carried out in a federal government agency; this study cannot be referred to directly.

educated people have more contact with the operation of these laws? Because they were in the working classes. Now it was known that educational status and occupation or income were correlated. Further, it was found that wealthy people had less knowledge about the social security laws in 1940 than they had in 1936, although this drop in knowledge did not occur for highly educated people in the upper- and middle-income brackets. Someone was able to call attention to the fact that in 1936, when the social security laws were being passed, there had been a barrage of propaganda against them, and a good deal of discussion about them, among people at the upper economic levels. In retrospect it seemed that it was this propaganda and discussion among those at the upper economic levels which had been responsible for the correlation found in 1936. The explanation in terms of education was incorrect, and it was realized that there had been no justification in the first place for holding education constant when the relation between economic status and knowledge about the social security laws was examined.

What might be called the "administrative value" of the simple correlation is that within the population studied the simple correlation informs the student of the existence and extent of a relationship. He can learn, for example, that the poorer a district is, the fewer people it contains who know about the provisions of the social security laws. If it is desired to disseminate knowledge about these laws, the administrator then knows that he must direct his greatest effort at the poorer districts. Nothing need be inferred about the causal relationship between poverty and knowledge about social security laws. No more can really be inferred about the causal nature of the relationship when education is held constant than when it is not held constant. It could be, as suggested in the example, that wealthy people know more about social security legislation because they have been barraged with propaganda against it, rather than because they are more educated. The administrative value of simple correlation is best known in prediction by interpolation in the line of regression.

The simple correlation is understood to be a measure of covariation without any implications of causal relationship. The partial correlation is widely misconceived to be a step in the direction of causal explanation. It is thought to be similar to holding factors constant in a physical experiment. But this is true only when there is independent

outside knowledge that the factor or factors held constant are causally related to the factors studied. Even if a factor known independently to be causally related to the factors studied is held constant in
a partial correlation, nothing can be said about the direction or degree
of causal relation between those factors from the sign or size of the
coefficient of partial correlation. This is true because still other factors
not held constant can be obscuring or even reversing the true relationship of the factors studied.

Let us take another example. A student found a significant correlation between a measure of "social participation" and a measure of
social status, but the correlation was not perfect, of course. He also
found a smaller but still significant correlation between social participation and distance of residence from the center of the city and a
similar correlation between status and distance. Thinking that distance from the center of the city might be "really" an inhibiting
factor in social participation, and therefore that the "intrinsic" relationship between participation and status was higher, he calculated a
partial correlation between the latter two variables, holding distance
constant. He was surprised to find that the coefficient of partial correlation was smaller than the coefficient of simple correlation between
participation and status. What had happened was that in holding
distance constant he was in effect holding part of social status constant. Distance of residence from the center of the city was both a
cause and an effect of status, and to hold it constant was equivalent
to holding some of the variation in status constant. To make his case,
the student should have performed an experiment. He should have
moved people of a certain status closer to the center of the city, and
measured any increase in their social participation. This is physically
(and socially) extremely difficult, of course, but the partial correlation
was no substitute for the experiment.

It has been my experience in sociological studies that a correlation
will fall to zero as the number of variables partialed out are increased.
Theoretically, the partial correlation should come closer to 1.00 as
"extraneous" variables are successively held constant. This does happen in biology, and frequently in demography and economics, but
usually not in sociology because of the intrinsic and socially inseparable
relationships of many variables. The problem is akin to the one the
social statistician frequently has in trying to decide when forming a

scatter diagram which variable is to be considered the independent variable (that is, the cause). He puts aside the problem by saying that correlation does not indicate causation anyway, and therefore it makes no difference which variable is the independent one. That is true and is one of the advantages of simple correlation. But it is to be noted that the problem seldom arises in biological science, and not often in economics or demography. In these sciences it is usually definitely known which of two variables is the independent one.[4]

For example, when correlating the size of the crop with the number of sunny days, the agronomist knows—from plant physiology—that the number of sunny days is the independent variable or cause. This permits him to hold constant the number of sunny days (by partial correlation, since he cannot control sunshine and cloud formation) when he wishes to correlate crop production with the amount of a certain fertilizer used. In other words, partial correlation requires a clear specification of the independent and dependent variables in all the zero-order correlations that are used in the calculation of the partial correlation. Before a factor can properly be held constant by partial correlation it must be known that it is a cause, but not at the same time an effect, of one or both of the variables being correlated. It must be a "pure" measure of the cause, not contaminated by factors which should not properly be held constant. It must also be known to be an independent cause and not a component of one or both of these variables. When the independent variable (or cause) cannot be identified, because relationships are interdependent rather than one-way, partial correlation cannot be justified.

The question arises as to when independent outside knowledge of one-way cause and effect relationship exists in sociology, so that one may legitimately use the technique of partial correlation. An example has already been given of biology's providing such knowledge. In general, it could be stated that any science which provides relevant knowledge about human beings on a more elemental level than the one used in the study can provide such knowledge. Thus, studies of social relationships could sometimes rely on knowledge from psychology and economics, as well as from biology.

[4] Nevertheless, it was a statistician in the biological sciences who was probably the first to suggest the limitations of the technique of partial correlation. See Sewall Wright, "Correlation and Causation," *Journal of Agricultural Research*, 20 (1920–1921), 557–585.

Another source of independent knowledge is logic. Economics owes a great deal of its success in using partial correlation to logic. For example, it is knowledge from logic that tells the economist that with a fixed amount of goods the money value of the goods will vary in direct proportion to the amount of money in circulation (since money has value only in terms of the goods it will buy). When, therefore, the economist wishes to study the relation between price and demand for goods, he is justified in holding constant the amount of money in circulation.

Two minor technical problems may be dismissed with mere mention. Both involve the assumption of normality—necessary to all correlation—in the distribution of values for each variable. First, the relation between variables must be linear, and second, the correlation must not be caused by a small proportion of the cases. These problems are usually dealt with rigorously and without much difficulty in simple correlation, but they are often ignored in the application of partial correlation in the social sciences. Nonlinearity can be detected in partial correlation only with much effort and can be adjusted for only with a tremendous amount of mechanical labor. The detection of spurious correlation due to lack of normality also involves much labor. These problems are mere technical ones but they loom large in any practical application of partial correlation and they should not be neglected.

The matter of the "purity" of the measure of a variable to be held constant, which has only been touched upon since it is only a minor facet of the general problem raised, may be resolved by the use of unidimensional scales, factor analysis, and more careful observation.

In conclusion, it may be stated that partial correlation—or any statistical method of holding factors constant—is not a substitute for scientific experiment in getting knowledge about cause-and-effect relationships. Exceptions occur where there is outside knowledge that there is a necessary relationship between a factor to be held constant and a factor under study. The simple correlation, while it gives no knowledge about cause-and-effect relationships, has an administrative value which is not so often possessed by the partial correlation. The sociologist who uses partial correlation is guilty of fallacious reasoning unless he has independent outside knowledge of cause-and-effect relations—usually based on findings of the more elemental sciences or on logic—before he holds any factors constant.[5]

[5] Long after this article was completed, but before I decided to publish it, my attention was called to an article published in 1927 by the psychologist Barbara S. Burks, entitled "Statistical Hazards in Nature-Nurture Investigations," (*Twenty-Seventh Yearbook of the National Society for the Study of Education*, pp. 11–14). In a few pages of this article Burks makes the same basic criticism of partial correlation that I sought to make almost twenty years later. The exposition is different, of course, and there are some distinguishing minor points in both articles, but at first it did not seem worth republishing the same general idea. On thinking over the misuse of partial correlation since Burks published her critique, as well as the inadequate treatment in many textbooks, I decided to try publication. The interested reader is encouraged to look up Burks' paper and an even earlier exposition by Burks in the *Journal of Educational Psychology* (November–December 1926), pp. 532–540, 625–630, for a more mathematically oriented exposition of the basic weakness of partial correlation.

SECTION V

Some Specific Techniques of Sociological Research

18

Attitude Measurement and the
Questionnaire Survey

We *now turn from the controversial chapters of the last section to the constructive suggestions by way of research techniques of the present section. The first chapter is simply a summary of the considerations that apply in the use of a technique which has probably the most widespread use in sociology and social psychology. Although the questionnaire survey as a research technique for attitude measurement may seem, to the uninitiated, to be simple in concept and easy in execution, the following chapter suggests that it is not.*

MUCH of the basic raw material of social science consists of the beliefs and attitudes of men. These presumably exist in men's minds, and one task of the social scientists is to get a fair representation of them down on paper. Traditionally, this work of the social psychologist and the sociologist has been known as "attitude measurement," although recent commercial use of some of the techniques has popularized the term "public opinion poll."

To some outsiders, the public opinion poll looks deceptively easy: you just ask people questions and add up their answers, and you know what they are thinking. To other outsiders, a correct representation of men's thoughts is an impossibility: how can you ever know what people are really thinking simply by asking them a few questions, when it is so easy to dissemble and when even a psychoanalytic probing of two years' duration sometimes fails to get beyond all the conscious or unconscious defenses?

Three decades of research and testing prove both types of critics wrong; it takes many technical devices and a good deal of skill to measure attitudes with validity and reliability, yet we know that it can be done. The early doubt that you could "really" get at attitudes through questionnaires was justifiably based upon a lack of concern on the part of opinion measurers for anything but a check mark or a verbal statement. As attitude measurers became more interested in the meaning of their raw data, this criticism became less valid. This must not be taken to mean that every published study of attitudes or every newspaper poll should be taken at face value. There are still numerous charlatans in the field, both with and without college degrees, who find it either profitable or prestigious to publish unsound figures. This has been especially true since reports on public opinion have become salable goods—to businessmen, to special-interest groups, or to the general public through newspapers and magazines.

MAJOR REQUIREMENTS

Let us briefly review the major requirements of a sound public opinion poll. In the first place, the questions must be capable of being answered adequately. There is little purpose in asking people questions for which they do not have an answer, or for which they cannot readily formulate an honest and complete answer. To rely on a refusal to answer is not sufficient, since some people seek to avoid the appearance of stupidity or ignorance by giving an answer when they really have none, and other people hesitate to appear dogmatic or overcertain by stating their true attitudes and so say that they "don't know."

Words serve as a vehicle for the question, and most words have at least a bit of ambiguity. It is essential that the words have a minimum of ambiguity as well as that they be simple and understandable to persons of little education. Even the person who has had long experience with formulating questions will occasionally be amazed when he poses a question, which he thinks is straightforward and unambiguous, to a variety of people and finds several variant interpretations. American culture is so far from being homogeneous that even the meanings of words shift markedly from one group to another. The skilled attitude measurer is aware of these cultural variations insofar as they apply to the more common words. Yet no reputable investigator will permit a questionnaire to go into the field without having "pretested" it on a range of individuals, representing the principal social groups, and experimenting on word selection with them.

This raises the question of the reliability and validity of the questionnaire. These concepts have played a central role in the development of measuring instruments in psychology and the other social sciences. A measuring instrument is commonly said to have validity if it measures what it is supposed to measure, and it has reliability if it gives the same results consistently. Both validity and reliability are measured statistically. Validity is measured by the correlation between the results produced by the measuring instrument and results known independently to be accurate. Reliability is generally measured by the correlation between the results of successive administrations of the measuring device, or by the correlation between the results of the administration of equivalent forms of the measuring device.

Validity and reliability may also be tested by nonstatistical means, which is often preferable, since it provides clues for the improvement of validity and reliability. The measuring instrument concerned may be either a test for knowledge or a questionnaire to ascertain opinion.

The procedure referred to is a guided interview commonly known as a pretest, but it must be conducted in a rigorous manner which is not always followed in the usual pretest. The group selected for the pretest must represent the full *range* of persons among whom the measuring instrument is to be ultimately used. The purpose of this requirement is to avoid having some people misunderstand the questions because a cultural divergence causes them to define certain words differently. The *number* of persons interviewed must be large enough to give stability to any findings about validity and reliability, as well as to permit an adequate range of persons to be interviewed. The interviewer must constantly exercise his ingenuity so as to catch any misinterpretations of the questions and any ambiguities in their wording. The interview must thus be an "experimental" one rather than one that is formalized and fixed in advance.[1]

The following is meant to be suggestive as to how the interview should proceed. The interviewer should first inform the respondent that he is simply trying out some questions, to see if they are good questions, before giving them to several thousand people all over the country (or whatever geographical range is being used). When a question is read to the respondent it may be wise to let him read the typed question along with the interviewer. Since the interviewer is interested in determining the relevancy of a "free" answer to the question, the respondent should not be given any check list of answers.

[1] See the following chapter, "A Research Note on Experimentation in Interviewing."

The relevancy of the response is an index of the validity of the question. The respondent's answer should not only reveal whether he understands the question as the interviewer hopes he will understand it, but it should also give the interviewer suggestions as to what form his check list must take (if he plans to use a check list). Even if the respondent's answer is judged to be relevant to the question, the interviewer should ask him about the meaning of various key words in the question. This would show the interviewer the extent to which variant definitions of the meaning of his questions are reducing the reliability of the questions.

The whole process, finally, gives the interviewer an inkling of the degree to which the respondent has formulated his opinion (or is certain of his knowledge of the answer to a factual question). This information is important for a judgment as to the reliability of the answers.

The interviewer may find it convenient to try alternative wordings, so as to reduce the ambiguity and complexity of his question and thus increase its validity or reliability. Variations of wording must, of course, be tested on the full range of respondents. The end product will be a question (1) that is easily understood by all the types of persons likely to be questioned in the future, (2) that means the same thing to the respondents that it means to the interviewer, and (3) that elicits in the minds of respondents the same sort of responses which the interviewer has formulated in his check list. Such a question has as high a degree of validity and reliability as the subject matter of the question and the conditions under which it is asked permit. It is not possible, of course, to expect a question about a subject on which the public has not formulated its opinions to have a high degree of reliability, or to expect a question about a subject of which the public knows little to have a high degree of validity. The pretest interviews will, however, let the interviewer know which of his questions have a low validity or reliability for these reasons.

There are other problems connected with questionnaire formation. Even when the question is completely and correctly understood, its specific wording can influence the direction of the answer in most instances. It is only when people have thought through all the ramifications of an issue and have reconciled their conflicting motivations toward it that they will not be influenced by the subtle connotations of the words constituting the question. Most attitude measurers have sought to meet this problem by choosing only "neutral" words and in other ways seeking to avoid the "biasing" of a question. Other investigators feel that no question is unbiased in an ongoing social situation and therefore seek to probe an attitude with a battery of five or six questions, some biased one way and others another way. This has led to the development of the "attitude scale" (which we shall consider later). The recognition that answers to biased questions may be significant also led to experimentation with questions that indirectly reveal attitudes of which the respondent may be completely unaware. Life itself is full of suggestive influences, and it may be as important to know whether an individual will respond to a subtle suggestion as it is to know how he will respond to a straightforward, unbiased question.

The complexity of human motives has been exploited in questionnaire formation in other ways. Numerous studies have shown that the order of questions in a questionnaire will influence the response, and investigators must not only be wary of this but must adjust for it by varying the question order in any one study. The content, or subject matter, of the question is also important. Kornhauser has demonstrated, for example, that many studies of attitudes on labor issues used a content that sought only to get at negative attitudes toward organized labor.[2] If, instead of asking questions about strikes and monopolistic practices, the studies posed questions about security and bargaining equality, the conclusions regarding the status of unions in American public opinion would have been quite different.

After a questionnaire is formulated, a second major set of problems arises. How, and under what circumstances, shall the interview be conducted? There are innumerable empirical "rules" on how to establish a good relationship with an interviewee, varying from an admonition against interviewing anyone where a third person can hear the answers to an injunction against expressing the interviewer's own attitude either by word or subtle gesture.

Some critics who have done little or no interviewing themselves question whether people will truthfully answer questions, especially when the questions become intimate and personal. Those who have

[2] Arthur Kornhauser, "Are Public Opinion Polls Fair to Organized Labor," *Public Opinion Quarterly*, 10 (Winter 1946–1947), 484–500; also see the symposium "Is Dr. Kornhauser Fair to Organized Pollers," *Public Opinion Quarterly*, 11 (Summer 1948), 198–212.

experience in interviewing know that it is possible to question successfully about any subject if the interviewee is "approached in the right
way." With very few exceptions, people seem to like to talk to strangers, especially if they feel their answers have some value, if they
understand the purpose of the interviewer, and if they are convinced
that their identities will be kept confidential. The interviewer must
be sympathetic toward the interviewee so as not to inhibit him from
expressing an unusual attitude, but nevertheless must maintain his
social distance, since it is the impersonality of the interview situation
that seems to bring out full and and frank answers. Studies have been
made to check the validity and completeness of answers secured by
good interviewers when interviewing on very touchy and personal
subjects, and it is startling to see how correct the information is.

The problems of interviewing remain for most investigators, however, because of the difficulty in securing or training good interviewers.[3] Checks have had to be devised to curb interviewer cheating. A
disturbing finding was that interviewers drawn from low-income levels
secured answers different from those brought in by interviewers who
had middle- or upper-income backgrounds. Conscientious investigators
are now training their interviewers more carefully and are trying to
select interviewers with backgrounds representative of the general
population.

There is a difference of opinion as to whether interviewers should
rigidly follow a fixed schedule of questions or should be free to develop
their own questions after a fixed first question sets the subject for
discussion. The fixed schedule reduces interviewer bias and the need
for high interviewing skill. It also has the advantage of permitting
easy classification and tabulation of the answers for quick reading.
The flexible schedule permits probing for subsurface and complex
attitudes. It allows the respondent to state his attitude in more than
a phrase, and it prevents misunderstanding about the meaning of
questions. The resolution of this disagreement about the rigidity or
flexibility of questions seems to have taken the form of a general
recognition that both forms have greatest value for different problems
and different subjects.

[3] The most systematic analysis of interviewer performance is that by Paul B. Sheat-
sky, "An Analysis of Interviewer Characteristics and Their Relationship to Performance," *International Journal of Opinion and Attitude Research*, vol. 4, no. 4 (1950),
pp. 473–498; vol. 5, no. 1 (1951), pp. 74–94; and vol. 5, no. 2 (1951), pp. 191–220.

A new difficulty has arisen to complicate interviewing in recent years. When people have strong fears, they are too suspicious to be readily interviewed. This is why it has always been impossible to conduct a public opinion poll under a dictatorship. People will not talk freely to an interviewer who might be a threat to them. In the United States, until recently, this was significant only when interviewing Negroes, who were so afraid of expressing their true opinions to a white person that they either "played dumb" or told the white interviewer what they thought he would like to hear. Reliable investigators always met this situation by employing Negro interviewers and clearing their survey with Negro defense organizations or leaders. Since 1946 the same situation has arisen with a significant number of white respondents; they are suspicious of strange interviewers as possible Communists or as investigators for some selfish interest. Interviewers for such nationally known polling agencies as Gallup and Roper can easily identify themselves, but the problem remains for independent social scientists. The only partial solution that has been devised has been to clear studies with churches and civic organizations.

A third important factor in public opinion research is the selection of respondents. Only the Census Bureau has the resources to interview every family in the United States, and then only once in ten years. For all other studies, a sample of respondents must be selected, and the sample must be representative of the population about which the investigator wishes to generalize. The rules for drawing a representative sample have been well worked out by statisticians, but they are difficult to apply when human beings constitute the sample. When physical objects, or even plants or animals, are the subject of investigation, it is a relatively easy task to pick cases at random, and to make sure that each unit has the same chance of being selected as any other unit. When the people of the United States are the subjects of investigation, however, it is impossible to line them up for purposes of picking a random sample or to obtain equal access to all of them. There is not even a list of their names and addresses from which a sample list could be selected and then traced.

Two types of methods have been contrived to meet the problem of selecting a representative sample of people. One is the "quota" method, by which a sample is devised to match the distribution of the population in certain known traits, such as age, sex, region of country, and rural-urban residence. (This information is available from the decennial census, corrected for postcensual changes and for demonstrated errors.) Then interviewers are sent out to interview people who have the specified traits. They fill up the quota of each type of person (by age, sex, region, etc.) as fast as they happen to come across persons of that type.

This method of sampling is widely employed by commercial pollsters and was the one chosen by the one biologist who has elected to do a major social science study—Kinsey, in his study of sex behavior. The method has one grave weakness, however, in that the people *within* each of the quotas may not be representative. This is of no great importance if the biases of nonrepresentativeness within the quotas are not related to the subject matter of the interview. But if aggressive people happen to be chosen more frequently than passive people, it does make a good deal of difference, for example, if one is questioning about attitudes toward war. If working women are not available to a poll-taker because they are working during the daytime, it will make a great deal of difference in an election poll, since working women vote differently from housewives. The careful social scientists have therefore devised another method of sampling, called the "area" method. This involves dividing the population into small geographical areas, selecting some of these areas as representative on the basis of known traits, and using carefully controlled random sampling of people within each of the selected areas. This method is more difficult and more expensive to employ than the quota method, especially in rural areas where the dispersion of population makes random sampling hard to arrange. But it seems generally to be more foolproof than the quota method.

The problems of the attitude measurer are not done when he has devised his questionnaire, selected his sample, and secured his interviews. Then he has to boil down his mass of information into a comprehensible and readable form. This involves the steps known as "coding" and "analysis." Coding is essentially a process of classifying the diversity of answers, and the words in which the answers are couched, into a reasonable number of categories. Actual deviations must not be lost, but meaningless diversity must be submerged.

The planning of a code requires skill and knowledge; the application of a code takes a great deal of tedious work. The principal step in analysis is deciding how the coded answers are to be tabulated. Should answers to a given question simply be added up, or can answers to one question make sense only when put in the context of answers to another question? Are the facts for the population as a whole what is important, or is significance to be secured only by comparison of answers from different elements in the population? Do answers to a single question have any validity, or is it necessary to combine into a scale the answers to a series of questions all trying to get at the same attitude? These are some of the questions the analyst must answer as he tackles each study. He cannot wait to solve these problems until after the interviews are complete, but must have his solution fairly well worked out before he regards his questionnaire as complete and before he collects a single interview.

The interpretation of findings and the presentation of results offer a final set of challenges to the attitude measurer. No uniform standards have as yet been devised to handle this stage of the operations. Nor probably can any ever be, since each subject of study is somewhat different from every other. A few general principles have been set forth, and a variety of devices for presentation have been examined, but they are too detailed to go into here.

USES OF THE QUESTIONNAIRE SURVEY

What sort of information is the product of all these operations? Although the questionnaire survey grew up in an effort to measure attitudes, it now has a far broader use than that. In addition to detecting attitudes, it can reveal expectations, wishes, activities, facts, estimations, and so on. Let us translate these vague terms into examples of concrete uses to which the questionnaire survey has been put.

One is the simple determination of facts, such as the amount of liquid savings in the hands of the general public, which the U.S. Federal Reserve System regularly asks the Survey Research Center at the University of Michigan to determine.[4] Sometimes facts that are easily detected separately have no significance until put in context by a questionnaire survey. Certain army officers in the Mediterranean Theater were disturbed at the sloppy appearance of American soldiers from the replacement depot at Pozzuoli until a survey determined

---

[4] See George Katona, *Psychological Analysis of Economic Behavior* (New York: McGraw-Hill, 1951).

that not only were there no QM laundry facilities available at the depot, but there was no soap available at the PX and the military police did not allow soldiers to take clothing out of this camp for fear they would sell it on the Italian black market. The Kinsey study of the distribution of different types of sex expression is another example of fact determination, in which the main interest lies in comparison of different groups in the population.

The preference type of study is most frequently employed by large industrial concerns. A great deal of money is spent every year to determine what various consumers find most pleasing to the eye, to the nose, to the palate. The government has also used the preference survey when it has a choice and wishes the decision to be made in accord with the preferences of the citizenry. In planning its postwar education program, the Army used a sample interview survey as the equivalent of getting a filled-out commercial order. The social scientist seldom has any direct use for a preference survey, except when preferences can be used as indices of attitudes. Many of the early studies of attitudes toward minority groups, for example, involved the respondents' making statements of preference for one group as compared to another, in different social situations. The psychologist L. L. Thurstone developed a complicated technique for transforming such preference statements into a scale of attitudes reflecting the status of minority groups, vocations, and other rankable social traits.[5]

The knowledge type of questionnaire survey is very much like a school examination, except that it is given to the usual representative sample of the population and its purpose is not to rank. Rather, its purpose is to determine whether a publicity campaign of one sort or another is successful in reaching the public or whether those who have greater knowledge about something also have attitudes more favorable to it. Government policy-makers—as well as manufacturers—are interested in such information. Social scientists have found use for many studies of the opinion or personality correlates of knowledge. In general, they have found that those with more knowledge about a given subject have fewer emotional prejudices against that subject.

Other types of cross-classification are employed in an effort to get clues to the causation of attitudes and behavior. In one study of

[5] L. L. Thurstone, "The Method of Paired Comparisons for Social Values," *Journal of Abnormal and Social Psychology*, 21 (1927), 384–400; "An Experimental Study of Nationality Preferences," *Journal of General Psychology*, 1 (1928), 405–425.

venereal disease, not only was there cross-classification of incidence of this disease with knowledge of preventive techniques but also with facts about drunkenness when having extramarital intercourse and with beliefs about the ability of newly discovered drugs to cure the disease. The findings confirmed the hypothesis that little knowledge, drunkenness, and overconfidence in modern drugs were strongly associated with the incidence of venereal disease. Correlations by themselves are insufficient for imputing cause, and so experiments were carried out to test the tentative findings. Information was given about techniques of preventing venereal infection and about the uncertainties of available drugs, with the object of determining whether this would result in a reduction of the venereal rate.

Most experimental studies in the social sciences require attitude measurement at every phase. The usual procedure has been to administer a questionnaire to matched experimental and control groups. Then the social stimulus is directed at the experimental group, sometimes quickly, but more often over a period of time and without obvious connection to the questionnaires. After this, the same or equivalent questionnaires are administered to the same groups, and changes in the attitudes of the experimental group are compared to changes in the attitudes of the control group, if any. The questionnaire may be repeated after an interval of several months to see whether the effect of the stimulus has worn off. Sometimes several stimuli are directed at different experimental groups at the same time and a comparison is made of their relative influence. Such, for example, was a study of the relative effectiveness of emotional and logical propaganda. For the particular groups and subject matter chosen, it was found that the emotional appeal had greater success than the rational appeal, but that the latter was more effective than no appeal at all. Some experimental studies are "evaluational" when the stimulus investigated is a program that someone desires to evaluate.

Another type of attitude survey might be called a "definitional" study. Definitions are usually set by a tradition or by operational convenience, but sometimes it is valuable to conduct a little study before formulating a definition. One such study might be to determine whether people generally make the same distinctions between terms or set the same limits on terms that the scientist does. A certain study translated the numerous current definitions of the term "morale" into a questionnaire in order to determine the extent to which high morale in one sense was related to high morale in another sense. Such diversity was discovered that it was necessary to formulate several distinct definitions of morale and to note that they were not the same thing. Some investigators find important social science data in popular definitions, and they conduct surveys where the questions allow the respondent to formulate his own definitions.

A final type of study that must be mentioned has prediction as its primary purpose. One prediction study may simply be an extrapolation of attitude trends. Another may be based on influences from causes discerned from the correlational or experimental types of studies. A workable schedule on such a basis has been prepared by Burgess and Cottrell to predict the future marital adjustment of engaged couples.[6] A third may be a questionnaire survey in which respondents are asked to state or estimate their future plans. Some valuable clues to the future of the consumers' market have been discovered by asking people their plans for buying radios, automobiles, or household equipment. The election pollsters have this last type of purpose—to predict simply by asking people what they intend to do. But the method is risky if not carried out in conjunction with questions about motivation and intensity of attitude, and if careful analysis is not made of the "undecided" voter.

Sometimes a prediction study can be used as a selective technique to prevent the predicted events from occurring. Such was a study carried on in the Army during World War II to predict which newly inducted soldiers would develop psychoneuroses. After it was determined which traits, experiences, and reactions predisposed a man to psychoneurosis, those inductees who had a high score on the predisposition test were sent to a psychiatrist, who either rejected them for army service or marked them down for further observation.[7]

There is an increasing range of uses for the questionnaire survey. Each time there is a new use or a new criticism, there is development or refinement of techniques. In 1944 Hadley Cantril brought together existing knowledge about techniques in this field in his book *Gauging*

[6] E. W. Burgess and L. S. Cottrell, Jr., *Predicting Success or Failure in Marriage* (New York: Prentice-Hall, 1939).

[7] S. A. Star, in Samuel A. Stouffer *et al.*, *Measurement and Prediction* (Princeton, N.J.: Princeton University Press, 1950), Chaps. 13 and 14.

Public Opinion.[8] Developments have been so rapid, however, that already many sections of the book are out of date. Even the periodical literature is somewhat behind, as one can observe when he attends the annual meetings of the World Congress for Public Opinion Research, the American Association for Public Opinion Research, the American Statistical Association, the American Sociological Society, or the American Psychological Association. The presentation and discussion of new techniques are carried on under the most favorable conditions of open-mindedness and high interest. Those practitioners with a scientific orientation know their own limitations. The field appears to have a most interesting future.

[8] Hadley Cantril, *Gauging Public Opinion* (Princeton, N.J.: Princeton University Press, 1944).

19

A Research Note on Experimentation
in Interviewing

THE *methods of interviewing presented in the previous chapter have a cut-and-dried character to them, except for the suggestion which forms the subject matter of the present chapter. The strange tendency of social scientists to confuse objectivity with neutrality—noted in another context in Section II of this volume—can be seen in the purely technical context considered in the following discussion. The goal of social science is objective knowledge. Objective knowledge can sometimes be better secured with biased questions than with neutrally worded questions. It depends upon the specific problem for investigation.*

THE EMPHASIS on objectivity has, in one respect at least, seriously restricted the information which social scientists have been able to get from interviews. This drive toward objectivity has taken the form of setting up restrictive mechanical rules rather than of demanding conscious honesty on the part of the scientist. The interviewer is supposed to present uncolored questions and to take down the subject's answers as given, that is, to act as a combined phonograph and recording system.

This technique may be essential when untrained or unsophisticated interviewers are employed to get data for analysts working independently of them. It is equally essential at the beginning of an interview while the interviewer is seeking the basic framework of the subject's attitudes. It is again useful when the interview is covering topics that are simple or are of little significance. But when the subject's attitude must be fully known, then the interviewer must take an active role.

The interviewer must not only invite frankness and gain rapport, as is generally recognized, but he must also experiment verbally with the subject. (The word "experiment" is used advisedly, since experimentation during an interview consists of introducing a novel stimulus and noting the response to it.) Experiments may take many different forms: (1) a question, using either biased words or neutral words; (2) an expression of an attitude of the interviewer, either real or assumed; (3) volunteered information, presumed either to be unknown to the subject or not taken into account by him in formulating his attitude.

A primary rule of experimental interviewing is that it be designed by the interviewer during the course of the interview. It can be assumed that if a topic is of some importance to a person his attitude with respect to it is related to many of his other attitudes; therefore, to understand fully a person's attitudes, the inteviewer must probe into the nature of their relationships. But frequently so many possible relationships exist that no prediction can be made in advance as to what question, or fact, or statement of attitude should be employed in the experiment. Also, the type of experiment which would elicit the most information about the attitude of a particular person cannot be predicted until the interview develops. Furthermore, the experiment may be a complex one—containing several elements and administered in several stages—and, as a result, its form cannot be specified in advance of the interview.

The following are some experiences in experimental interviewing:

1. Many attitudes are based on misinformation. During the course of the interview an interviewer who finds that some person's attitude is due to misinformation can provide the correct facts and note any change of attitude. Such an experiment would not only reveal the basis of the subject's attitude, but it would also provide clues as to the effectiveness of providing information of a certain type.

2. Attitudes which are not considered quite respectable, or which are considered unusual in any way, may not be fully revealed. However, the interviewer may get an inkling of their existence and encourage a full expression of these hidden attitudes by presenting them, in a matter-of-fact tone, as commonly held attitudes or as attitudes of the interviewer himself. I have even been able, by such an experiment, to elicit an expression of hope that World War II would continue for a considerable time in order that certain personal privileges could be continued. In the course of an interview with a visiting foreigner, who

was politely concealing his attitude toward American foreign policy, the conversation was turned to support for research in the United States by the armed services. The investigator remarked that this subsidy was a kind of imperialism comparable to American aid to Europe. The subject immediately objected, "But in your research here it is benevolent, whereas in Europe your Army is there to control us!"

3. If any seeming inconsistencies or illogicalities or any other "peculiarities" appear in a subject's statements, the interviewer should probe for the premises of his attitudes. It is wise to assume that a subject considers himself to be thinking logically and consistently. Intensive questioning in certain areas of subject matter may be found valuable in uncovering the roots of certain attitudes. The questions that the interviewer uses under these circumstances depend on the apparent inconsistencies and are usually best directed toward trying to make the inconsistencies apparent to the subject.

4. Certain assumptions can be made during an interview that, if accepted or rejected, reveal more about the subject than answers to straightforward questions where the subject may not wish to reveal his attitude. For example, when union members were asked if they had read their union contract a large number claimed that they had. A significantly smaller, and probably more accurate, figure resulted from the question, "Do you intend to read your union contract?" Four answers were now possible instead of two: the blunt "no," the casual "don't know," the face saver "intend to read the contract," and "have read it."

The purpose of experimentation in interviewing is to find out as much as possible about attitudes, and the bases and premises of attitudes. Such information is needed when a relatively full understanding of a problem is desired, when ideas are needed for further research, when the subject is a key person, or when the basis of an observed relationship needs to be understood. Nothing said here about the value of experimentation in interviewing should be taken as condemnatory of questionnaires or of formal interviewing when the purpose is to determine the prevalence or distribution of attitudes within a given group. Findings from a questionnaire depend on the realism of the questions and on the interpretation made of the answers. Although the experimental interview cannot provide a statistical description of the distribution of attitudes within a group, it can furnish information useful in making the questions realistic and in interpreting the answers.

20

The Use of "Informal Small Samples" in Mass Communications Research

ONE *of the long-time controversies in social science methodology has been over the use of "case studies versus statistics," as it used to be known. Everything that can be said about this now dying controversy probably has already been said. The following chapter does not take up the argument or present much that is new. Rather, it attempts a fairly systematic presentation of the possibilities in studying small unrepresentative samples, showing the advantages of this technique over the use of large samples for some types of research and indicating the kinds of information that can be secured from informal small sample studies.*

FOR THE purposes of this chapter, "informal small sample" studies will be taken to be those which do not permit statistically reliable conclusions, not only because an insufficient number of cases is used, but also because the sample is not representative. "Small sample" is, thus, not used in the ways that either R. A. Fisher or Hadley Cantril use the term, but in the sense of those who have advocated a "case history" approach. In this definition, "small sample" cannot include the entire universe,[1] but rather a nonrepresentative "chunk" of the universe. Although this chapter is limited to small sample studies, absolutely no implication is intended that large and representative sample studies may not be more valuable in communications research.

A. REASONS FOR USING INFORMAL SMALL SAMPLES RATHER THAN LARGE SAMPLES FOR SOME TYPES OF RESEARCH

1. *Need for speed.* Sometimes the communication has to be disseminated before an adequate test can be made on a large and repre-

---

[1] There are at least two types of studies in which the "universe" includes only a few cases: (a) when a small group—e.g., a club—is the only object of interest, and (b) when a group of key people—e.g., leaders of a community—can give all the information about a larger group of people that it is necessary to know.

sentative sample, and it is better to have a rough answer regarding its probable effect than no answer at all.

2. *Low cost.* Small sample research can generally be done at considerably lower cost than large sample research.

3. *Other administrative reasons.* Among the other administrative reasons for using small samples are small size of research staff, research personnel located in one part of the country when the communication is to be distributed throughout the country, etc.

4. *Simplicity of answers.* There are relatively simple or obvious answers for some questions, and therefore no need for a careful detailed study. (E.g., such a question might be, "Does the title of this cartoon use understandable words?" Interviewing among unselected passers-by on a downtown street corner or at a railroad terminal may be sufficient for such a study.)

5. *Complexity of problem.* Sometimes a problem is so complex psychologically that it cannot be analyzed adequately with any currently available statistical methodology. In such a case a small sample study of the probing type can often elicit more information than any other type of study.

6. *No need for large sample.* Some questions, regardless of their simplicity or complexity, can be answered as well by a study of a small number of properly selected cases as by a study of a large number of cases. For examples, see section B below.

7. *Quick check of previous studies.* Sometimes previous studies or general knowledge provide answers about the impact of a communication of a given type and only a brief check is needed to see whether the communication in question belongs to the type.

B. TYPES OF INFORMATION THAT CAN BE SECURED FROM AN INFORMAL SMALL SAMPLE STUDY

1. *Hypotheses and ideas for further research.* A hypothesis should be more than a mere guess. The development of an intelligent hypothesis, in a framework of existing knowledge, should be one of the most important steps in research. Especially when tackling a new problem, informal small samples are valuable for arriving at a first approximation as to what the relevant variables are. Significant hypotheses cannot be developed with preplanned surveys of large representative samples, although of course they can often be tested by such means.

2. *Ideas for improving practical techniques to make propaganda more effective, just as hypotheses are formulated.*

3. *Range of attitudes, or reactions, to pieces of propaganda.* This requires the sample of persons to be as heterogeneous as possible, at least to include some members of each of the groups which the propaganda is ultimately intended to reach. Very frequently, the most blatant errors and misunderstandings crop out; for example, in the study of the understandability of a certain cartoon, the few Catholics in the sample were quite sufficient to point out that Catholics found it difficult to conceive of a layman criticizing a priest for his sermon. Areas of confusion and misunderstanding are revealed, and the meanings behind, or reasons for, check-list answers can be clarified in the interviews.

4. *Ideas as to the psychological mechanisms underlying the reactions which appear.* This requires intensive interviews, usually conducted on an individual rather than on a group basis, although the latter can sometimes be useful. It may be necessary to extrapolate or to interpret the facts. Such extrapolation or interpretation should be done openly and consciously, and by the interviewers as well as by an independent judge who reads the record of the interview.

5. *Estimation as to how opinions are linked together and rationalized —similar to recognition of psychological mechanisms.*

C. ANALYSIS OF THE STEPS INVOLVED IN DOING AN INFORMAL SAMPLE STUDY

When doing small sample studies, some social scientists tend to slip over into the methodology of large sample studies. Properly, the methodology of the small sample study differs at every stage from the methodology of the large sample study. For this reason, the steps of a small sample study will be briefly outlined and certain distinctions between them and the steps of a large sample study noted. It should be noted that the small sample study is useful for studying not only the comprehension of communications material but also its effects, its attention-getting value, etc. The small sample study may not be nearly as good as the large sample study to get at these things, but when done with ingenuity it can secure some relevant information.

When examples of studies are used, they will usually be selected from research on the comprehension of propaganda.

1. *Formulating the problem.* Only those problems should be set up that are capable of being answered with a small sample study. For example, in a propaganda comprehension study, the problem should not be set up in terms of whether people understand or how many understand or what group affiliations they have, but in such terms as these: (a) What are the obstacles to understanding? (b) What are the processes involved in understanding or misunderstanding? (c) What psychological associations are made during understanding?

2. *Formulating the research design.* The usual way of measuring effect has been to give the same questionnaire to a group of people before and after their exposure to the mass communication. The statistically reliable difference in responses on the two questionnaires is considered to be the measure of effect. This procedure has the defect that the participants might become aware of what is expected of them after seeing the material and perhaps respond in terms of this expectation rather than their "real" attitudes. In general, the major problem in setting up a study is to find some ingenious means whereby the respondents are likely to indicate their "real" attitudes rather than what they think the researcher wants.

   A. Some users of before-and-after written tests have succeeded in creating situations in which the respondents were highly unlikely to realize that they were objects of experimentation. That is, the situation in which they were exposed to the communications material was kept psychologically distinct from the situation in which they took the tests. Of course, it usually also required a large sample to measure effect by means of before-and-after tests.

   B. Sometimes a test on a matched sample can be used instead of a before-test, and the experimental group is given an after-test only. The matching should be done not only on relevant background traits but also on unrelated social opinions. If the matched group is practically identical with the experimental group on all unrelated opinions (or consistently variant from it), and is different only on the opinions which the communications material might reasonably be expected to change, the implication is that the communications material caused this difference. It is extremely difficult, of course, to match groups satisfactorily, and very often it cannot be done at all.

c. Nonstatistical indications of people's reactions to the communications can be had by certain indirect devices. Since these devices cannot be applied in a mass manner like a questionnaire, a small sample study is the only kind feasible; but this is not detrimental, as the findings cannot be put in statistical form anyhow. A few examples of indirect devices may be given by way of illustration.

(1) After showing a film or cartoon to a person, the investigator should ask him to tell what he saw, just as he would if he were talking to some specific group of which he is a member.

(2) After exposing the subjects to a mass communication (let us say a film in this case) and using the program analyzer,[2] the investigator should tell the group that he would like to turn to something else entirely different. If the film dealt with some aspect of intergroup relations, for example, he should start a discussion about a different aspect of intergroup relations that is close to the participants' own experiences. (For example, he should find out whether they think Jews and Negroes should be allowed to live in a housing project, if the respondents have been selected as applicants for apartments in the project.) In the discussion, the investigator should bring up all the messages which the film has been trying to get over, but make no reference to the film itself. He should watch particularly for spontaneous references to the film and for any points mentioned which go directly counter to the messages of the film.

[2] The "program analyzer" is a mechanical-electrical device whereby a subject can indicate his reactions to an ongoing communication (i.e., film or radio program) at each moment without interrupting his attention to the communication. It has the advantage over a questionnaire administered after the communication of not relying on memory and of permitting "spontaneous" reactions not encrusted with rationalizations and afterthoughts. It has the disadvantages of requiring some training before effective use and of permitting only a single continuum of reactions during the course of an absorbing film or radio program.

(3) The investigator should select a sample of persons who saw
the film in a commercial movie house the previous week
as part of a regular film program (i.e., the persons went to
see an entertainment film and saw the short propaganda film
incidentally). He should get them to discuss all the films
they saw the previous week, observe to what extent they
remember the propaganda short, and seek their reactions
to the short film.

(4) After showing a film, the investigator should conduct a
formal debate between two persons who are known to be
prejudiced (from previously administered scales) and between two persons who are known to be unprejudiced.
Each team should evaluate the film from the standpoint
of prominority and antiminority positions. After the debate, the rest of the audience could be brought in for additional points; each person could be asked, "What else
would you have said if you had been in A's place?" or
"What did you think of A's arguments?"

3. *Selecting the persons in the sample.* At several points in the preceding discussion, the need for a heterogeneous sample has been
made evident. That is, there is a need to reach at least one or two
representatives of each of the major types of social groups that
the communications material is intended to reach. Also there is a
need to tap a wide range of personality types.

It is conceivable that a panel of persons who could be interviewed again and again over a long period of time would be the
best sort of sample for many types of research using small samples.
If persons can be found who can be demonstrated to have the same
sorts of reactions as the great majority of persons in the groups
which they are used to represent, these persons may be used over
and over again to test propaganda. Such persons presumably are
"aware," consciously or unconsciously, of how their community or
social group feels and thinks on all sorts of issues. These persons
may be community leaders or persons who have a lot of social
contact or simply persons of great insight but little influence.
Sometimes they should be approached with questions about what
they themselves think, sometimes with questions about what they
think their social group would think. The possibility of using a

group of this sort brings out the similarity between what we do when we make small sample studies and what anthropologists do when they study a community. The panel is a heterogeneous group, but since its members are interviewed individually, they do not inhibit one another from talking. An obvious prerequisite of the use of a panel in communications research is a specification of the groups in the general population which the mass communication is expected and intended to reach.

4. *Preparing instructions for interviewing.* In general, the advantages of specific, set questions to be used by the interviewer is that the answers can be considered as equivalent responses to the same stimulus and so can be coded and tallied. A small sample study, however, has no value for giving statistical findings, and therefore the tallying of answers based on small samples has no value. The obvious strength of non-set, or modifiable, questions is that they can be used for purposes of "probing" into the attitudes of the respondent or of "experimenting" with him.[3] The major instruction to the interviewers is that they should look for new ideas and follow up any leads. When individual interviews are conducted, the interviewers should write up the whole case and add their insights and interpretations to the formal answers. All this requires trained interviewers. The analysts should always do part of the interviewing. Special consideration to interviewing problems should be given before each study is taken out into the field.

Periodically there should be objective checks on each interviewer's bias. The whole problem of bias in research personnel is perhaps more important in small than in large sample studies because of the greater freedom in question asking and the absence of statistical tallying. Therefore more checks are needed on this bias, and insofar as the checks are made objective they increase the reliability of the findings. However, such checks must be carried out in such a way as to avoid inhibiting the researcher's tendencies to devise new questions spontaneously and to interpret the respondents' answers.

5. *Analyzing the data.* As was suggested previously, an informal small sample study should not analyze respondents' answers by

---

[3] See "A Research Note on Experimentation in Interviewing," Chapter 19. The distinction between "probing" questions and "experimental" questions is that the former are neutrally worded whereas the latter are deliberately leading or biased.

coding and tallying. A single answer can be valuable for itself in providing a hypothesis, an idea for improving propaganda techniques, an example of the working of a known psychological mechanism, etc. One answer, therefore, can outweigh a dozen answers. Every answer must be explained, and consequently a "universal" generalization is sought, not a statistical generalization in which one type of answer is pointed out to outweigh another type. While a universal generalization is sought, it must be made clear that the informal small sample study does not *attain* these generalizations in a verified form.

Complete reports on individual interviews are valuable to reveal the ways in which specific attitudes are tied up with whole personalities or whole opinion structures. If a check list is devised for a question to be included in a large sample study, coding is desirable, but one answer is as statistically important as five or ten if the total is only fifty cases.

As a check on individual bias, more than one analyst should make the interpretation. An inventory of psychological concepts used in comparable studies would be helpful in eliminating the individual bias which creeps in because of confused terminology.

A special effort should be made to find practical suggestions, and to find some positive values in the propaganda technique being studied. Interviewing of certain kinds of persons can be especially valuable here. For example, in studying the effect of a piece of propaganda designed to reduce race prejudice, sometimes interviewing of nonintellectual, nonprejudiced persons can be of greatest help.

D. REVIEW OF A SPECIFIC "INFORMAL SMALL SAMPLE" STUDY

To the above point-by-point exposition, a word will be added on a procedure using an "informal small sample" for the purpose of achieving a description of the pattern of communication and participation in a city of 50,000 inhabitants. The ultimate purpose of the study was to evaluate the effectiveness of a specific action program, but it was felt that some general description of communication and participation in the community had to be obtained first at great speed and low cost. Information about communications and participations is relatively difficult to secure for any but the smallest of American communities, since there is no set pattern of expectations which can be discerned

in a few selected interviews nor is the information collected systematically through such formal organizations as the United States Census
or a local department of public welfare. The best way of securing the
information is by means of an interview, using a detailed, preformu-
lated schedule, conducted with a fairly large representative sample.
While this means is the best for securing *facts* about communication
and participation, it sometimes leaves something to be desired regarding the interrelation or "meaning" of these facts. A more serious drawback of the method is that it is expensive and time-consuming.

A substitute method—an application of which will now be reported
—is to interview a limited number of community leaders. A schedule
of questions is worked out in advance to make sure that all aspects
of communication and participation are covered, but the questions
are not to be thought of as either fixed in form or all-inclusive. Rather,
considerable probing is done, and the questions are reordered as the
interview develops. In general, the interview procedure follows that
worked out by the Survey Research Center of the University of
Michigan.[4]

The selection of community leaders to be interviewed, indeed the
designation of certain persons as leaders, presents quite a problem.
According to the definition of "leader" adopted, different lists of persons
would be formulated. The most significant distinction is that between
formal and informal leaders. A good case can be made that the real
leaders of a community are those who hold no formal position
of leadership—either the "grass roots" leaders or the "powers behind
the thrones." But, for our specific purpose, the formal leaders of the
community are the ones deemed best to interview, for the following
reasons:

1. *Overlap in leadership.* There is a large overlap between formal and
   informal leadership. In small or medium-sized communities there
   are almost no "powers behind the thrones" and the formal leaders
   have little opportunity to get too far from the grass roots. Although not substantiated by sufficient investigation, an assumption can be made that the smaller the community, the more the
   formal and informal leaders coincide.
2. *Ease of designation.* The formal leaders are relatively easy to desig-

[4] E. E. Maccoby and R. R. Holt, "How Surveys Are Made," *Journal of Social Issues*,
2 (May 1946), 45–57; also see *A Manual for Interviewers* (Ann Arbor: Survey Research
Center, University of Michigan, November 1947), mimeographed.

nate, because they hold certain offices which are common to most communities. To determine who the informal leaders are would almost require a public opinion study in itself, which is what we are trying to avoid.

3. *Knowledge of whole community.* The formal leaders usually have knowledge of the community as a whole, since they are frequently in meetings with representatives of most of the community's groups. The "grass roots" leaders may know their own particular groups better, but they usually have much less opportunity to learn about other groups.

4. *Outside contacts.* The formal leaders tend to have more contact with the world outside their community, since they are usually better educated and are more frequently chosen as emissaries to other communities. They are thus better able to select the respects in which their community differs from its neighbors or from others of comparable size, function, etc. They also know more about communication between members of the community and those outside the community.

5. *Access to data.* The formal leaders generally have access to all the compilations of data which have been made in the community for some other purpose but which are relevant to the researcher's needs.

Each leader has a bias, since he knows more about some groups than about others. But if all the leaders interviewed cover all the groups and activities in the community, the divergent biases will tend to cancel out and a true picture emerge of relevant aspects of community life.[5] Thus, the leaders should be selected to represent the various types of groups and activities in the community—political, social welfare, religious, business and banking, labor, social, cultural, ethnic, and publicity. Many of the individuals selected for this particular study were "obvious" leaders—the mayor, the president of the Chamber of Commerce, the business agent of the two largest local unions in town, the editor of the town's sole newspaper, the manager of the leading radio station, the director of the public library, the director of the museum, the commissioner of public welfare, the director of the City Planning Commission, the director of city parks and playgrounds,

[5] This methodological principle follows a broader one enunciated by Karl Mannheim, *Ideology and Utopia* (New York: Harcourt, Brace, 1936).

the Negro community's only professional man, the director of the Jewish community center, the president of the Parent-Teacher Council. In cases where there was a choice—for instance, among businessmen, lawyers, ministers, or heads of voluntary civic associations—the investigator chose those whose names he heard most frequently in his other interviews. In making these choices he was aided by a personal friend who lived in the town and by the editor of the town's newspaper.

The list of persons interviewed cannot be said to be statistically representative of the city's leadership, largely because there is no way of equating the influence of, say, a minister and a businessman. But insofar as coverage of a range of activities is concerned, and the selection of at least outstanding names within each of the activities, the list can be said to be fairly representative. In terms of the experience of the investigator, the names of the persons interviewed are among those who are most frequently mentioned in the community and who are most frequently found on boards, committees, etc. While these people are in a *position* to influence most of the other people in the city, nothing is known of their actual influence. All of them were in a position to *know* a great deal about the community, and when they did not believe they knew, they were often responsible and objective enough to say so. A total of thirty-three community leaders were interviewed, with each interview lasting between one and two hours. Appointments were made by telephone and were kept in the respondent's office or home. No person selected refused an interview outright, but one postponed several times and was finally dropped from the list. Not only because the people interviewed were not statistically representative, but also because they were too few in number, it is not justifiable to report their answers to questions in statistical terms. Nevertheless, either unanimity or sharp diversion on their part in answer to a given question is of interest because of the position these people have. Each statement was also judged in terms of what was objectively known about the town in terms of its geographic location, census statistics, local histories, and so on.[6]

[6] For a report on the findings of the study, see my "Communication and Participation in a Small City as Viewed by Its Leaders," *International Journal of Opinion and Attitude Research*, 5 (Fall 1951), 367–390.

21

Popular Logic in the Study of Covert Culture

This chapter suggests ways of getting information about a highly inaccessible subject matter. It is impossible to know the extent of covert culture and its relative importance—as compared to overt culture—in the determination of human behavior. But some anthropologists and sociologists as far back as Durkheim have been aware of its existence. Covert culture cannot be studied by the usual techniques of investigation; if it is important enough to study, new techniques will have to be developed to reach it. Anthropologists like Kluckhohn have made many important contributions in this direction. The present chapter attempts to extend them, based upon my research experience as a sociologically trained social psychologist.

STUDENTS of society have often observed a tendency for various parts of a culture to be dependent on one another in a logical fashion, and some students have used this observation as a methodological rule for the study of a given culture. The functional anthropologists have made greatest use of this rule. Among sociologists, Sumner ("drive toward consistency"), Durkheim, and Parsons have been outstanding in their reliance on it.

Without necessarily taking a thoroughgoing functionalist point of view, we can perhaps agree that there are certain areas of our culture which can profitably be studied in terms of an assumption of logical arrangement of parts. It is not the purpose of this chapter to present a comprehensive list of these areas, but to suggest the possibilities of an approach based on this assumption in the study of popular ideology. Perhaps the approach to be suggested works best in those areas of culture which are most static, but evidence will be offered to prove that the approach has some value for the study of nonstatic aspects of culture.

In a study of the attitudes of whites toward Negroes in the United

States,[1] conducted during the early 1940s, it was found that southern whites had a systematic and integrated "theory" about Negroes that pervaded most of their actions and words with respect to Negroes. This popular theory has its keystone in the doctrine that no Negro blood can be allowed to infiltrate into the white race because the Negro race is inherently inferior to the white race. The doctrine is used to justify all sorts of separation between the races and all sorts of discrimination against Negroes. It is not claimed that a sincere belief in this doctrine is the "real reason" why southern whites act as they do toward Negroes, but it is claimed that the doctrine will be found to be behind most arguments and rationalizations given by southerners to explain why they act as they do toward Negroes. The postulation of the doctrine permitted the students to discern two important corollaries, both of which were later substantiated by facts:

1. Southern whites exhibit emotional reaction to violation of the rules of separation in a degree which corresponds to the closeness of the violation in question to violation of the sex taboo. For example, there is greater reaction to a case of a Negro and a white eating together than to a case of a Negro and a white working at similar jobs in different locations.

2. Southern whites are willing to compromise and let Negroes have equal privileges in certain areas of life to a degree which corresponds to the distance of connection between the areas in question and the area of sex relations between Negro men and white women. For example, southern whites are more willing to permit economic equality than social equality.

Another segment of life where a highly developed popular theory behind social behavior has been discerned is the Army. Based perhaps on the medieval caste distinction between nobility and commoners is the distinction found in many modern armies, including the United States Army, between officers and enlisted men. The heart of the theory is that officers are gentlemen and that enlisted men are not gentlemen. Many personnel policies in the Army are primarily determined by that distinction. One can almost deduce the implications of the theory without knowing the facts, and then find that the facts substantiate the logical deductions. Some examples: (1) Officers can be trusted to carry out any orders; enlisted men cannot be trusted,

[1] Gunnar Myrdal, with the assistance of Richard Sterner and Arnold Rose, *An American Dilemma* (New York: Harper, 1944).

and a constant and detailed checkup must be made to see that orders are carried out. (2) No enlisted man can become an officer through promotion; this fiction is maintained in the American Army by giving an enlisted man an honorable discharge a day before he is to be commissioned. (3) An officer can use an enlisted man to perform personal services for him, even though that is contrary to official Army regulations. (4) One of the most severe punishments meted out to officers who have violated orders or rules is forced resignation or dishonorable discharge from the Army (depriving him of his status of "gentleman"). But such punishment alone is practically never given to an enlisted man (resignation is not permitted and dishonorable discharge is always accompanied by a prison sentence).

Many other logical implications of both these theories could be stated, but enough have been given to illustrate their general nature. Also, other examples could be given of the sway of complex, logical, popular theories in other areas of modern society.

Thus, in certain areas of our culture, it would seem that a complex, logical ideology—which may be called a "popular theory"—can be used to predict various sorts of behavior. Like all ideal types, popular theories do not yield perfect predictions; other influences come into play and changes occur all the time. Enough can be predicted, however, to make recognition of the popular theory an essential for understanding the area of culture. The existence of popular theories would suggest that there is a tendency for people to think and to organize their social behavior logically and systematically.

The two examples given of the logical character of group thought are areas where relatively little social change has occurred for scores of years. A somewhat different sort of example will be given to illustrate the logical character of group thought in areas where change is rapid. In a study of rumor,[2] the hypothesis found most adequate—out of a half dozen proposed by different writers—to explain the growth and spread of that short-lived phenomenon was the one expressed in terms of a rumor's usefulness in filling in logical gaps in public information. When something is of interest and importance to a group of people, and the regular sources of news do not provide adequate information about it, people are inclined to blow up little clues into a full-fledged story which plausibly ("logically") explains

[2] Arnold M. Rose, "A Study of Rumor," unpublished M.A. thesis, University of Chicago, 1940.

what is happening with respect to the thing of interest. The rumor's truth or falsity depends on the adequacy of the clues and of the other premises taken for granted from which the rumor is deduced.

Perhaps I am misusing the word "logic" in this chapter. What I mean to point out is that group thinking and action seem to be based on deductions from premises, whether the premises are true or false. The premises are elements (meanings and values) of the culture or subculture, on the one hand, and any perceived "facts," on the other hand. The deductions are made by various people who come up against different situations, and if their deductions seem to follow from the basic premises—which are accepted by most members of the group—they become group practices. What is being discussed here, then, is not the logic of the logicians, but what might be called "popular logic." When it is commonly said that the masses of the people do not think "logically," what is meant is that the factual *premises* of their thinking are false or that their value premises are not made explicit. Given the premises as they are, group thinking does involve logical deduction from these premises.

Popular logic is always logical, but logic has nothing to do with the realism, consciousness, or rationality of an idea. That is why the average man can always argue that his thinking is logical, and yet the social scientist finds it so fascinatingly irrational. Rationality is the trait of an idea which has been thought through, with or without the aid of others, so that all premises and implications of the idea are clear and explicit. When the anthropologist says that different logics prevail in different cultures he means that different premises are taken for granted in different societies, not that the rules of reasoning (logic) from these premises differ from one culture to another. Popular logic permits people to perceive their social behavior (including thought) as logical and rational, even when the objective observer does not so perceive it. Individuals have to learn to think and behave logically, and probably a minimum of intelligence is required, although animals used in the psychologist's laboratory seem to have sufficient intelligence to learn this. There are rewards, in the form of making accurate predictions, for logical behavior and thus it is learned universally.

If these hypotheses concerning popular theory and popular logic are true, a suggestion for methodology may also be made. When studying an area of group behavior, an effort must be made to determine the premises of the group thought behind the behavior. When these premises are found, the behavior will be seen to have a certain consistency and logic, although initially it seemed disconnected and irrational. The main value of such a procedure is that it permits prediction as to how people will usually act under certain conditions. In other words, a method based on an assumption of popular logic is suggested for arriving at a statement of a popular theory which has been found in some instances to permit accurate prediction of social behavior. The main weaknesses of this methodological suggestion are: (1) It may lead to an exaggeration of the stability and consistency of the behavior. (2) It may not be applicable to wide areas of behavior.

There are probably several ways in which the basic premises of a popular theory can be discerned by the student. One technique will be described here. Since a popular theory is logical, any apparently odd, inconsistent, or illogical statements or practices on the part of many members of a group should serve as clues to the premises. That is, if the end result of popular thinking is seemingly odd, inconsistent, or illogical, and yet it is based on logical deduction, the premises must be the source of the apparent peculiarities, and an analysis of the end results will lead to the premises. Oddness, inconsistency, and illogicality are noticed by the observer to the extent that he does not work under the same premises that the group he is studying works under. Such objectivity may be a result of contact with a different culture or of ability to divorce oneself sufficiently from one's own culture to look at it as an outsider would look at it.

Examples may be the best way to explain how apparently odd, inconsistent, or illogical statements or practices serve as clues to the basic premises of a popular theory. In the case of the southerners' relations with Negroes, the observer may note the following practices: refusal to call Negroes "Mr." or "Mrs.," revulsion from eating at the same table with them but not from having them serve the food, giving as the ultimate and unanswerable argument to a plea for equality of almost any sort the equivalent of "Would you want your daughter to marry a nigger?" In the case of the theory behind army organization, the observer may note the following practices: officers getting around regulations insofar as they consider it useful or desirable while at the same time insisting upon rigid adherence to regulations on the part of enlisted men, officers calling enlisted men by their first names but forbidding any reciprocal intimacy, officers regarding it as their privilege to ask personal favors of enlisted men without reciprocating. In the case of rumors, the clue is the rumor itself and it serves to lead the observer to the gap in public information which is considered important.

Psychiatrists have long been aware of the essentially logical character of behavior even when they speak of it as "nonrational." Freud, for example, regarded neurotic behavior, forgetting, getting into "accidents," flying into tantrums as symptoms which could be regarded as clues for logically tracing the underlying repressed desires, thoughts, and impulses which he regarded as the sources of the maladjustive overt behavior. Harry Stack Sullivan once remarked, "If I were asked in a moment of weariness, 'What is the outstanding characteristic of the human being,' I believe I would answer, 'His plausibility'." [3] The method suggested here has a certain similarity to the method of psychoanalysis, broadly conceived, except that it is the group, or the society as a whole, which has repressed the premises of the popular theory rather than the individual. Some sociologists and anthropologists have long been aware of hidden premises in culture, which they call covert culture, or latent culture, even though they have not called attention to the logical character of social behavior. [4]

The techniques of the psychiatrist, the clinician, and the anthropologist for discovering the covert may have some value for the sociologist:

1. Clinicians have used projective techniques for comparing the unstructured responses of "normal" and "abnormal" persons. Perhaps these techniques can also be used for comparing the unstructured responses of "normal" persons in different cultures, and for comparing the unstructured responses with the structured responses (to specific, "meaningful" questions) within our own culture.

2. Psychologists have discovered that convictions, wishes, and fears produce distortion in syllogistic reasoning, and at least one group of

[3] Harry Stack Sullivan, *Conceptions of Modern Psychiatry* (Washington, D.C., 1946), p. 26.
[4] F. Stuart Chapin, "Latent Culture Patterns of the Unseen World of Social Reality," *American Journal of Sociology*, 40 (July 1934), 61–68; Edward Sapir, "The Unconscious Patterning of Behavior in Society," in E. S. Dummer (ed.), *The Unconscious: A Symposium* (New York: Knopf, 1928). Clyde Kluckhohn, "Patterning as Exemplified in Navaho Culture," in L. Spier, A. I. Hallowell, and S. S. Newman (eds.), *Language, Culture, and Personality: Essays in Memory of Edward Sapir* (Menasha, Wis.: Sapir Memorial Publication Fund, 1941), pp. 109–128; Laura Thompson, "Attitudes and Acculturation," *American Anthropologist*, 50 (1948), 200–215.

investigators have suggested that "such distortion could be used to provide a means of determining the opinions of persons toward current issues without asking them directly what they believed about those topics."[5]

3. Psychiatrists consider neurosis, delusions, and "unusual" behavior generally as symptomatic or "symbolic" of underlying complexes of wishes, fears, and thoughts and use the overt peculiarities as leads to the underlying problems.

4. Anthropologists since Sapir[6] have used an analysis of the structure and content of language as a guide to unexpressed cultural premises.

5. Sapir suggested that fashions and other expressive elements in culture could be used to trace hidden cultural values and strains.[7]

6. Functional anthropologists—especially those in the tradition of A. R. Radcliffe-Brown, who in turn received impetus from Durkheim —assume that parts of the culture have a necessary, not an accidental, relation to each other, and that therefore "missing" parts are simply hidden.

The technique of tracing cultural premises with the aid of "popular logic" could become one of the sociologist's contributions to the scientific uncovering of the covert.[8] This would, of course, involve overturning an old assumption among sociologists and making the new assumption that man generally thinks logically.

Sociology emerged as a separate discipline partly as an attempt to account for certain nonrational factors in human behavior. While some sociologists have pointed out the consistency within a given culture, the assumption of inherent nonrationality in the things they were studying led most sociologists to ignore the fact that there is a certain "popular logic" in many of these things. If the existence of this popular logic is recognized, it may be found useful in several kinds of sociological investigation.

[5] J. J. B. Morgan and J. T. Morton, "Distorted Reasoning as an Index of Public Opinion," *School and Society*, 57 (March 20, 1943), 333ff; J. J. B. Morgan and J. T. Morton, "The Distortion of Syllogistic Reasoning Produced by Personal Convictions," *Journal of Social Psychology*, 20 (August 1944), 39–59.

[6] Edward Sapir, "The Status of Linguistics as a Science," *Language*, 5 (1929), 207–214.

[7] Edward Sapir, "Fashion," *Encyclopedia of the Social Sciences* (New York: Macmillan, 1931), VI, 139–144.

[8] I have attempted a tentative application of the technique in setting forth the hypothesis of my "Anti-Semitism's Root in City-Hatred," *Commentary*, 6 (October 1948), 374–378.

22

A Deductive Ideal-Type Method

SOCIOLOGISTS *have shied away from systematic use of the ideal-type method and have never attempted the extensive use that the economists have given to it. This chapter, which borrows heavily from economics, presents some of the possibilities in the method for sociologists and other "empirically oriented" social scientists. These groups may find some of the suggestions disturbing, but it is the same kind of concern they feel when they try to get into a significant conversation with economists. Social scientists who engage only in empirical research may not find much use for the suggestions, but others who also have theoretical interests may find that the technique has important values for the development of our discipline.*

CHARACTERISTICS OF THE METHOD

THE PURPOSE of this chapter is to indicate how a method which has received wide application in economics can be applied to some sociological problems. In economics a deductive method was developed by Adam Smith, the utilitarians, Jevons, Marshall, and others before Roscher, Veblen, Commons, and later "institutionalists" arrived at an inductive method.[1] The deductive method is still in wide use in economics, but little effort has been made to apply it in sociology. Sociologists like Weber, von Wiese, and Becker have made significant

NOTE: I wish to thank A. G. Papandreou and Michael Scriven for a critical reading of this chapter.

[1] These two methods are perfectly antithetical only in a logical sense and not in actual application. The greatest of the classical economists were keen observers of actual life, and the institutionalists did not forget their classical training. It should not be taken that the classical and institutional methods are the only ones used by economists. Another important method combines induction and deduction into a method that goes under the name "mathematical," exemplified by the work of Henry Schultz in *The Theory and Measurement of Demand* (Chicago: University of Chicago Press, 1938). It is also necessary to recognize that adherents of each of the methodological schools which we are considering were not in perfect agreement with one another as to the specific nature of their method.

application of ideal-type methodology, but they have not considered it within their province to associate deduction with it.

The inductive method in economics used by the German historical school and the American institutionalist school consists in observing an economic phenomenon with a variety of instrumental aids—such as statistics, interviews, and participant observation—summarizing it descriptively as a historical phenomenon, and stating causal relations as a set of functions of unknown magnitude. For example, the American labor movement might be described in terms of the number of persons belonging to unions, the types of leadership and internal organization, the means of achieving its aims. Usually, a conclusion of such a study would be in general causal terms: The strength of the American labor movement varies with the numbers who join, the "friendliness" of the courts, the degree of organization or monopoly by the employers, the number of unemployed, etc., and each of these things is causally dependent on the other. This sort of conclusion could be put in the form of the following type of mathematical equation: $Y = a + bX_1 + cX_2 + \ldots zX_n$, where Y is the strength of the labor movement; X_1, X_2, and X_n are causal factors or interrelated sets of causal factors; b, c, and z are the "weights" (or measures of importance of their respective factors), and a is a constant.[2]

In contrast, the deductive method was based less on observation than on rigorous logic and on truisms, that is, tautologies, called by some logicians "pragmatically a priori propositions" and popularly called "self-evident truths." Observation was necessary only to set some fairly accurate and simple assumptions. The crucial point in deductive economics was to arrive at a significant truism within the limits set by the assumptions. It was not easy to arrive at practical truisms, since they had to be stated in terms of a few basic and manipulable variables. The following are two of the most important truisms developed by deductive economics: (1) If the demand for and supply of an item can be put in the form of a price-frequency schedule, the price of that item will occur at the point at which the amount demanded equals the amount supplied. (2) The total amount

[2] This type of equation can, of course, be put into an "ideal" form, plotted, and compared with observable empirical conditions. This became the "mathematical" method, used successfully in biophysics and the older natural sciences and introduced into economics by Walras. The type of deductive equation considered in this chapter follows the pattern of the English "classical" economists rather than that of Walras and his successors in the "mathematical" tradition.

of money spent in a given time will equal the sum of the prices of all the items purchased with that money. Or, in another form, the total national income equals the total money value of the national product. To exemplify the deductive method, the latter truism will be developed here because it is the easier one of the two and because it provides two distinct sets of deductions and predictions.

The assumptions underlying the second truism are these: a circumscribed economy involving exchange of goods for money, the practical absence of barter and gift, the practical absence of hoarding, the possibility of allocating resources and money to producers' goods as well as to consumers' goods, and the possibility of varying prices and the amount of money and goods. We say that these are assumptions of the truism, even though a truism is universally true, because without them the truism is only a logical exercise and therefore useless.[3] It is to be noted that these assumptions are validated for the most part by actual conditions in Western countries. There is some barter, gift, and hoarding, but not enough to make the truism useless. To the extent that actual conditions deviate from the assumptions, the truism becomes useless, and no useful predictions can be deduced from it. These assumptions are very much the same as those necessary for the first truistic law of economics—the law of supply and demand. It was the limitations imposed by the assumptions which prompted the economist Adolph Lowe to remark, "Far from presenting a pure theory appropriate to any social conditions, so simple a law as the law of supply and demand, as soon as we take it in its exact meaning, depicts the essential features of a very concrete society: the liberal society of early capitalism." [4]

The first statement of the truism is valuable when it is cast into the form of the equation of exchange: $MV = PT$. That is, the amount of *money* in existence multiplied by the *velocity* of its turnover (MV represents the total amount of money spent) is equal to the average *price* of an average item [5] multiplied by the number of *transactions*

---

[3] A logician, Michael Scriven, informs me that logicians are accustomed to thinking of what I call assumptions as part of the definitions of the terms in the tautology. This is, of course, simply a terminological difference and makes no substantive difference. We can understand that the assumptions regulate the application and meaning of the terms in the tautology.

[4] Adolph Lowe, *Economics and Sociology* (London: George Allen & Unwin, 1935), p. 59.

[5] This abstract term "average price of an average item" is more commonly known as the "price level."

of that item (PT represents the sum of all the prices of all the items
sold for money). This "equation of exchange" is a predictive tool of
the economist. It enables him to predict, for example, that any increase of money, say by printing or by importation, which is actually
used to buy goods will result in a rise in the price level because an
increase in one side of the equation automatically means an increase
in the other side of the equation. Any increase in the circulation of
money, such as is involved in a general increase of wages, unless there
is a corresponding increase in goods produced, will also result in an
increase in the price level. It is to be noted that the equation is not
based upon a statistical summary of a large number of cases or upon
historical examination of the factors which create a given price level
at a certain time. The equation is based, rather, upon pure logic:
Assuming a closed economy in a specified period of time where money
is used as a medium of exchange, we find that the total amount of
money passed from hand to hand is equal to the sum of the prices of
all goods and services exchanged. This proposition is necessarily and
inevitably true. It is, in fact, a tautology, since the last part of the
statement simply repeats, in different words, the meaning of the first
part. Predictive statements, in this case the equation, based on
tautologies are logical deductions and are therefore inevitably true.
However, no known economy is completely closed, and there are such
items as hoarding or a foreign demand for dollars that can prevent
the issue of new money from driving up the price level under many
circumstances. Probably there has never been a time or an economy
in which a change in the amount of money circulating is followed by
an exactly proportional change in the price level. Nevertheless, in our
society the equation is constantly used for prediction, and the predictions come true—unless "some new factor enters."

The second statement of the truism has been employed by Wick-
sell and Lindahl[6] in the following form: $I - S = CP$. That is, that
part of the total national *income* which is not *saved* is always equal
to the amount of *consumption* goods sold, multiplied by their *price*
level. To arrive at this statement, the economists had to break up the
national income into the amount "spent" and the amount "saved,"
and the national product into "consumer goods" (e.g., food, luxuries)
and "producers' goods" (e.g., machinery, construction). It is truistic

[6] See Gunnar Myrdal, *Monetary Equilibrium* (London: William Hodge, 1939), p. 22.

that money can only be saved or spent and that money which is saved goes for producers' goods—since no hoarding is assumed—and that money which is spent goes for consumers' goods. With this tool the economist can predict, for example, that an increase in savings will lower the price level of consumers' goods.

Thus, in economics, truisms which are significant in terms of realistic assumptions and controllable variables have been used to deduce very useful relationships. Valid predictions have been made from these logical deductions. While probably most economists find the method useful, practically no contemporary economist would claim that it is the only scientific method or that it should be used independent of empirical observation. The best uses of the deductive method have been made by those who have been the keenest observers of what is significant in actual social life, and much of the current criticism of the method among economists points to the frequent failure to relate the assumptions to concrete social reality. Sociologists, on the other hand, have long been aware of the need to test every assumption and hypothesis with empirical evidence. But they have not yet taken advantage of the deductive method so brilliantly employed by the theoretical economists.[7]

POSSIBILITIES OF THE METHOD FOR SOCIOLOGISTS

Sociologists thus far have used inductive methods analogous to those employed by historical and institutional economists, and their conclusions are usually in the form that the causes of a given phenomenon are such and such. Speculation has been employed by sociologists, but largely to arrive at hypotheses which can be tested by inductive methods or to generalize from empirical data. Where speculation has been used by sociologists in connection with the ideal-type method, it has followed Max Weber's injunction to engage in *Aufsteigung*—or "stepping up" to an extreme certain characteristics of an observable phenomenon. The stepped-up ideal types have two characteristics in common with the truisms discussed in this chapter: (1) They are almost never realized in actuality. (2) They are tools

[7] Instead of studying one another's methodology for techniques which might be valuable for their own science, many economists and sociologists have resorted to denouncing each other. See, for example, Frank H. Knight, "Anthropology and Economics," and Melville J. Herskovits, "Economics and Anthropology, A Rejoinder," *Journal of Political Economy*, vol. 49, no. 2 (April 1941).

found valuable in gaining an understanding of important variables. The ideal types differ from the truisms in that they do not take the form of an equation and in that they have not been employed deductively.

In looking for situations studied by sociologists to which the deductive method might be applied, two unusual difficulties were encountered. First, sociologists do not agree as to what are the central phenomena of their discipline in the way that economists regard price and exchange. Second, sociologists do not have a central and universal unit in the way that economists have the dollar (or its equivalents in foreign currencies). Because of these unusual conditions, I was forced to be arbitrary in the choice of subject matter and units. This arbitrariness may nullify the conclusions of the present chapter in the eyes of some sociologists; others will recognize, however, that the arbitrariness does not make for intrinsic weakness in the deductive method, but simply reflects current weakness in sociological theory.

The first sociological example is the following truistic proposition: If action is based on prejudice (or sentiment) rather than on rational self-interest, then some action works against self-interest. Whether or not *all* prejudiced or sentimental action works against self-interest is not important; it is sufficient to define prejudiced or sentimental action as not being based *solely* on rational self-interest. This simple proposition can be put into the following equation form: $A - PT = R$, where A is all action of a given individual or a given group or society, P is action based on prejudice, T represents the proportion in which prejudice is based on pure tradition or sentiment (that is, the proportion of prejudice which is not in accord with rational self-interest), and R is rational action for self or group protection or enhancement. By transposing the second element in the equation, the reader can see that the proposition takes the form $A = R + PT$; that is, all action can be classified into rational and irrational action, and—in respect to intergroup relations—irrational action can be considered as prejudiced action (P) to the extent (T) that it is irrational or based on sentiment or tradition.

Let us specify the conditions under which the proposition would be strictly and completely applicable (methodologically, such conditions can be treated as assumptions): (1) The individual or group places a high value on self-protection and self-enhancement. (2) The individual or group is not psychopathically bent on self-destruction. (3) The individual or group is not so rigid that its patterns of behavior cannot be changed. (4) Some of the prejudiced behavior is irrational in motivation in the sense of being based on tradition or sentiment (the more this is true—that is, the closer T is to 100 per cent—the more useful is the proposition). (5) An outside force arises to threaten the individual or group.

These assumptions are fairly applicable to the United States today, and therefore the proposition should permit a correct prediction about the behavior of the American people as a group. Some prejudiced behavior of the dominant group in the United States works against the group self-interest. For example, discrimination against minorities in industry and the armed forces prevents the most efficient use of their manpower; the presence of disaffected minorities in the population weakens national unity, or at least gives the dominant group the feeling that it does; preoccupation with giving vent to sadistic or other discriminatory behavior against minorities takes attention and time away from a real outside threat. According to the proposition, a need for increasing rational action to meet the force of an outside threat should either reduce prejudiced behavior (P) or reduce the proportion of prejudiced behavior working against rational self-interest (T).

This prediction has been borne out in the past;[8] whenever the United States has faced an outside enemy, its prejudiced behavior against minorities has declined, at least temporarily. The Revolutionary War led to a strong movement, successful in all northern states, to abolish slavery and to the constitutional provision outlawing the slave trade after 1808. The Civil War led to the abolition of slavery, to the enlistment of Negroes as "necessary" for the successful prosecution of the war, and to the movement to secure the franchise and civil rights for Negroes. World War I opened factory jobs to Negroes, secured for them higher positions in the armed forces, extended their acceptance in limited areas of life, reduced peonage, and re-extended the franchise to a small proportion. World War II greatly increased the job opportunities of Negroes, extended the franchise, and made the treatment of whites and Negroes by the judicial and executive

[8] Facts supporting the historical conclusions of this paragraph may be found in summarized form in Arnold and Caroline Rose, *America Divided* (New York: Knopf, 1948), esp. Chaps. II and XI.

arms of the government more equal. Correspondingly, there have been lapses into increased prejudiced behavior as memories of these wars have receded.

A critic of these observations would probably admit that the Mexican and Spanish-American wars represented too little threat to the United States to have any effect, but he would raise the realistic question, How does the proposition explain the increased anti-Negro behavior in the South during the War of 1812 and as the Civil War drew near, and the anti-Japanese behavior during World War II? These occasions of tightening the caste restrictions represent the second possibility of the proposition—namely, the tendency to eliminate all sentimentality from prejudice (T approaches zero) so that unremunerated work or wealth is exacted from the minority groups at the same time that the group is much more rigorously bound into a separate caste so that it cannot endanger the majority group.

The proposition helps to clarify certain aspects of current developments. The United States considers Russia to be a serious outside threat and probably at no time since the Revolutionary War has the feeling of this threat penetrated so deeply to the masses of the people. Under this circumstance, insofar as the United States desires and intends to meet this felt threat with a show of opposing power, the prediction is that either (1) the prejudiced behavior restricting the efficient use of minorities and diminishing their loyalty will rapidly decrease, or (2) a fascist-like development will ruthlessly suppress any change toward integration of minorities into various areas of life and will force them into a highly exploitative slavery (such as the South did with its Negroes between 1830 and 1864), herd them into concentration camps (as was done with American citizens of Japanese ancestry during World War II), or kill them off (as Germany did the Jews and other alleged "internal enemies"). Comparable developments can be expected to occur in the U.S.S.R. It will be especially interesting to observe whether events conform to these predictions or not, because the general expectation today seems to be that the position of minorities is unlikely to change at all or that reductions in prejudiced behavior will occur only gradually. Such expectations arise from simple extrapolation of past trends rather than from logical analysis of forces working in a certain type of situation.

It is to be noted that the prediction says nothing about the *attitude* of prejudice itself but simply speaks about prejudiced *behavior,* sometimes called "discrimination." A certain amount of empirical evidence exists to indicate that a change in behavior is followed by a conforming change in attitude.[9] To determine whether or not the changes in behavior predicted by the logical proposition will result in changes in the attitude of prejudice will require further empirical study, not simply logical analysis. The logical proposition under consideration simply indicates that where certain conditions (assumptions) exist certain consequences logically follow. These conditions seem to exist in significant degree at the present time—and empirical measurement should be carried on to see to what extent they actually do exist— and therefore certain predictions about human behavior seem to be in order. Assuming the continuance of these conditions, therefore, it would seem likely that prejudiced behavior will be diminished rapidly (P declines) or that prejudiced behavior will be rapidly systematized and deprived of traditional or sentimental elements (T declines).

To illustrate the application of the deductive method to an entirely different area of social behavior, a proposition mentioned incidentally by Burgess and Locke[10] will be examined. These authors distinguish three components of personality: biogenic, psychogenic, and sociogenic. The psychogenic component consists of noncultural reactive tendencies determined by prenatal and postnatal conditioning. These tendencies grow out of the contacts the baby has with his external world when there is no social communication. Sociogenic traits, on the other hand, grow out of social communication with other persons and are therefore largely determined by the existing state of society and culture. Marital conflict, say Burgess and Locke, may arise out of conflict between roles of husband and wife either on a psychogenic level or on a sociogenic level. Their proposition is that to the extent that a society is disorganized, interpersonal conflicts are likely to result mostly from clashes of nonmeshing sociogenic roles. Conversely,

[9] There are, for example, the studies supporting the James-Lange theory of emotions, which show that a change in expression is usually accompanied by a change in mood (e.g., deliberate laughter is usually accompanied by a happier mood). There is also the process of rationalization whereby a forced or accidental change of behavior is accompanied by verbal justification of the change; see, for example, the study by Gerhart Saenger and Emily Gilbert, "Customer Reactions to the Integration of Negro Sales Personnel," *International Journal of Opinion and Attitude Research,* 4 (Spring 1950), 57–76.

[10] Ernest W. Burgess and Harvey J. Locke, *The Family* (New York: American Book Co., 1945), pp. 559–560.

to the extent that a society is well organized, interpersonal conflicts are likely to result mostly from clashes due to psychogenic differences.

This proposition is a truism, or tautology, and one which allows valid predictions to be made. Its tautological nature is revealed by the assumption that a disorganized society is one in which communication is hampered by differences in values, in frames of reference, and in the very meaning of words. There is also the assumption that the biogenic component of personality is relatively fixed. In such a society sociogenic personalities cannot mesh properly since there is inadequate communication between them, and there are no strong cultural demands which define for both persons how they should behave toward each other. Conversely, in a society in which cultural demands are strong and are clearly understood by all members of the society and in which interpersonal communication is facilitated by everyone's having the same values and meanings, interpersonal conflict is at a minimum and whatever there is of it is due to psychogenic differences which are not subject to much cultural control. The usefulness of this proposition, at least insofar as it applies to "disorganized" American society, is seen in its directing investigators of interpersonal conflict to seek its causes primarily in a conflict of assumed social roles.[11]

On the basis of extensive investigation of drug addicts, Lindesmith[12] concluded that there were certain conditions that inevitably led to uncontrollable drug addiction. These conditions included taking a "habit-forming" drug a number of times (usually to assuage pain), experiencing withdrawal symptoms (the usual physical pains and mental depression), recognizing that the withdrawal symptoms would be relieved if the drug were taken again, and then actually taking the drug once again. Lindesmith could not find a single exception to his finding that a person who experienced all these conditions would, sooner or later, revert to use of the drug. Apparent exceptions were found actually to be persons who did not know what it was they had taken at first, or who did not connect the withdrawal symptoms with not taking the drug, or who did not realize that taking the drug again would remove the withdrawal symptoms.

[11] See Leonard S. Cottrell, "Roles and Marital Adjustment," *Publications of the American Sociological Society*, 27 (1933), 107–115; see also Ernest W. Burgess and Leonard S. Cottrell, *Predicting Success or Failure in Marriage* (New York: Prentice-Hall, 1939).

[12] Alfred R. Lindesmith, *Opiate Addiction* (Bloomington, Ind.: Principia Press, 1947).

While Lindesmith did important empirical work in his study, his central generalization seems to be a specific form of a truism. One must accept the validity of the truism even if one might reject Lindesmith's empirical conclusions. In its most general form, this truism can be stated thus: If one remembers a past experience and it has significance for him, that memory plays a role in all his future actions. A more specific form of the truism is this: Given the fact that an addict wishes to avoid withdrawal symptoms, if he knows how to do so he will take such action as will avoid them. One assumption behind this truism is that a mental state is a cause of outward behavior, which assumption is entertained by practically all psychologists. Another assumption is that people can take action on the basis of their knowledge and their desires or values. The main value of the truism lies in the suggestion it gives to look for the behavioral consequence of a memory. It also declares that every memory has a compulsive influence on behavior and that there is always a one-to-one relationship between memory and behavior if they are analyzed in the proper way. Lindesmith has provided a brilliant example of this type of analysis as it applies to the memory of how a drug relieves pain and depression and to the mechanism of drug addiction, even though he fails to distinguish the truistic from the empirical elements in his conclusion.

Starting from an empirical generalization by the anthropologist Oscar Lewis,[13] I have developed the following truism: If the possession of wealth is an important basis of status in society, and if there are conditions making for differences in the wealth of various members of the society, then status differences (social class) will vary directly with wealth differences. From this proposition we can predict that if wealth differences increase, class differentials will be sharper, and that if wealth differences are reduced, class lines will become blurred.

Some examples of unwitting use of truisms can be given from the writings of psychologists as well as sociologists. Festinger, Schachter, and Back state:

The magnitude of change the group can induce [on its members] will be equal to or less than the magnitude of the resultant force on the member to remain in the group. If the magnitude of the change the group attempts to induce is greater than the resultant force on the individual to stay in the group (the algebraic sum of all forces acting

[13] This was mentioned to me in a personal conversation in May 1948.

on him toward and away from the group), the effect would be to have the member leave the group. We may thus derive that the ability of a group to function without breaking up is not only dependent upon the cohesiveness of the group but also upon the magnitude of the change which the group attempts to induce in its members.[14]

While showing a fine appreciation of the role of logic in the formulation of theory, these writers fail to specify the truism which underlies their theory: An individual is willing and able (or is attracted) to remain in a group to the extent that the forces on him (or within him) to remain in a group are greater than the forces on him to leave the group. This can be expressed by the equation $W = Fi - Fo$ (where W is willingness to remain in the group, Fi is the sum of forces to remain in the group, and Fo is the sum of forces to leave the group). From this truism, specifying all the assumptions that the authors do specify, it may be predicted that when Fo becomes larger than Fi, the individual leaves the group (since willingness to remain in the group becomes negative) and that when the group increases Fo without simultaneously increasing Fi, individuals are likely to leave the group.

Robert Sears[15] states as an inductive proposition what is really a truism: "Effective aggression by one person toward another is always a frustration for the latter." It is a truism because Sears follows Dollard et al.[16] in defining aggression as "an act whose goal response is injury to an organism" and he uses "effective" to mean "that which leads to its goal-response." Since Sears and his fellow psychologists at Yale accept the assumption (general proposition) that frustration always results in aggression, Sears is able to deduce the following prediction from his truism: "Aggression elicits counteraggression."

IMPLICATION OF THE METHOD

While many other examples could be cited, the general character of truistic propositions can now be summarized. Their essential character is that they are based on logical relationships rather than on empirically observed ones. Thus they can never be proved, although they can be improved. Since they are inherently true, the criterion of a

---

[14] Leon Festinger, Stanley Schachter, and Kurt Back, *Social Pressures in Informal Groups* (New York: Harper, 1950), p. 166.

[15] Robert Sears, "Frustration and Aggression," in P. L. Harriman (ed.), *Encyclopedia of Psychology* (New York: Philosophical Library, 1946), pp. 215–218.

[16] Dollard et al., *Frustration and Aggression* (New Haven, Conn.: Yale University Press, 1939).

good truism is not its truth but rather its relevance and its usefulness, on the one hand, and the fact that it rests on true or at least plausible assumptions, on the other hand. It may be useful to clarify certain relationships by pointing out their logical character, to suggest certain types of facts to look for, and to make valid predictions if the assumptions on which they are based have some correspondence with reality. The deductive method may aid in building up a systematic theory of sociology, as it has done for economics—but of this we cannot be sure until it is tried. Since a useful truism is based on realistic assumptions, empirical research can aid significantly in indicating which truisms are likely to be useful. But the method itself is essentially an exercise in logical deduction. Finding that a deductive proposition does not allow for valid predictions does not help much in locating the source of the error; invalid predictions indicate that one or more of the empirical assumptions is wrong but it does nothing to indicate which one or ones.

The relation between inductive and deductive theory remains to be worked out; the logicians have failed us here because they do not concern themselves with induction and deduction as actually used in science and because they are usually partisans of either inductive or deductive theory but not both. A guess may be hazarded that the kind of deductive propositions we are concerned with here—the tautologies —can be considered as a special type of inductive propositions. All of them *can* be transformed into inductive propositions, and the definitions, assumptions, and general propositions from which such inductive propositions are deducible can be specified.[17] But the amount of work to do this can be staggering, and the deductive form of propositions sometimes has certain merits which the inductive form does not.

At least some of the differences between the two forms of proposition may now be specified:

1. Historically, deductive propositions have been used in physics (although not always deliberately) and in economics, whereas inductive propositions have enjoyed exclusive sway in biology, psychology, and sociology.

2. Procedurally the two kinds of propositions are formulated in different ways. Deductive propositions of the type we are considering are formulated first as truisms, then the "assumptions" are worked

---

[17] See Chapter 1, "A Theory of Social Organization and Disorganization," for a specification of the nature of inductive theory.

out as logical conditions under which the truism is valid, and then these assumptions are compared (usually casually, but now with increasing precision) to empirical conditions of real life to determine whether the truism has relevance and usefulness. Inductive propositions, on the contrary, are the last stage in a procedure of casual observation, perhaps systematic description, and definition of concepts which are believed to be significant and relevant. Also, individual inductive propositions are generally tested empirically before they are related to (integrated with) each other.

3. Deductive propositions *always* take the form of an equivalence (or identity); inductive propositions *never* take this form and apparently only some of them can be transformed into an equivalence form (these latter, of course, are then deductive propositions). It is for this reason that deductive propositions are probably a special case of inductive propositions, and it is also the *logical* reason for distinguishing the two types. Inductive studies test the hypothesis that b follows a under specified conditions. Deductive studies seek to specify the conditions (assumptions) under which b must logically and inevitably follow a, and they pose for empirical research the question of the relevance of these conditions to any observable phenomena.

4. Pragmatically, for the probably few subject matters where they can be used, deductive propositions are easier to handle than are inductive propositions. The *existence* of certain factors is easier to ascertain than is the *relationship* between factors under controlled conditions. Where techniques are not yet available to measure certain factors, it is safer to guess or postulate their existence than it is to guess or postulate their relationship. This is one important reason why economics has thus far been more successful in making predictions than sociology has been. It is also a major reason for suggesting that sociology might do well to borrow the deductive method of economics for certain subject matters.

It would be a mistake to conclude from anything in this chapter that the basic methods of social science research should not remain inductive. Detailed observation and systematic fact-collecting in conjunction with carefully developed theory will and should continue to be the main ways of getting information about social life. Statistics, experiment, and historical summary will and should continue to be the main ways of drawing generalizations. It is quite possible that the deductive method lends itself only to very limited areas of investigation. But this method of logical, ideal-type deduction may have a future role as a way of drawing out more implications, and more useful implications, from existing knowledge than we have hitherto thought possible. Also, a specification of the nature of the method allows the social scientist to distinguish a logical generalization (a truism) from an empirical generalization and to formulate a systematic theory of discrete empirical generalizations. An excellent example of this can be drawn from a paper written some years ago by the distinguished anthropologist Radcliffe-Brown. While he indicates that he hopes to establish four hypotheses on an empirical base, actually we can see that propositions (2) and (4) are really deductions from propositions (1) and (3), which are inductive. Propositions (2) and (4) are logically valid without empirical research, provided the assumptions contained in propositions (1) and (3) are demonstrated to be valid by empirical research:

Now if we leave aside altogether the question of the possible origin or origins of totemism, and try instead to discover its laws, we reach a theory of an entirely different kind, and if you will permit me I will illustrate the matter by a brief statement of my own theory of totemism, in the form of a few general statements which I think it may be possible in the future definitely to prove by the ordinary logical methods of induction:

(1) In primitive societies any things that have important effects on the social life necessarily become the objects of ritual observances (negative or positive), the function of such ritual being to express, and so to fix and perpetuate, the recognition of the social value of the objects to which it refers.

(2) Consequently, in a society which depends entirely or in some large measure for its subsistence on hunting and collecting, the various species of animals and plants, and more particularly those used for food, become the object of ritual observances.

(3) In differentiated societies of certain types (as, for example, tribes divided into sibs or clans, i.e., into groups of kindred) the different segments tend to be differentiated from one another by differences of ritual, observances of the same general type for the whole tribe being directed to some special object or class of objects for each one of its segments.

(4) Consequently, while in undifferentiated societies (such as the Andaman Islanders) the ritual relation to the animals and plants used for food is a general undifferentiated relation between the society as

a whole, in differentiated societies the general tendency is to develop special ritual relations between each of the social segments (clans or other groups) and some one or more species of animal or plant, or occasionally some special division of nature in which a number of species are included.[18]

It would thus seem possible that sociologists could develop a system of interconnected logical propositions from which important deductions and predictions could be derived that have as much validity as their original assumptions. The full development of such a body of propositions might have to await the determination of a basic unit of measurement, but experimentation with the method of deductive logic to find some simple propositions that are useful can proceed immediately.

[18] A. R. Radcliffe-Brown, "The Methods of Ethnology and Social Anthropology," *South African Journal of Science*, 20 (1923), 124–147.

Index

St. Scholastica Library
Duluth, Minnesota 55811